AF478261

el·e·gy

/eləjē/

JUSTIN KIMBALL ELEGY

RADIUS BOOKS

A CONTINUITY OF FRAGMENTS

Stanley Wolukau-Wanambwa

In *The Writing of Disaster*, Maurice Blanchot states that where "power does not reign—nor initiative, nor the cutting edge of a decision—there, dying is a living," suggesting that life without agency is itself a form of death. He continues that such a life is one "escaped from itself and confounded with the disaster of a time without present which we endure by waiting, by awaiting misfortune which is not still to come, but which has always already come upon us and which cannot be present."[1]

I cannot tell from picture to picture in Justin Kimball's *elegy* whether it was the mill that failed, or whether it is the prison that sustains the small town; whether in this place the crisis flowed from the plant, the river, the shale, or whether it suffers at the hands of some calculus located offshore. The pictures interweave a sense of weary anticipation for a future with a tone of deep lament for the scattered pieces of the past.

In Kimball's portrait of a decrepit green-and-white three-story house [PLATE 21] I cannot tell whether the roof collapsed under the weight of some external force, or whether load-bearing walls were gradually sundered until the structure folded in under its own weight. Both explanations seem plausible, since what has struck so many of the towns across this nation is a combination of systematic undermining from within, and external shocks from without. The disaster has in this sense already happened, continues to happen, can be seen nowhere, anywhere, and everywhere.

A sound repeated at a sufficient frequency is transformed into pure white noise: its generalization, its pervasiveness, its intensification by constant repetition renders all nuance utterly meaningless. As Blanchot writes of disaster itself, "The infiniteness of the threat has broken every limit. We are on the edge of disaster without being able to situate it in the future: it is rather always already past, and yet we are on the edge." It has become as indecipherable as white noise.

---

1. Maurice Blanchot, *The Writing of Disaster* [Lincoln: University of Nebraska Press, 1995]

The cover image of this book [PLATE 49] depicts a mishmash of disjunct elements arrayed in a flat matrix. It comprises—among other things—white patterned lace curtains, thick limestone bricks, a weathered wooden panel-cum windowpane, black lintels, a pinewood lattice, white vertical blinds, a black door, and the painted white façade of a brick building struck gold by reflected light. The image, and the piecemeal construction of the objects in it, provides a concise visual definition of the terms *bric-a-brac* and *bricolage:* they represent a miscellany of objects of little value, linked together to create a single discontinuous surface. The photograph itself harks back to the rectilinear structure of Piet Mondrian's early twentieth-century paintings, while its seemingly haphazard assemblage recalls the logic of collage, and the *merz* pieces of Kurt Schwitters.

Kimball's photographs often devolve around the structure of a grid that holds discontinuous fragments in uniform suspension. His pictures are simultaneously marked by the frequency of disjunctive combinations emerging from flattened space, and by the narrow margins of the world that they describe. In this way they show art imitating life's inherent artistry, as necessity trumps convention, and compels the needy to make virtue of disarray by insisting on the utility of that which is close to hand.

That this picture recalls the work of Mondrian or Schwitters, and with them the emergence of art forms such as collage, cubism, assemblage, and abstract expressionism, seems far from coincidental. The approximate half-century span of art history characterized by those art forms corresponds to the ascendancy of massed capital in modern American life. From the rapid expansion of national and international transportation networks to the proliferation of routinized labor; from the rapid spread of electrical and telecommunications infrastructure to the standardization of time zones, the period from approximately 1910 to 1960 is marked by the transformative spatial and social effects of capitalism. These effects can be traced in our landscape, our language, our living rooms, our individual and collective experience, and in our limited grasp of the multiple interrelations between those things.

In a startling group portrait found in the latter part of this book, four young men stand paused in the midst of a football game, each figure arrayed in its own separate segment of the frame [PLATE 62]. No two figures are of the same size, although two of the four sport nearly identical grey tee-shirts, while the other two are shirtless and pale in the vivid light. A cascade of rectangular shadows litters the grass in the foreground, echoing the distant shape of a modest grey stone memorial topped off with a globe and emblazoned with a brass plaque. The young men are transformed in this frame into separate but linked elements of a sundial, their bodies turned into discrete markers of time: the tallest a measure of adulthood; the smallest, with his bright red hair, a cherubic youth. None are connected to each other by gaze or by gesture, and in this they are rendered as discrete but coincident in a single exposure, which measures the differing phases of their lives.

Similarly, in a double portrait set against the deep but vibrant blood orange texture of a wooden garage wall, a woman in a brown hooded jacket and blue jeans seems to grimace and set herself to walk left out of frame as a man at the far right of the frame busies himself typing out a text message [PLATE 50]. The two figures are suspended in separate but contiguous orbits by the sharp edge of the garage wall, which divides the flatness of blood orange space from the receding depth of an alley at the right of the frame. The photograph's structure creates a division between stasis and mobility, which seems to carry a critical charge. This is to say that the contrasts between the two individuals are not merely trivial: neither of them can be described as experiencing comparable pressures, or occupying similar registers of time. They are cast as landlord and tenant, one restive the other impatient and disaffected, brought into a lateral correlation that reveals a profound disjuncture.

This dynamic of coincidence and separateness, modeled on the structure of a grid, recurs in another double portrait, of two women who sit atop a concrete step at the rear of a pale blue barn, each wearing dirty blue jeans and work boots, perhaps taking a moment's rest from labor [PLATE 34]. The woman on the left rests her back against a thick wooden beam, her brow furrowed, her left arm resting easily on her raised left knee in a posture that belies an underlying tension. The woman on the right is doubled over at the waist, her forearms resting on her knees, head buried beneath her hair, mouth resting on an arm. She is as shuttered up as the stables we might imagine behind the locked blue gate in front of which the pair rests.

In these and other Kimball portraits, bodies coincide in space but seemingly not in time. His pictures frame discontinuous unities, seeking out a poetry fashioned from restlessness set within the rupture of modern postindustrial experience. In both literal and metaphorical ways, his pictures address the interweaving of separateness and simultaneity, renewal and decline, proliferation and emptiness, entropy and the relentless cycles of capitalism. His pictures are made up of echoes and oppositions held in temporary suspension against the onslaught of time.

Consider some of the names of the streets in which these pictures have been made: Liberty Street, Prospect Street, Commerce Street, Country Road, West Mine Street, Creek Street, Elk Street, Roosevelt Drive, Lincoln Avenue, Bliss Street, Lark Street, Shenandoah, Way Street, Erie Street, Grand Street, Pearl Street, Liberty Hill Road . . . The names represent more than fact, region, or figure: they reflect the implicitly mutual bond of a promise. They are given not merely in celebration of a history, a hero, a landscape, or a function, but in the expectation of a future.

If this book is an *elegy*, then it is by definition a form of mournful lament, and thus it is an act of commemoration—a means of bringing something to remembrance. This last meaning is instructive, since it signals the effort of summoning into memory, recalling the collaborative work of drawing lost futures back into a common field of vision. The Italian philosopher Benedetto Croce wrote that "where there is no narrative, there is no history," and it is to this gap that the elegy addresses itself. It is a way of insisting on the proper weight and measure of our names, of our bodies, of our histories, and thus of our being.

If Kimball's book is elegiac, then it is in part because the photographs represent a refusal to wait without agency in a life Blanchot described as a "form of death." Rather, the book claims a restorative power through a form that allows us to create continuity from disjuncture, attempting—as in elegy—to sound the scattered pieces back into something whole.

el·e·gy (/eləjē/)

a poem of serious reflection

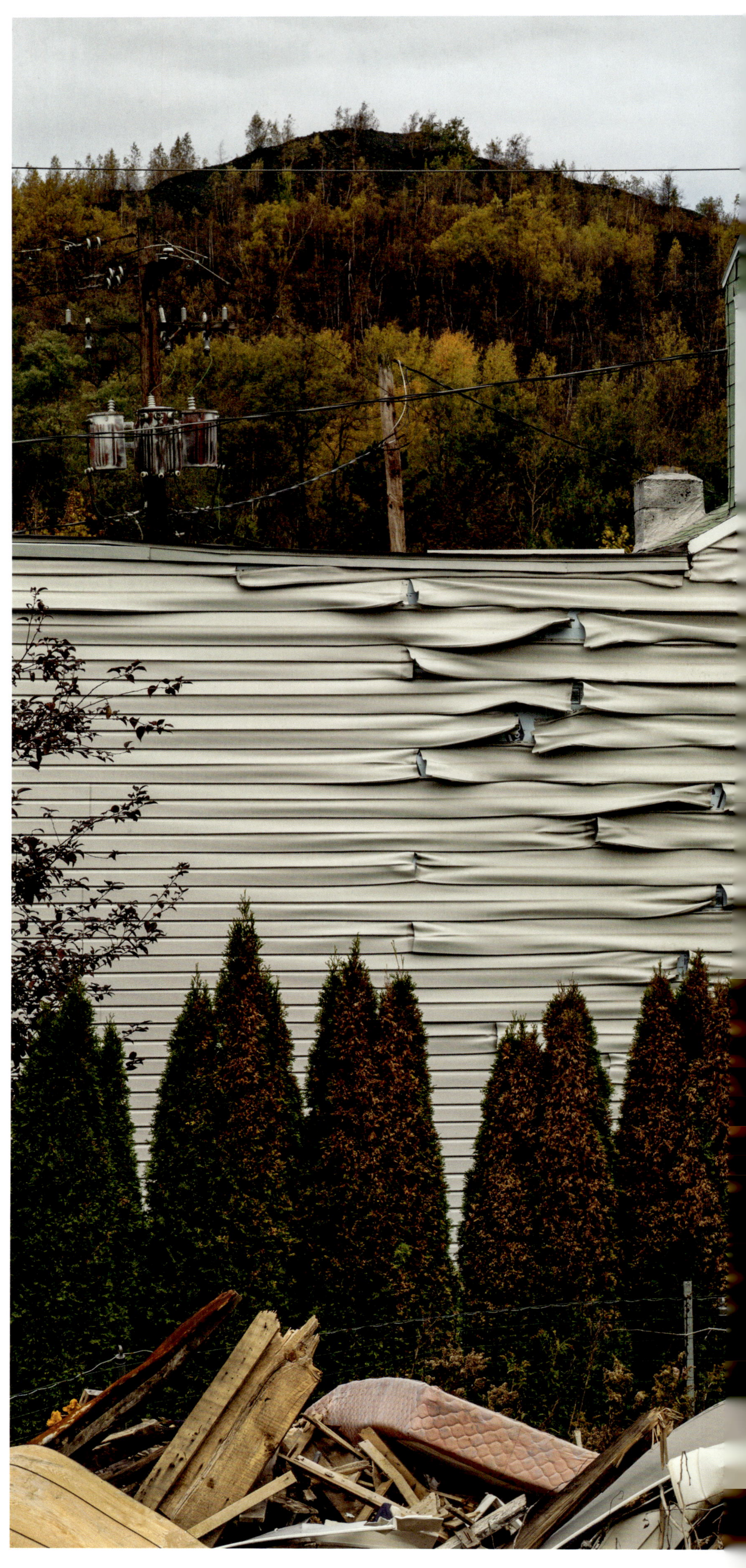

PLATE 1

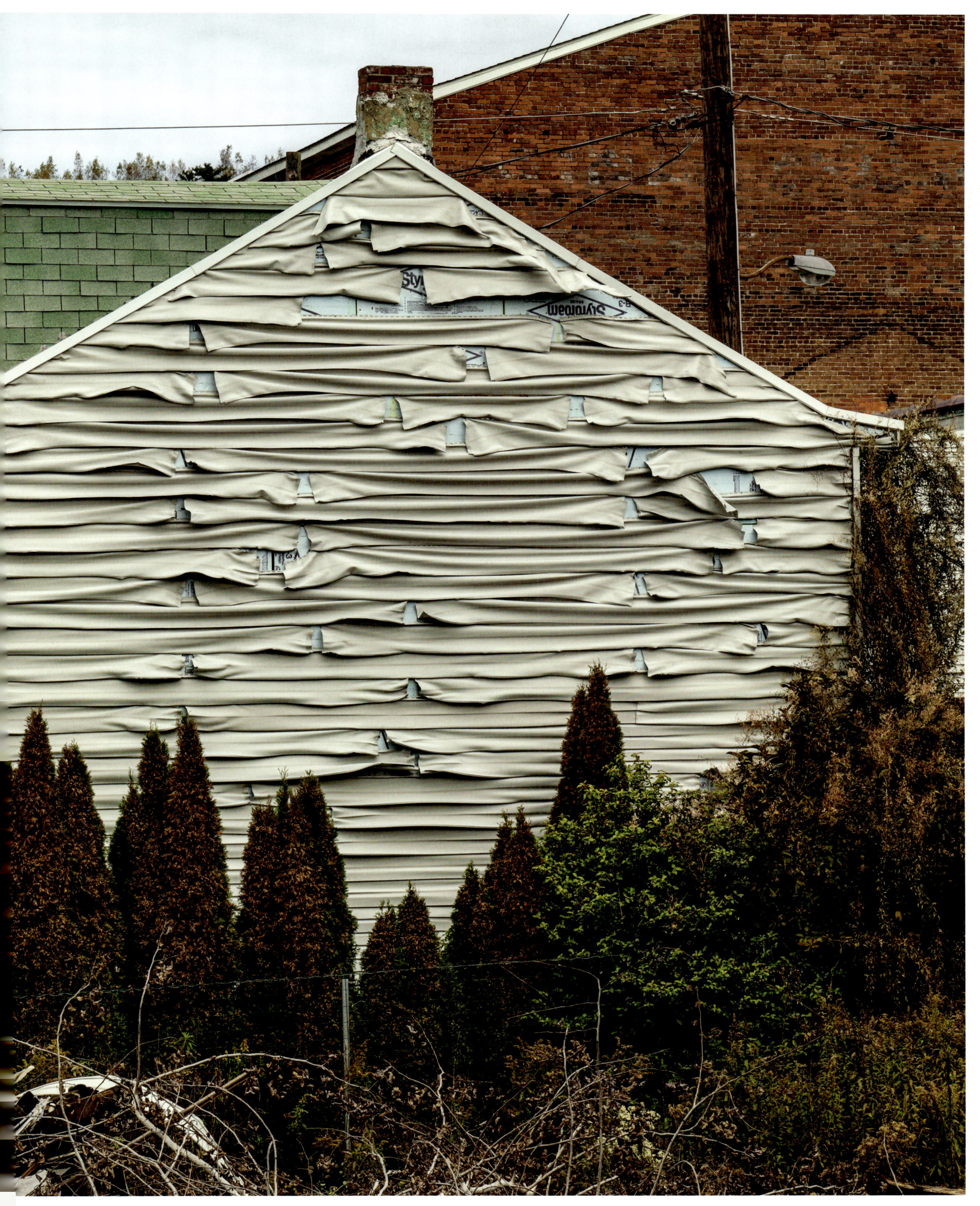

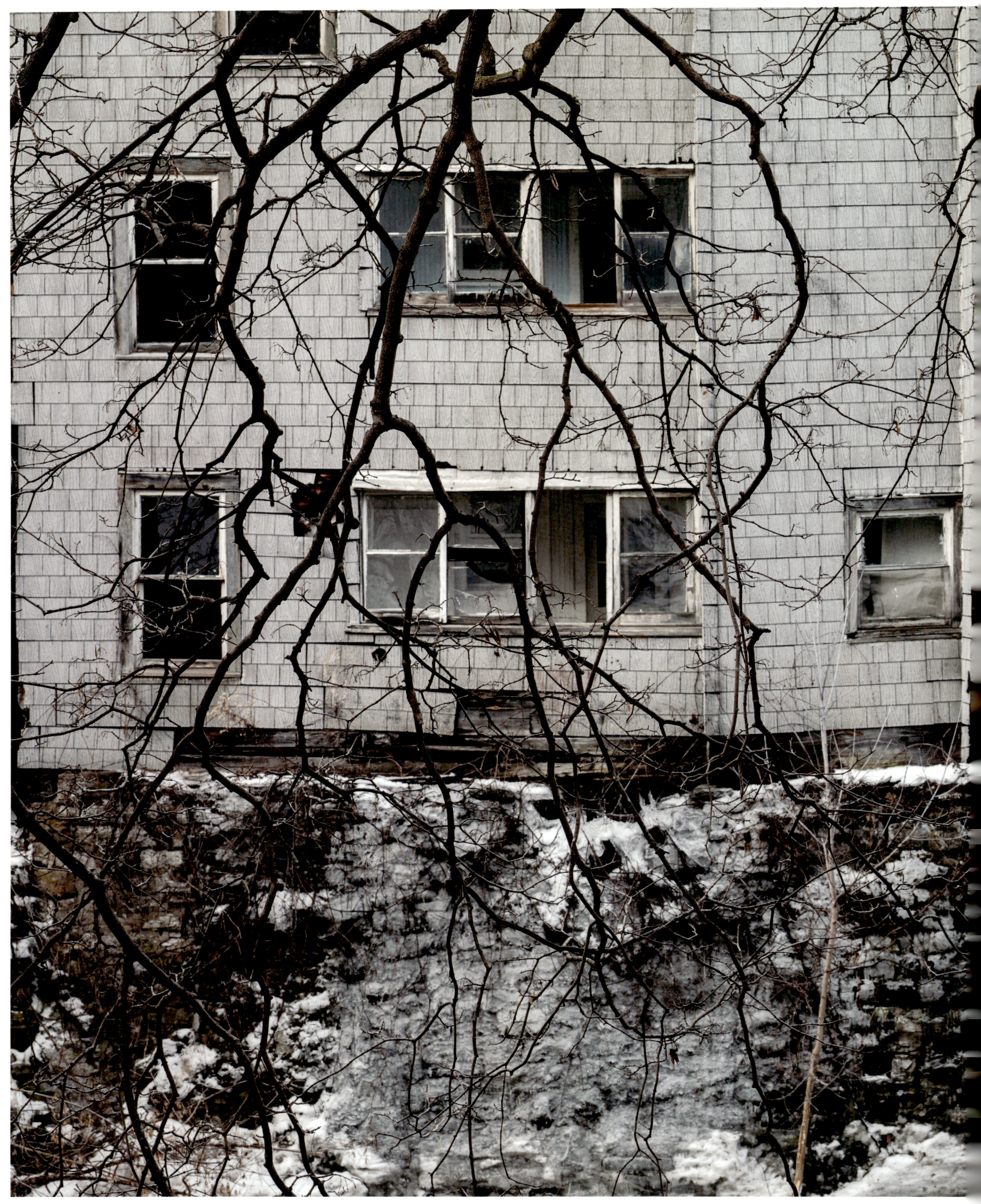

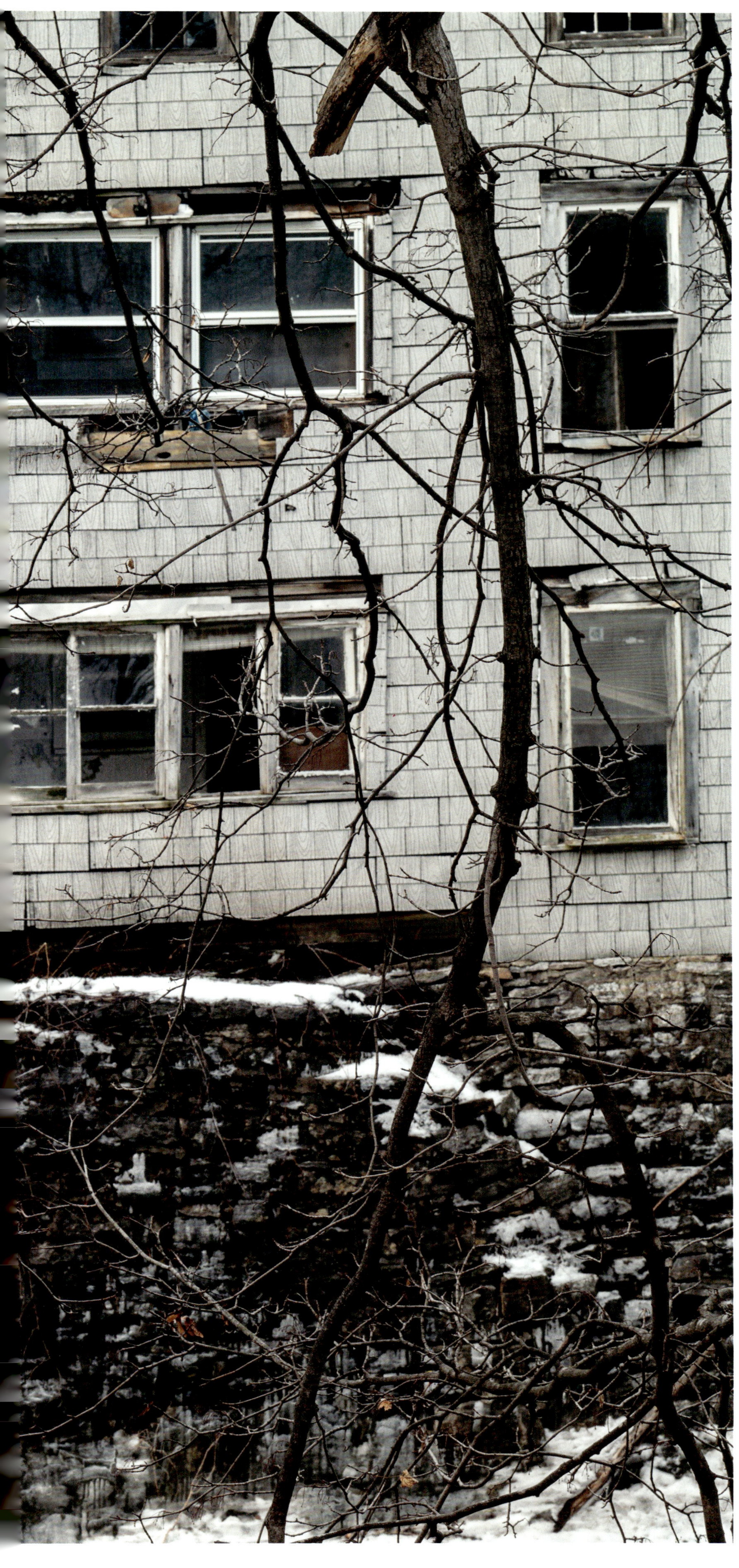

PLATE 2

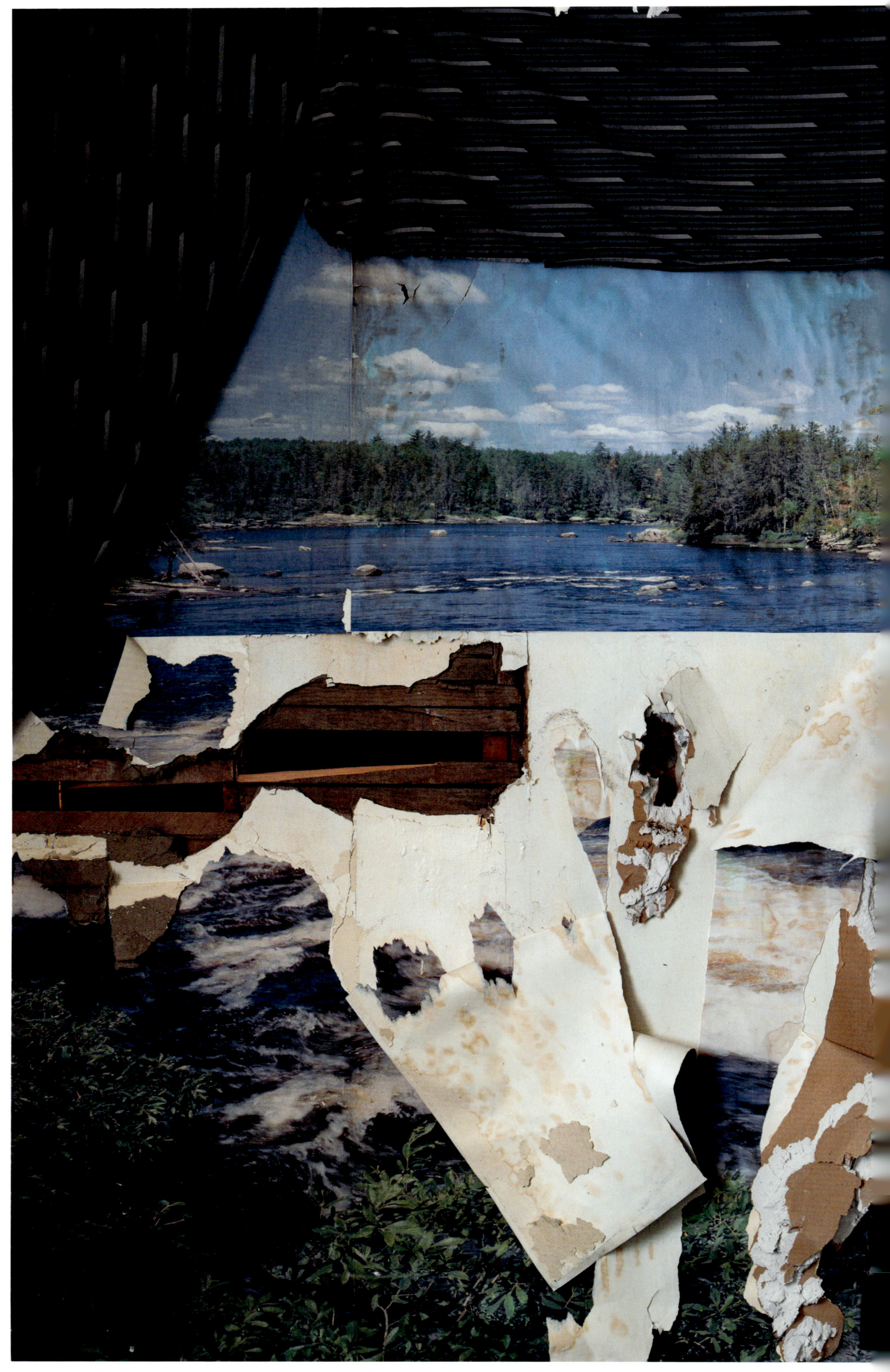

PLATE 3

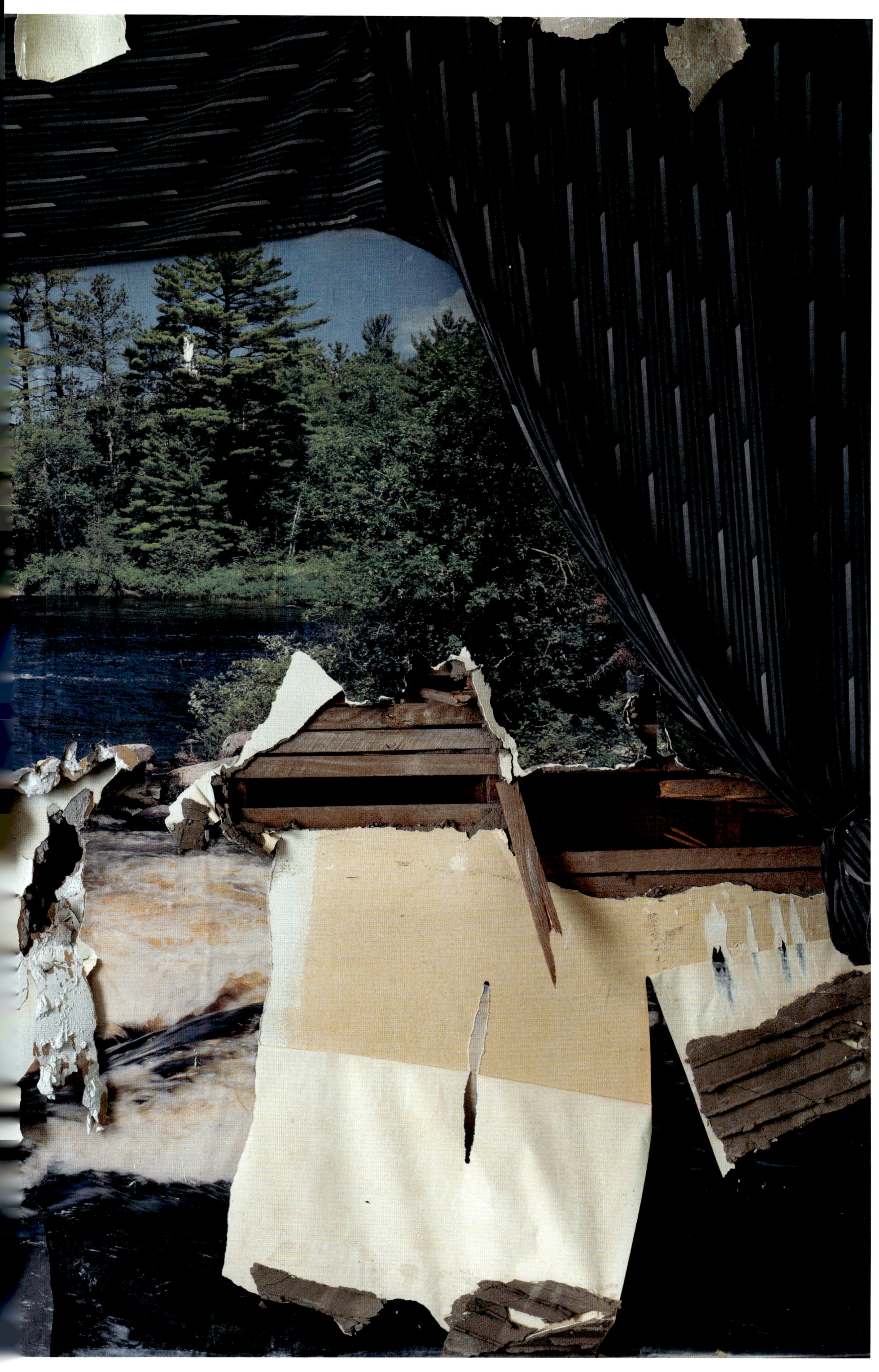

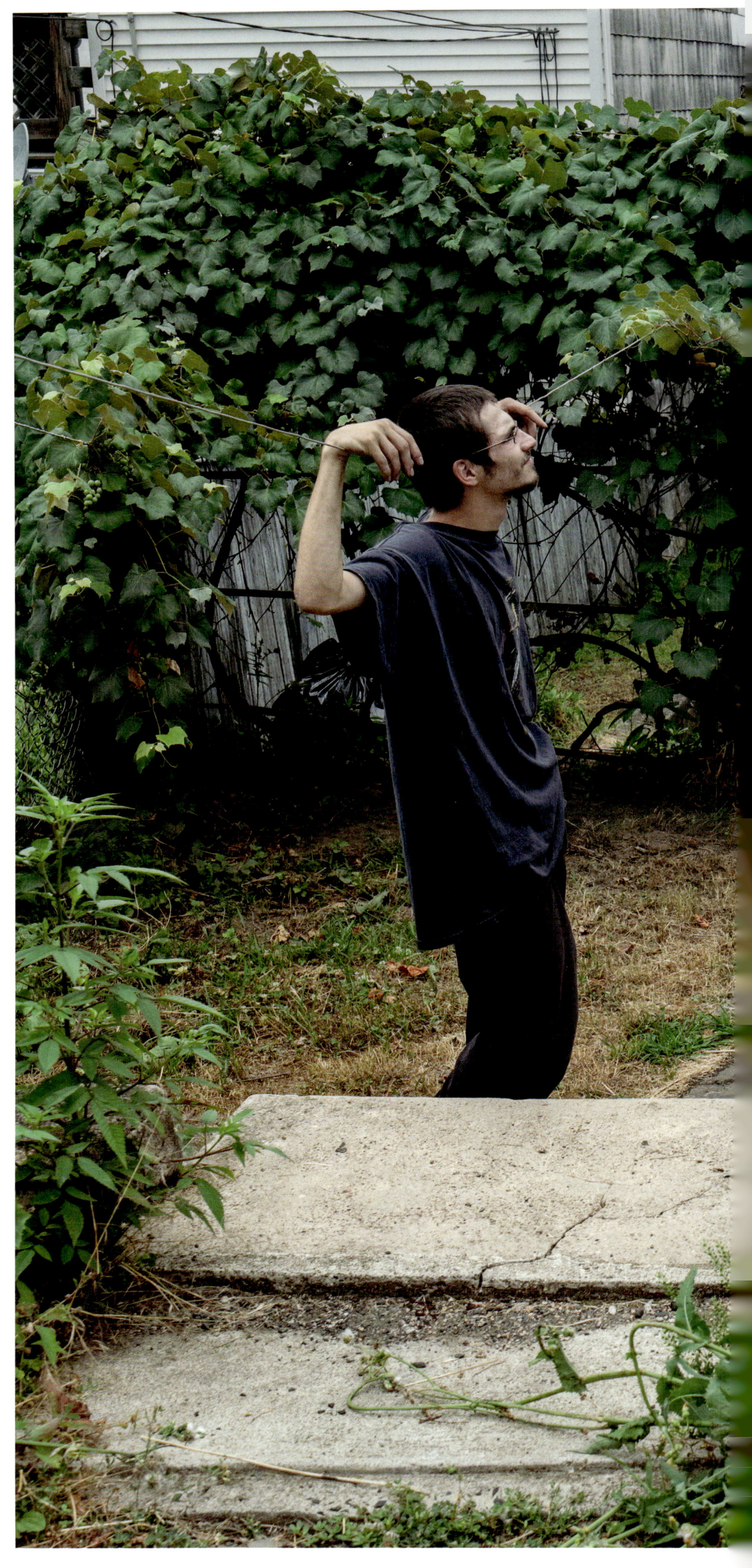

PLATE 4

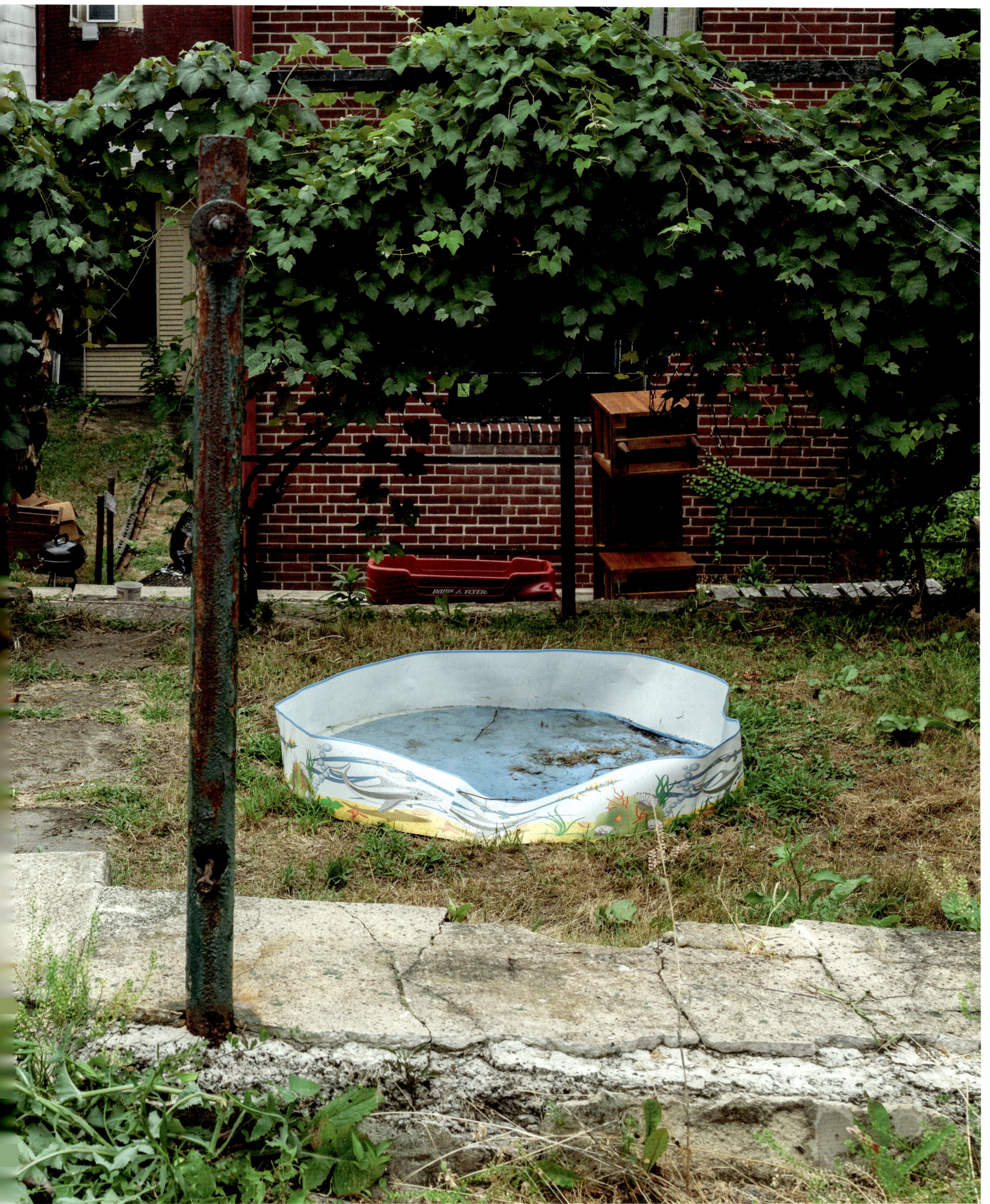
RADIO FLYER

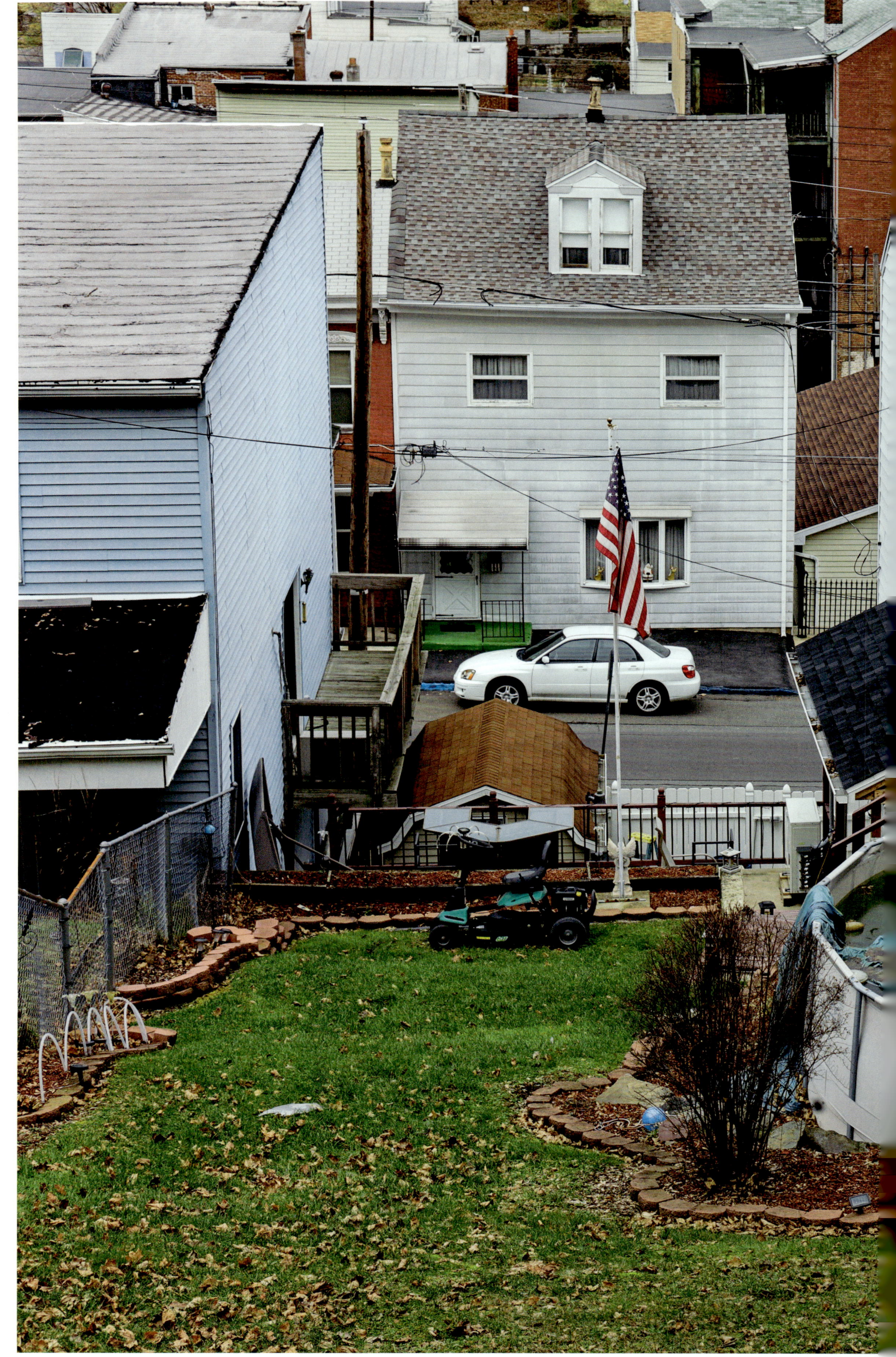

PLATE 5

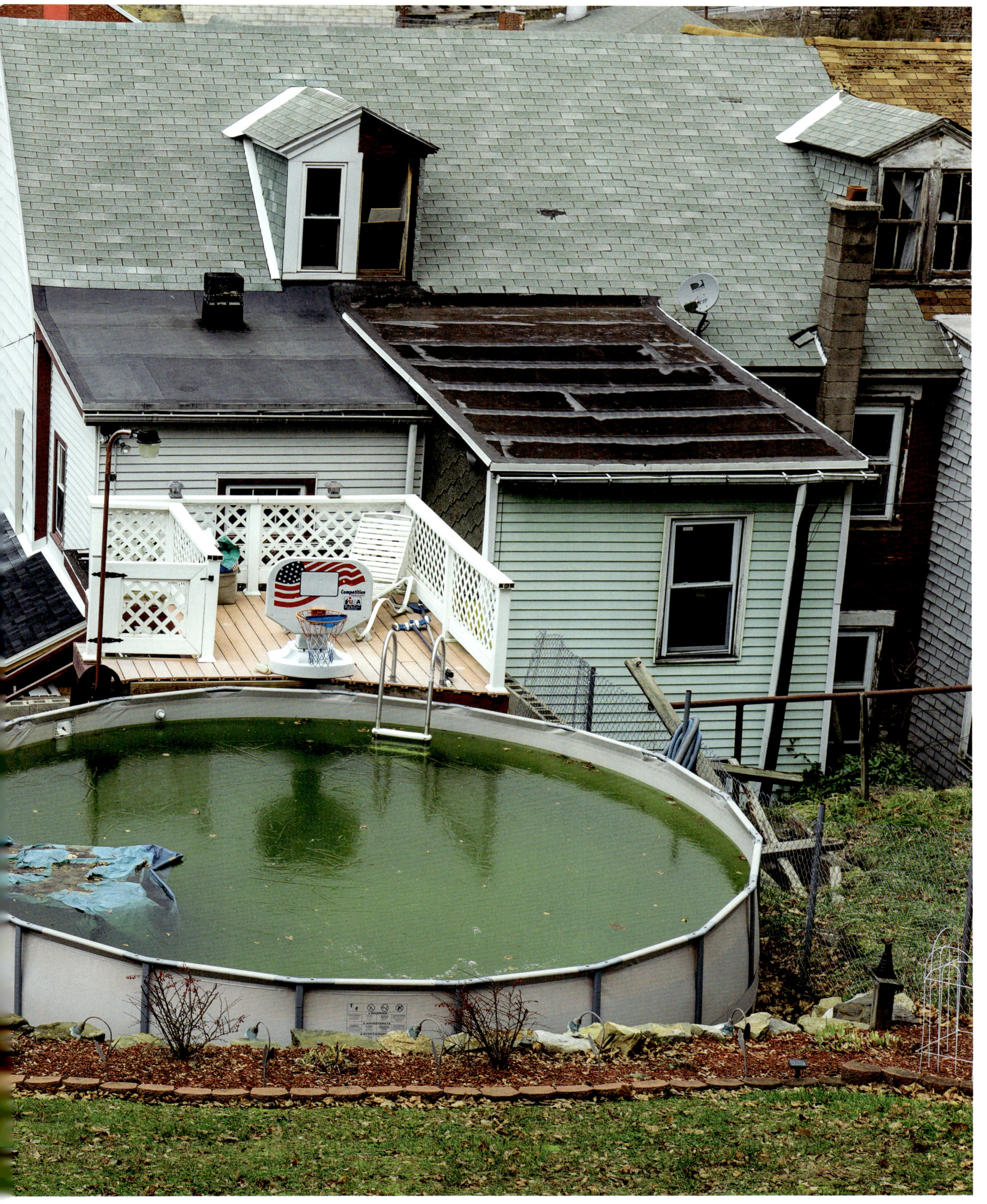
Competition

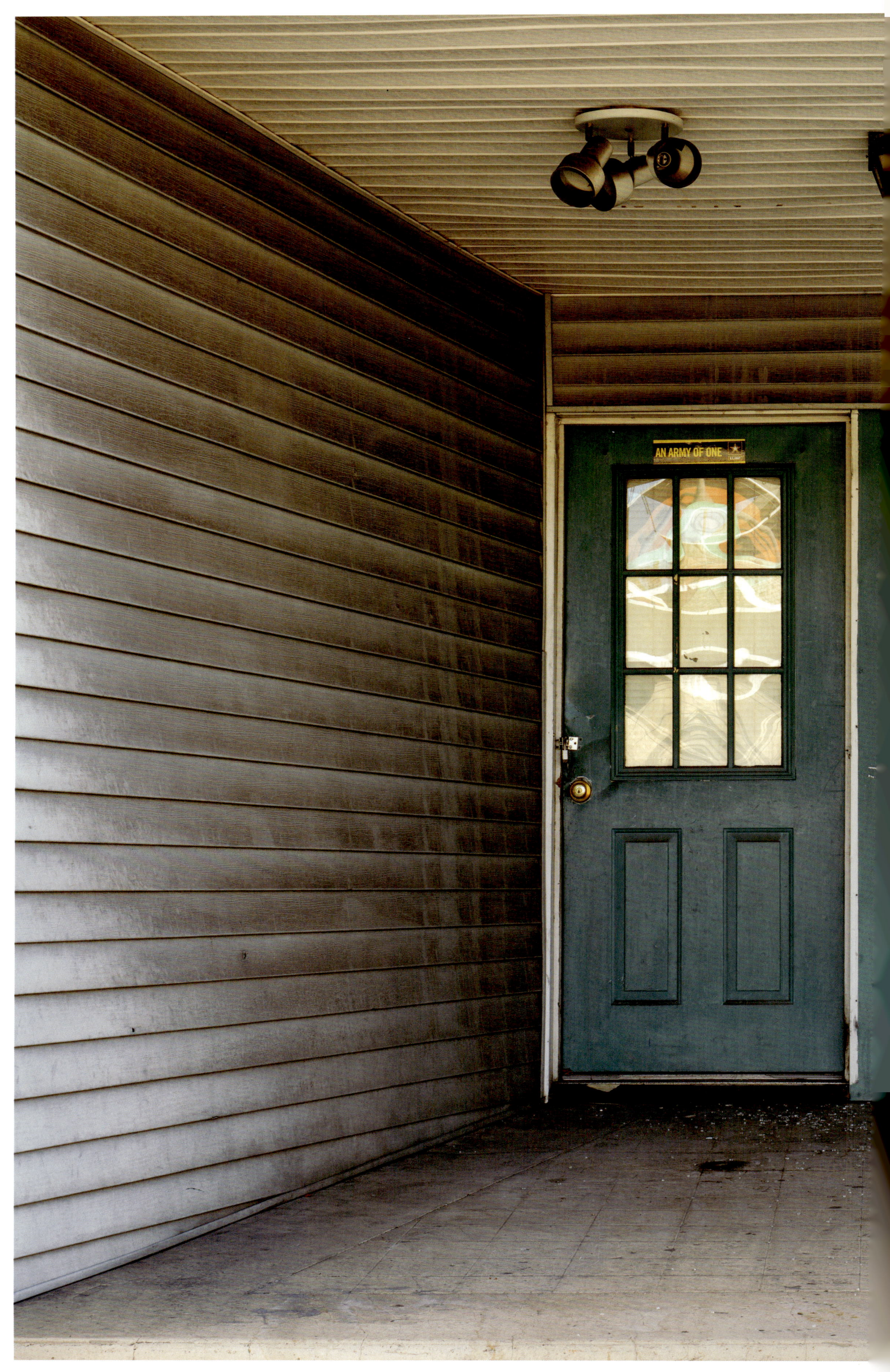
AN ARMY OF ONE

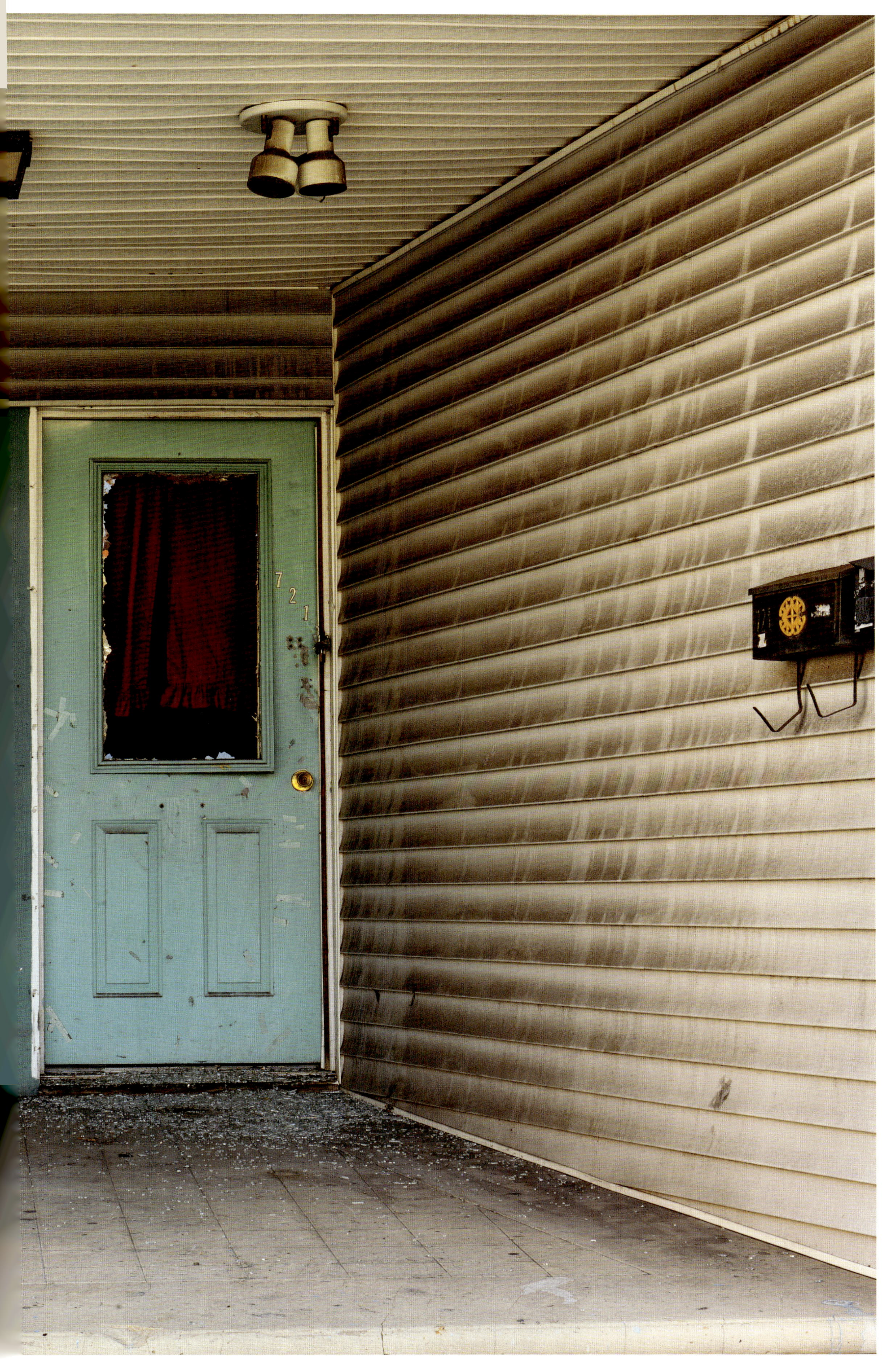

PLATE 6

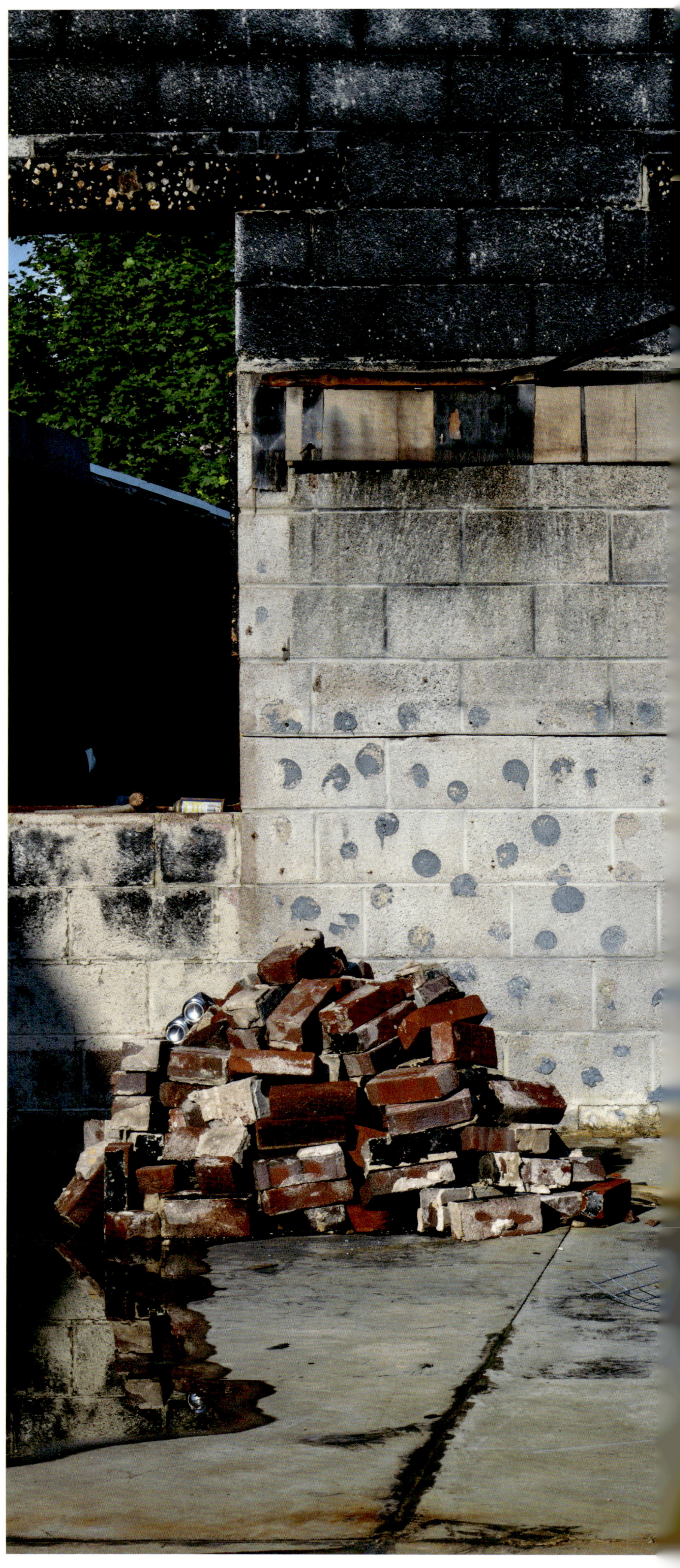

PLATE 7

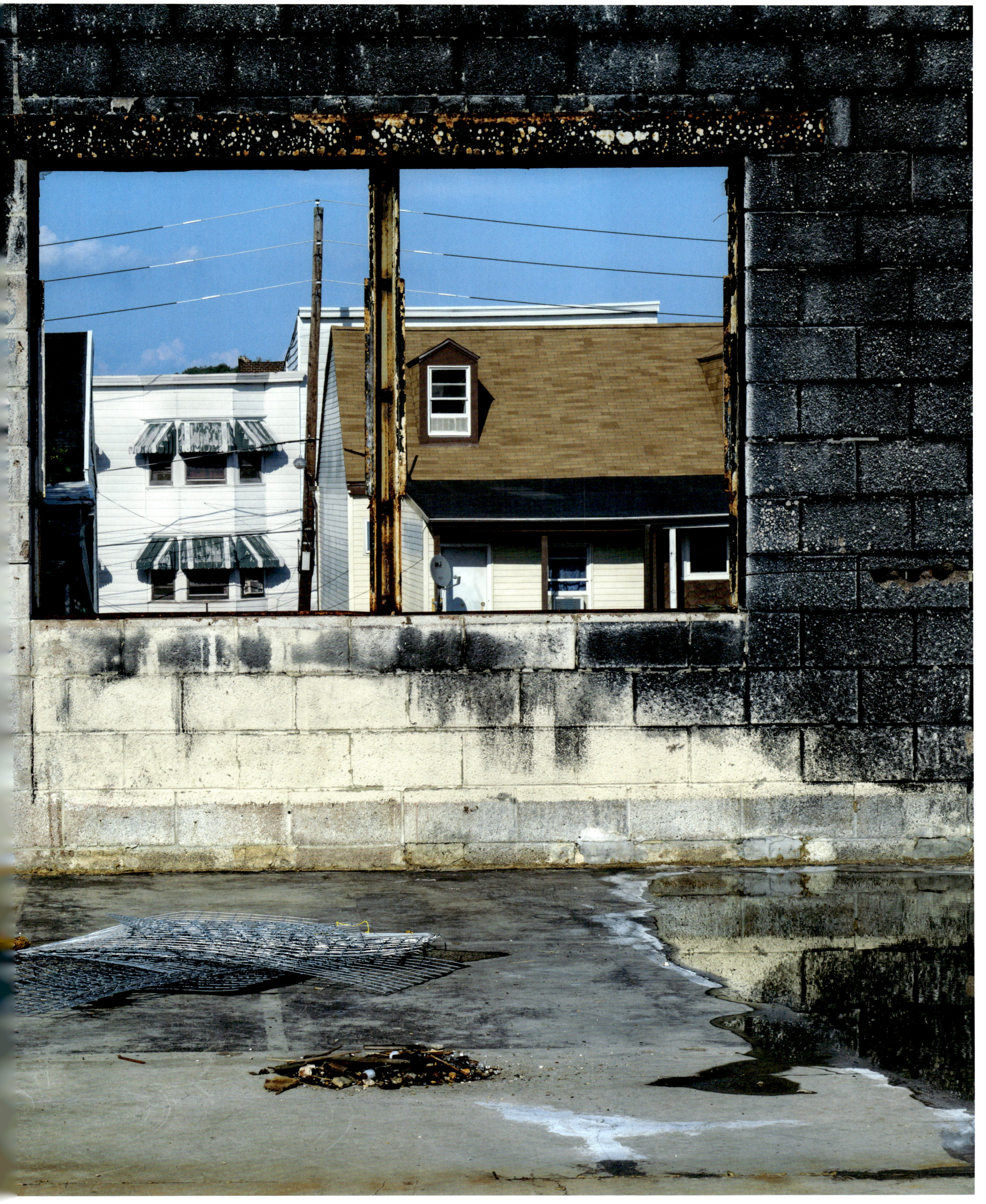

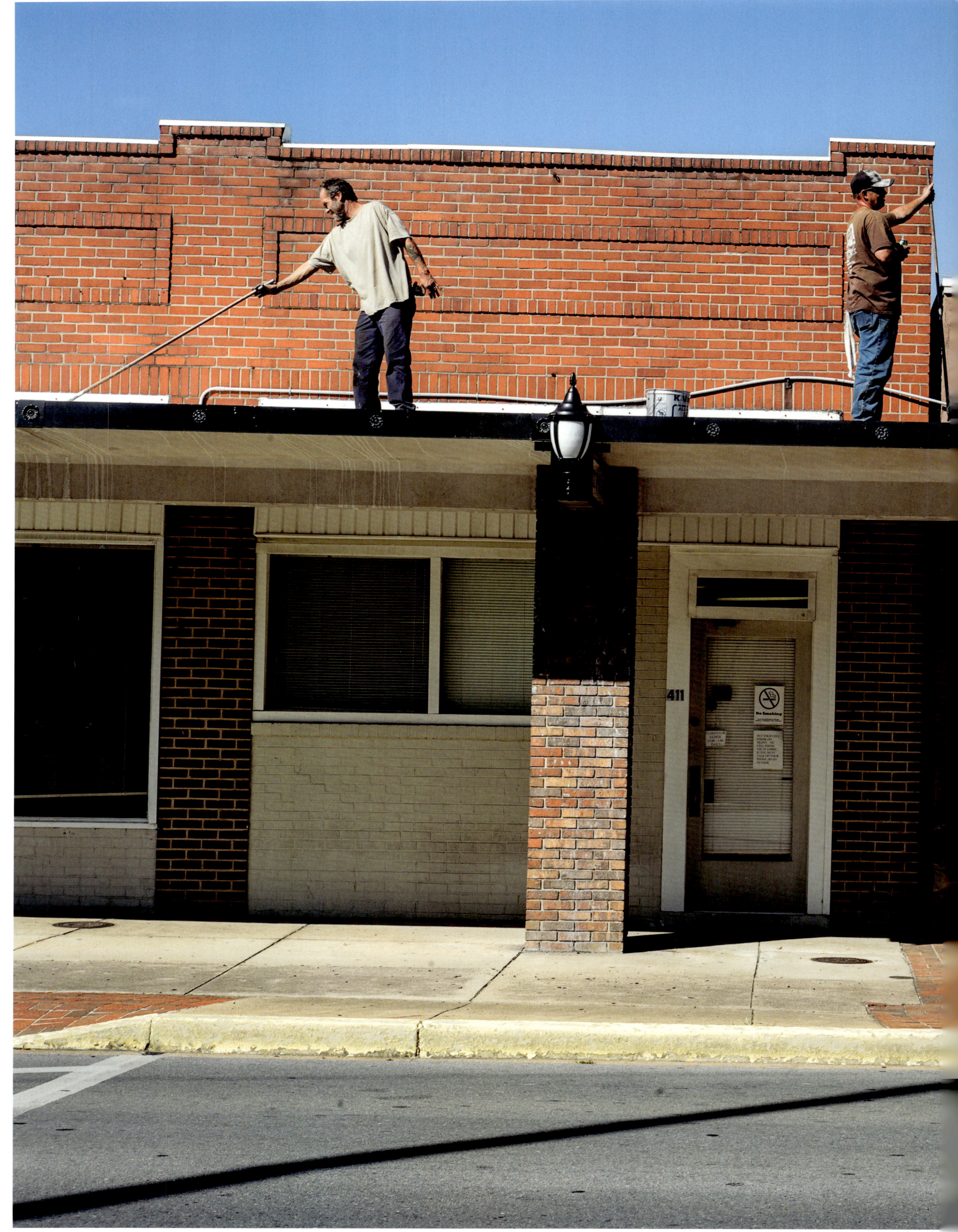
411
No Smoking

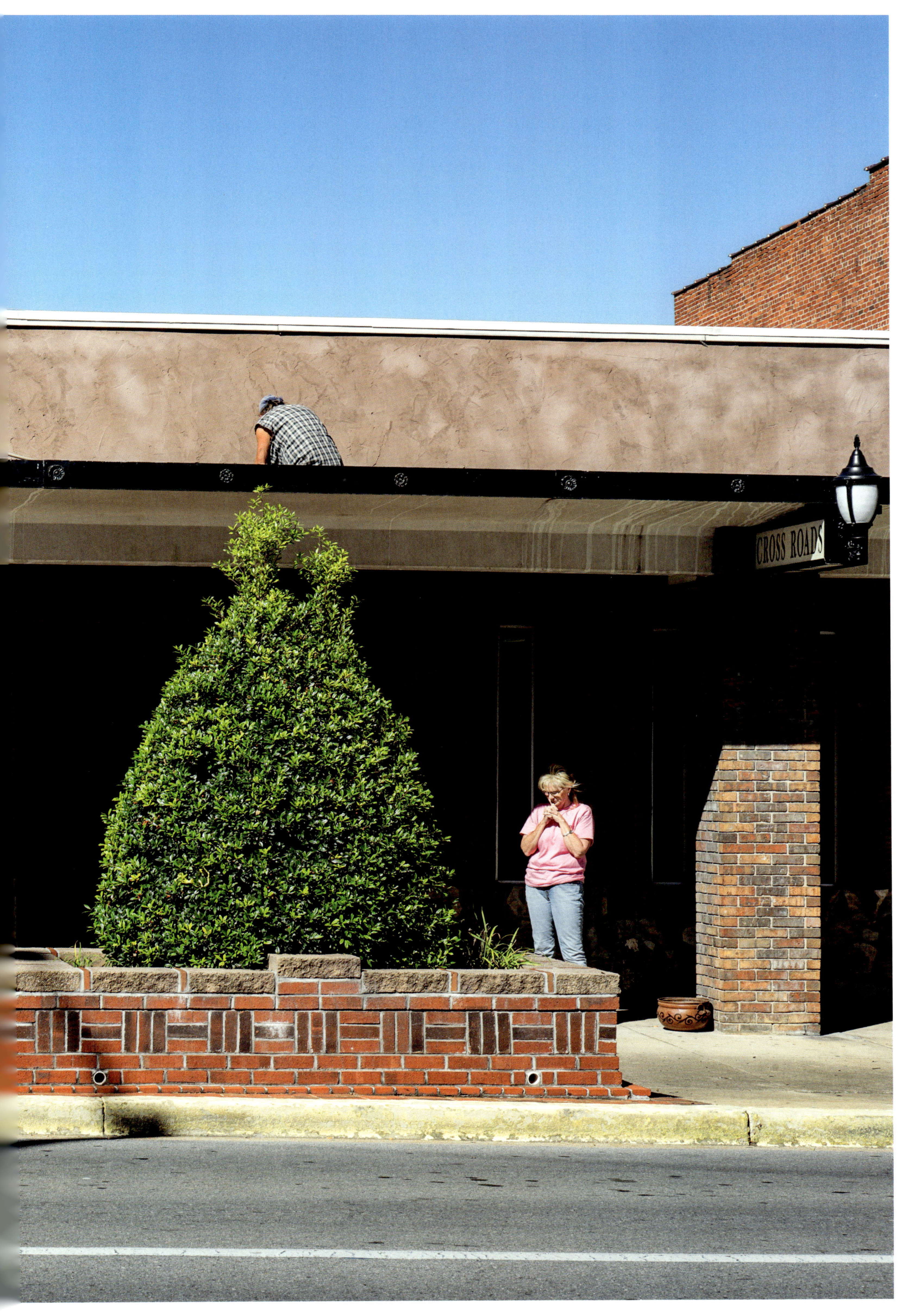

PLATE 8

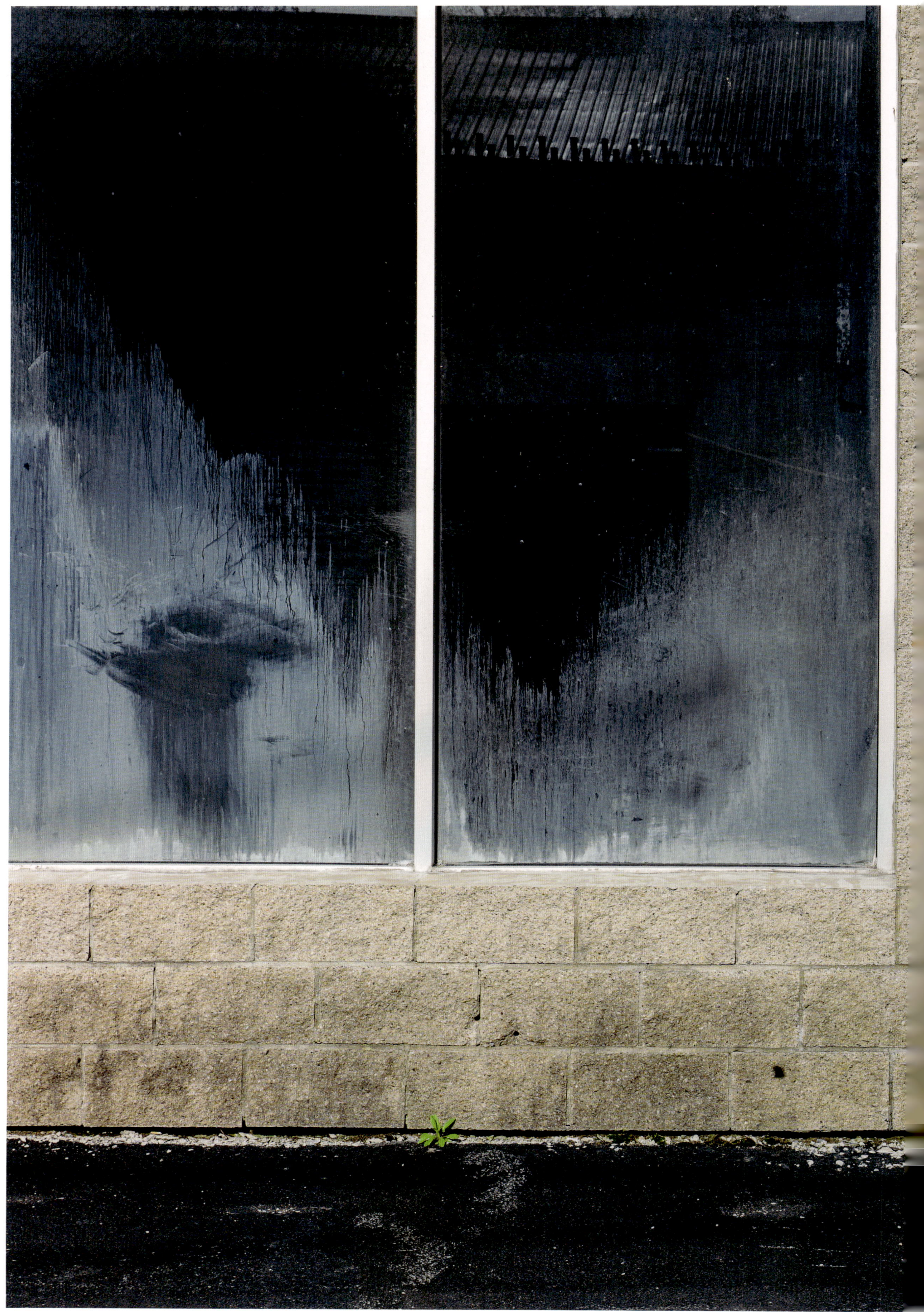

PLATE 9

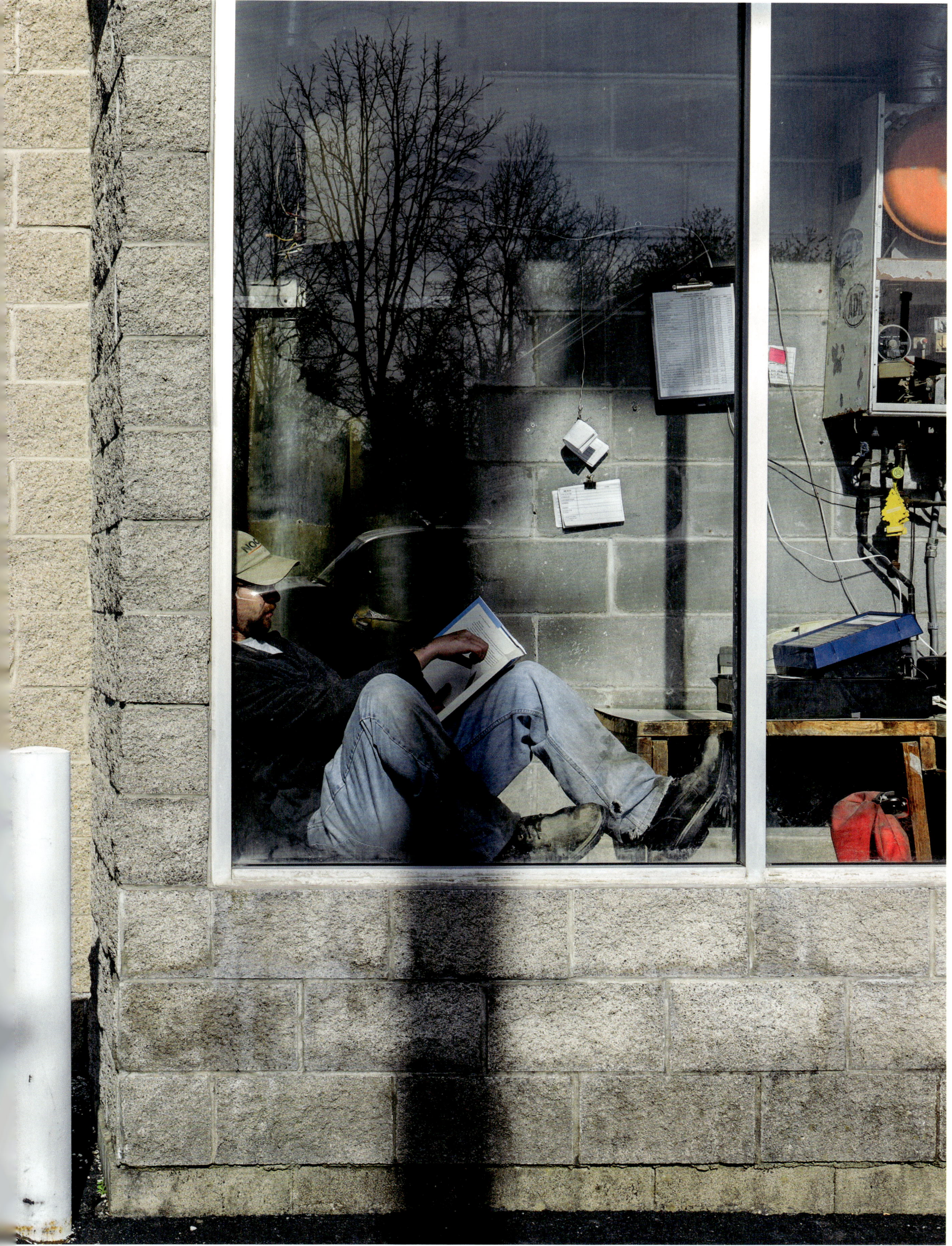

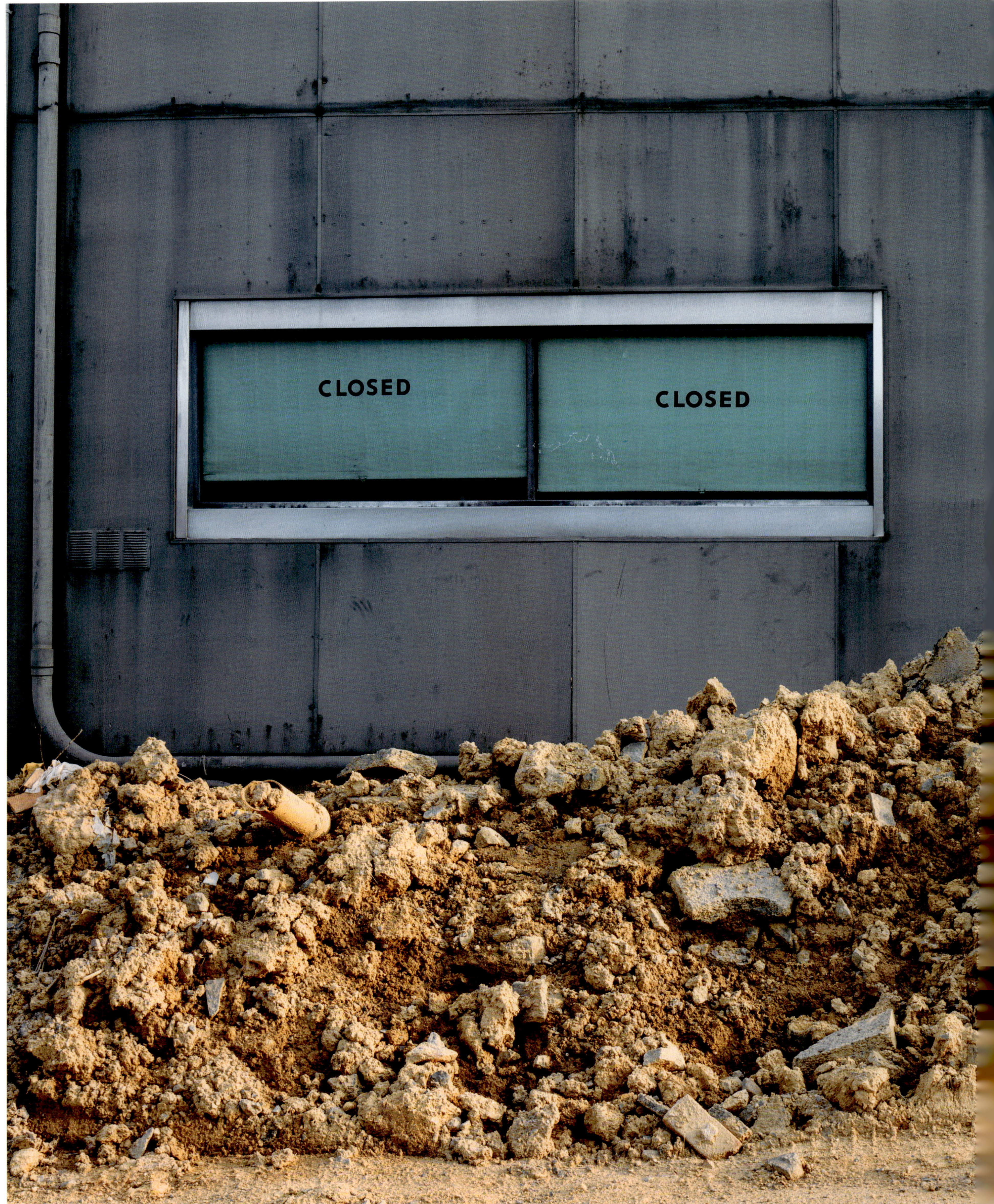
CLOSED
CLOSED

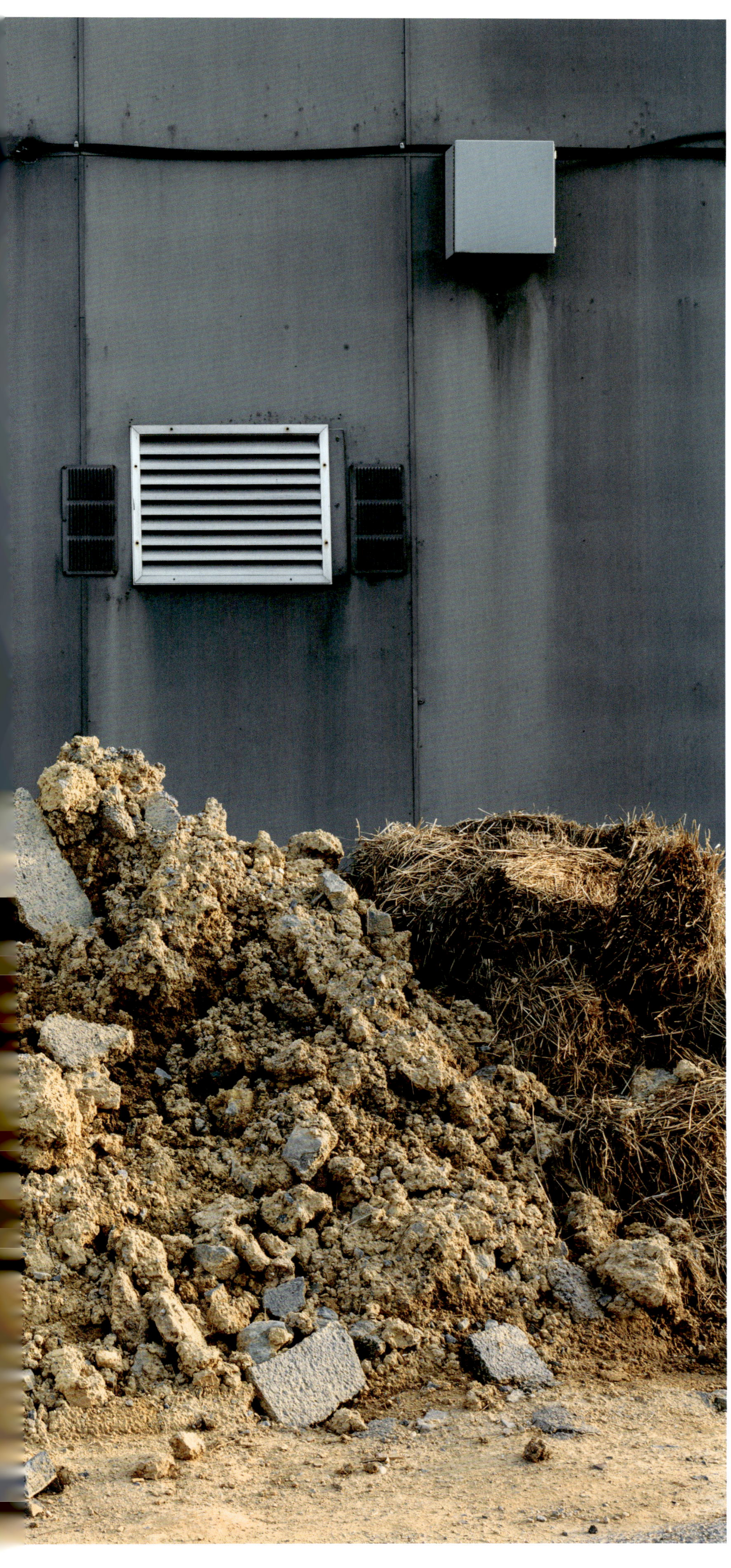

PLATE 10

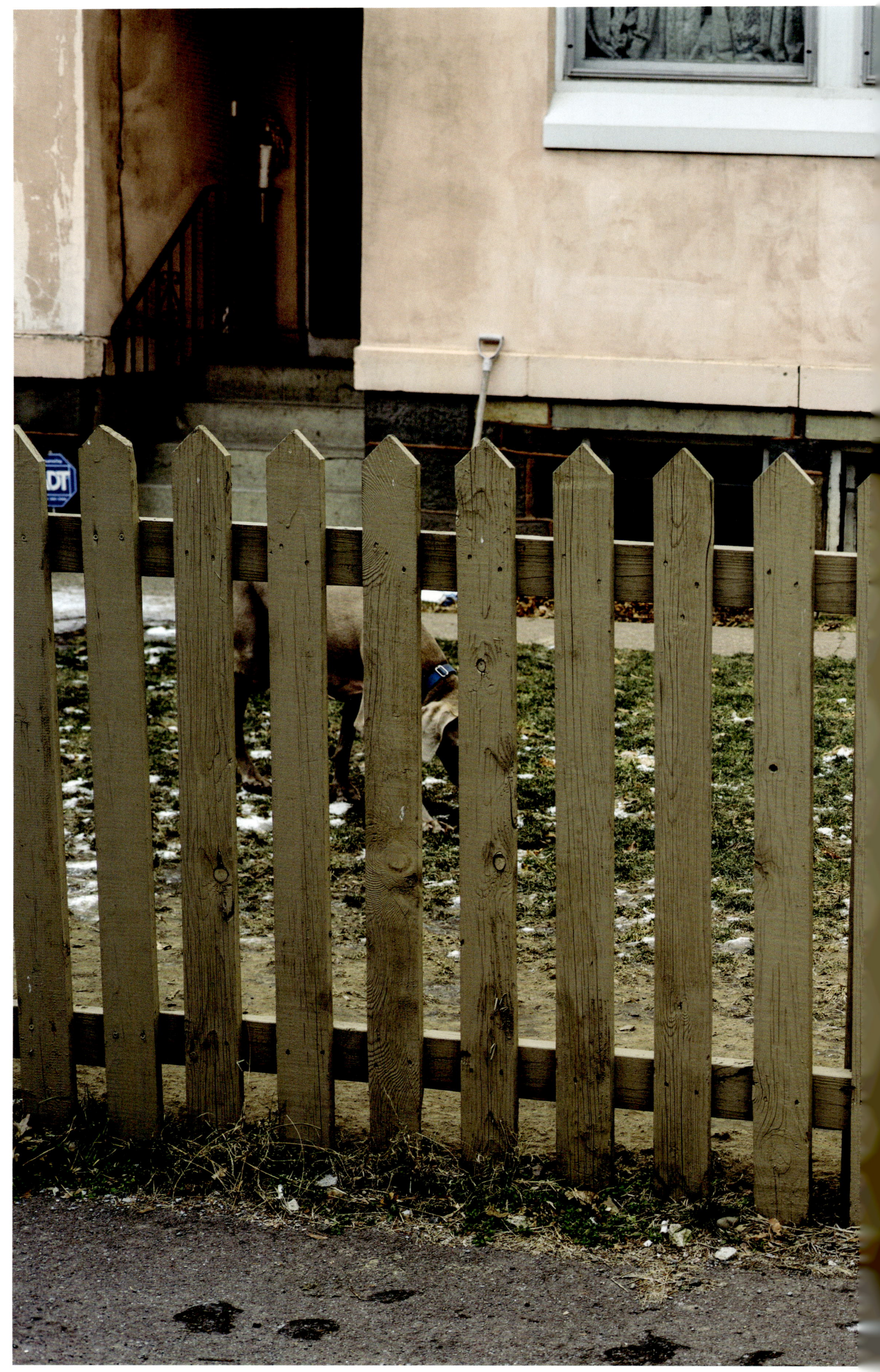

PLATE 11

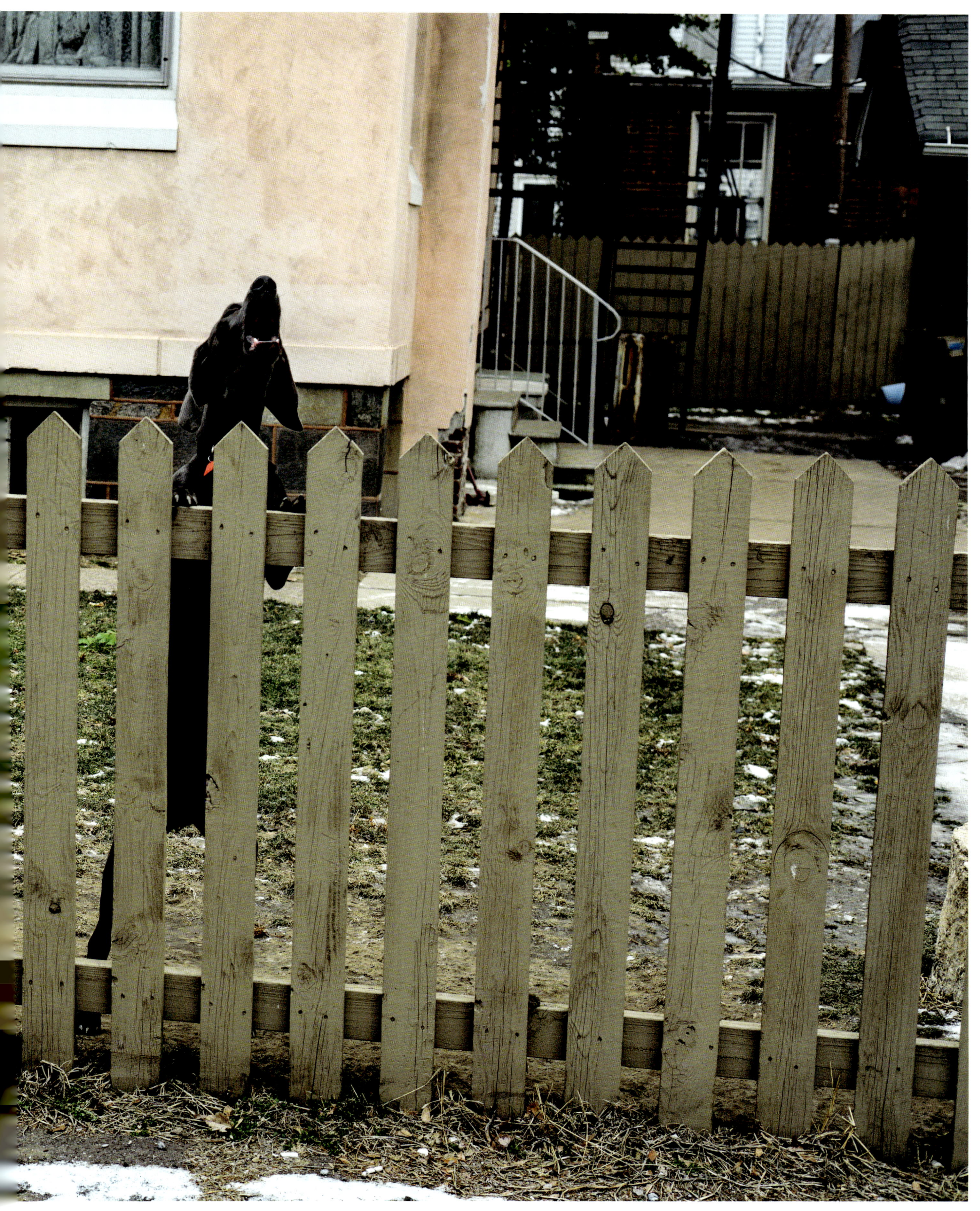

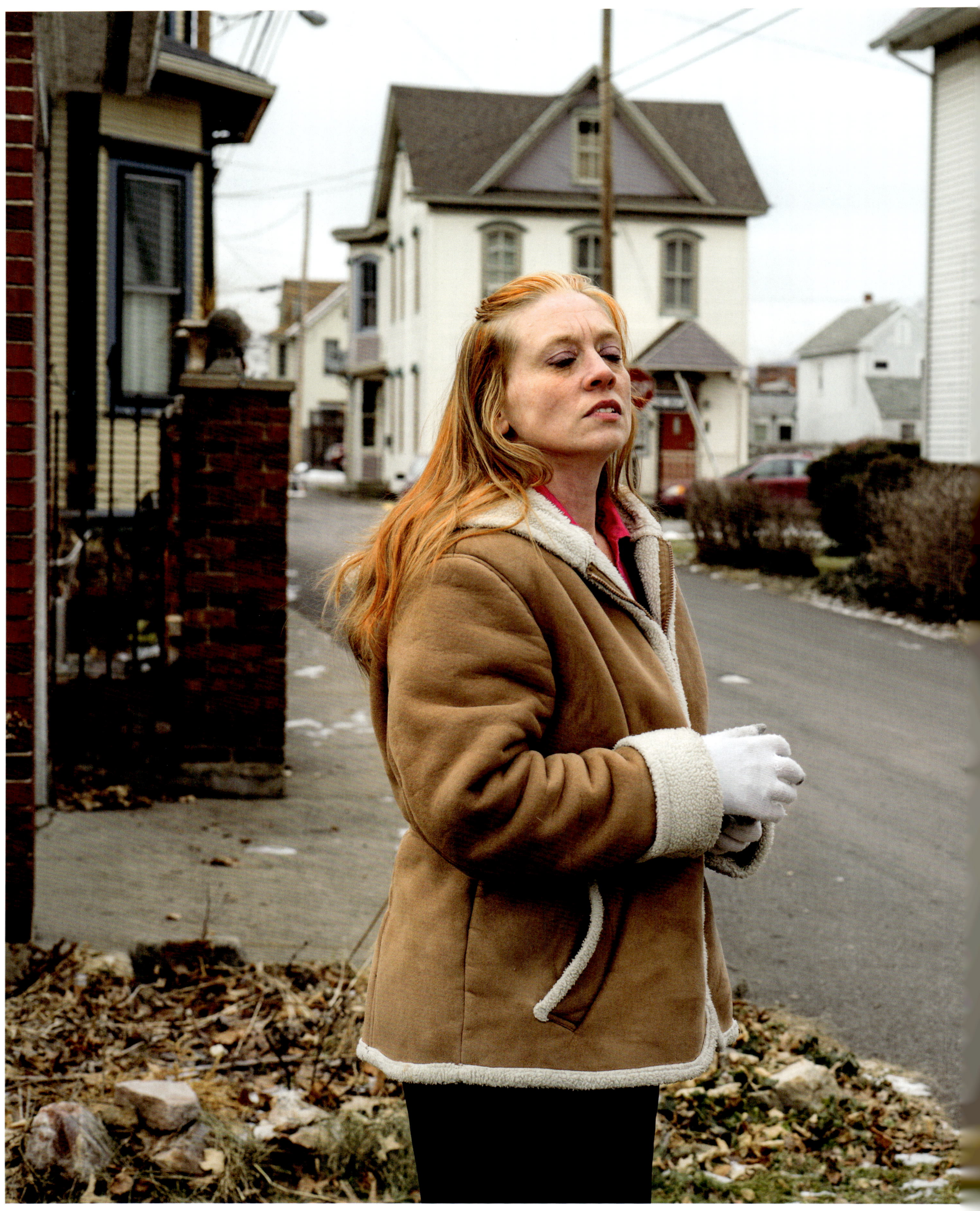

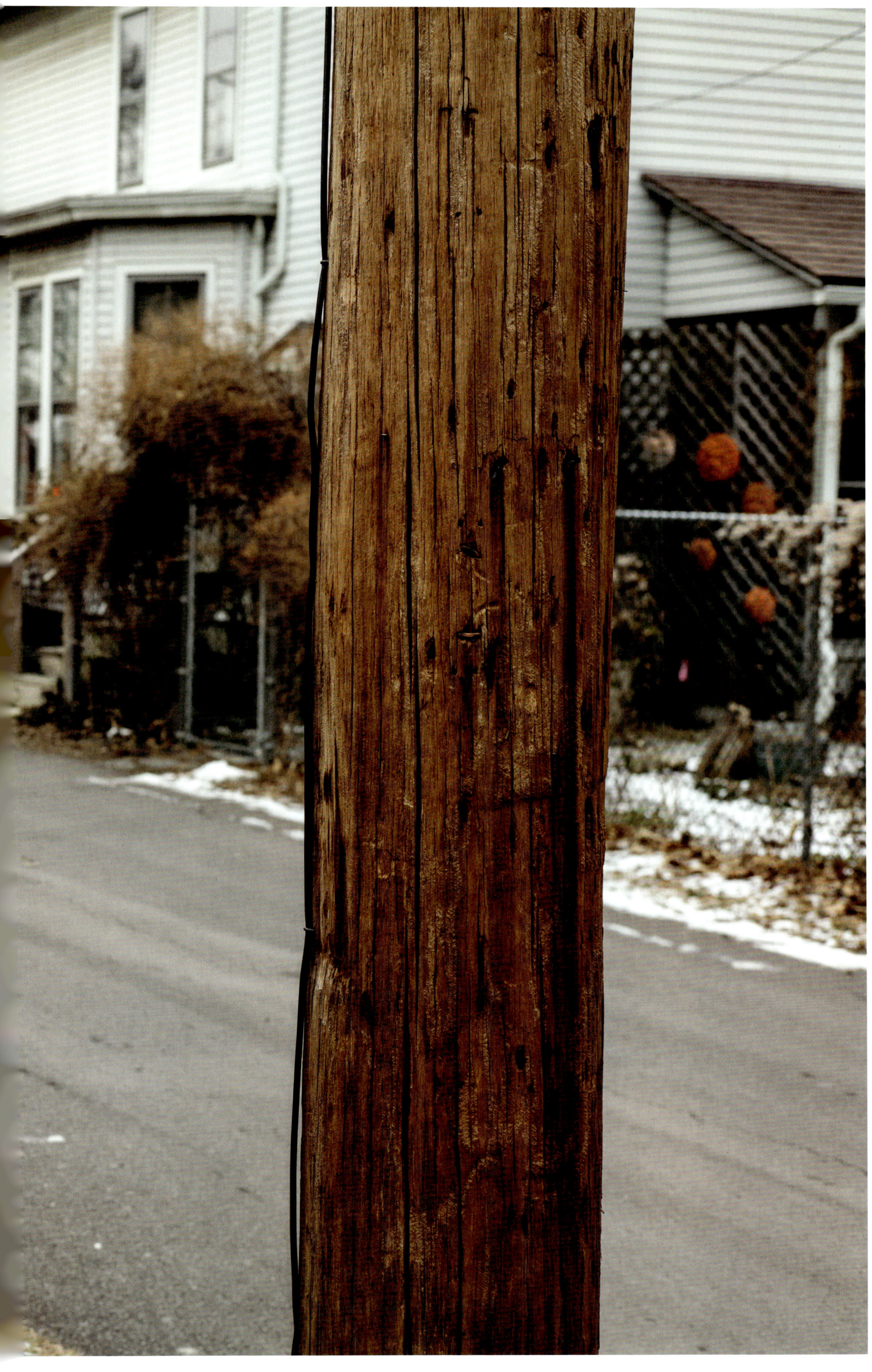

PLATE 12

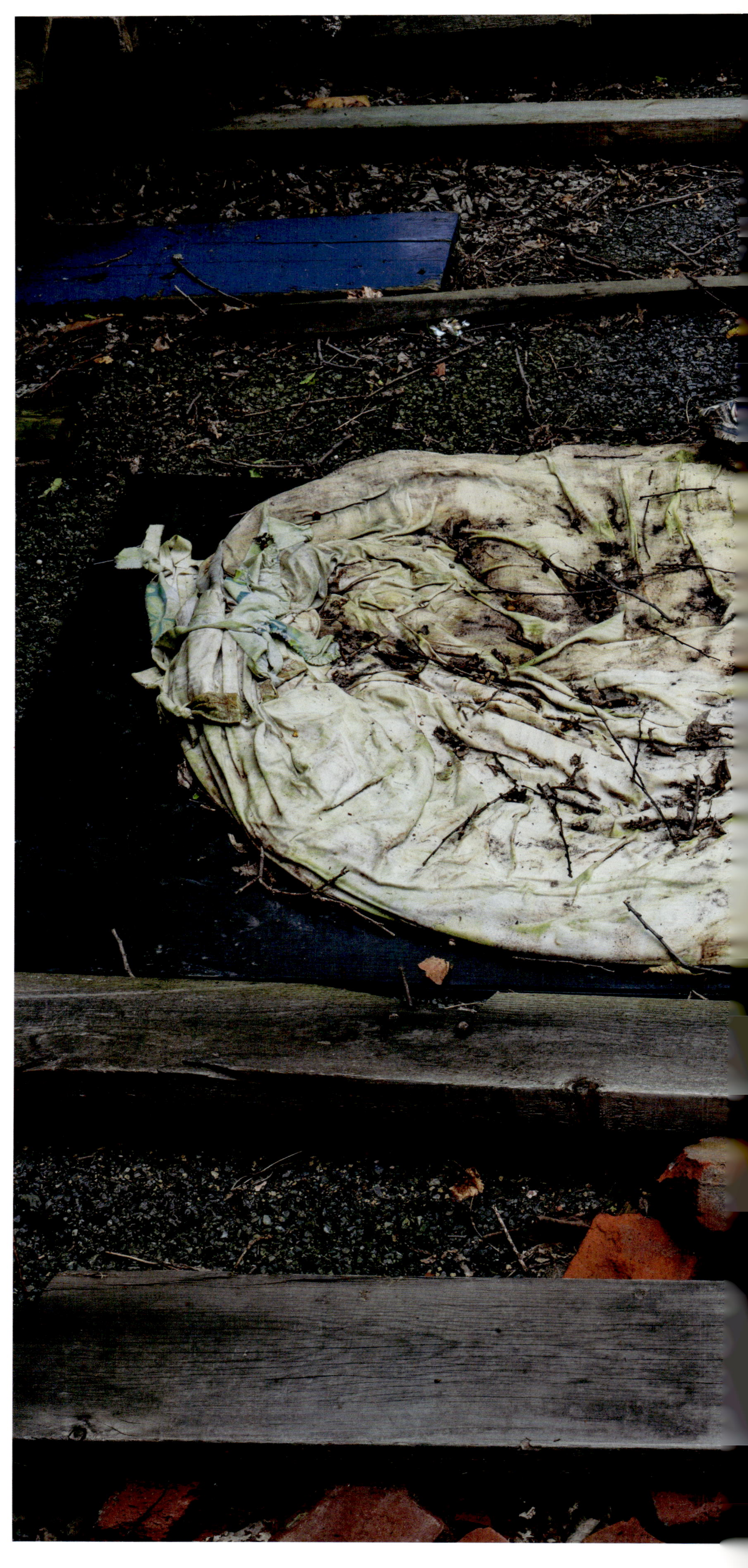

PLATE 13

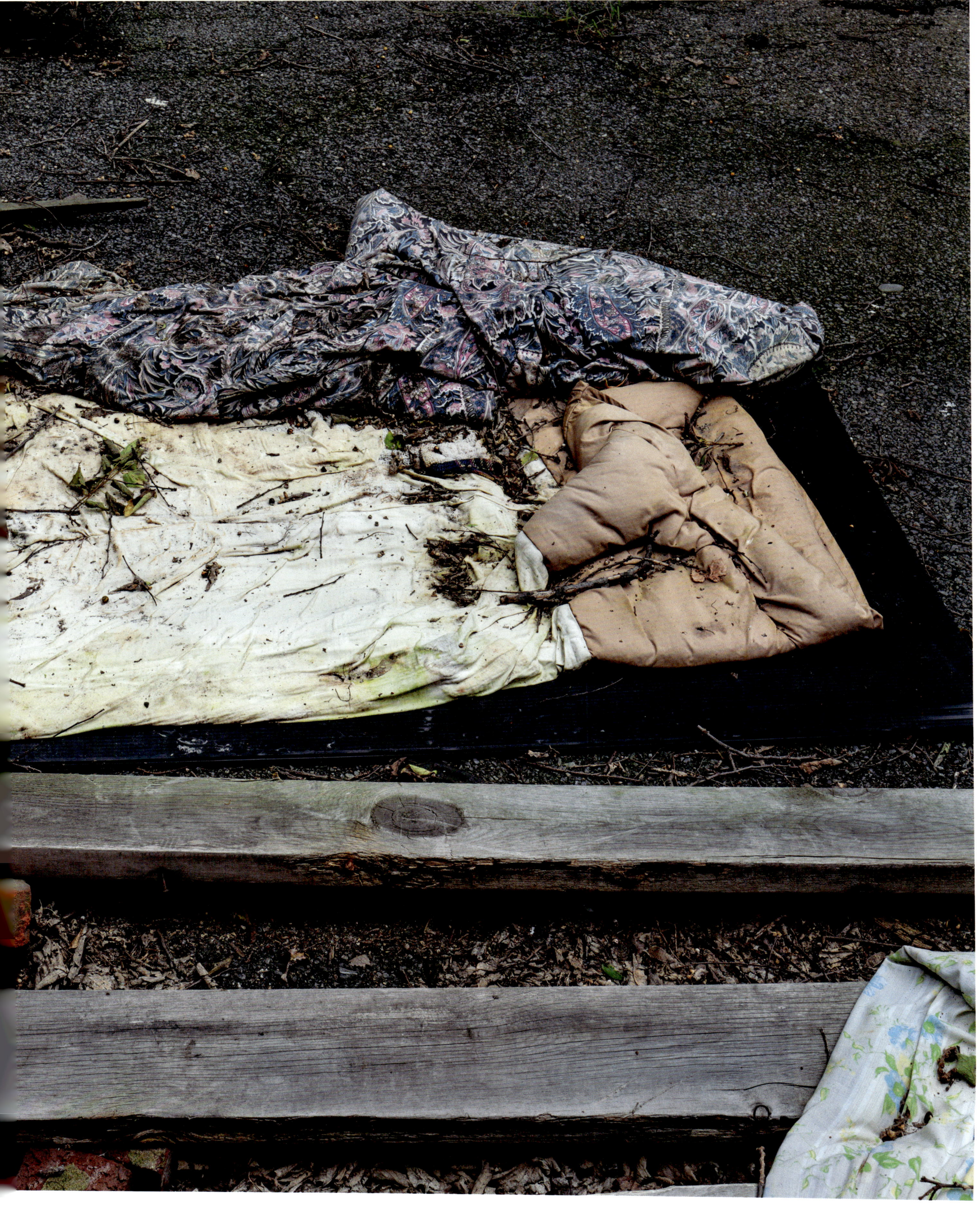

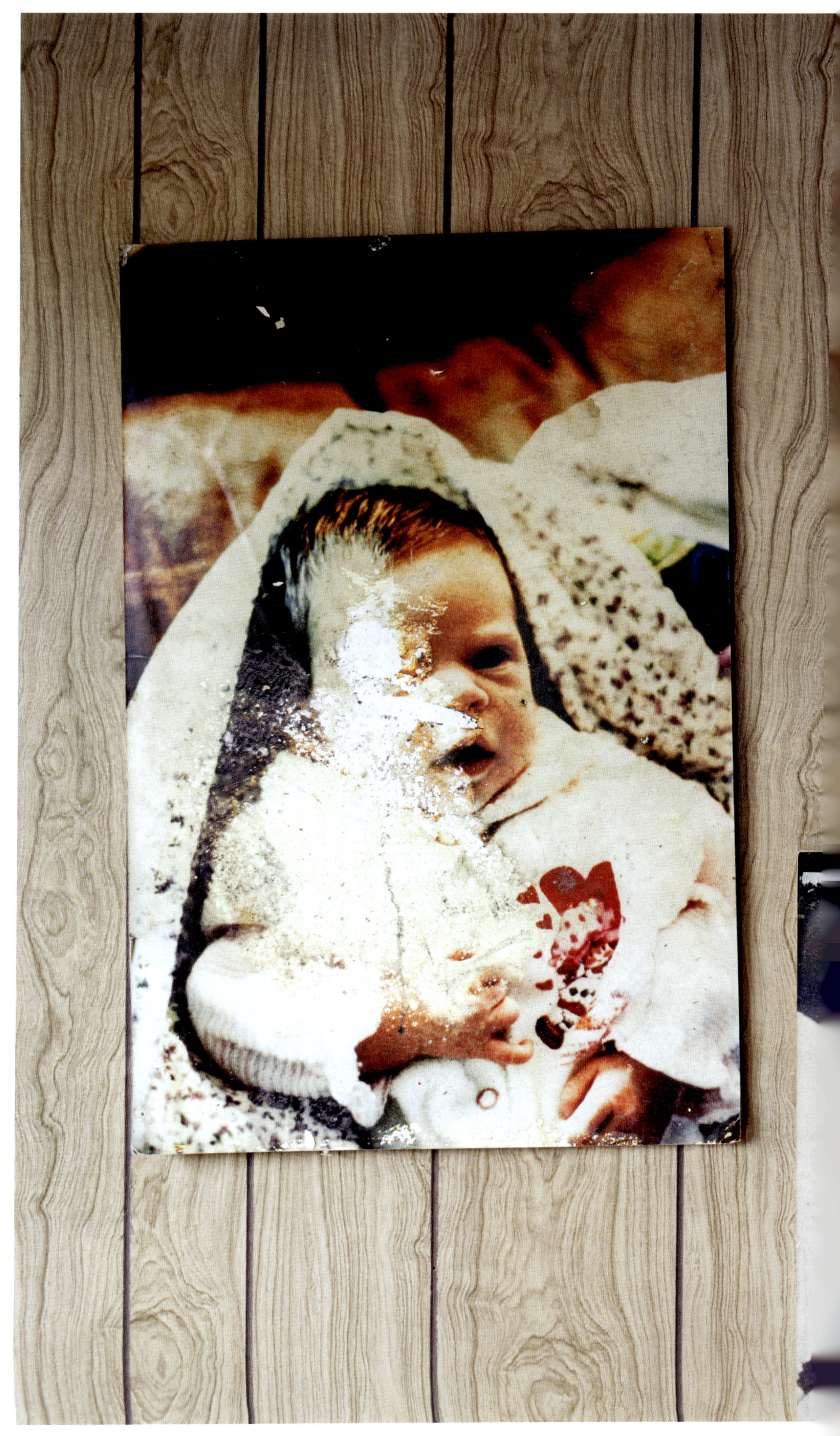

PLATE 14

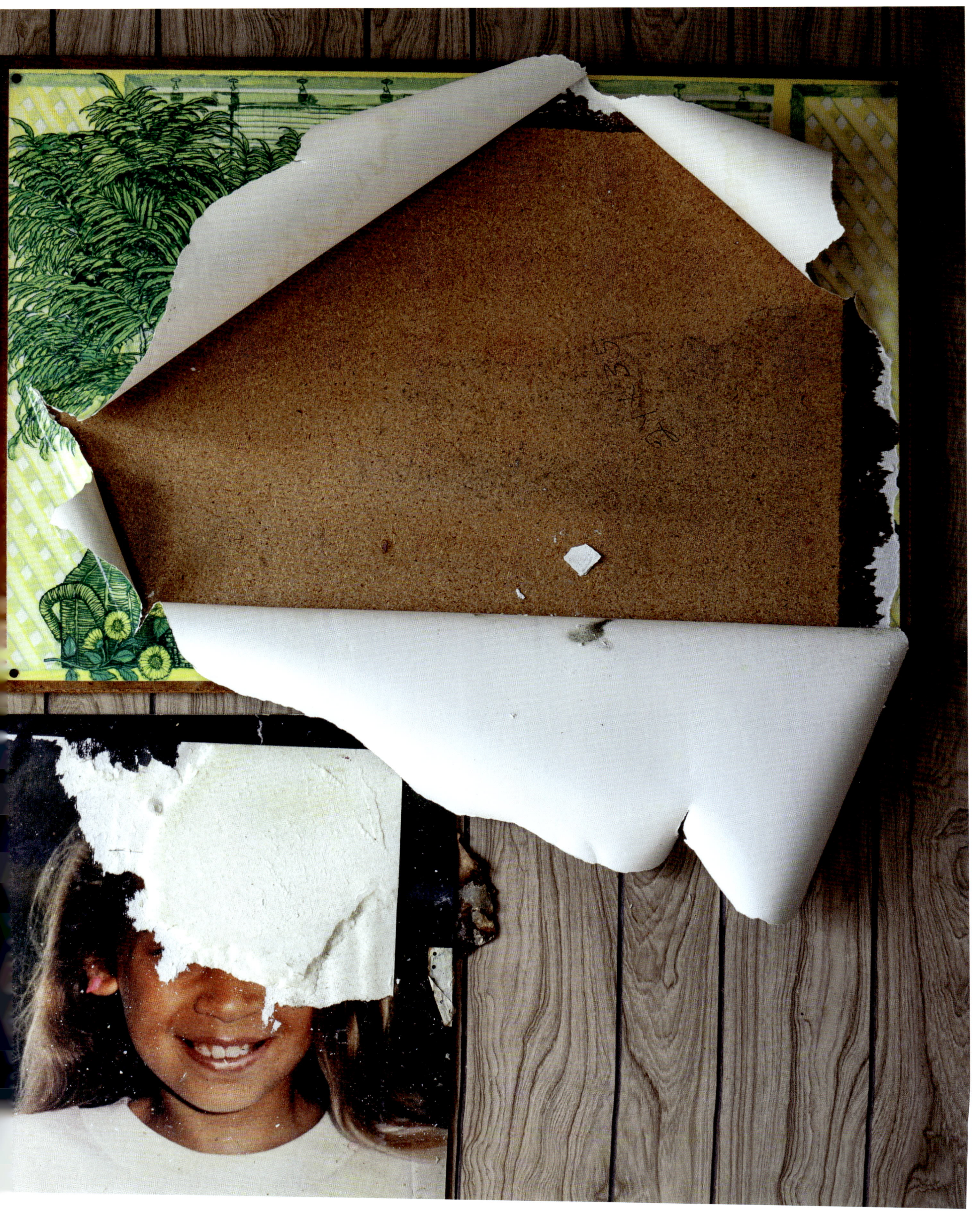

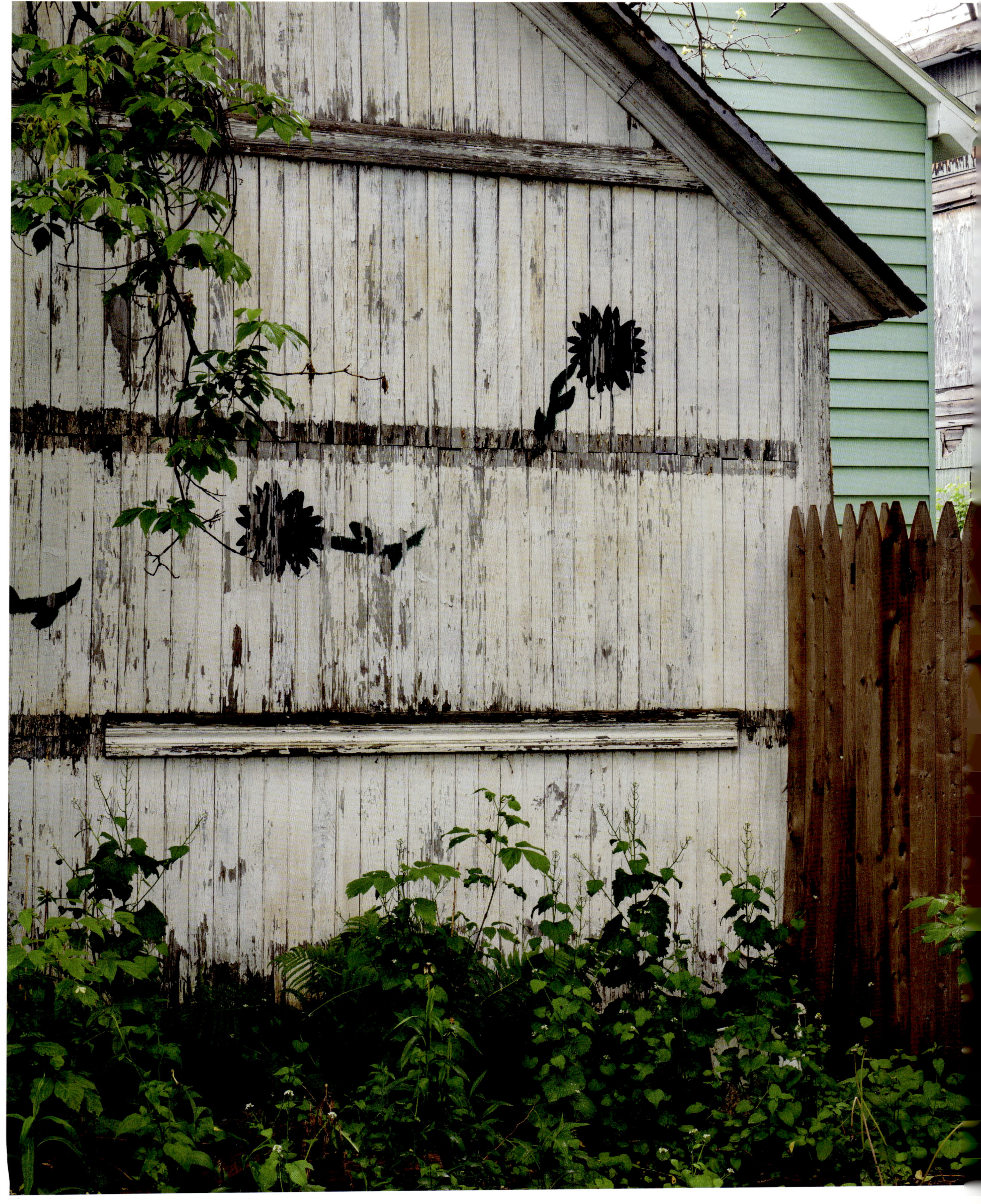

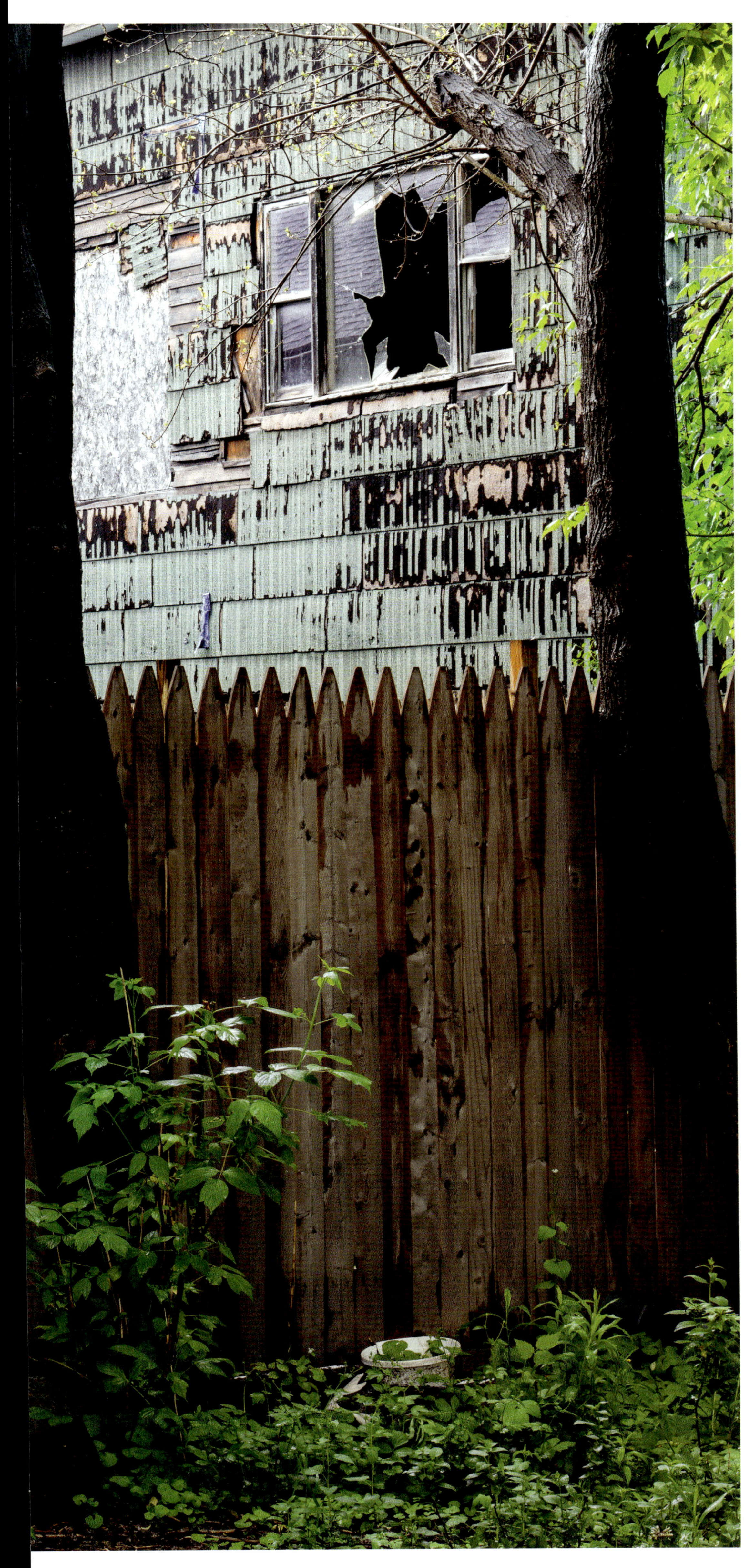

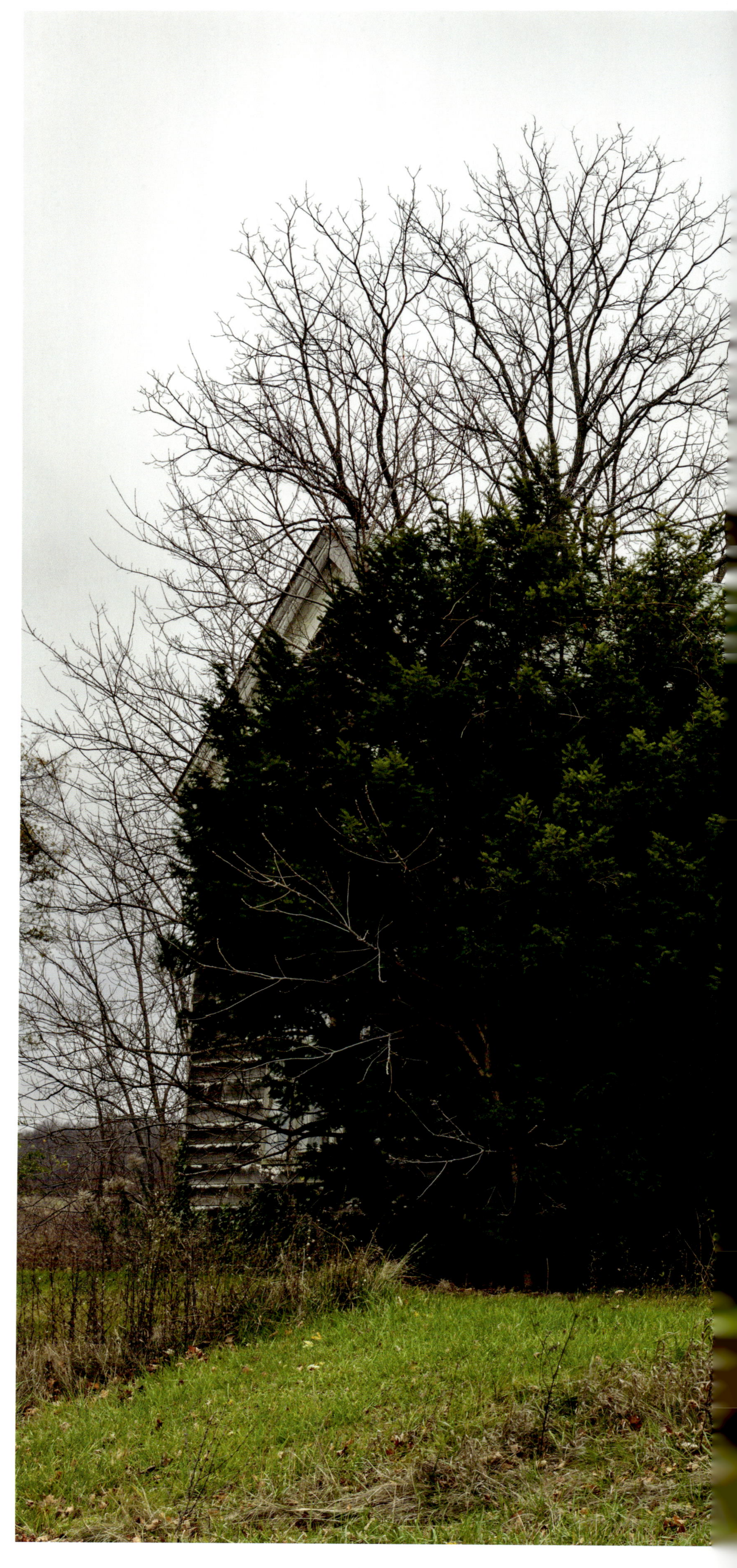

PLATE 16

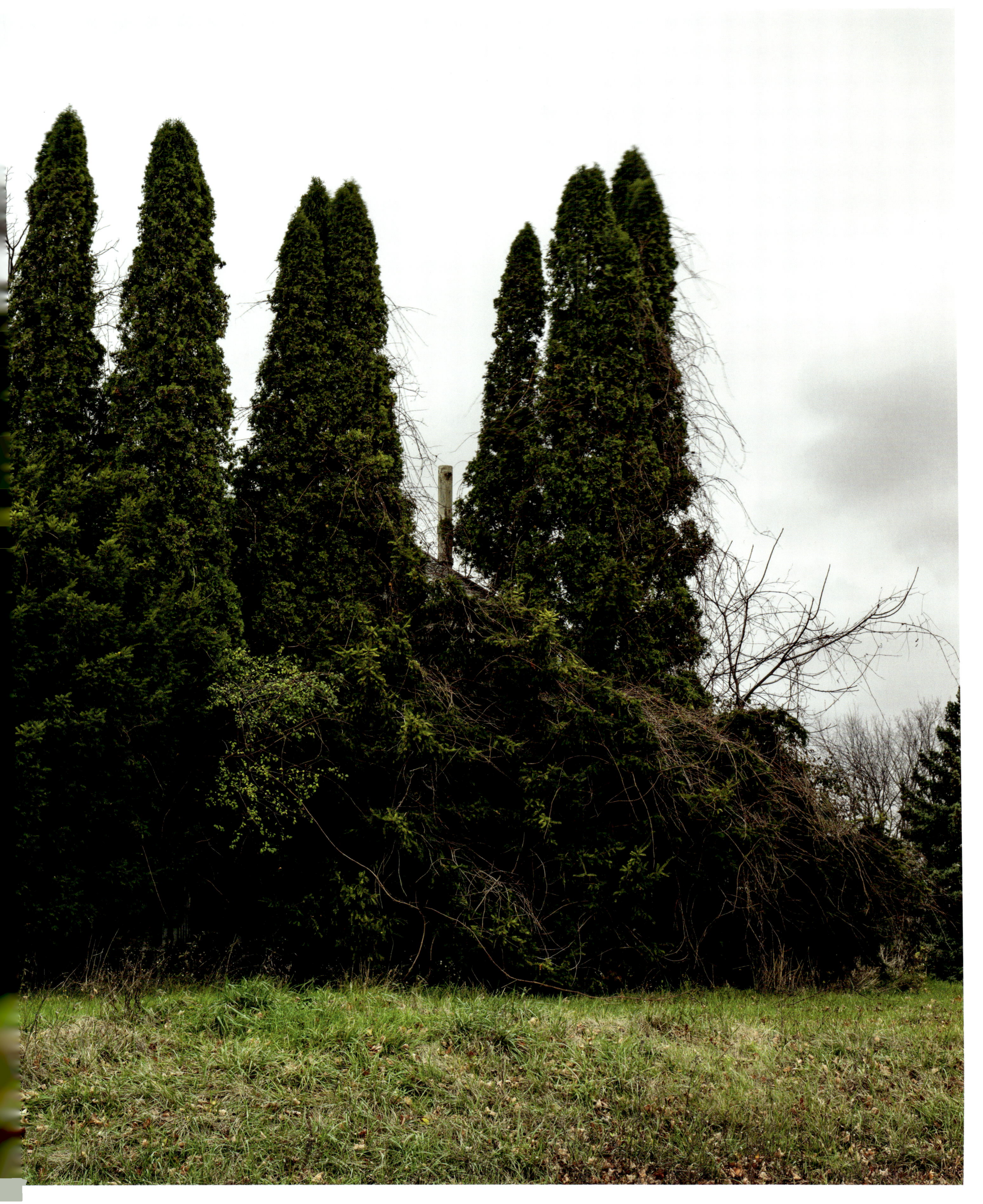

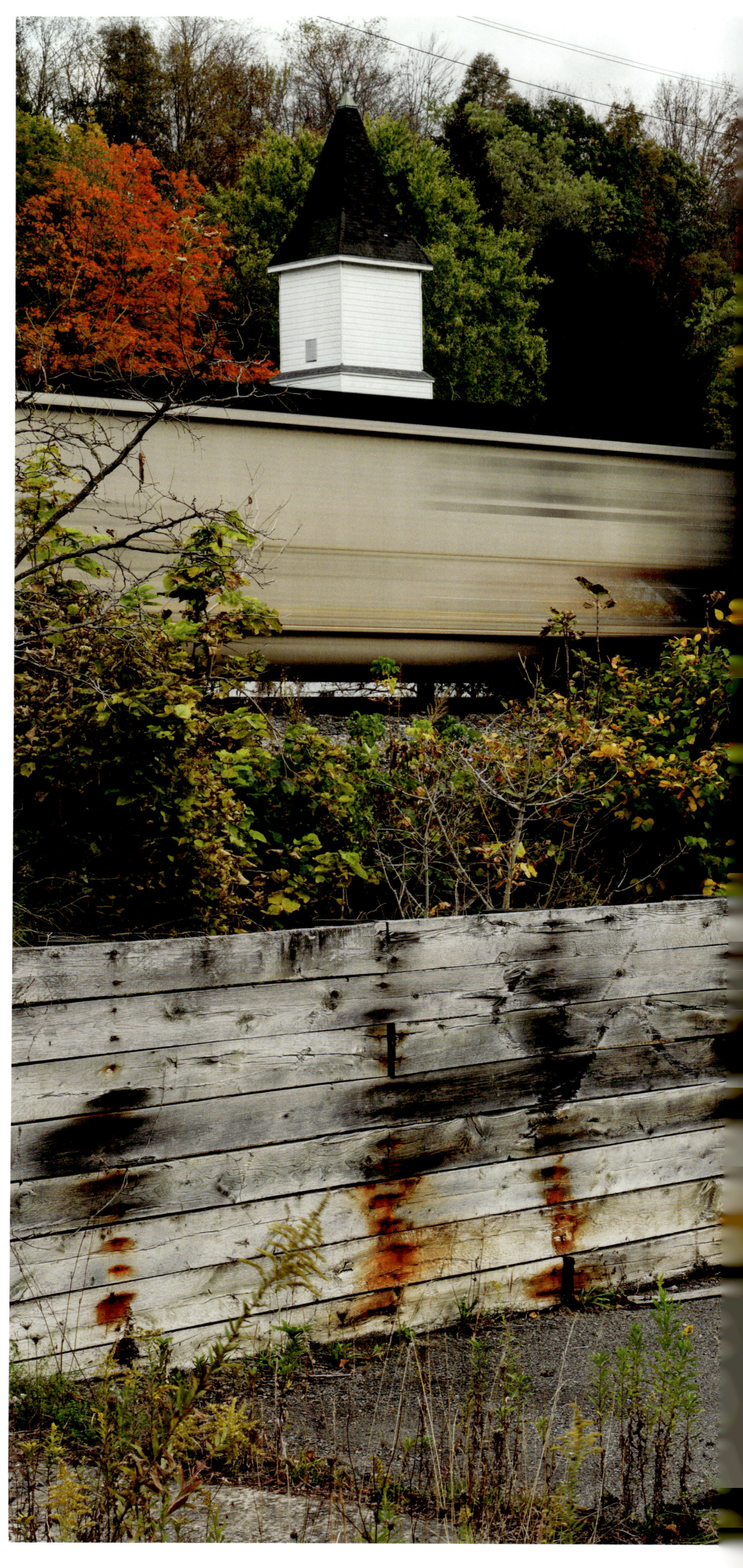

PLATE 17

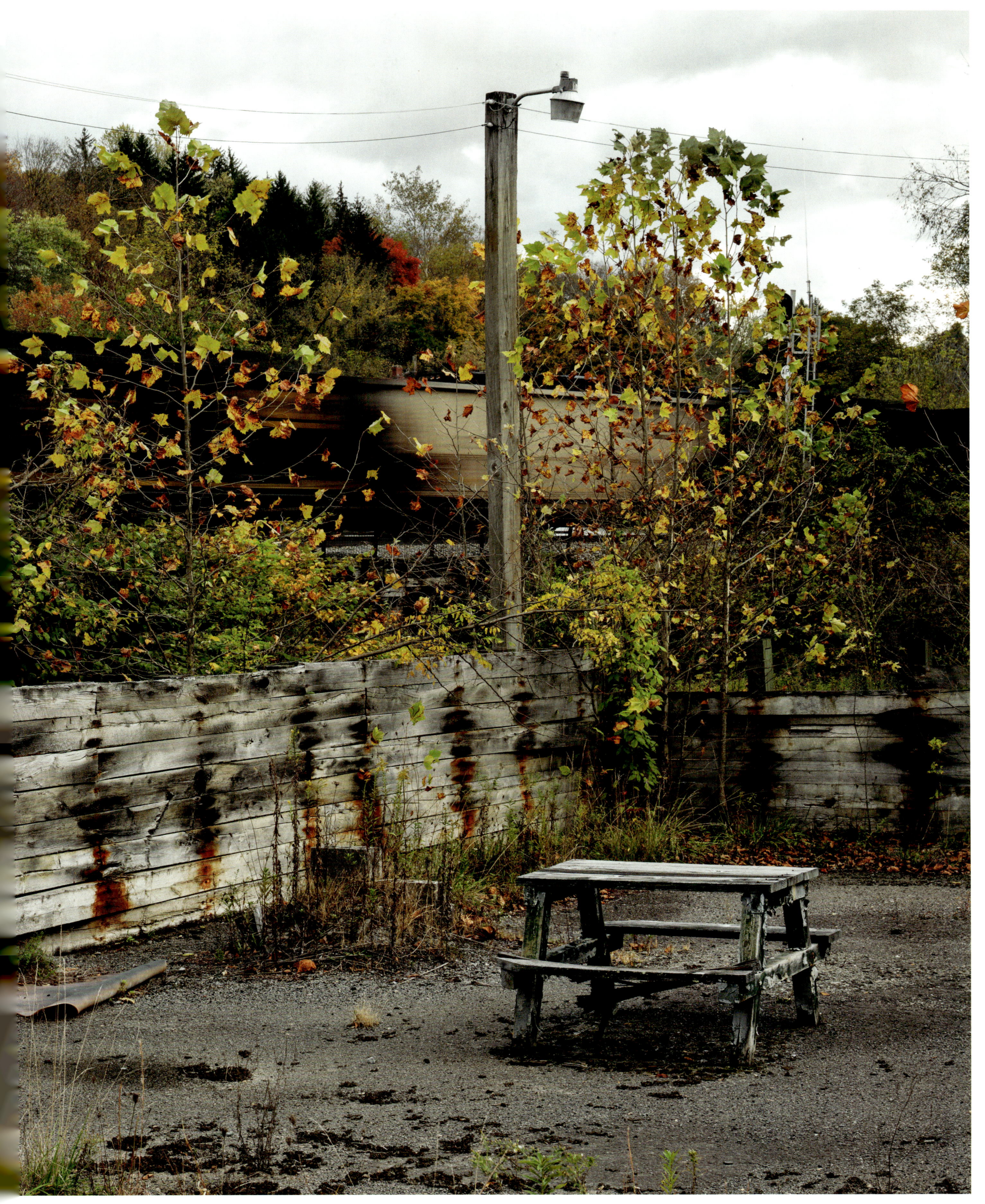

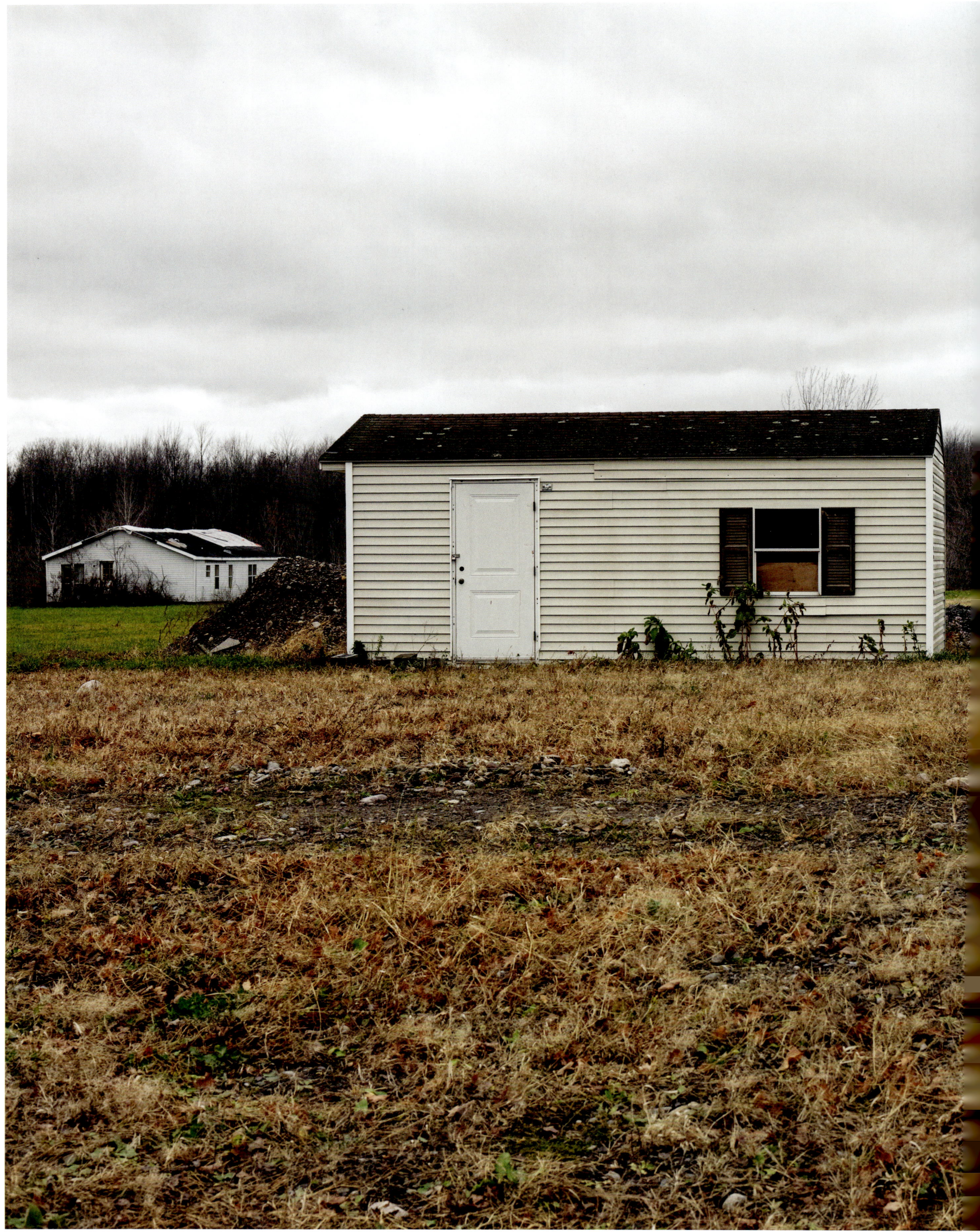

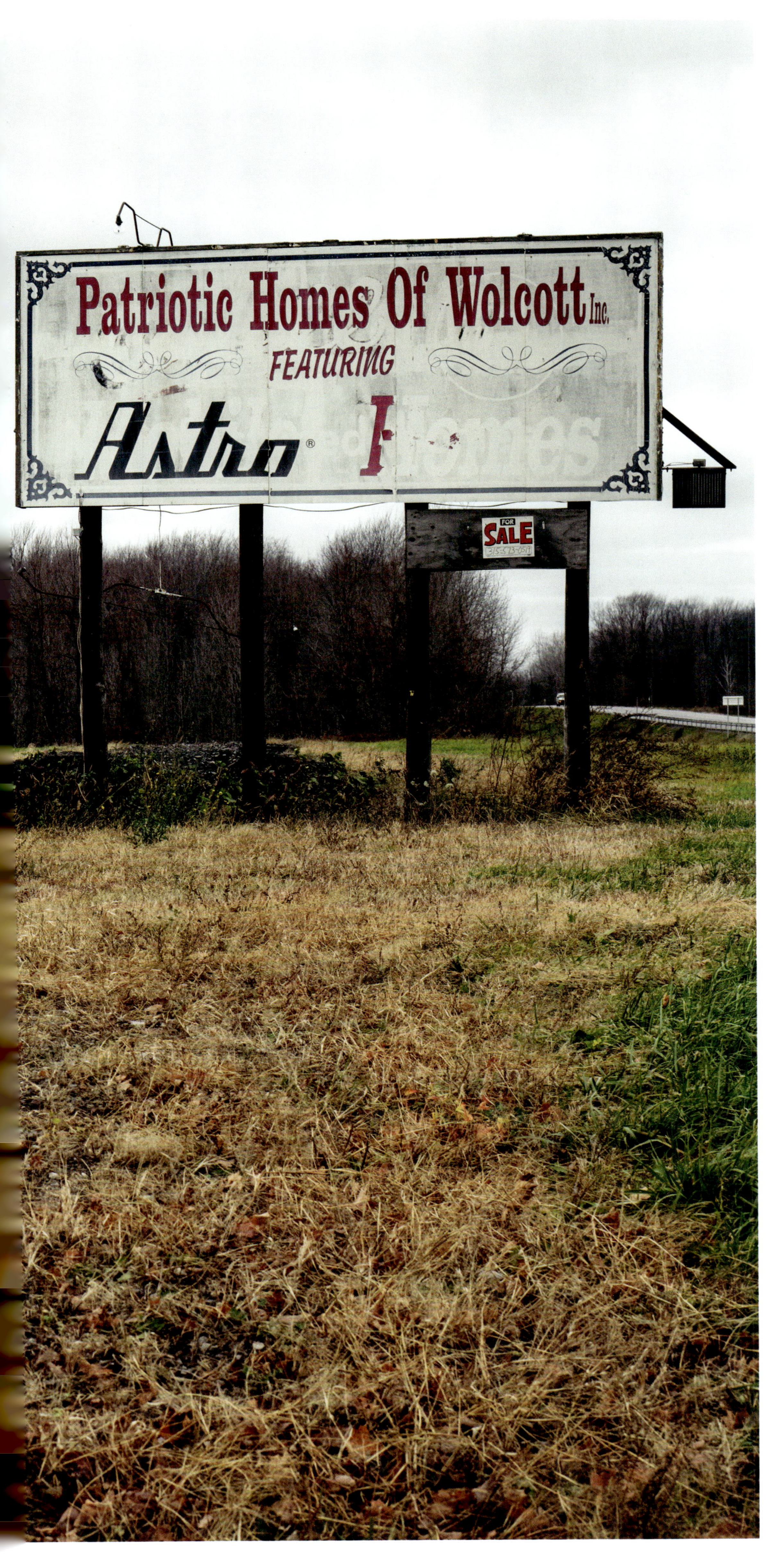
Patriotic Homes Of Wolcott Inc.
FEATURING
Astro®
FOR SALE

PLATE 19

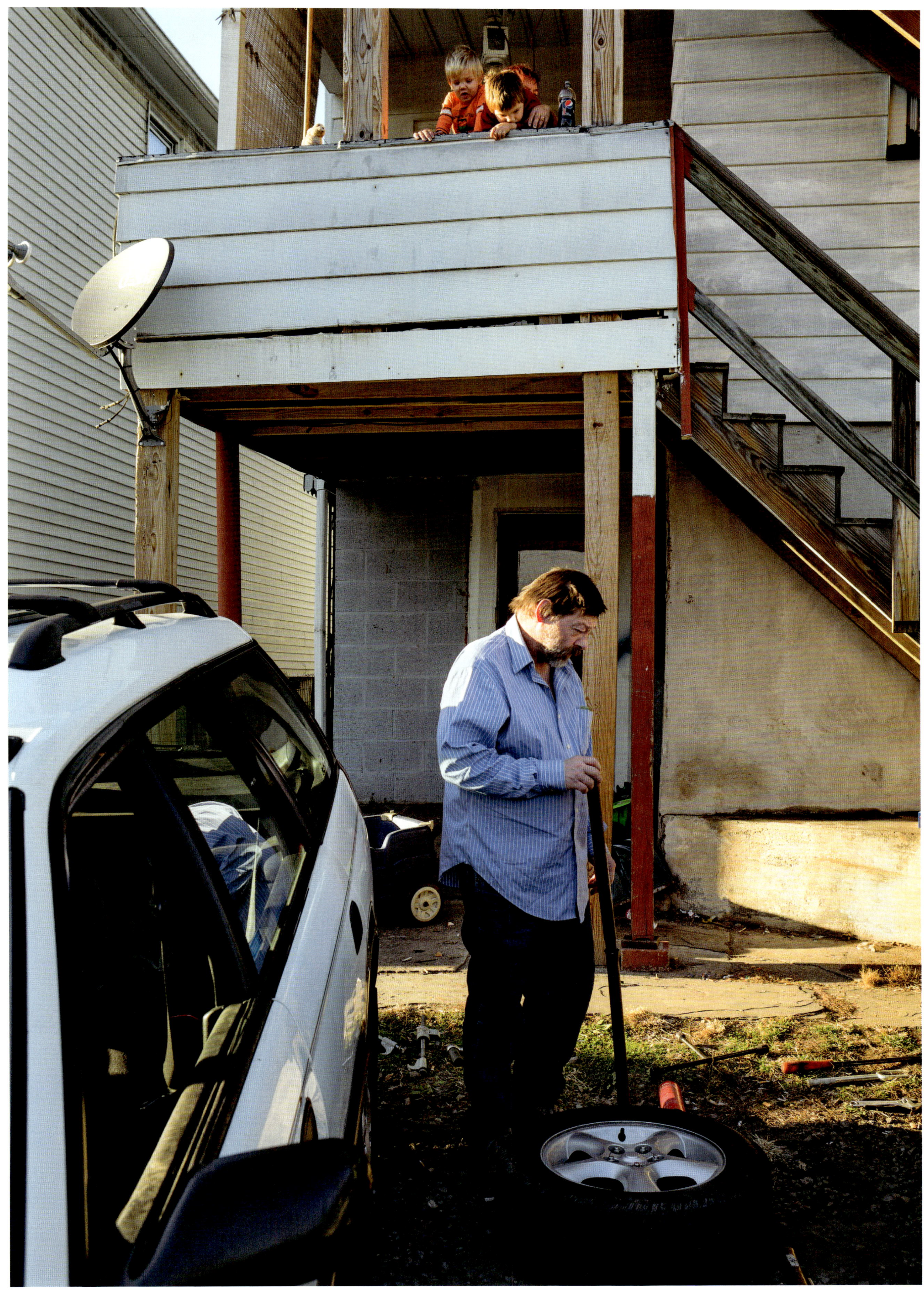

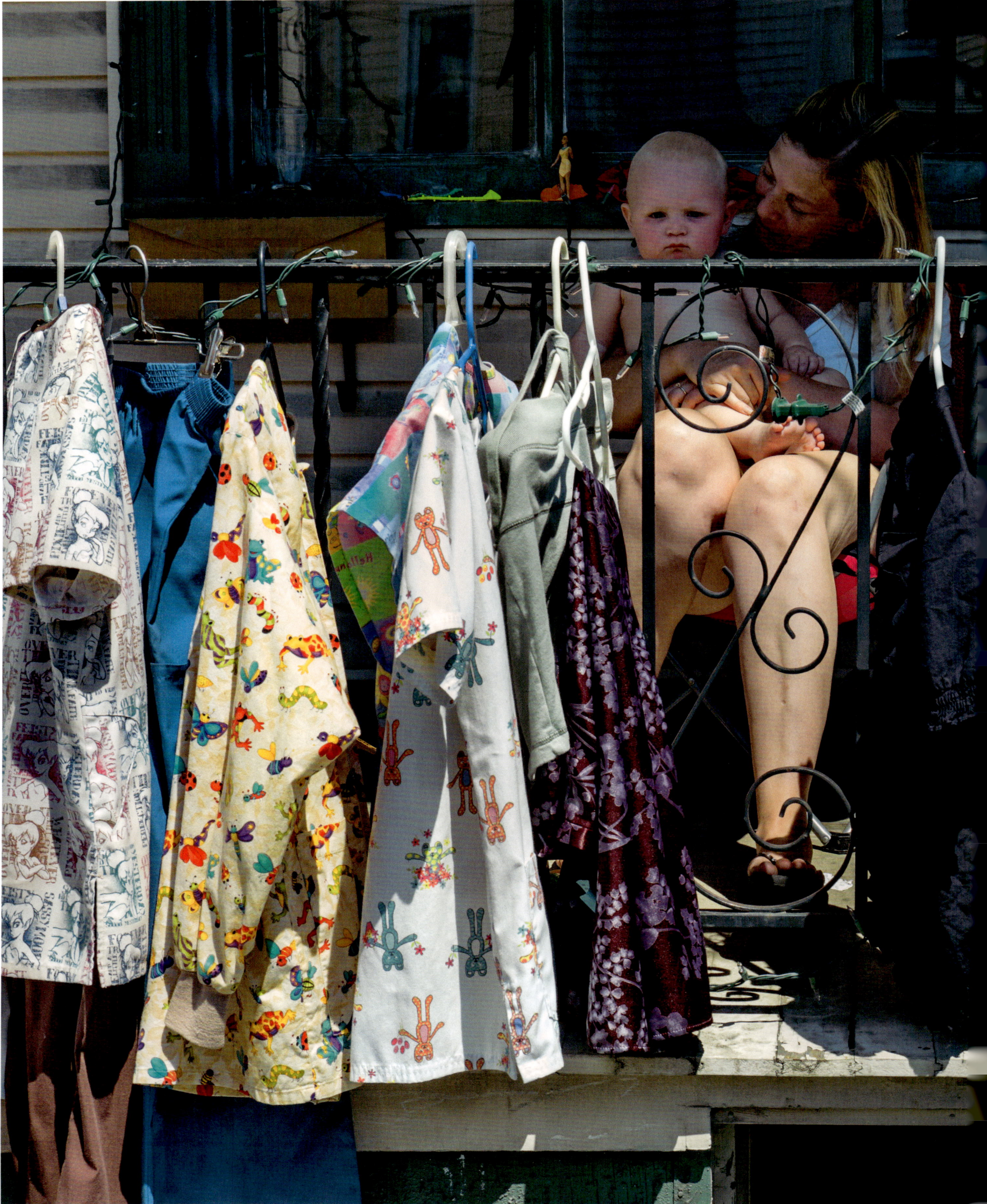

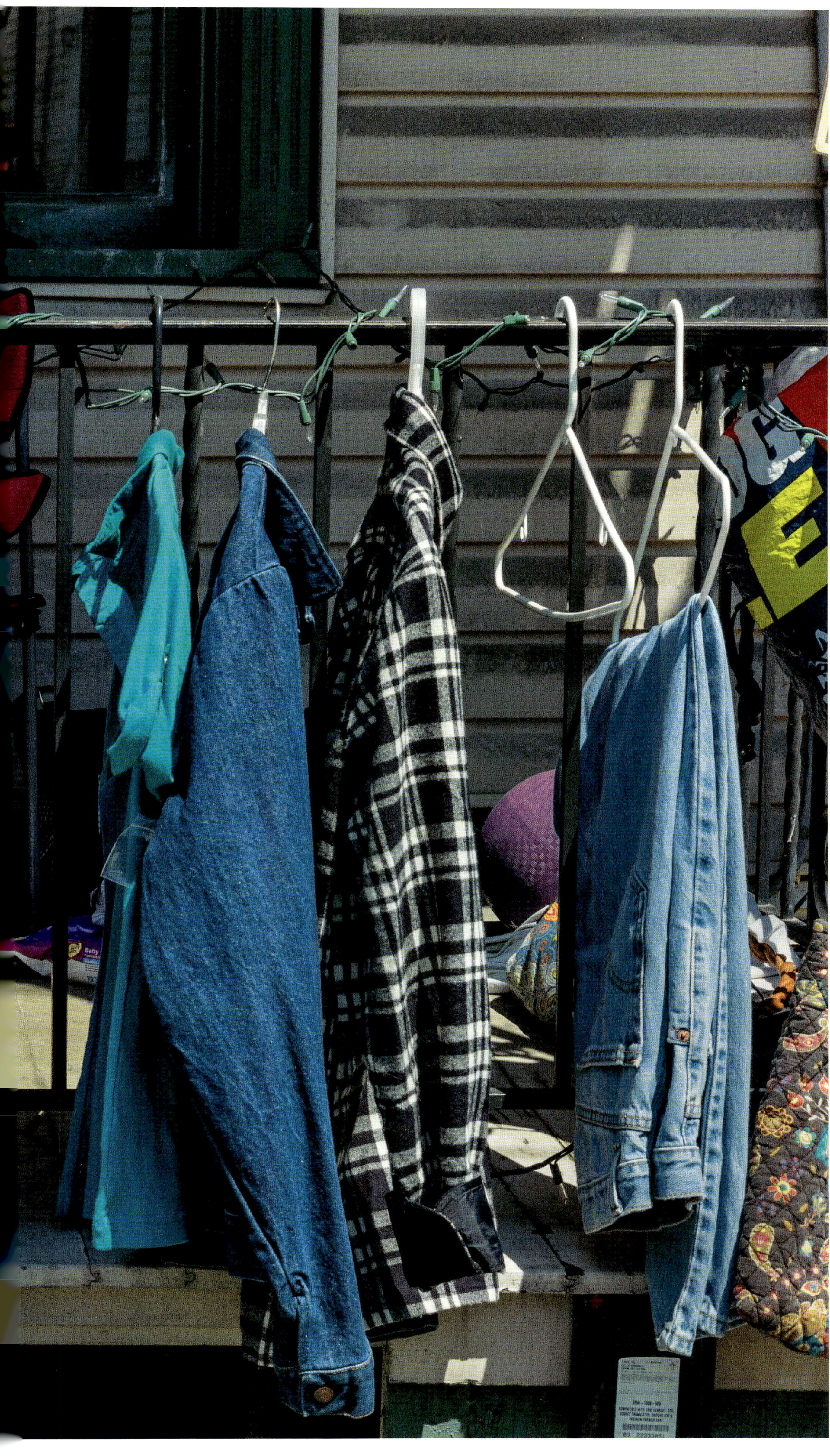

PLATE 20

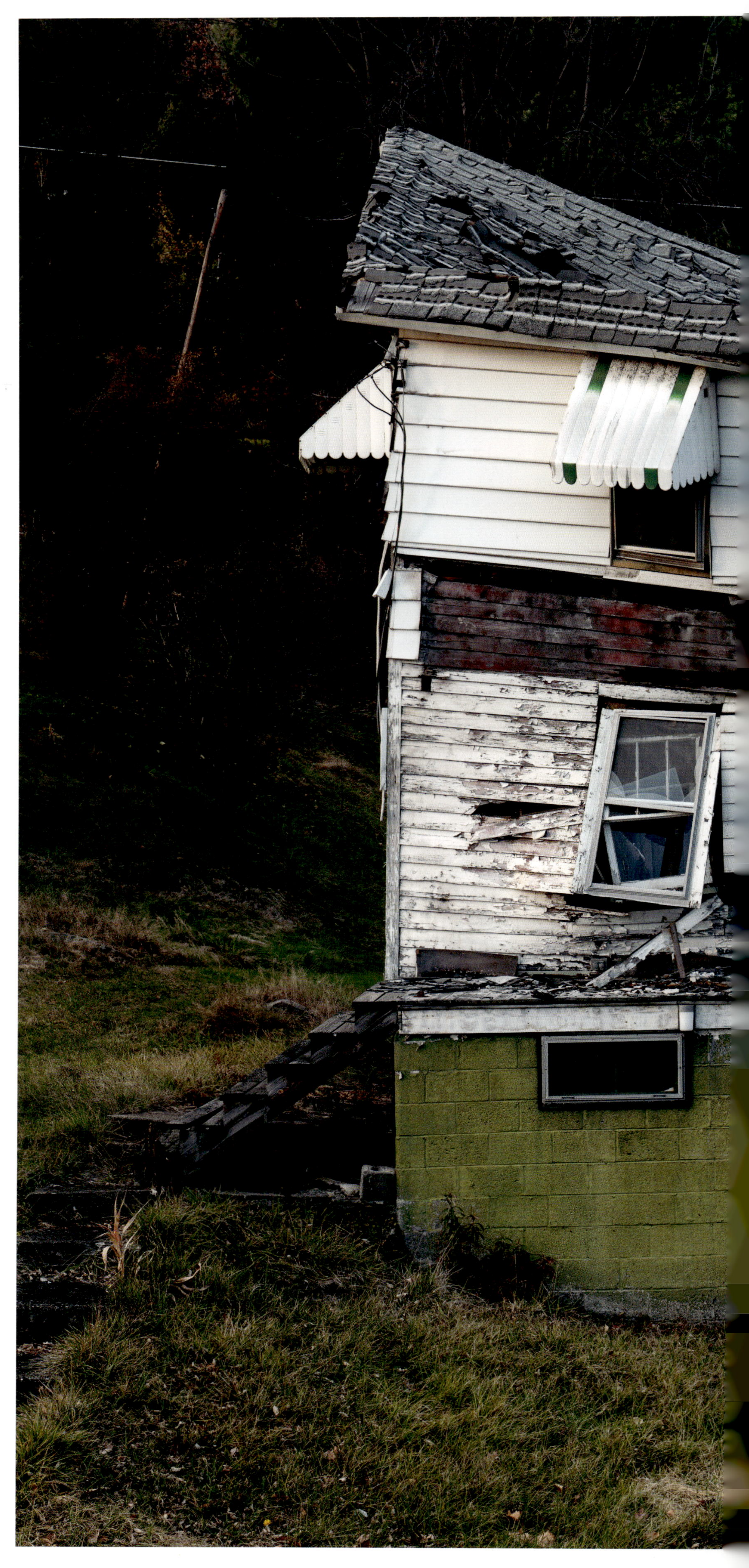

PLATE 21

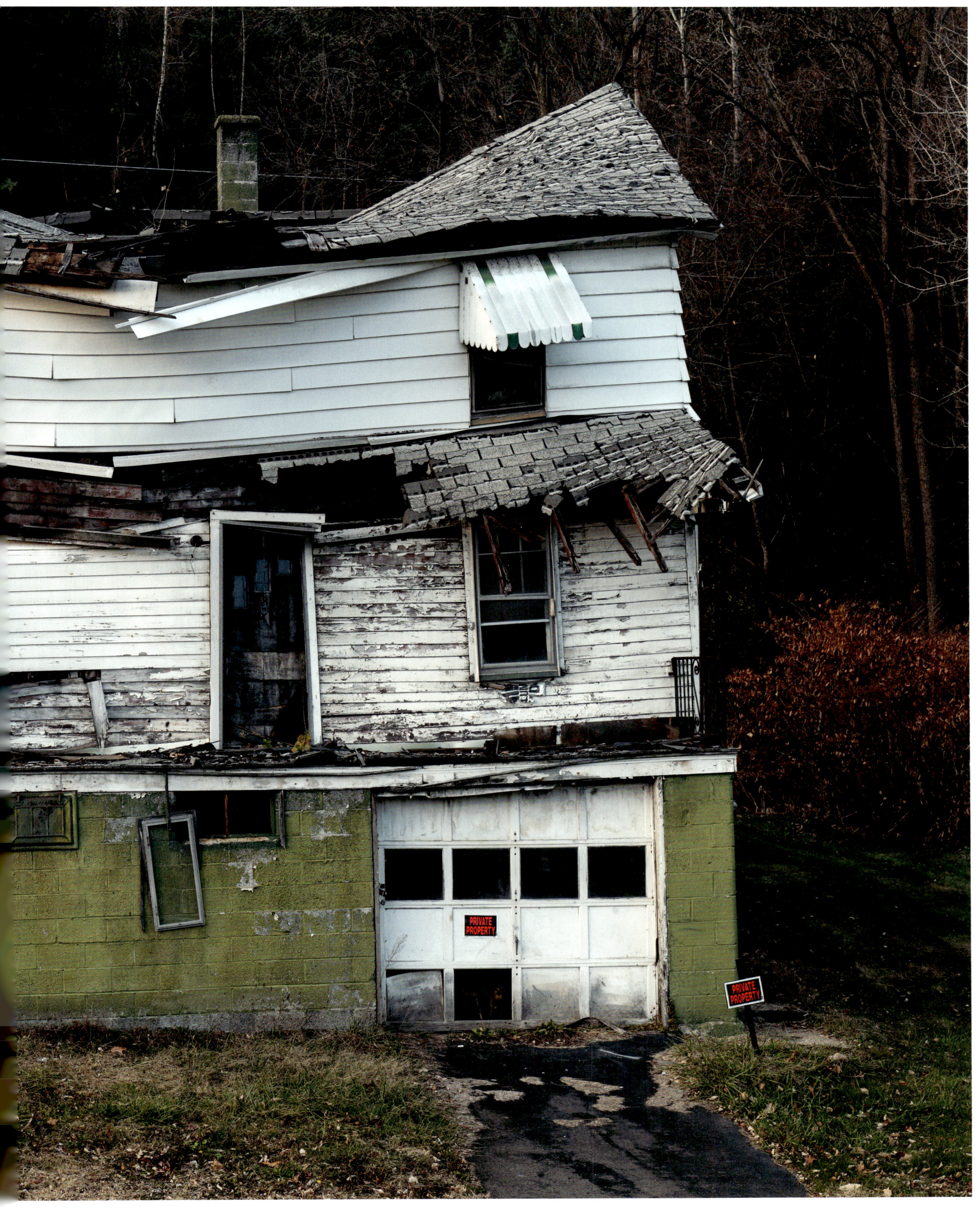
PRIVATE PROPERTY
PRIVATE PROPERTY

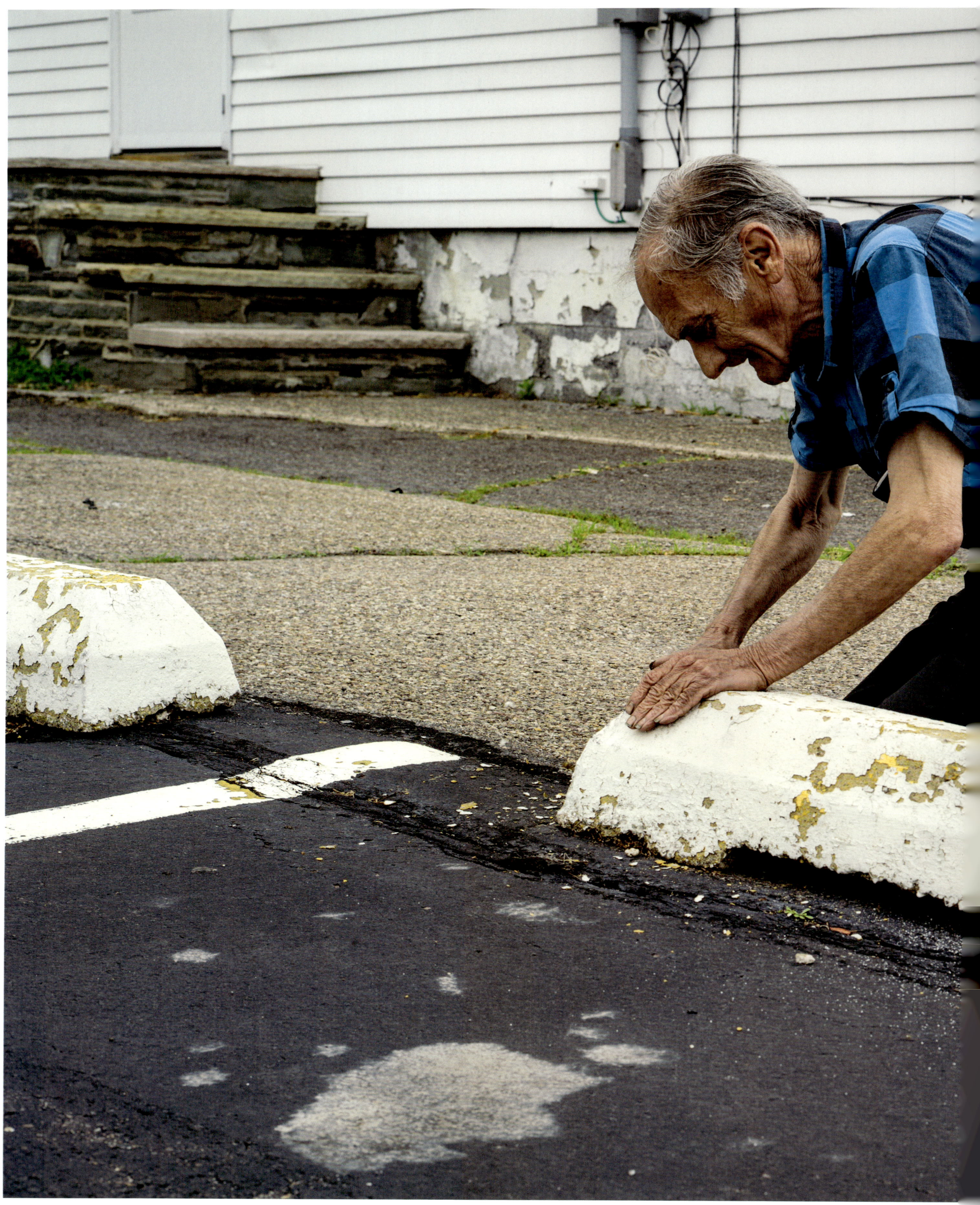

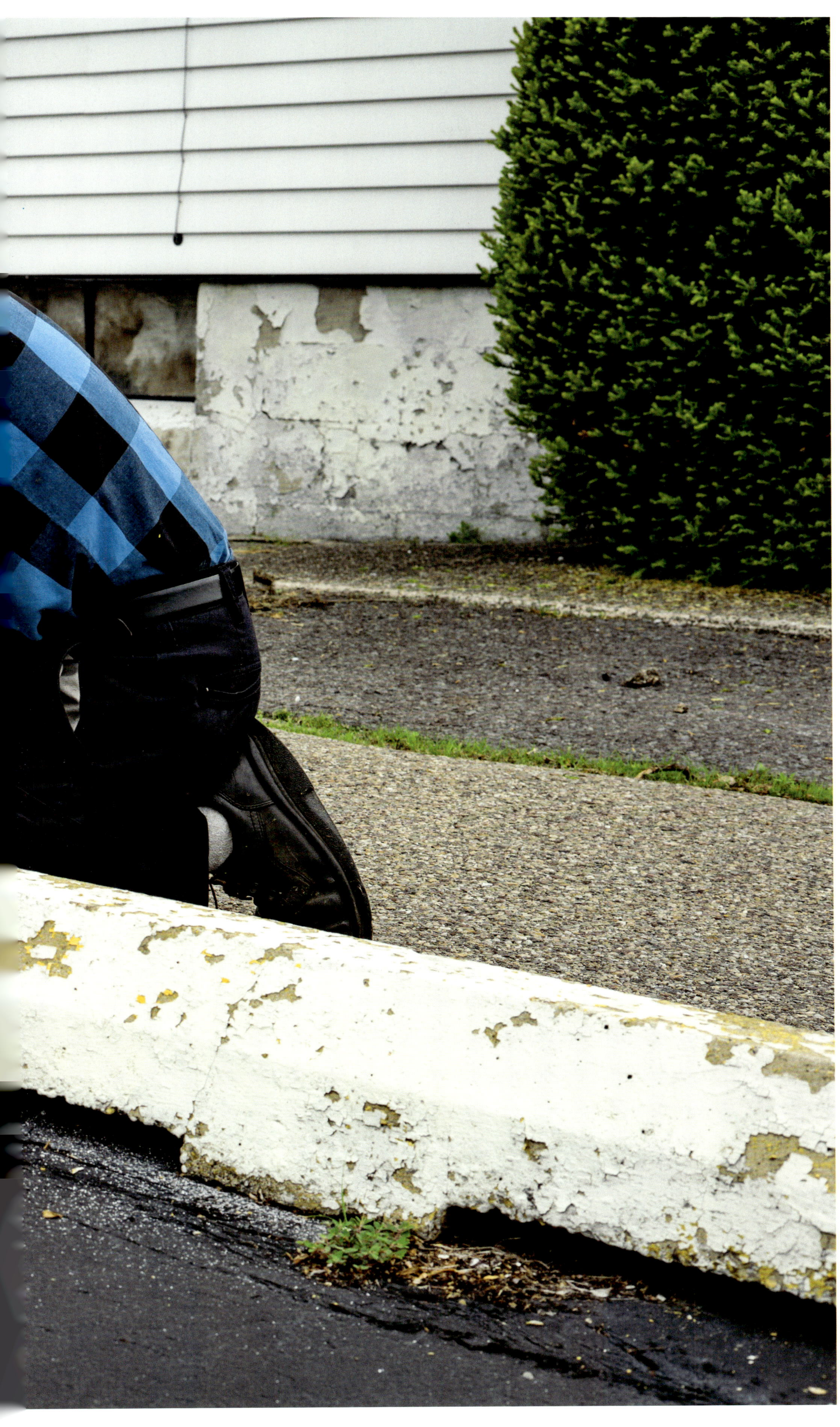

PLATE 22

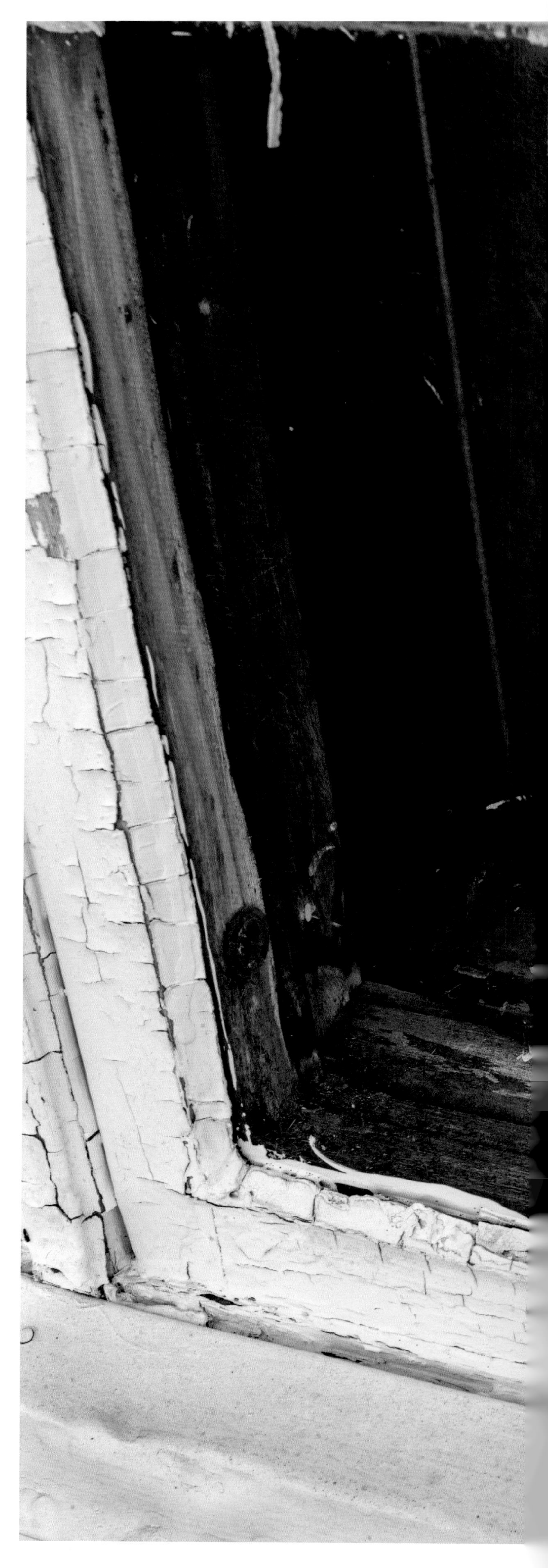

PLATE 23

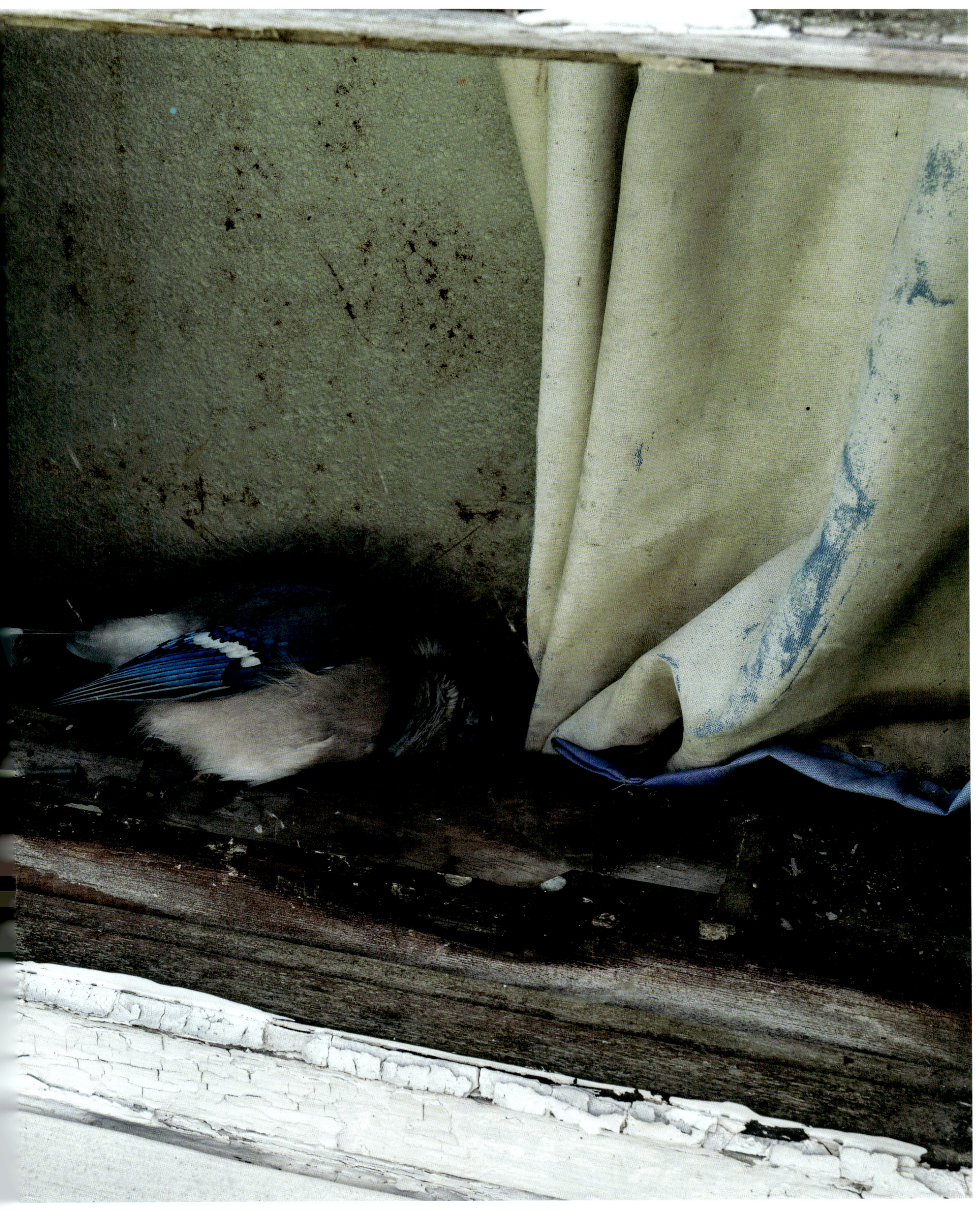

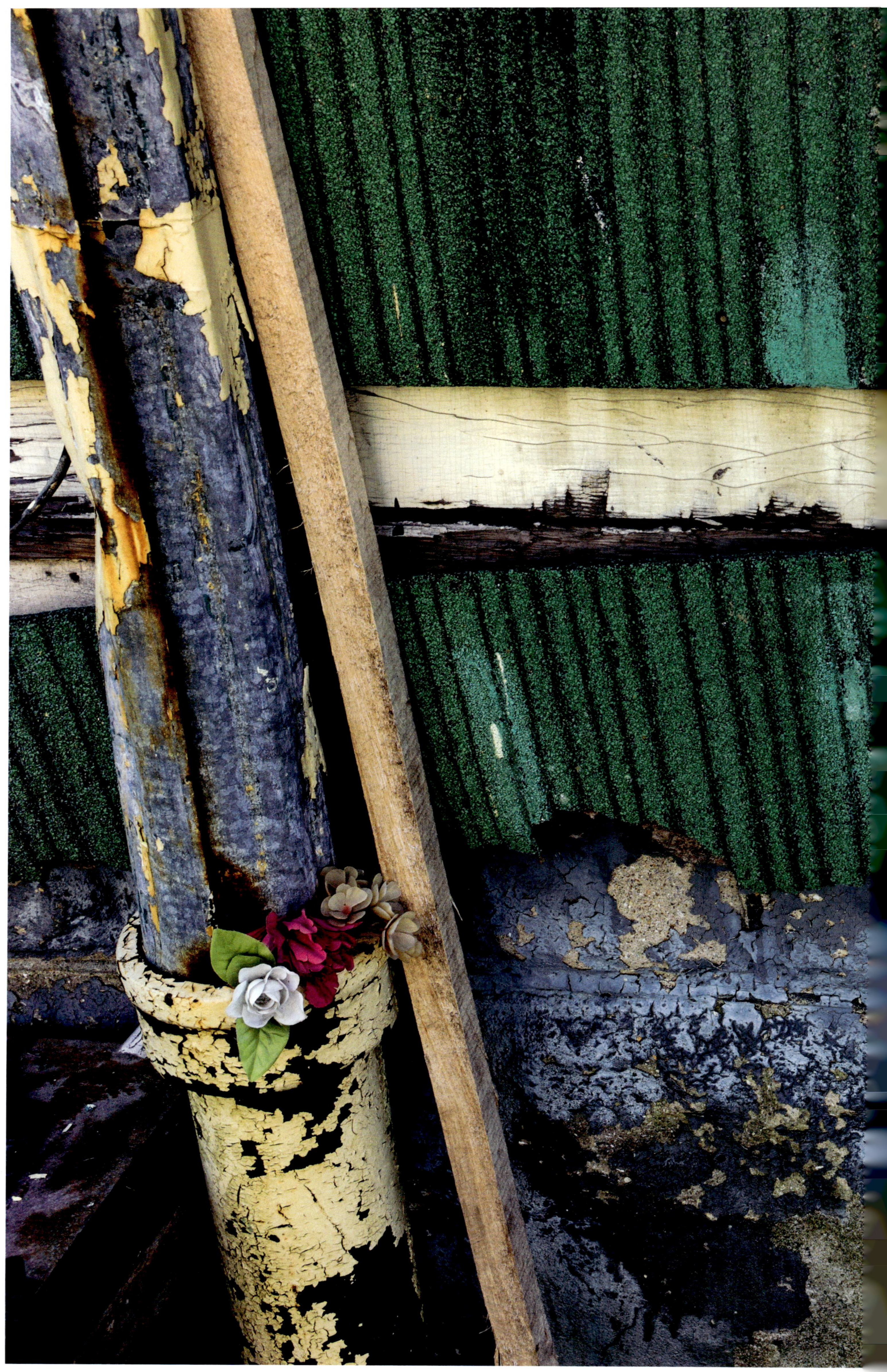

PLATE 24

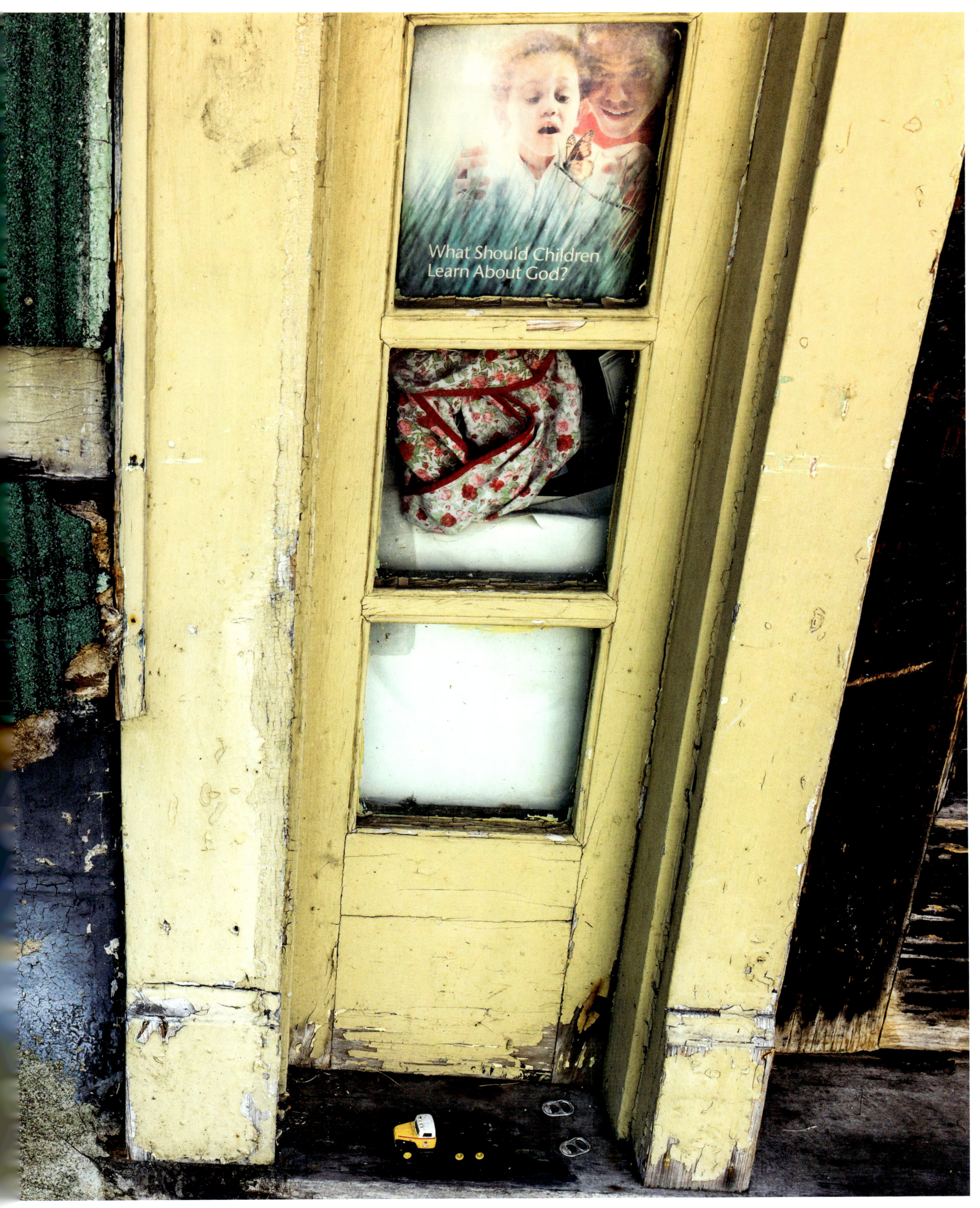
What Should Children
Learn About God?

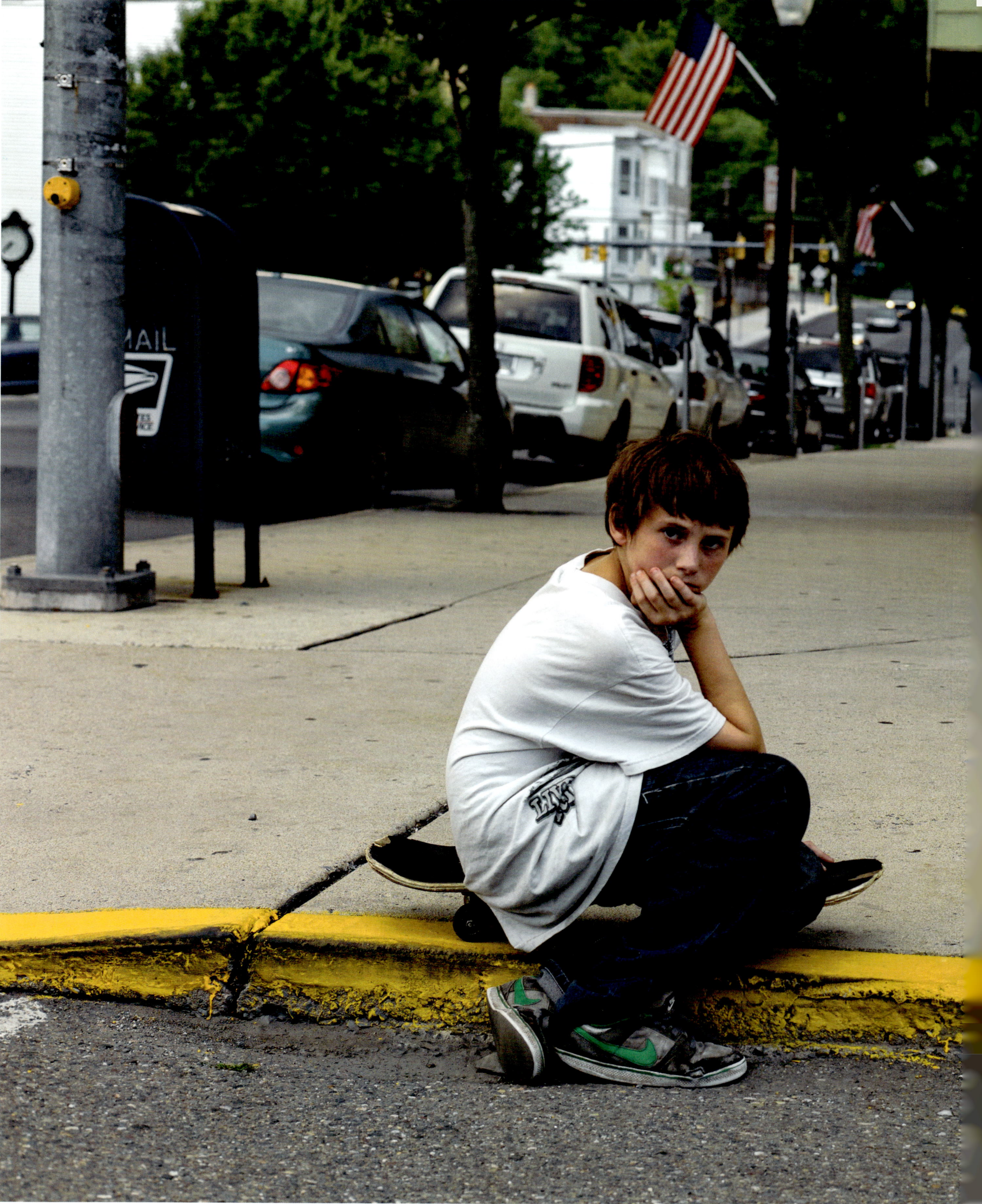
MAIL

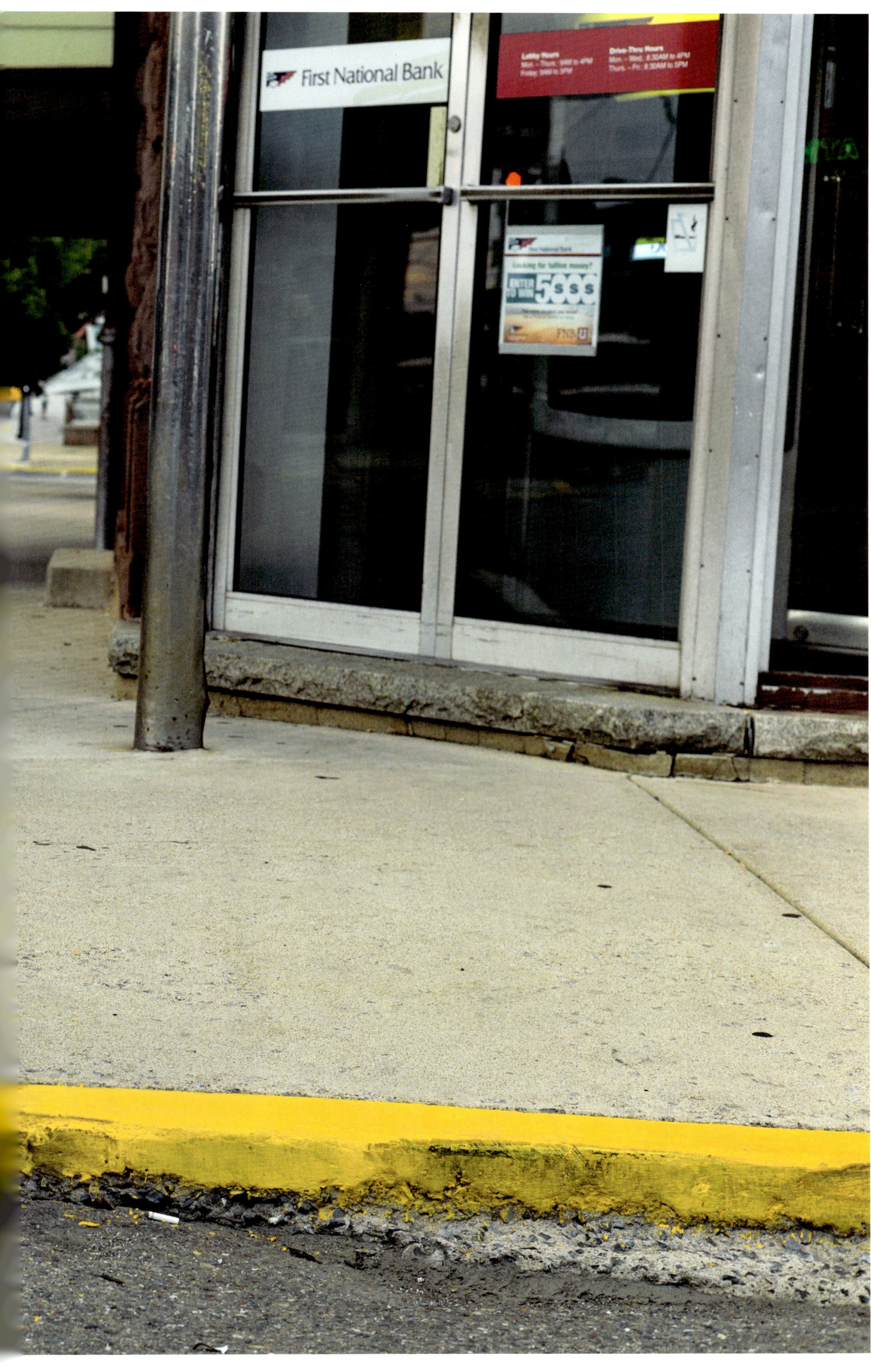
First National Bank

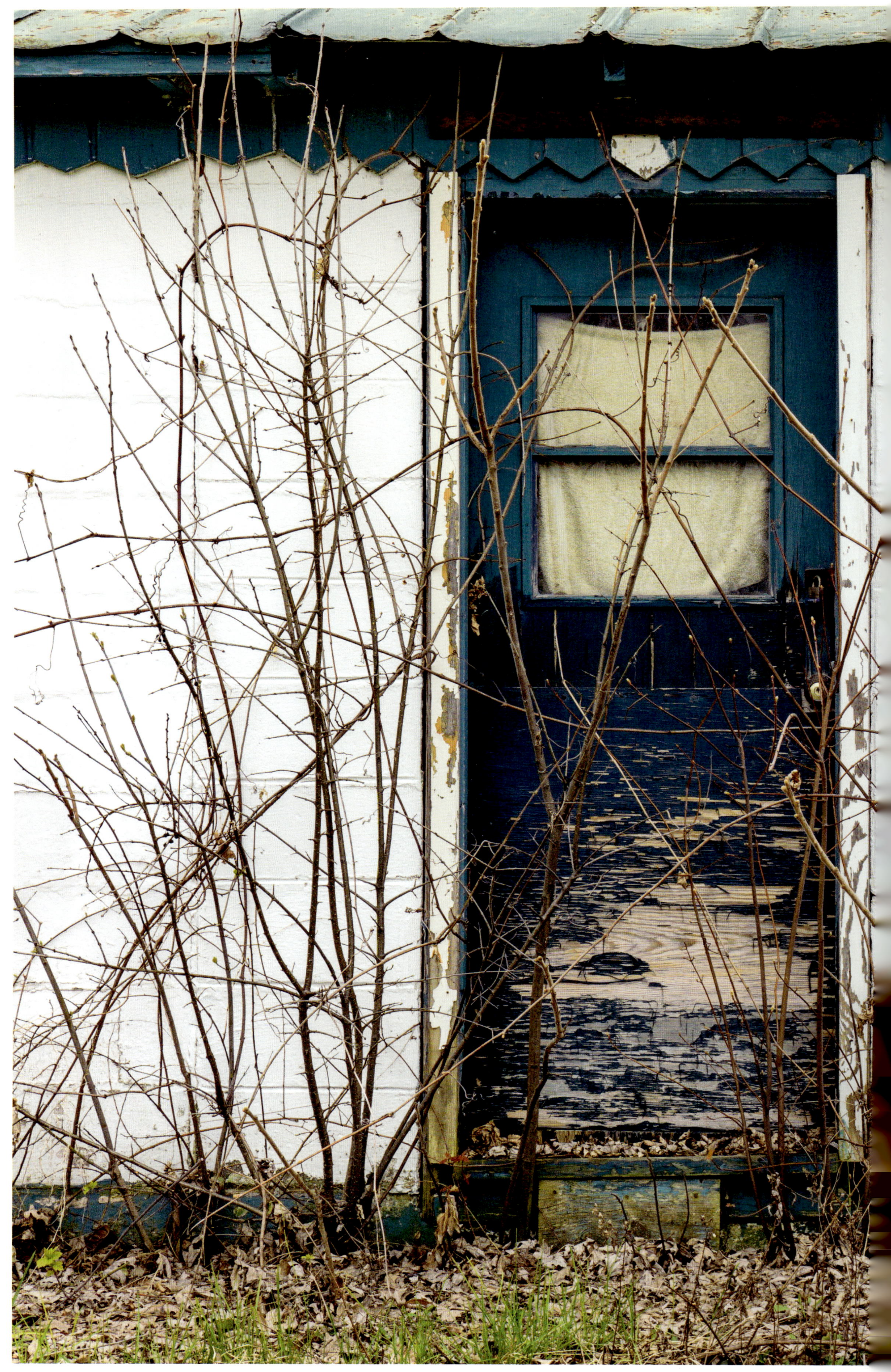

PLATE 26

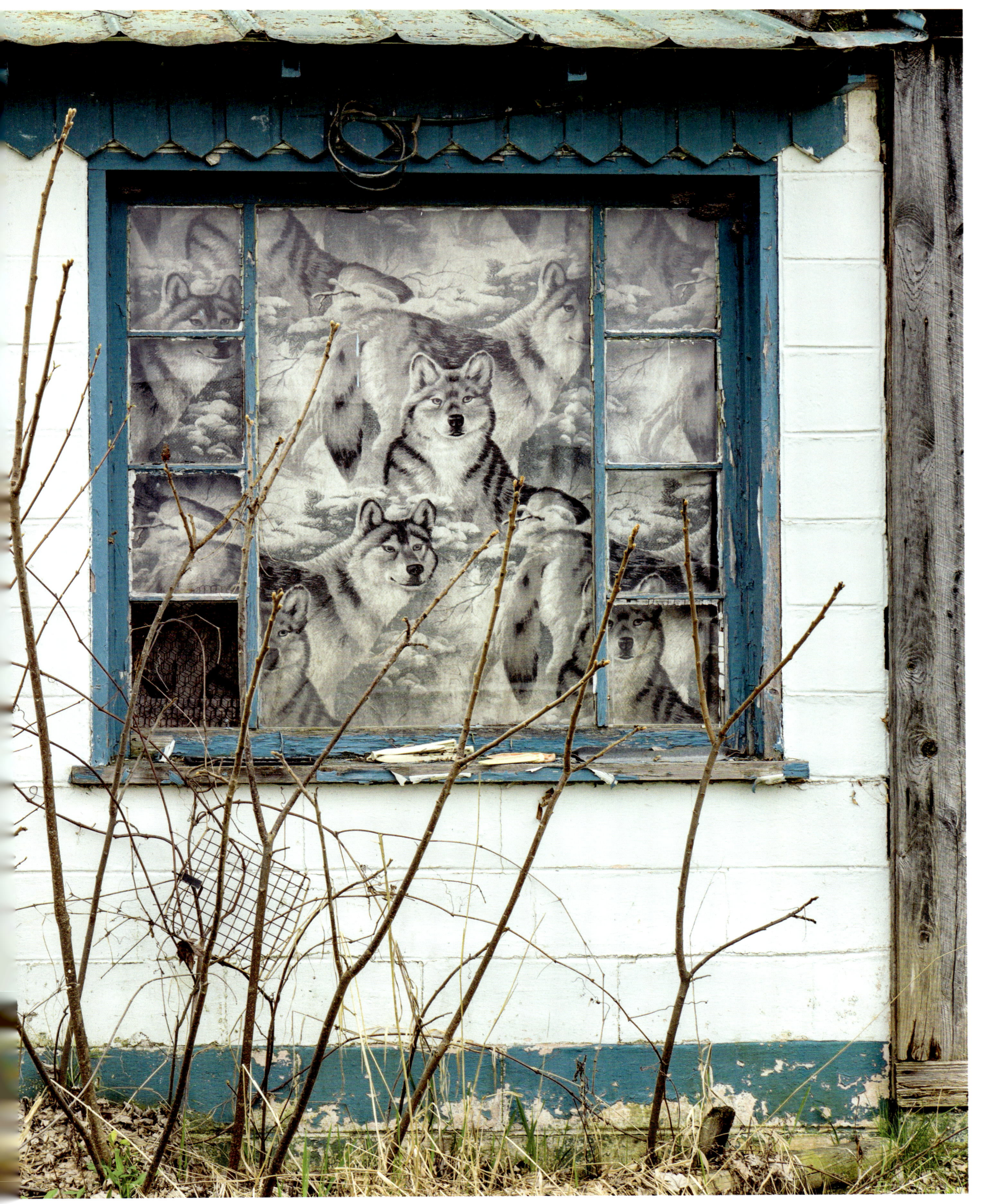

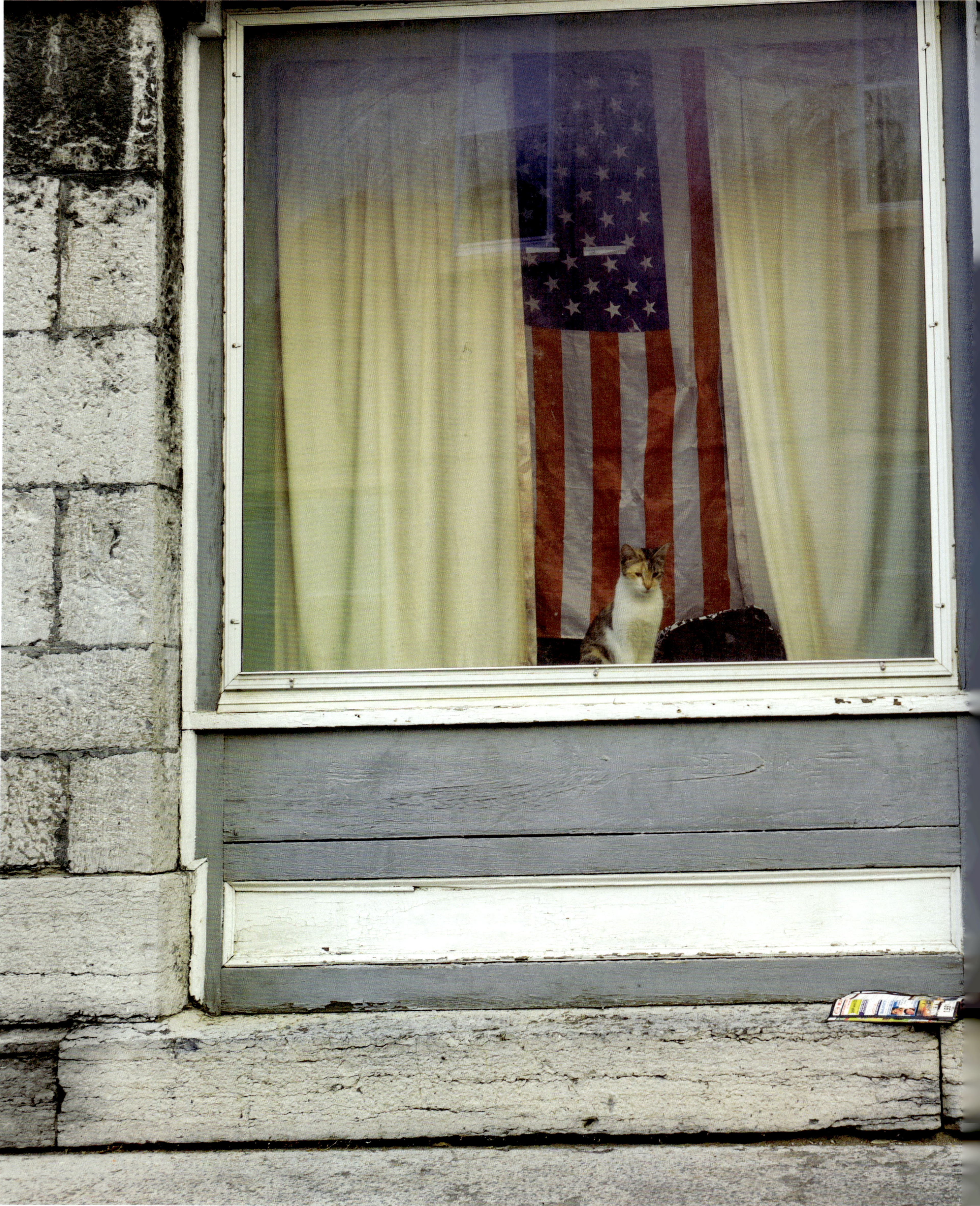

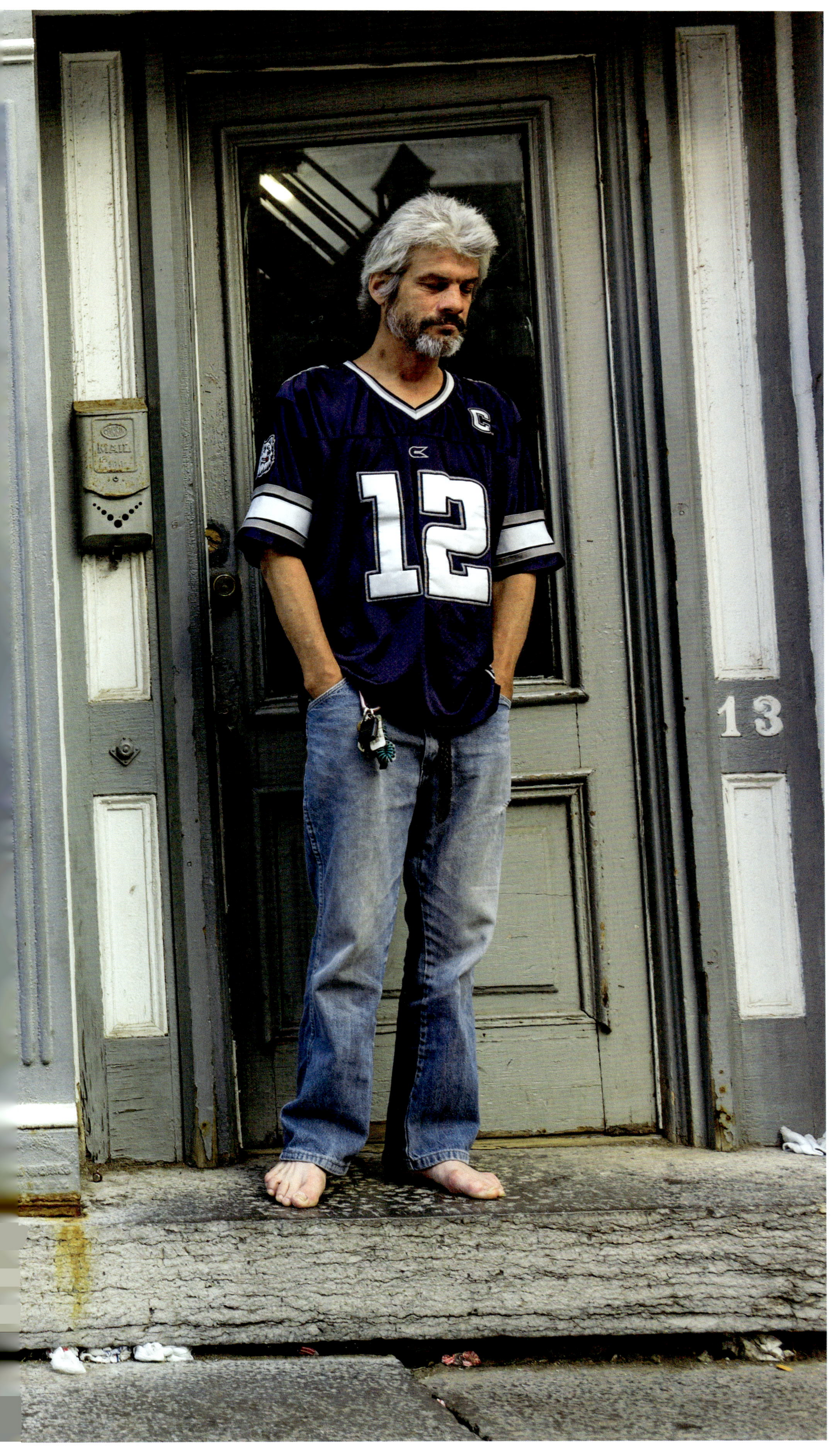

PLATE 27

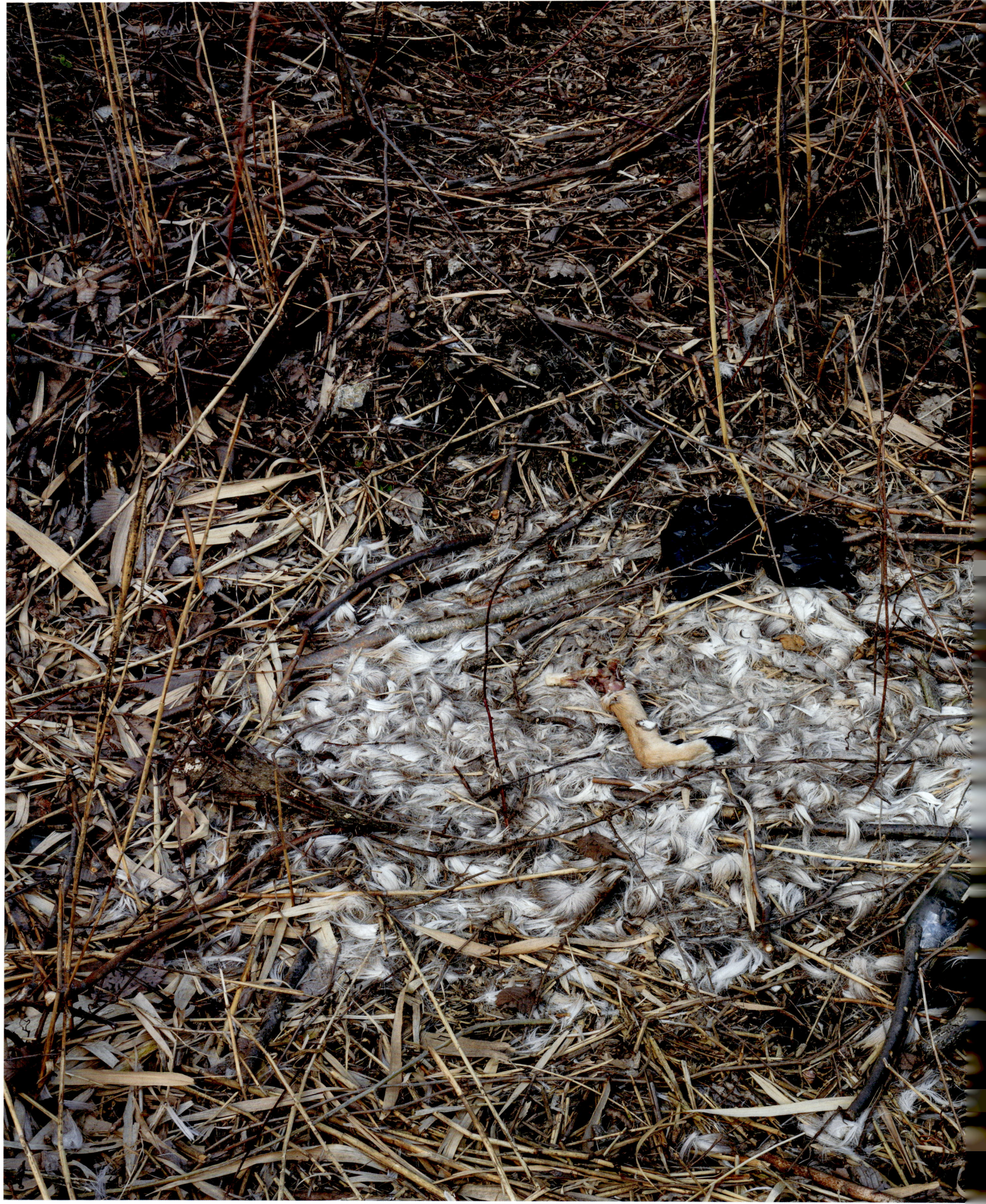

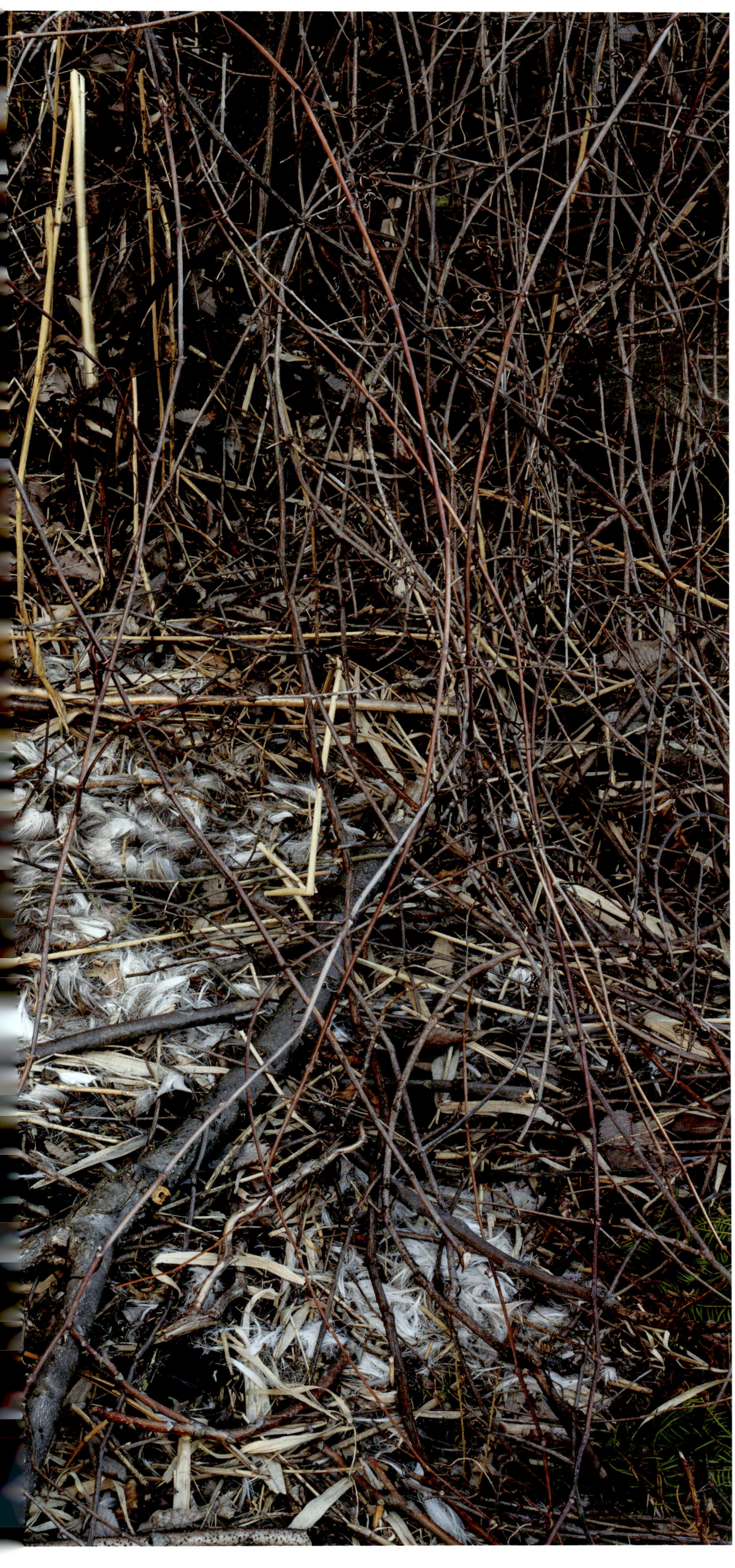

PLATE 28

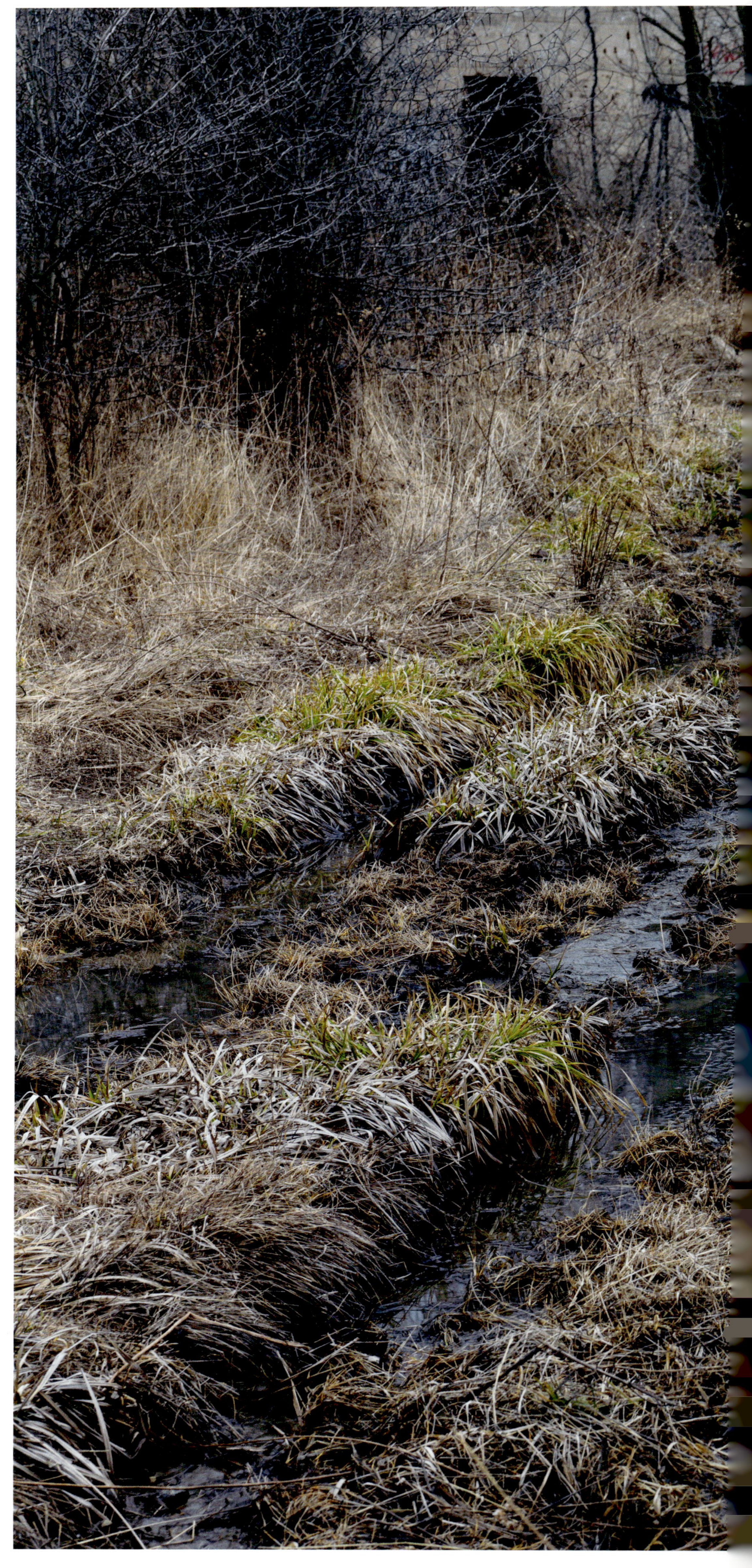

PLATE 29

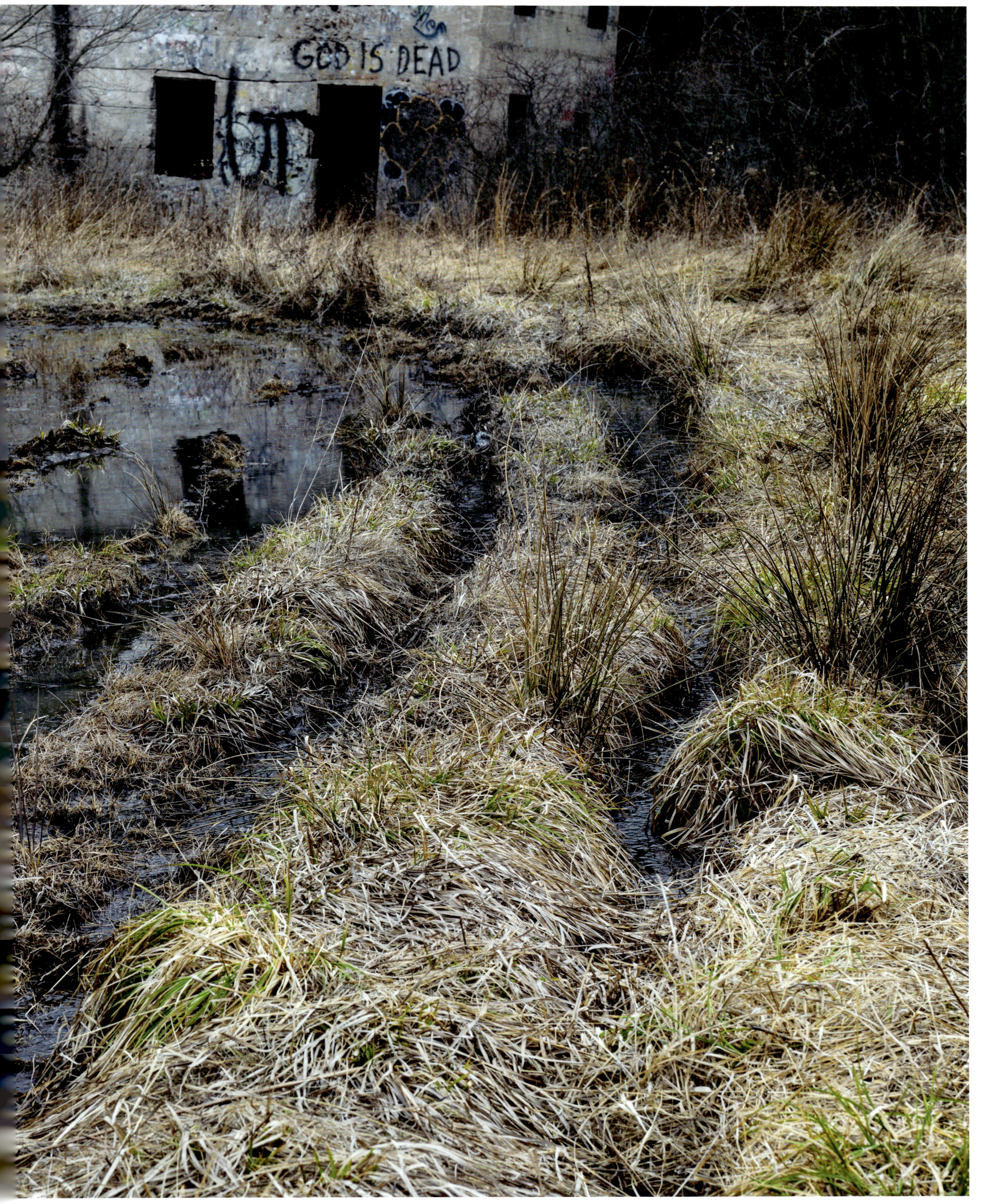
GOD IS DEAD

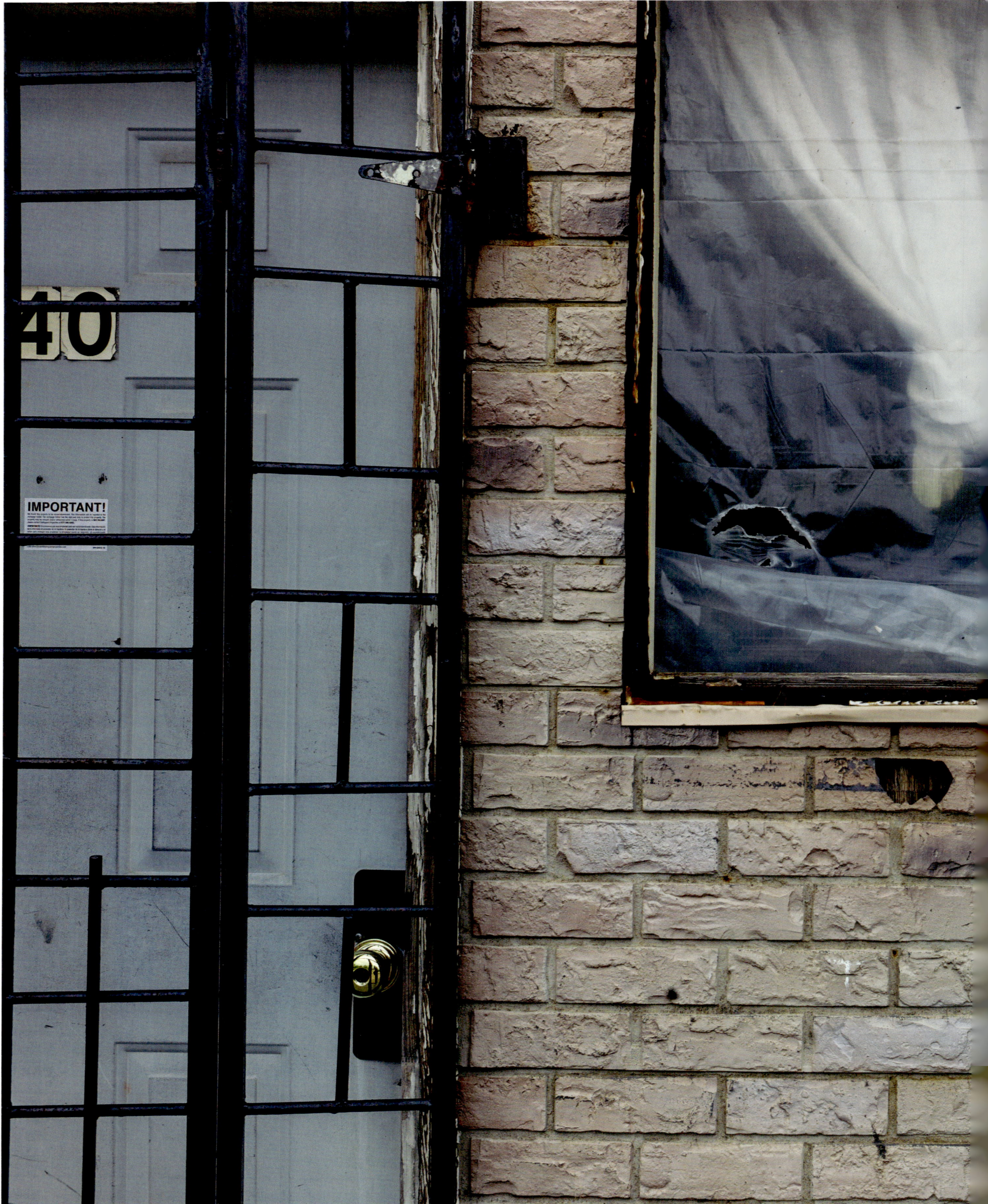
40
IMPORTANT!

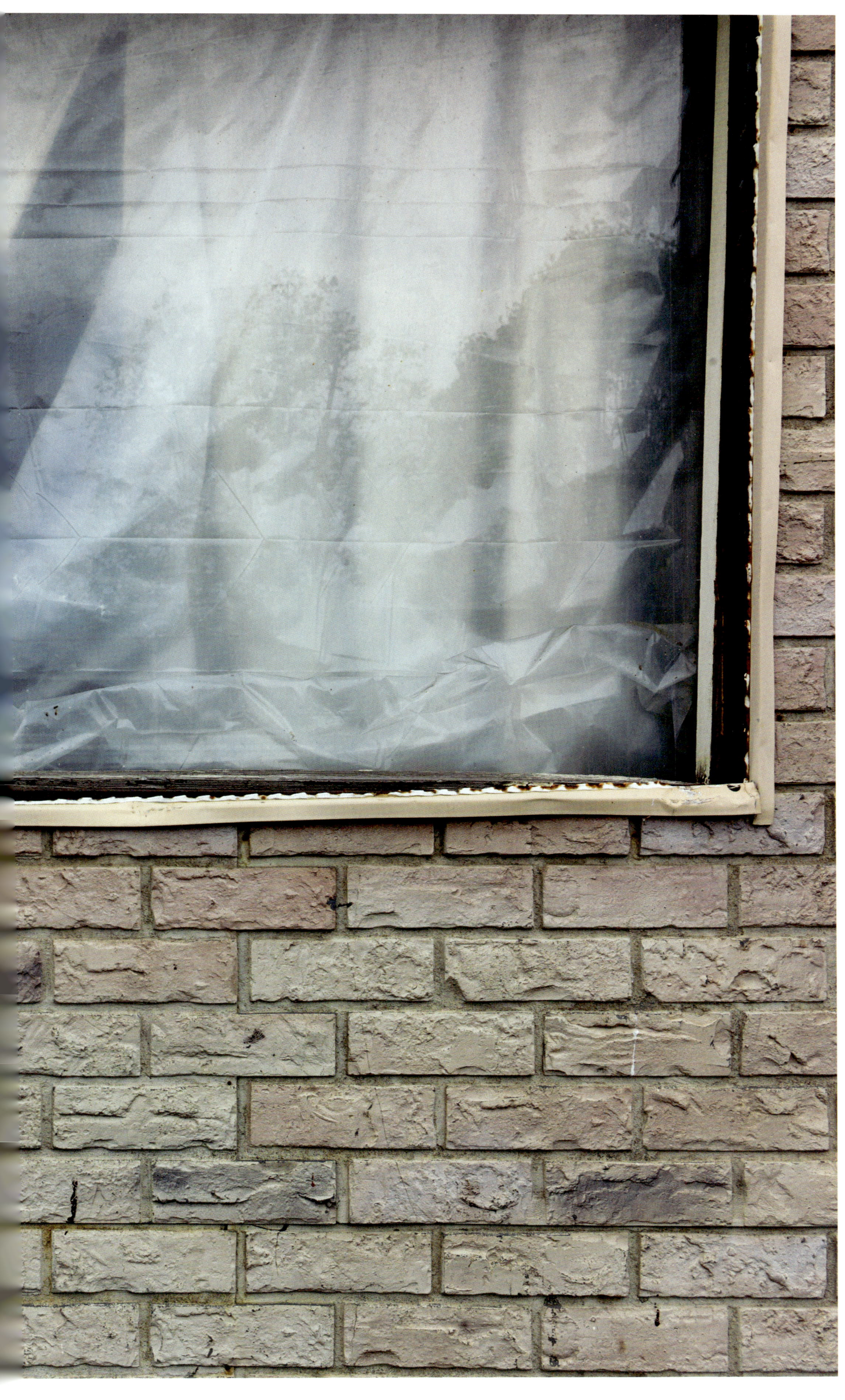

PLATE 30

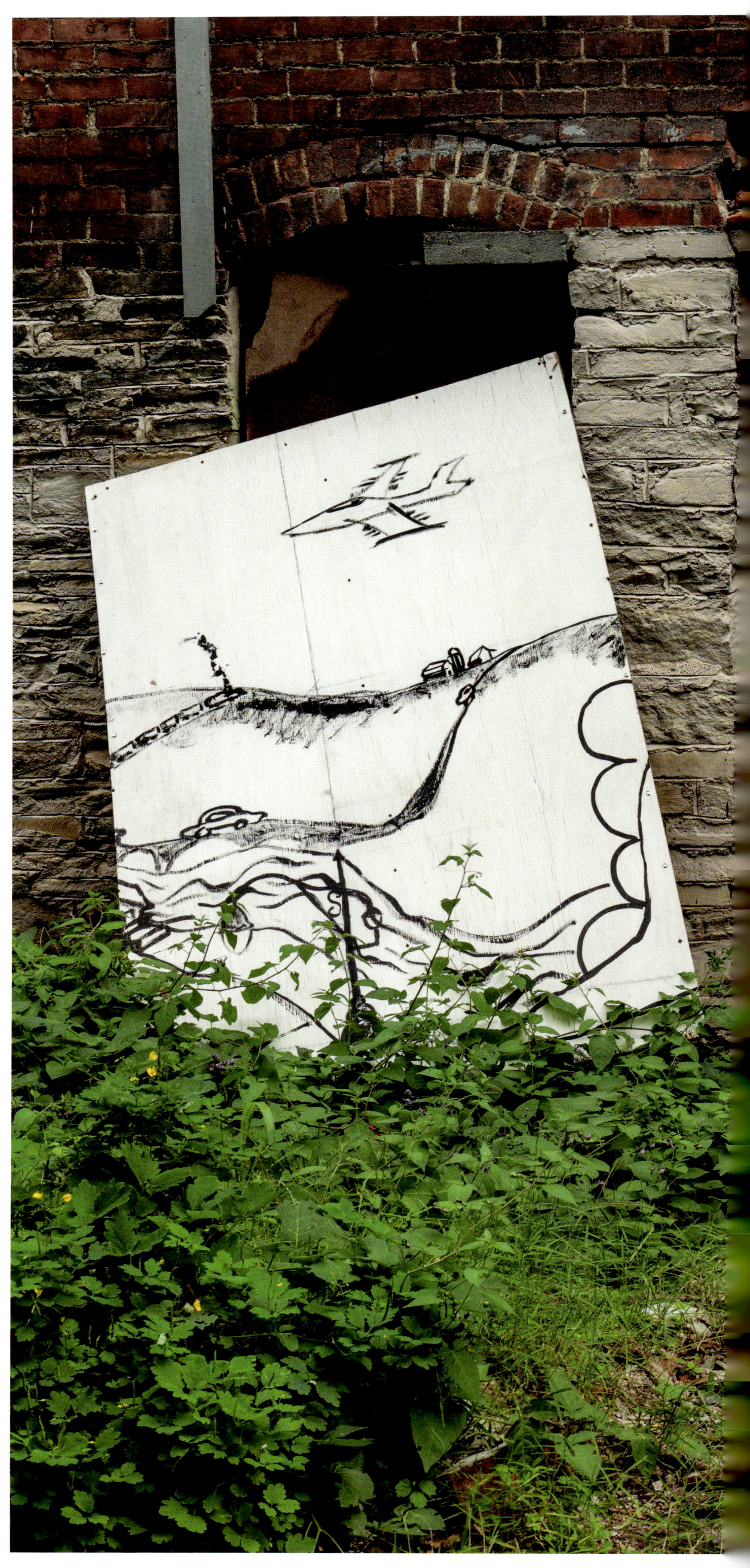

PLATE 31

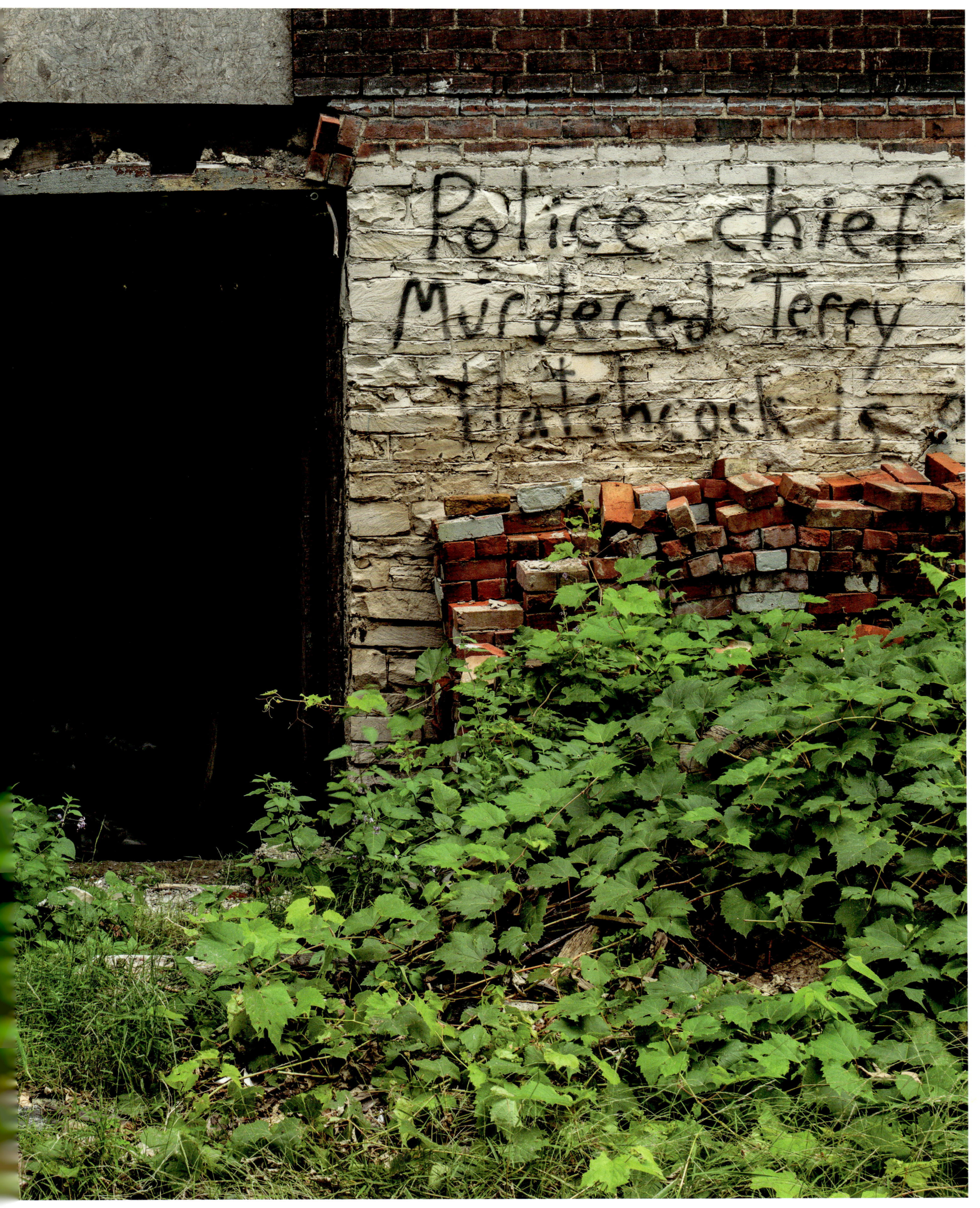
Police chief
Murdered Terry

PLATE 32

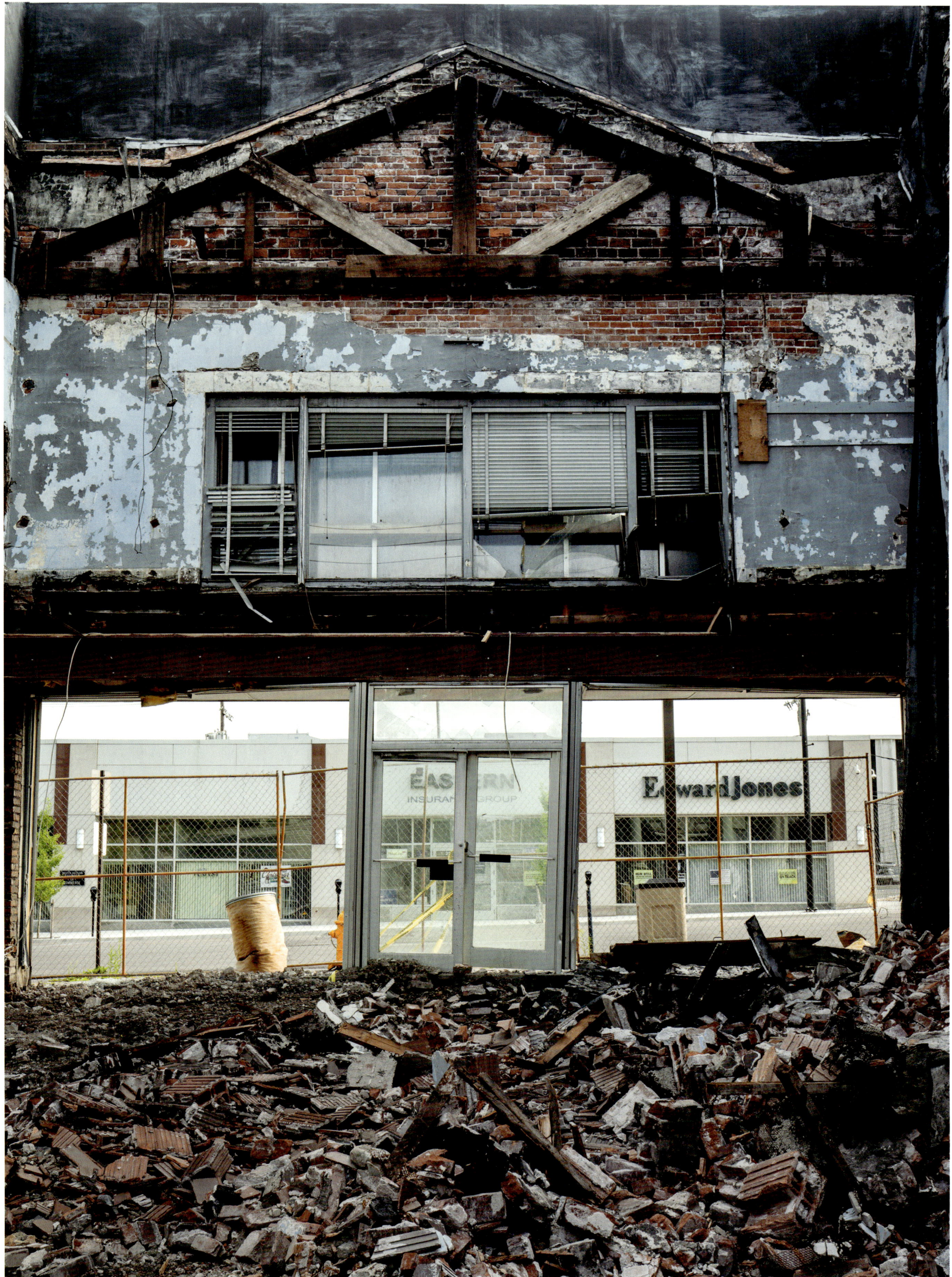
Edward Jones

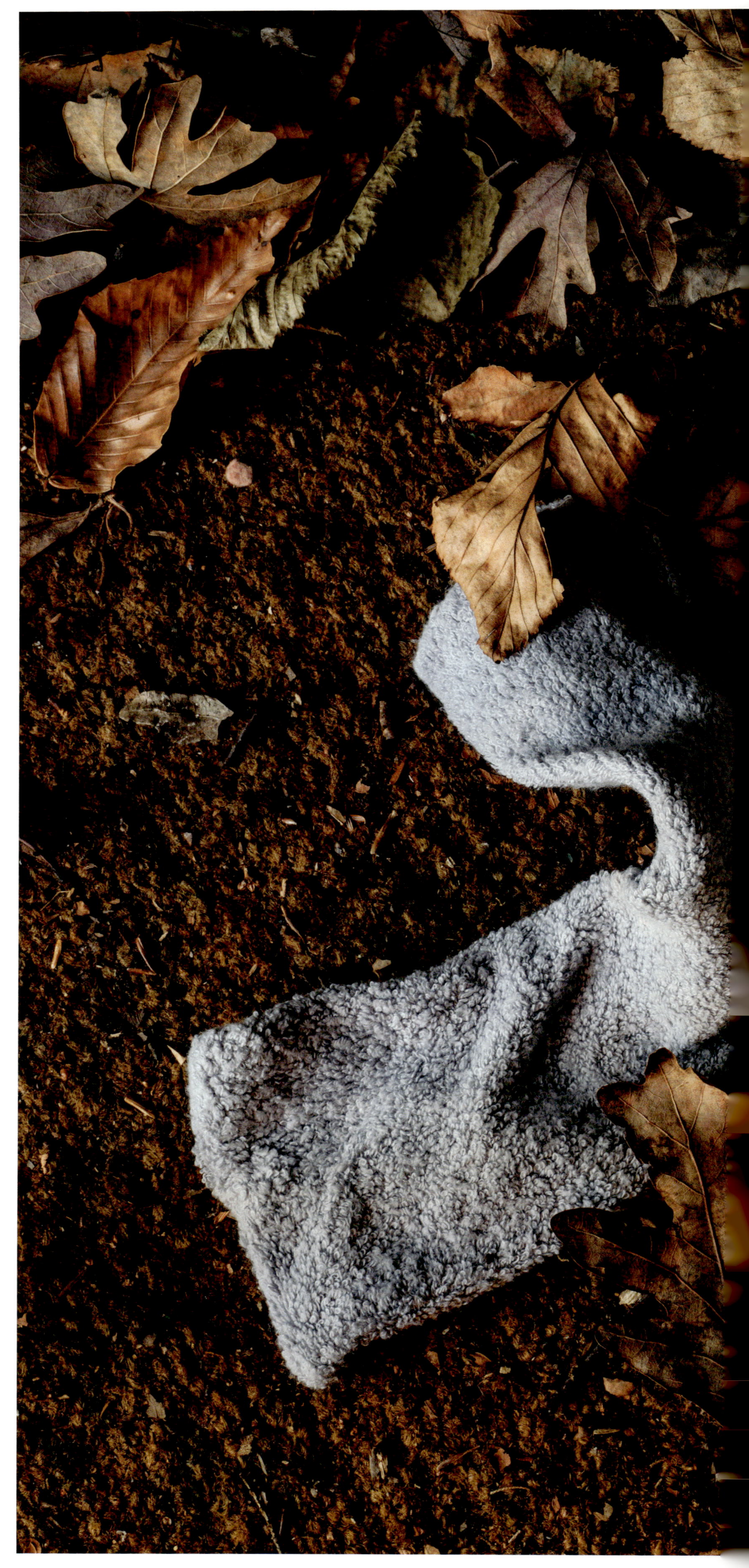

PLATE 33

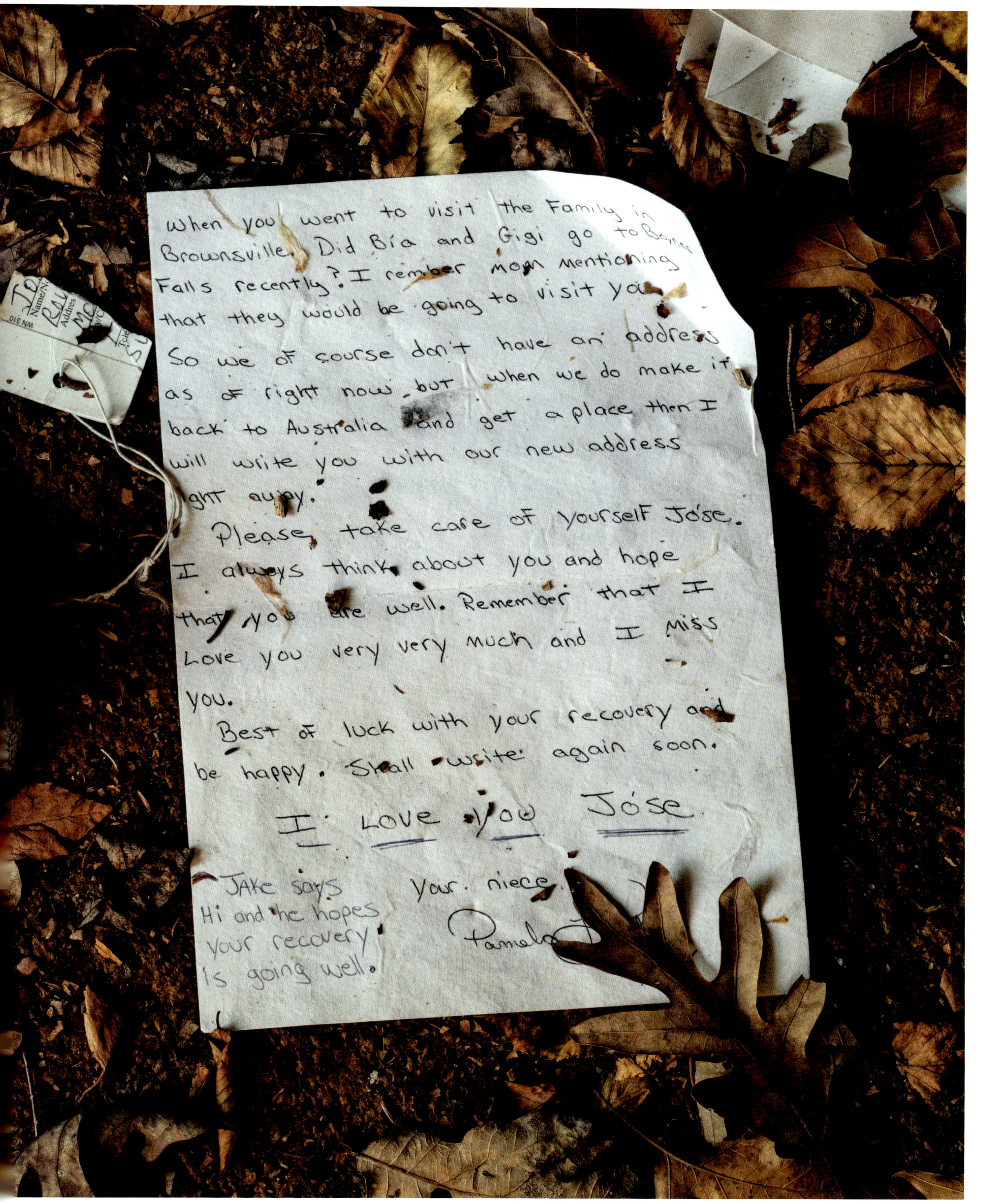

When you went to visit the Family in Brownsville. Did Bía and Gigi go to Bones Falls recently? I rember mom mentioning that they would be going to visit you. So we of sourse don't have an address as of right now, but when we do make it back to Australia and get a place then I will write you with our new address right away.

Please take care of yourself Jóse. I always think about you and hope that you are well. Remember that I Love you very very much and I miss you.

Best of luck with your recovery and be happy. Shall write again soon.

I Love You Jóse

Jake says Hi and he hopes your recovery is going well.

Your niece,

Pamela

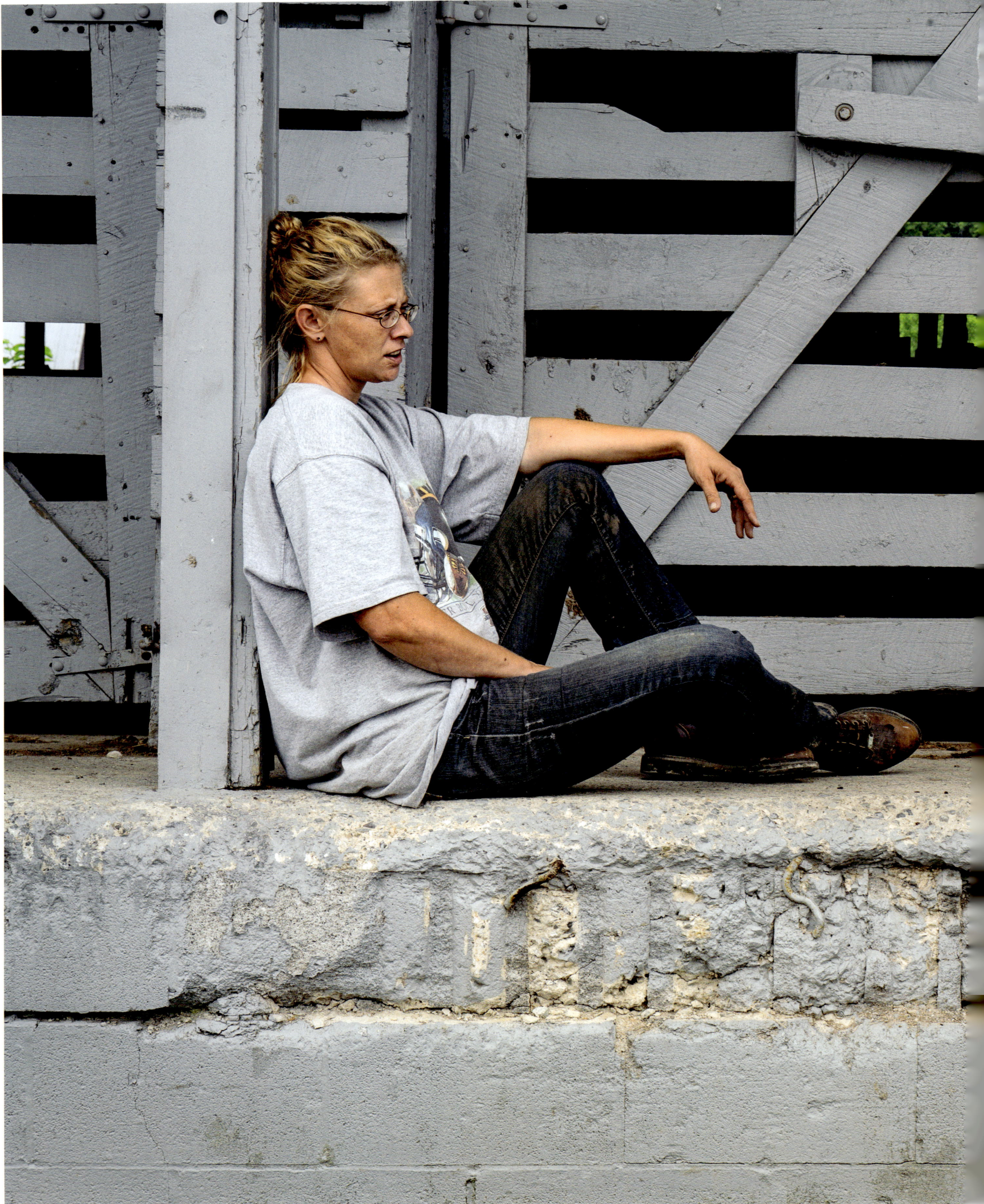

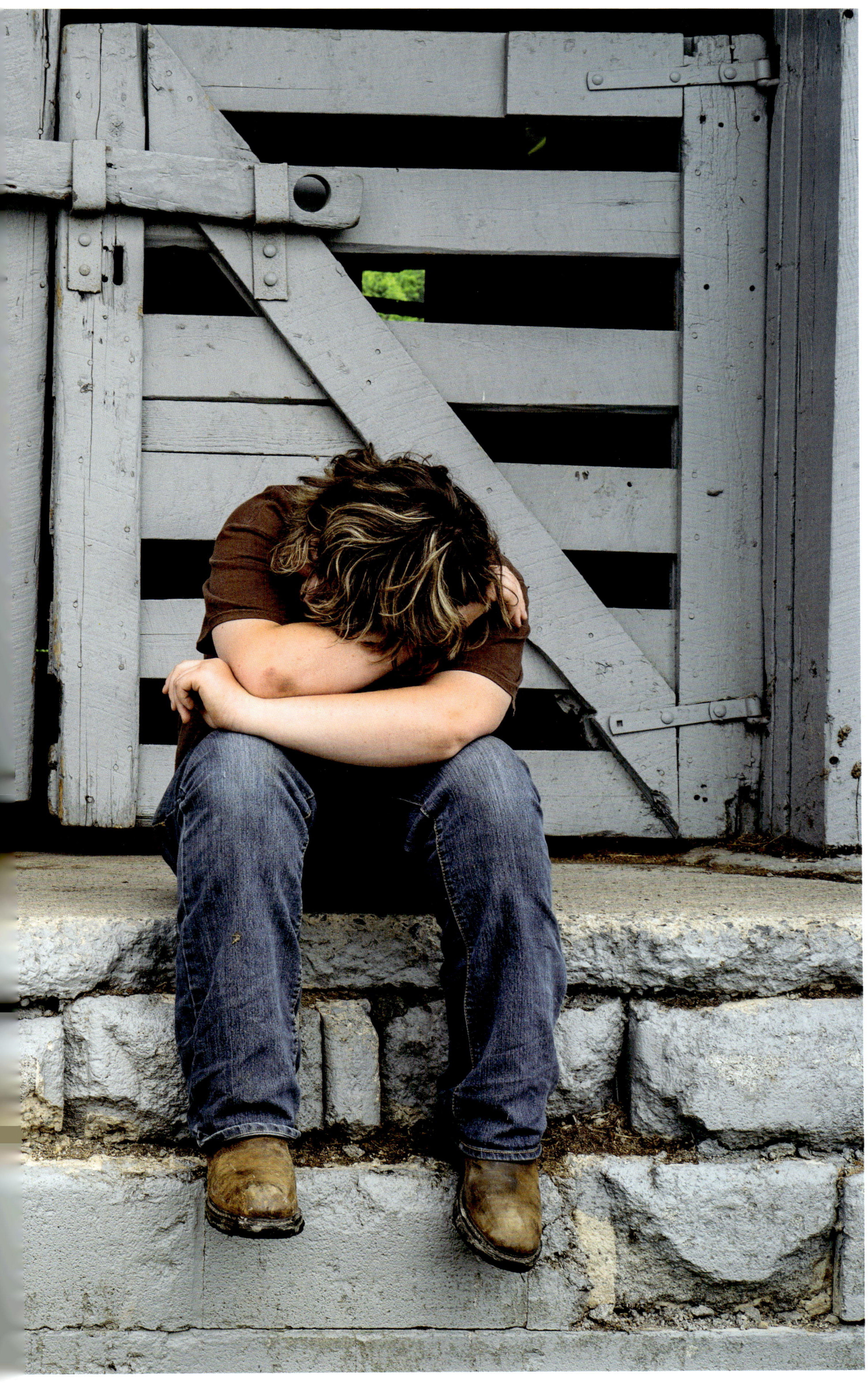

PLATE 34

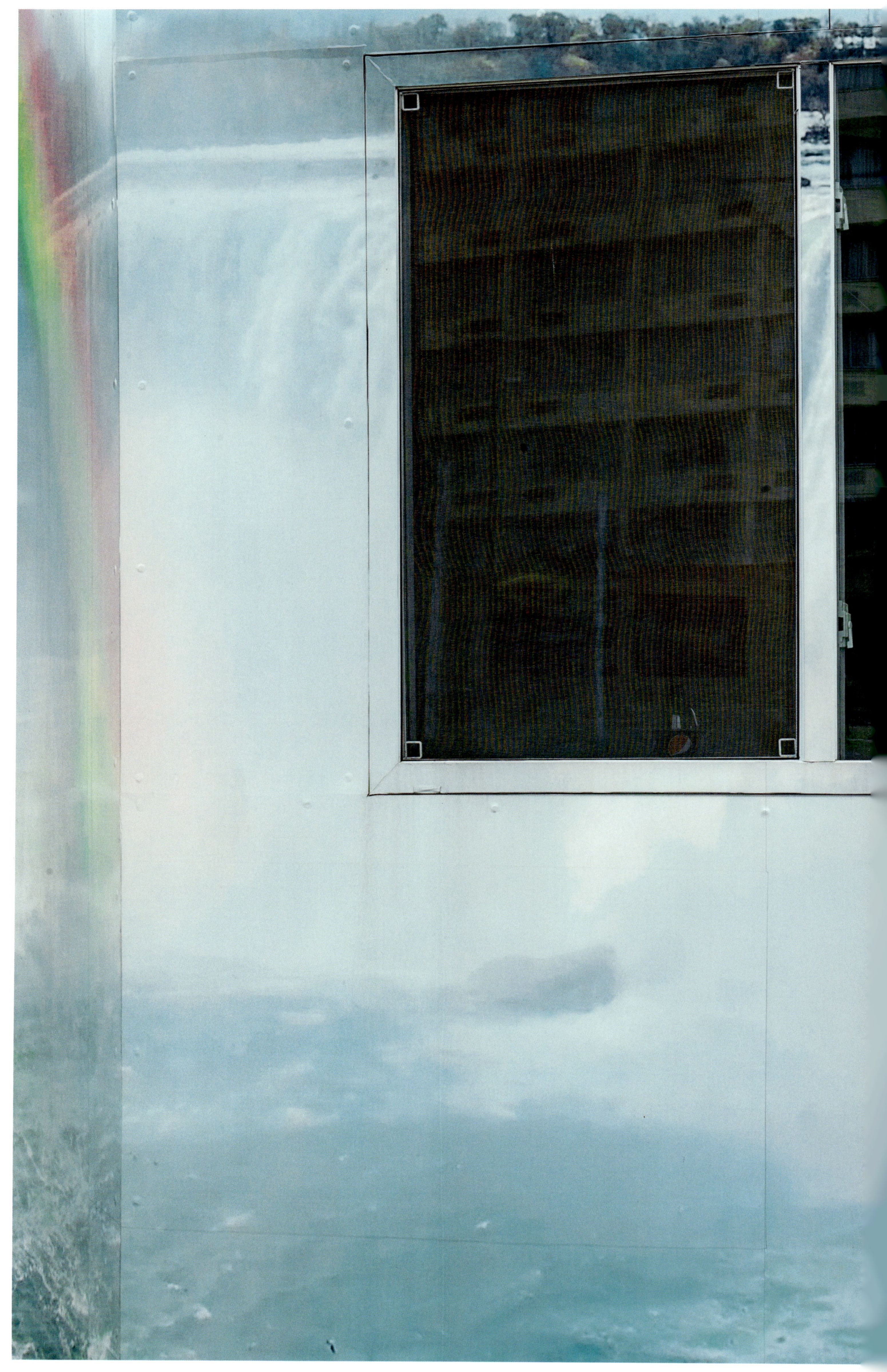

PLATE 35

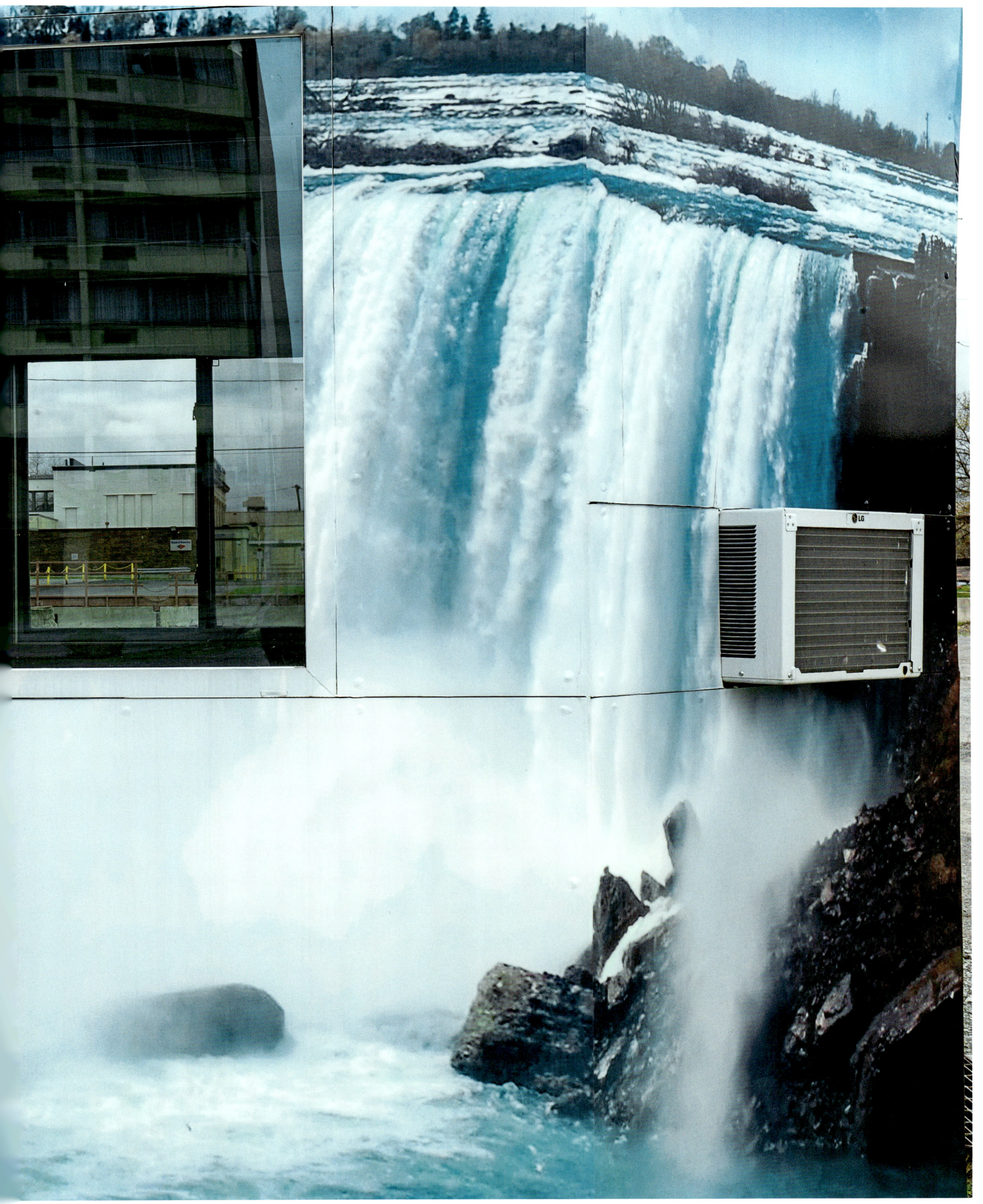
LG

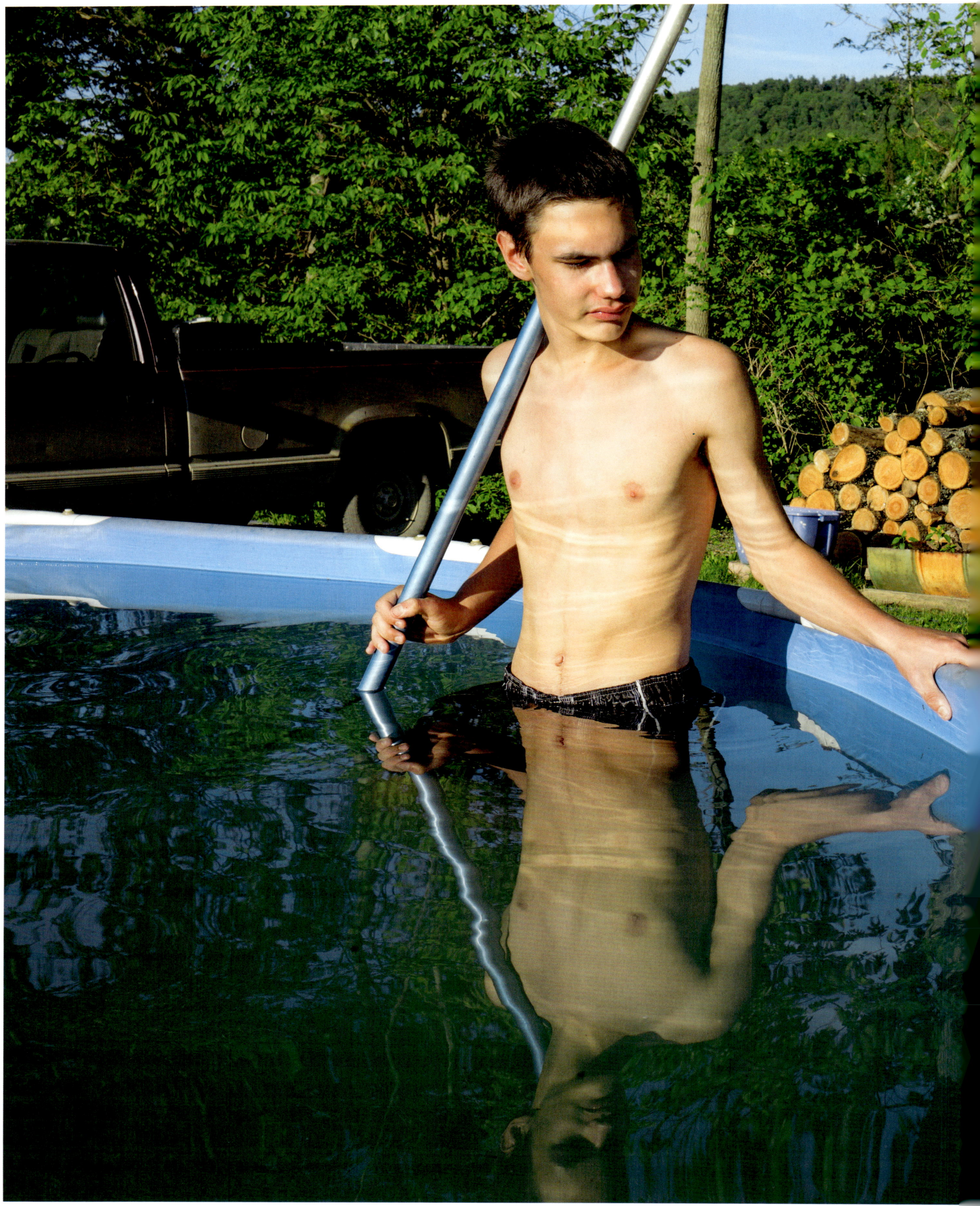

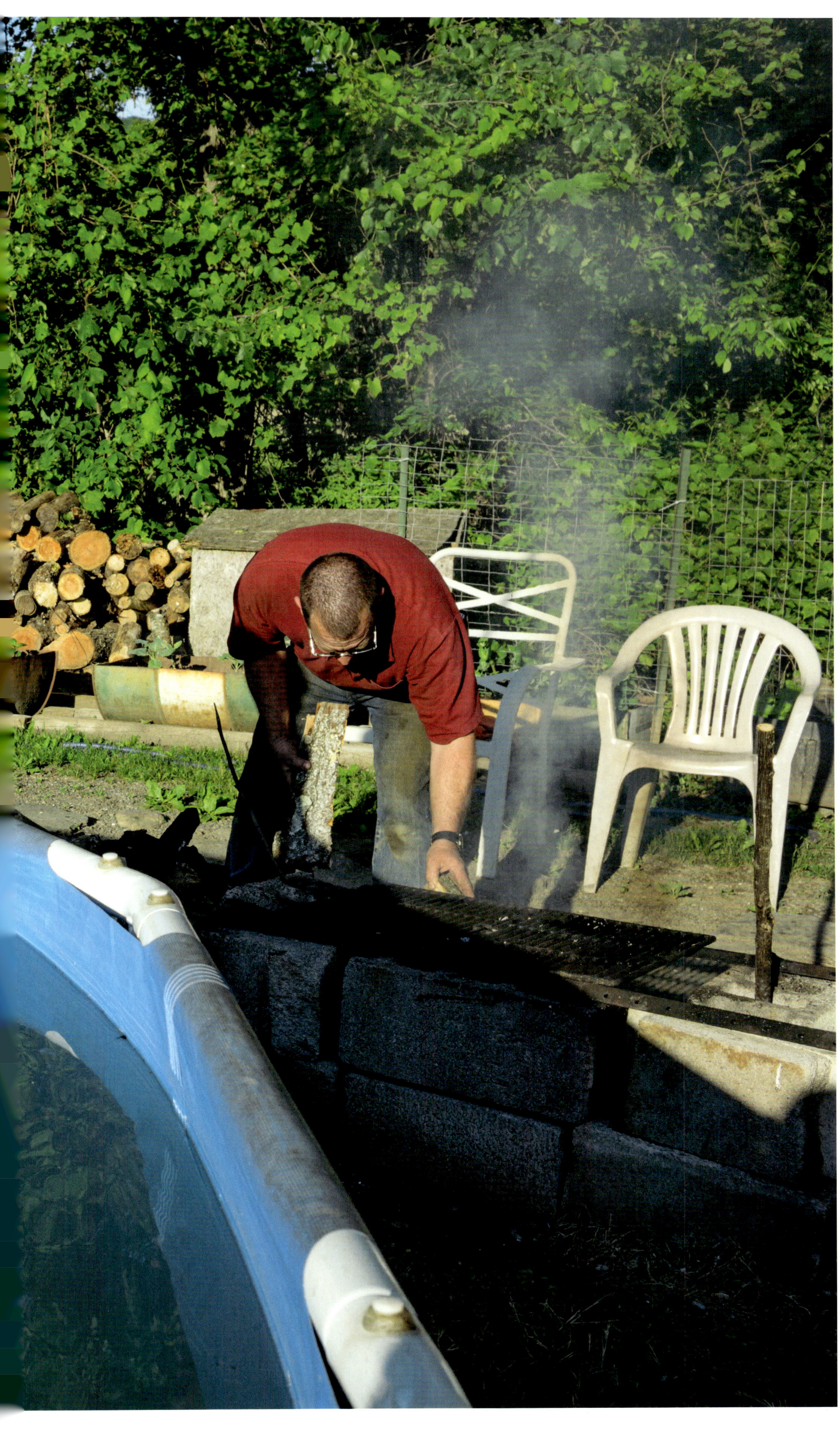

PLATE 36

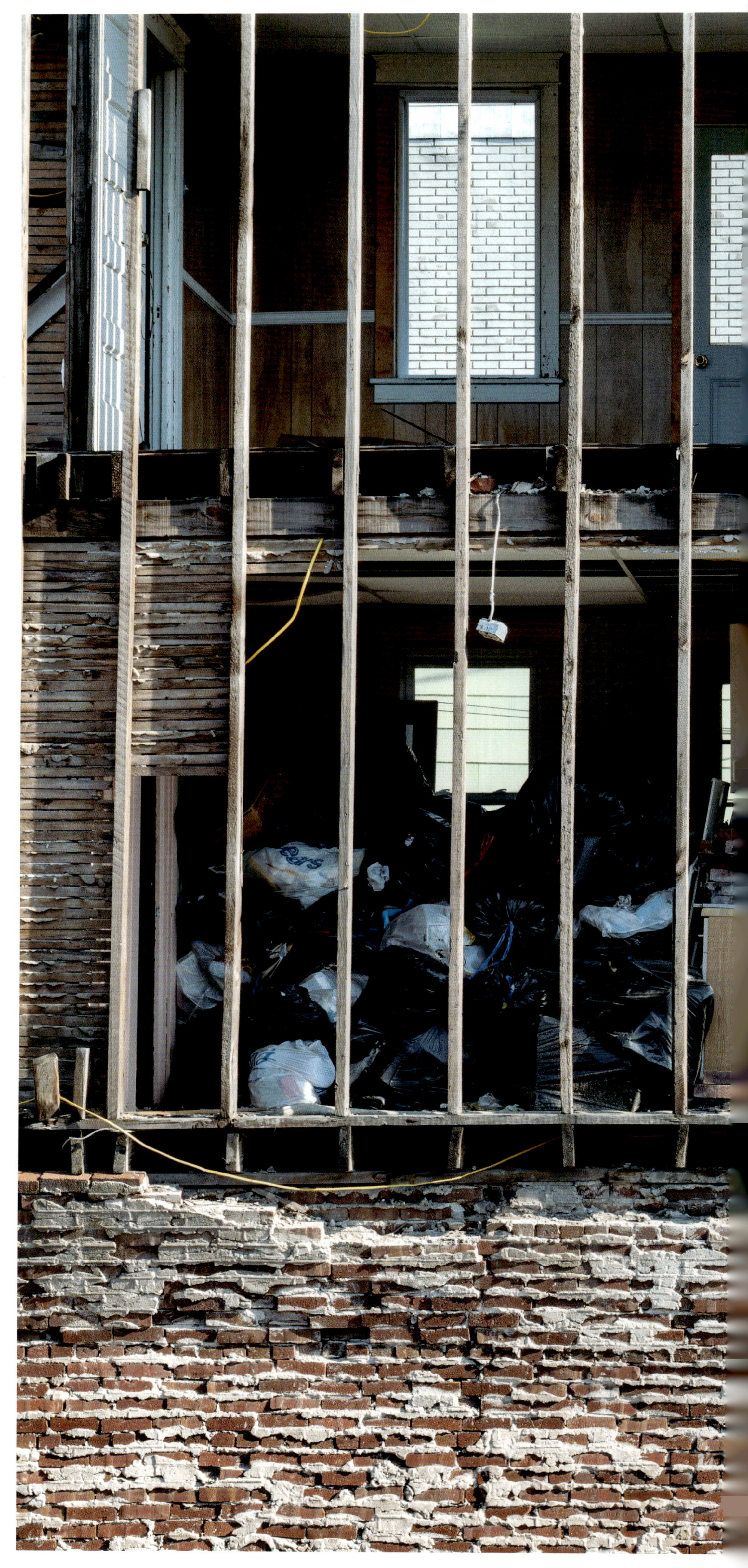

PLATE 37

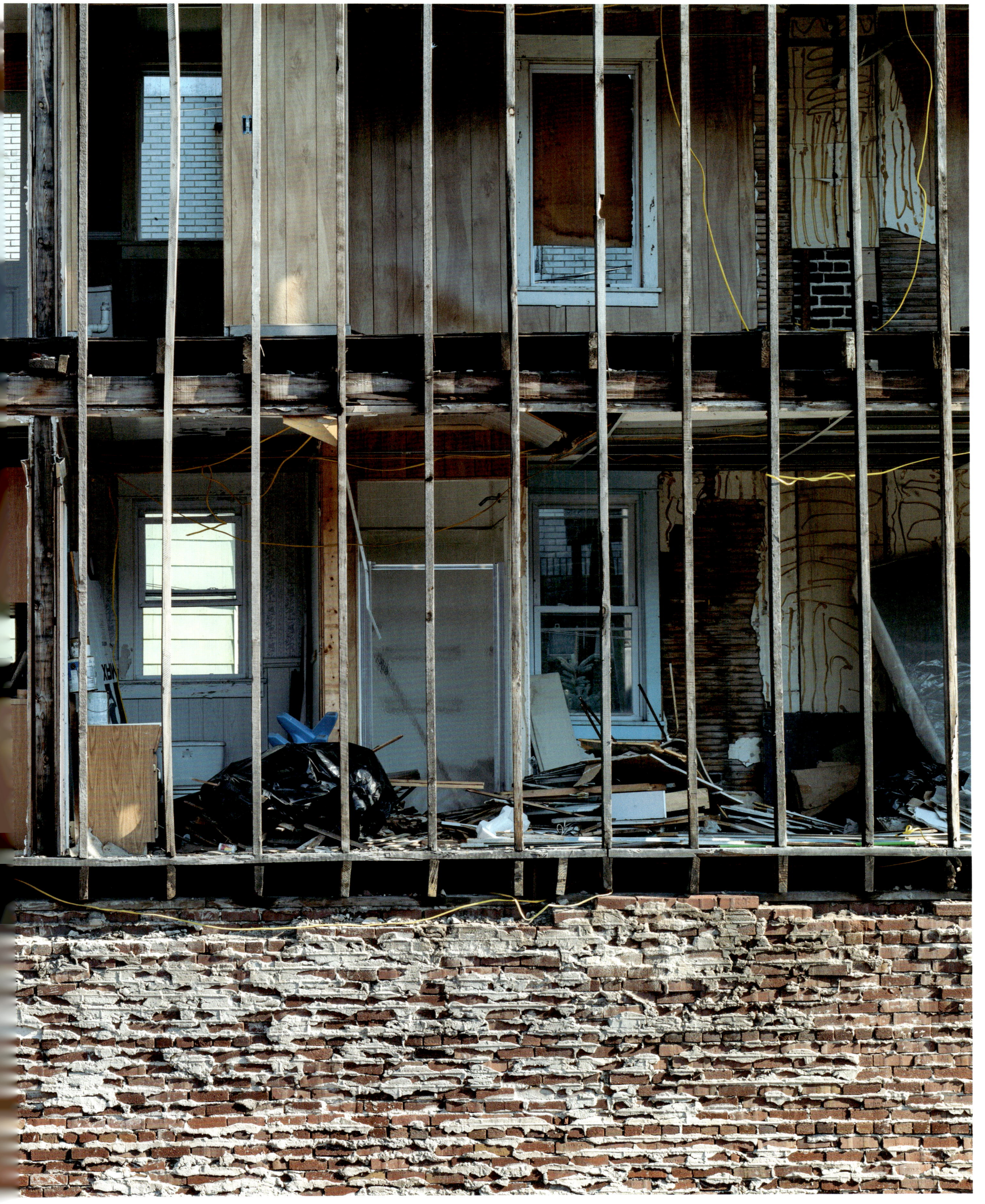

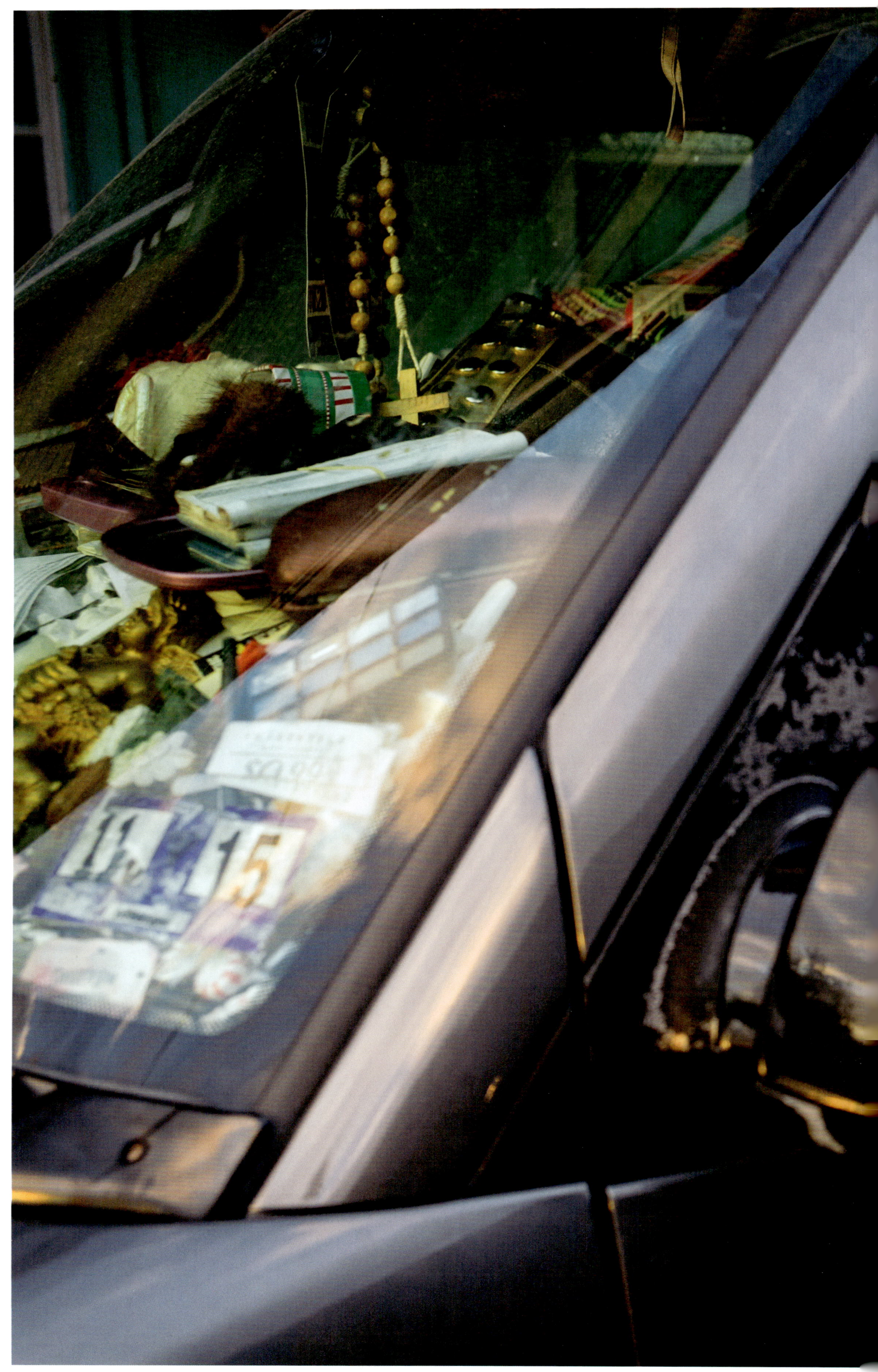

PLATE 38

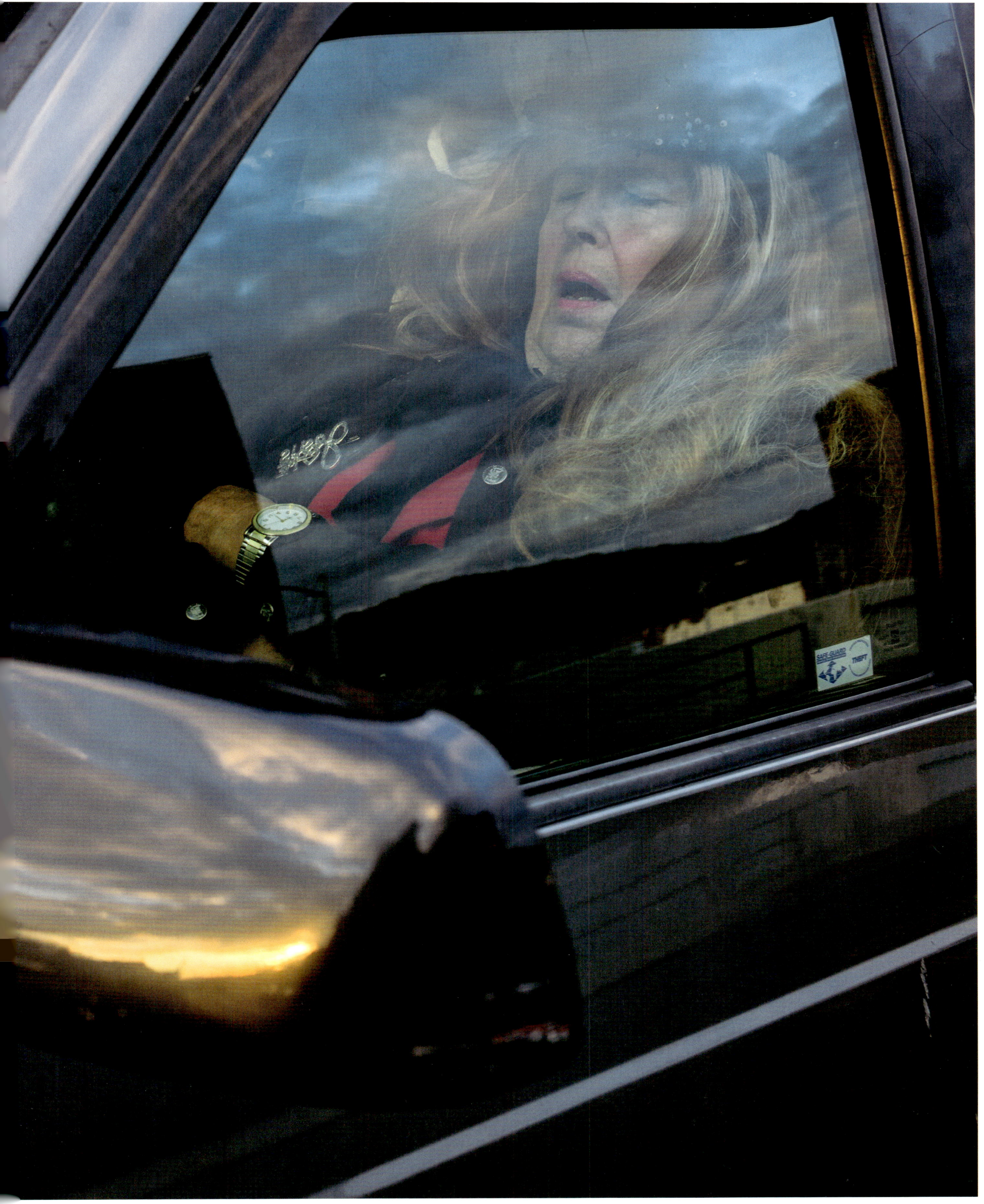
SAFE-GUARD
THEFT

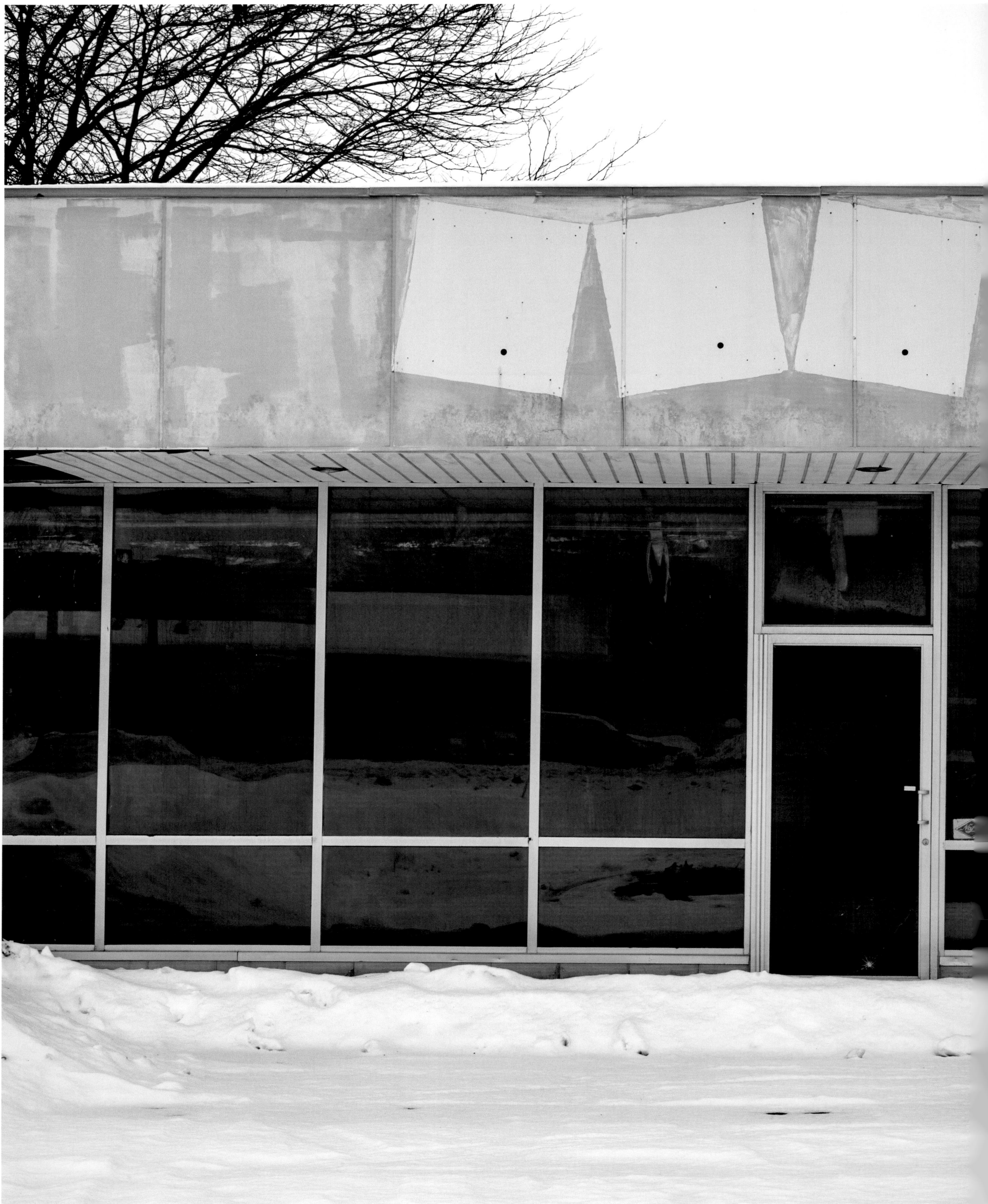

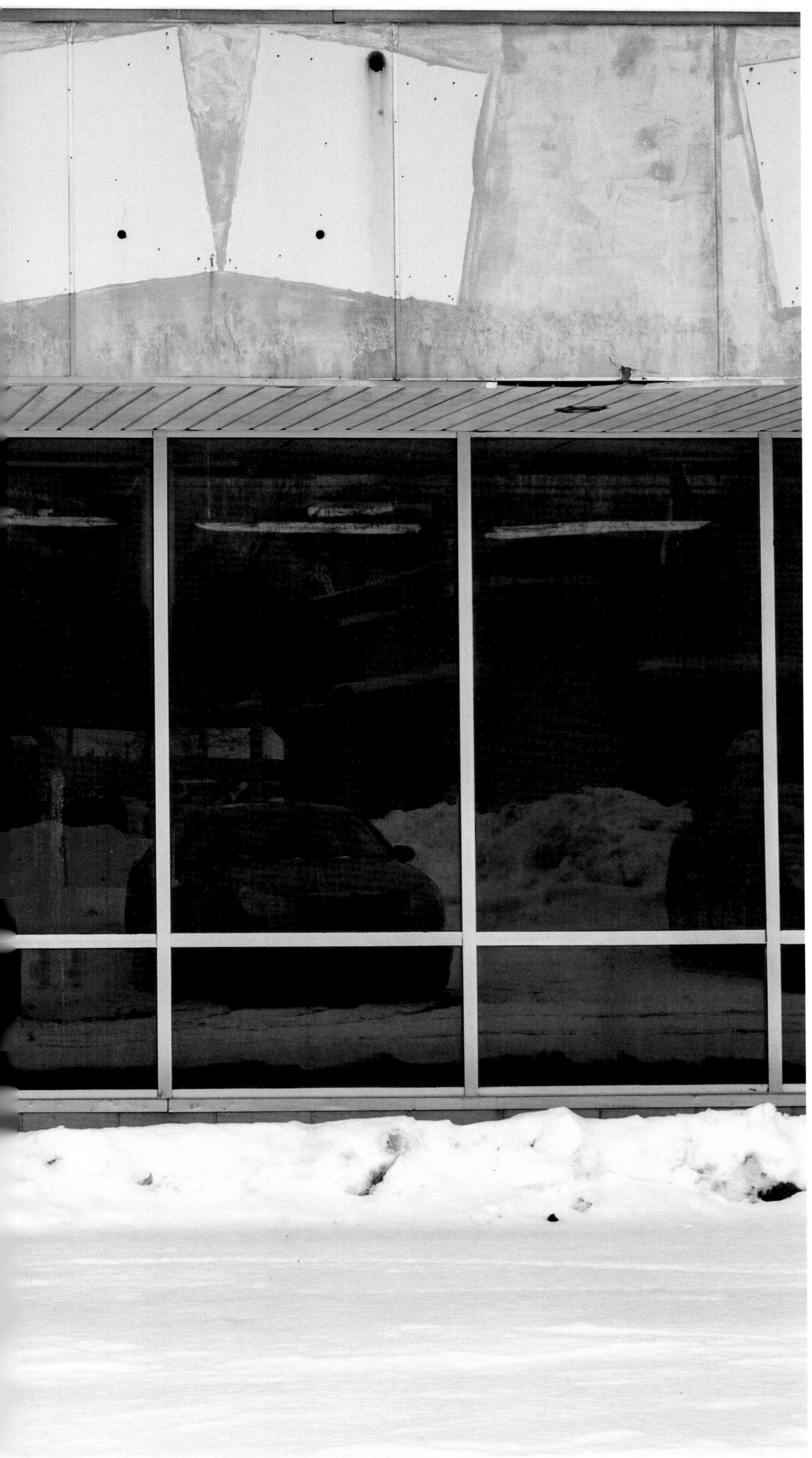

PLATE 39

PLATE 40

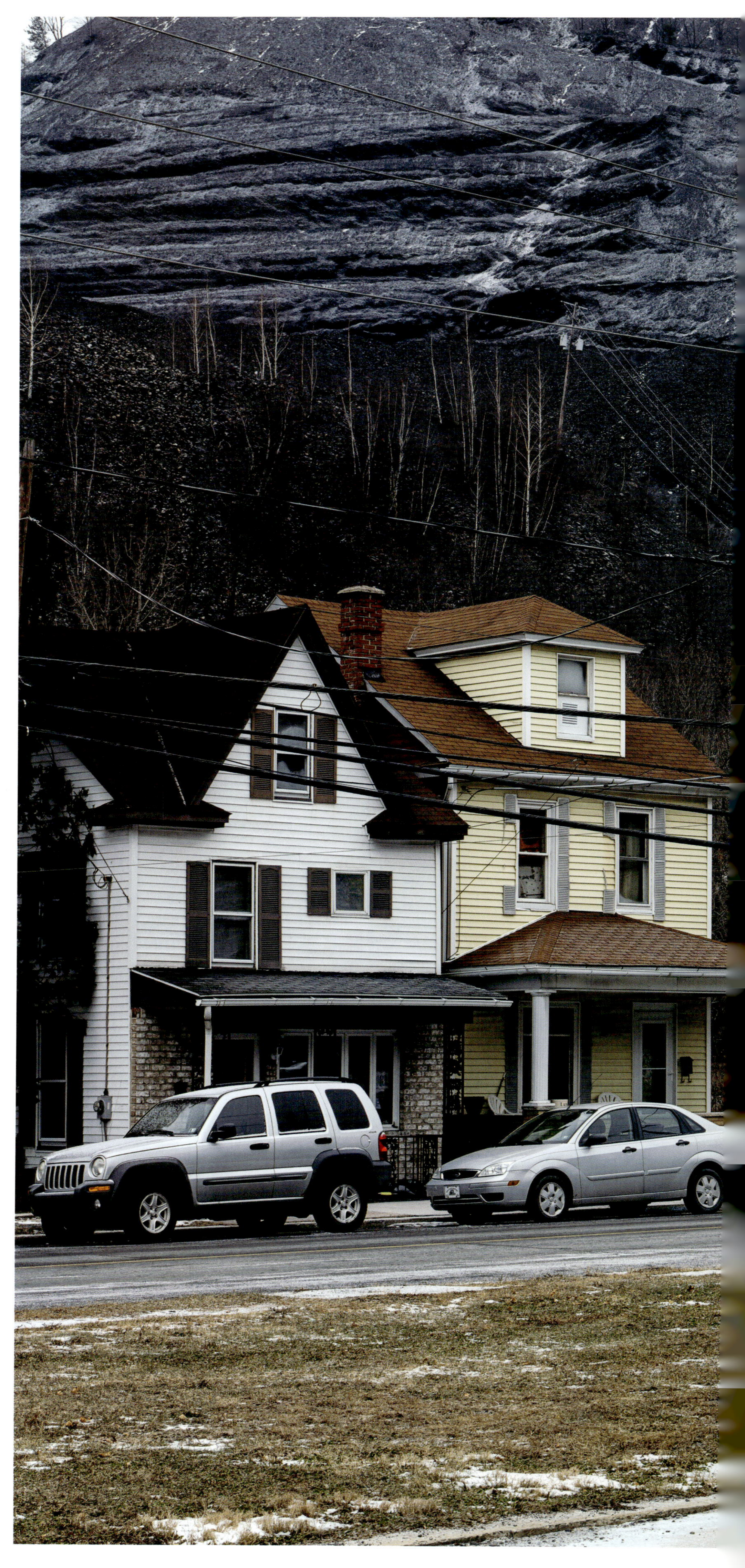

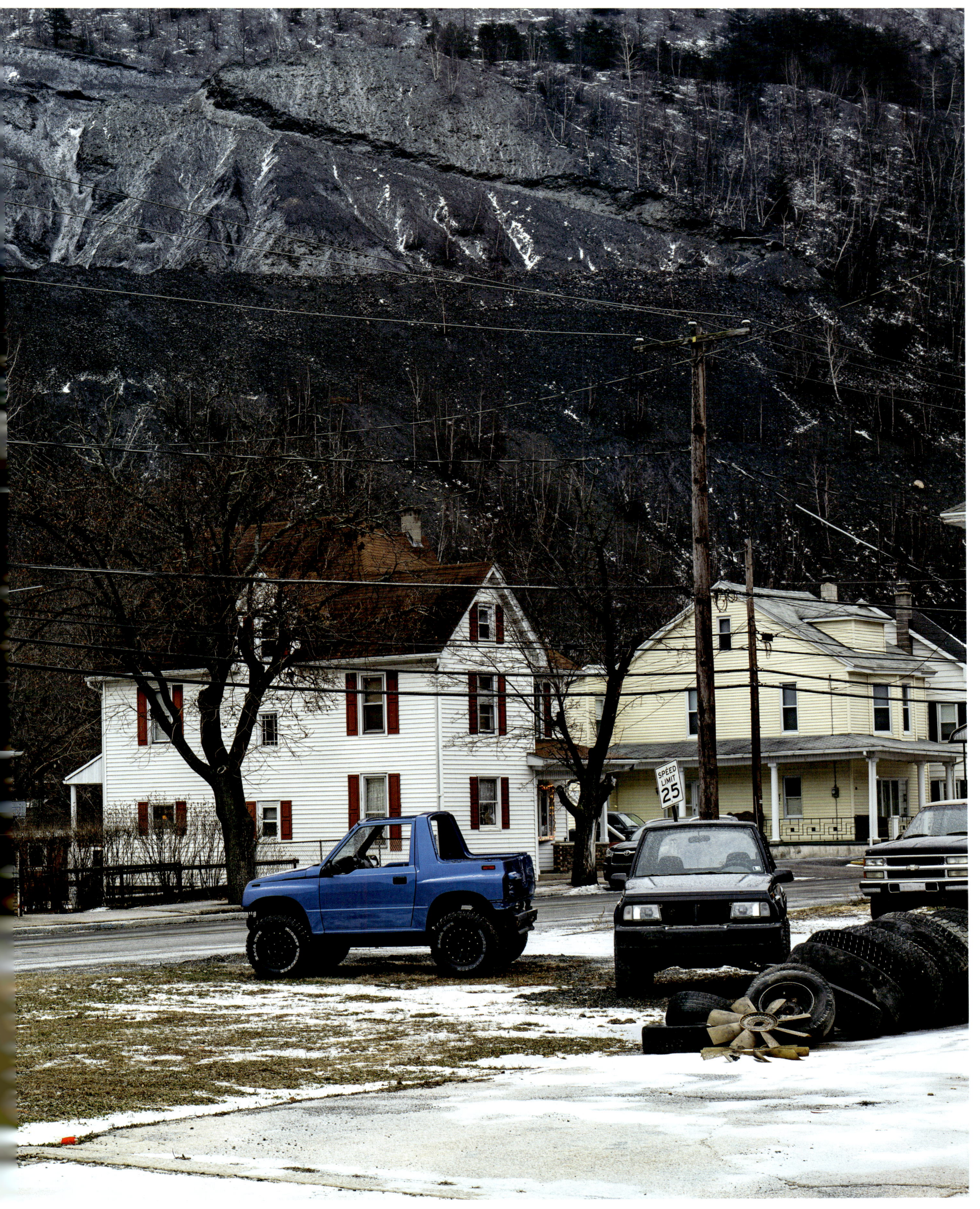
SPEED
LIMIT
25

PLATE 41

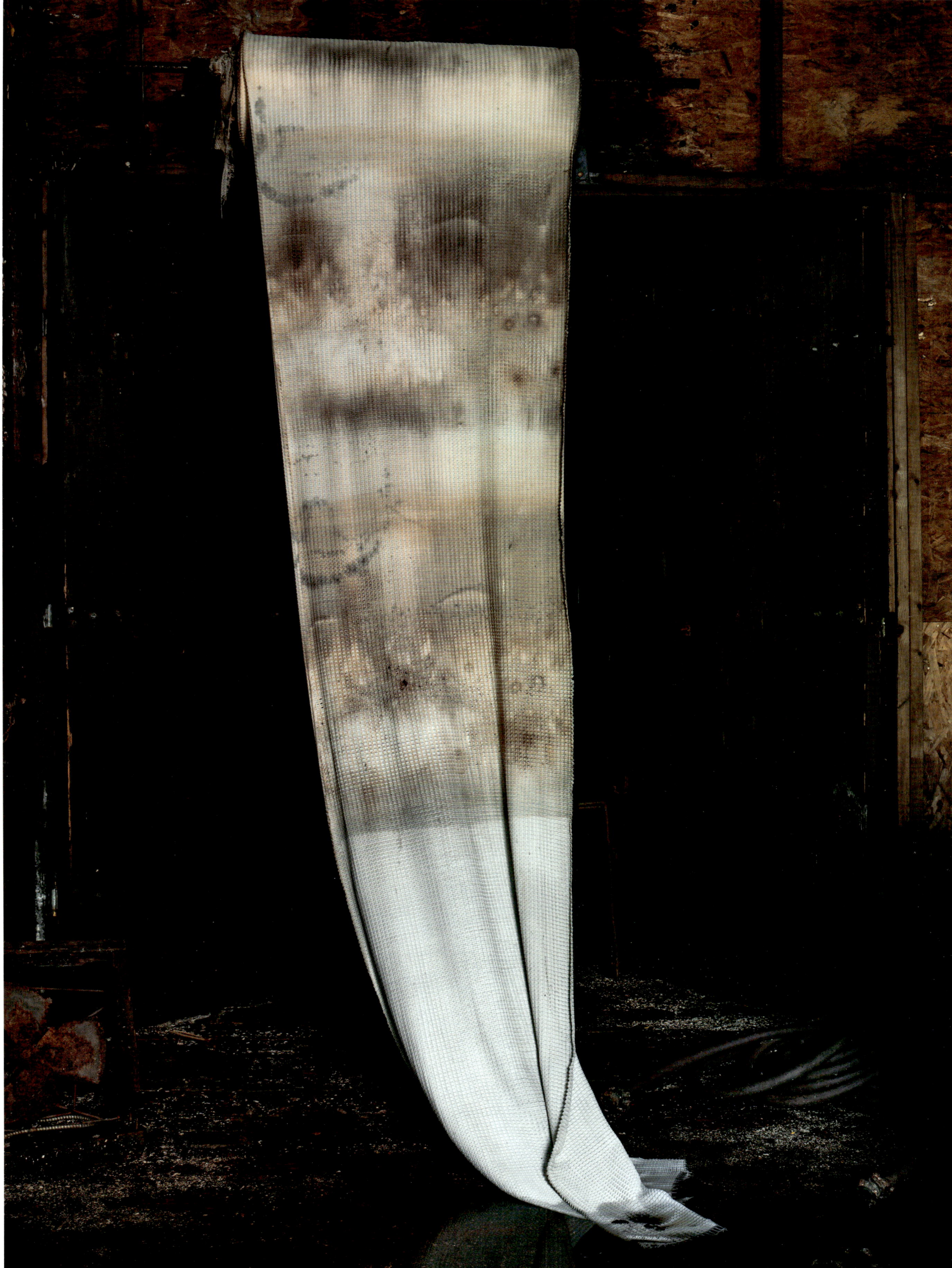

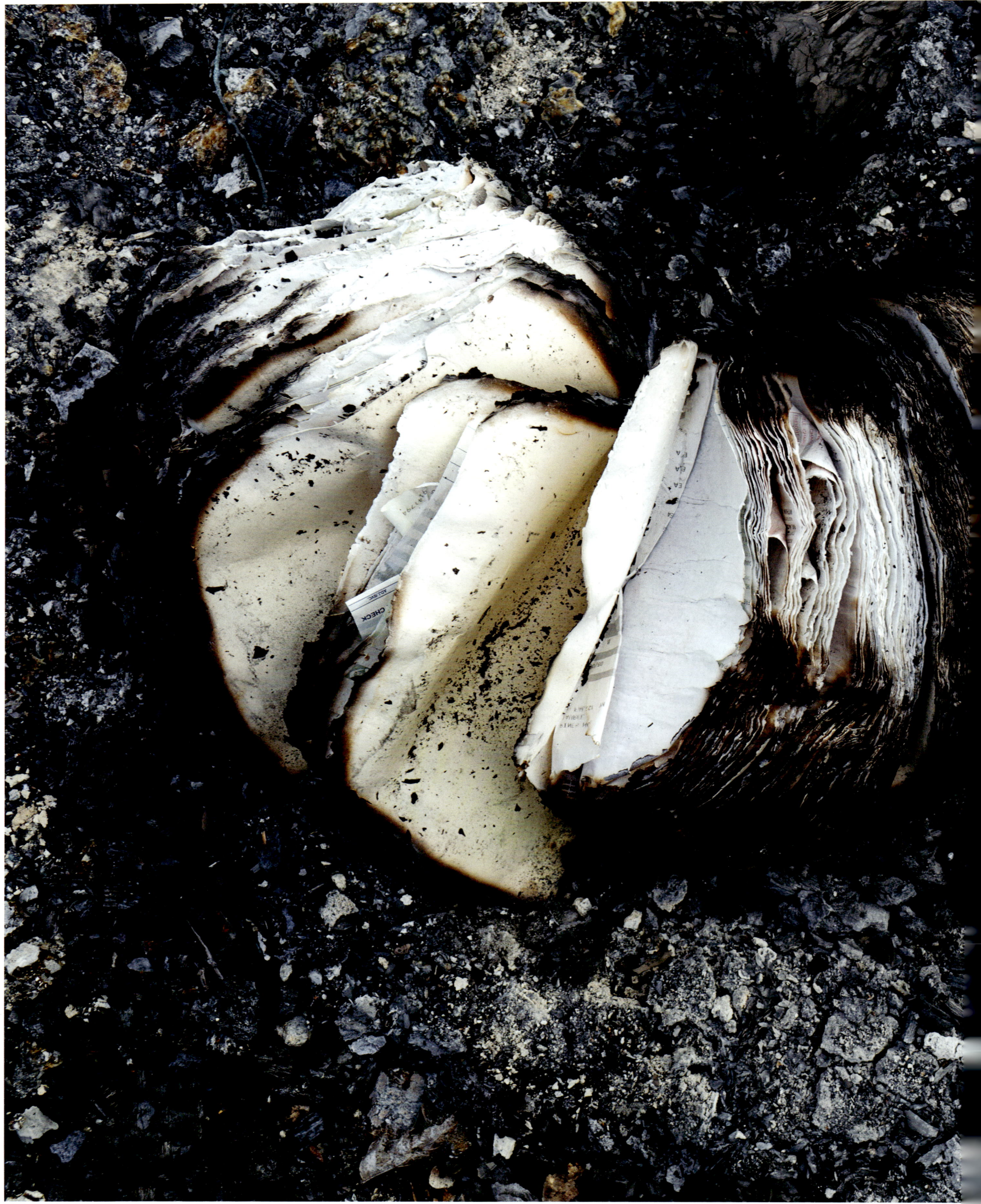

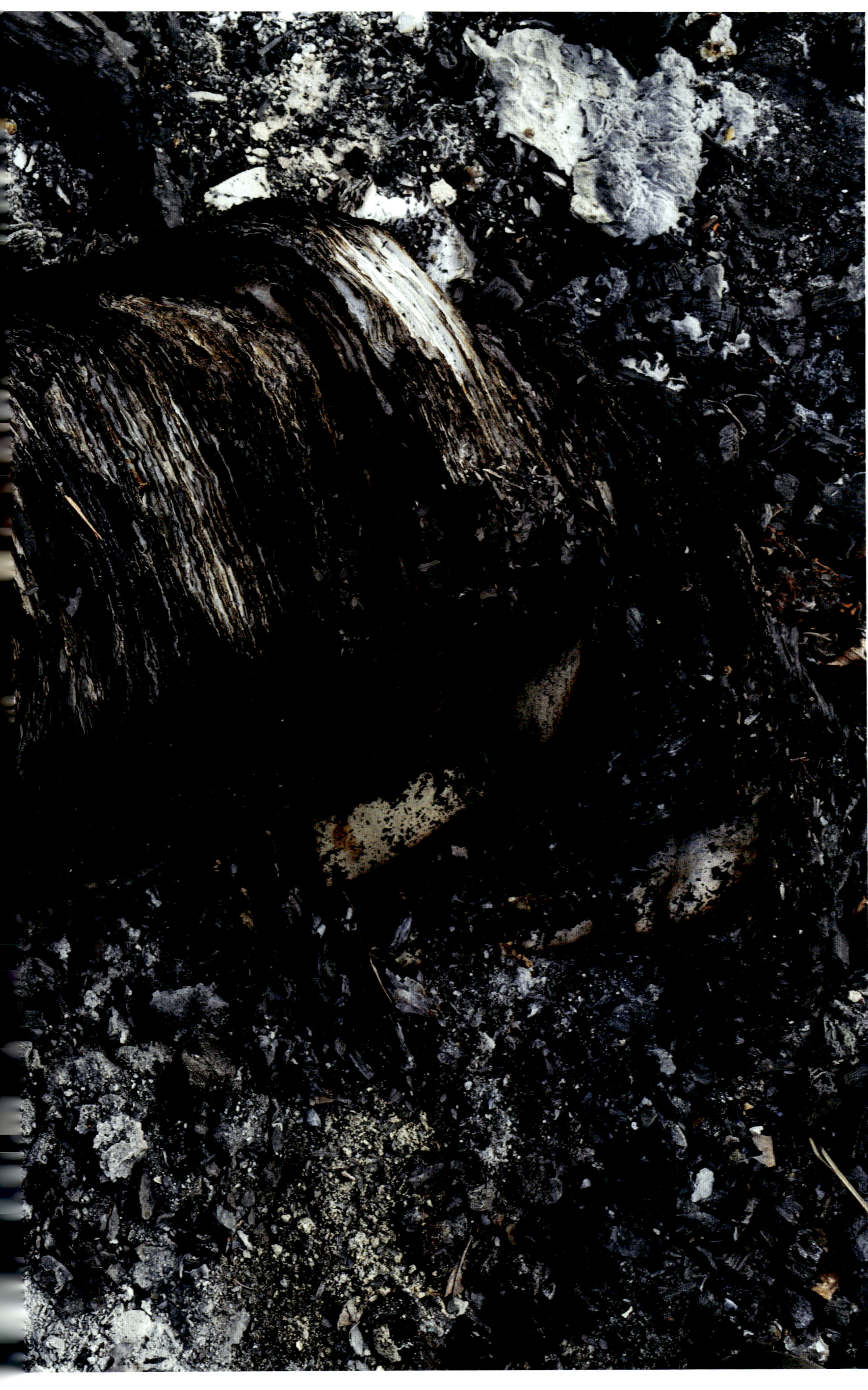

PLATE 42

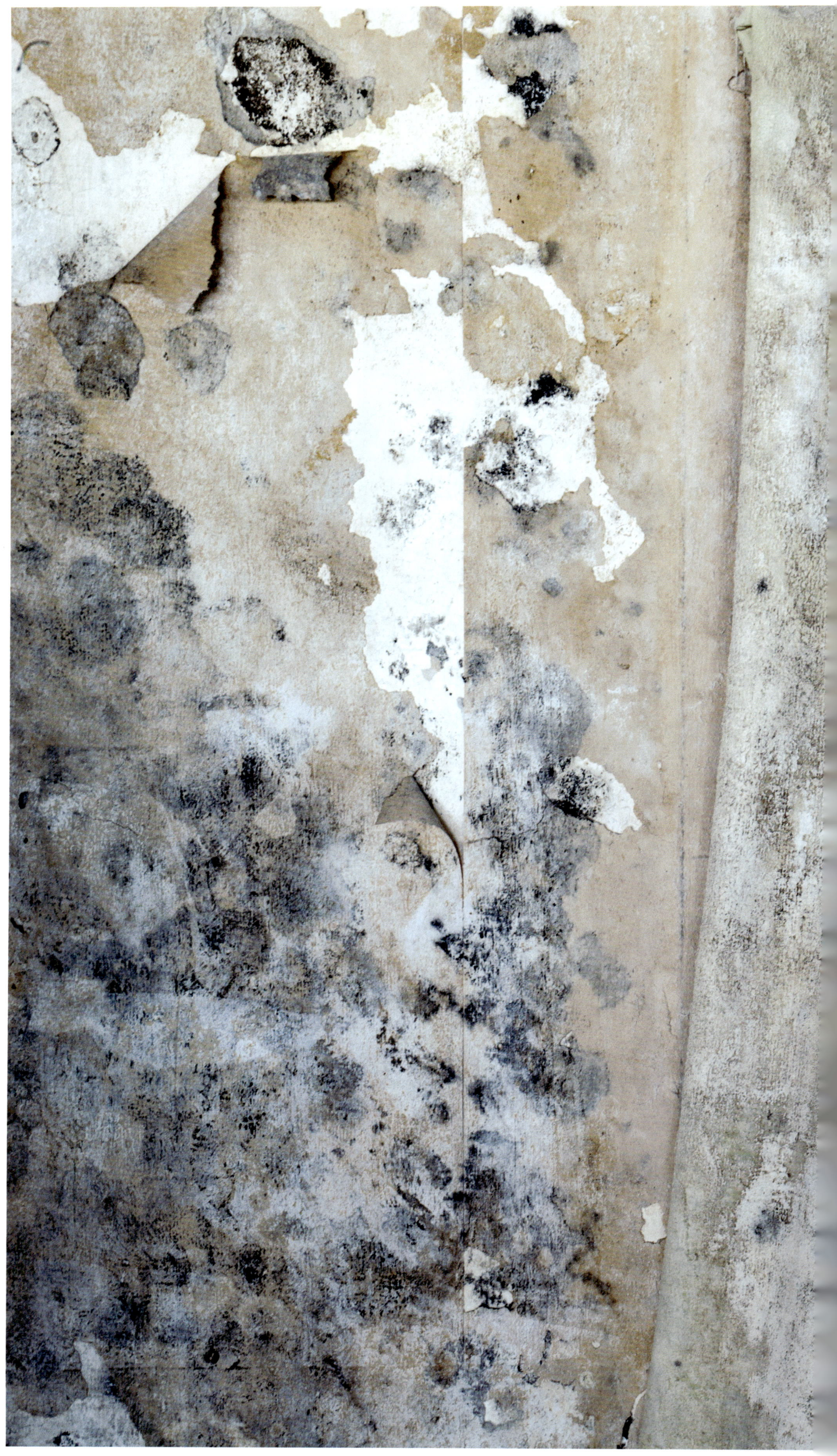

PLATE 43

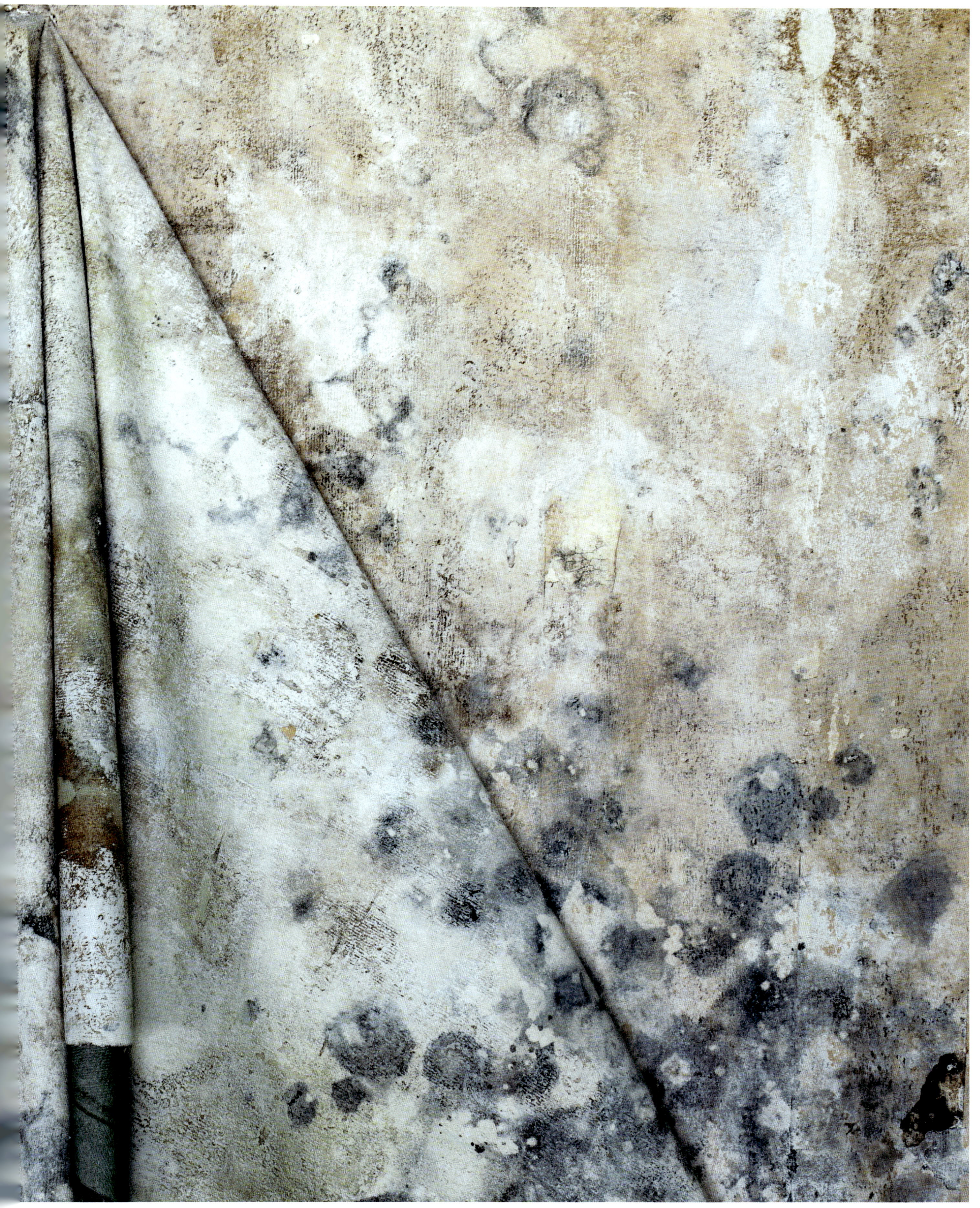

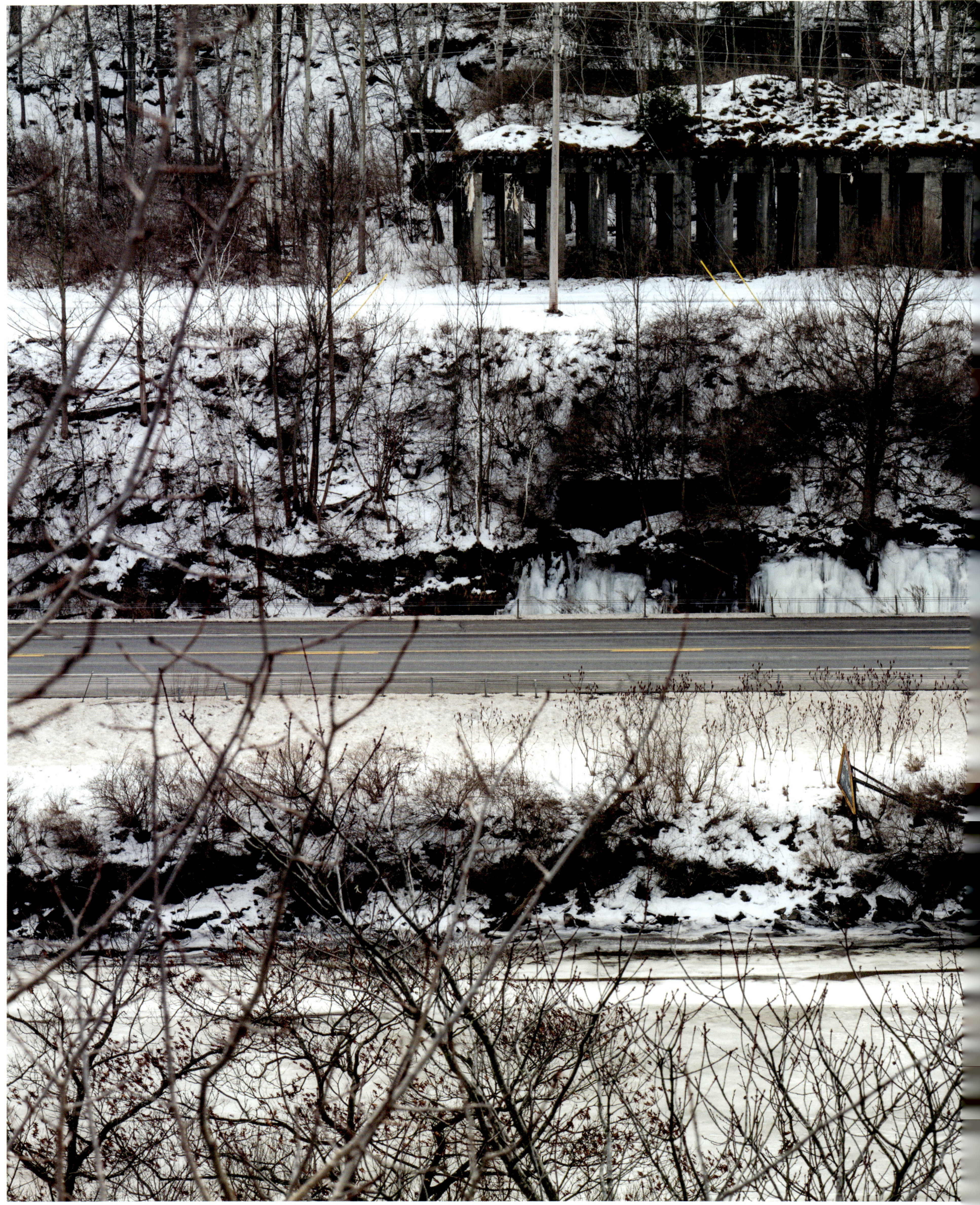

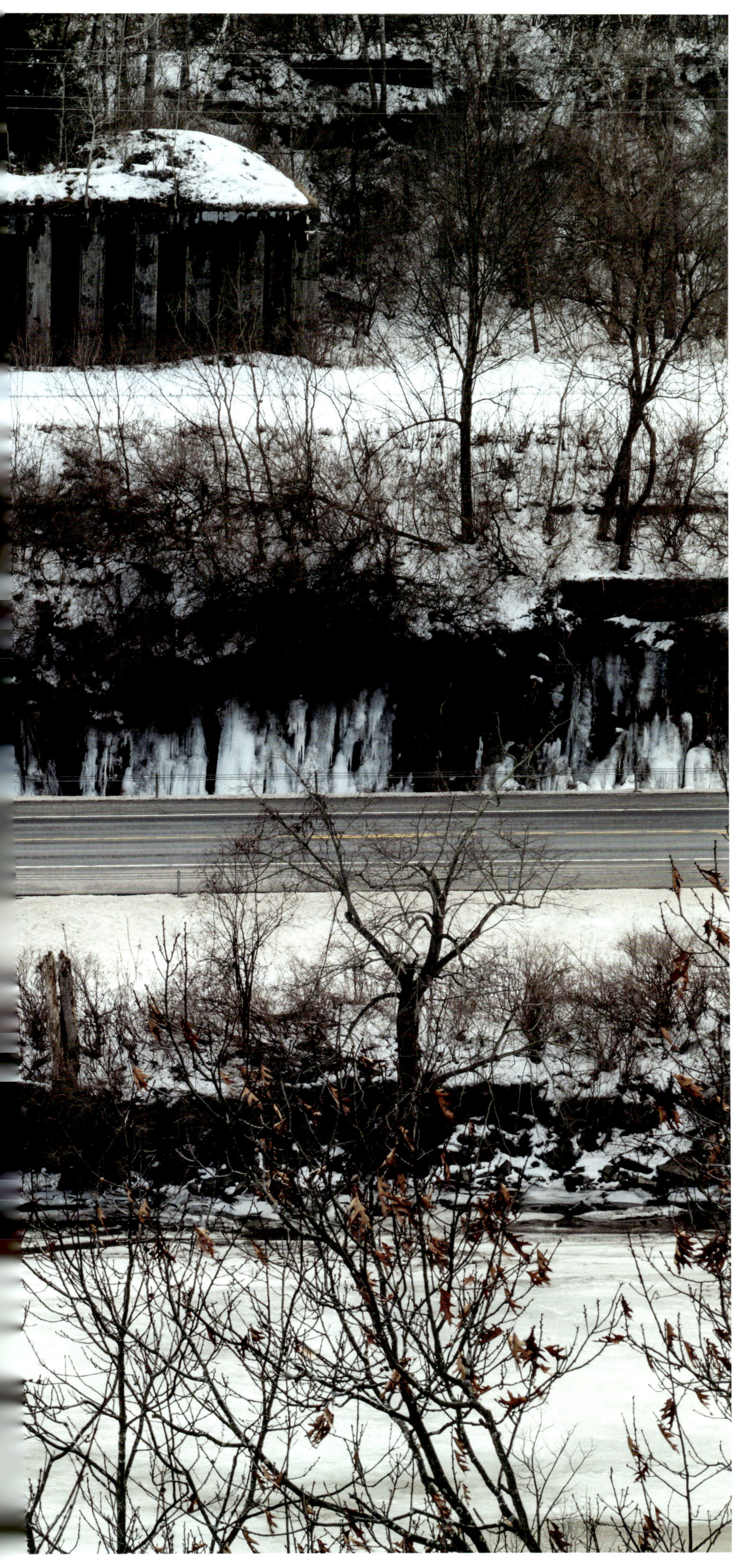

PLATE 44

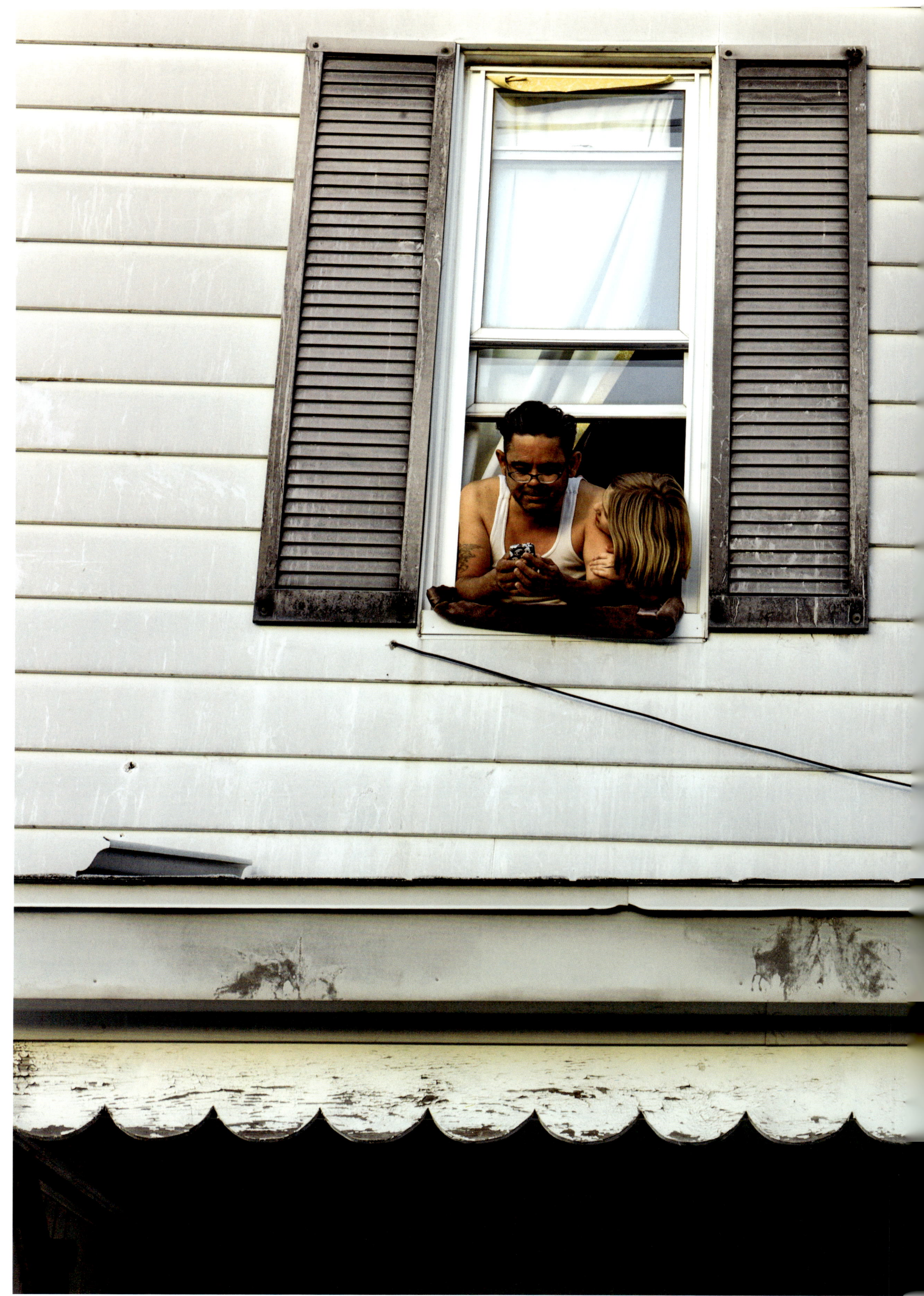

PLATE 45

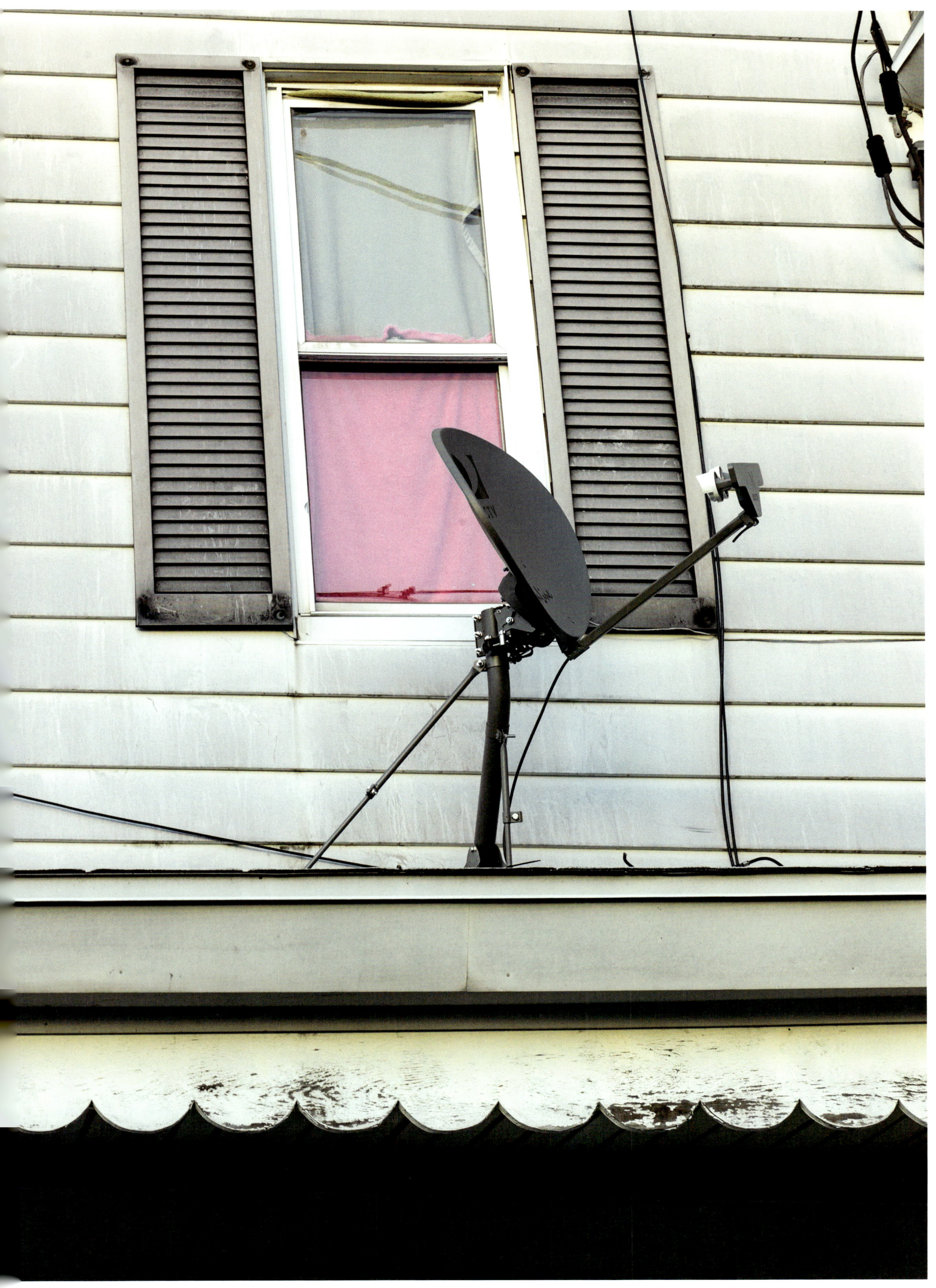

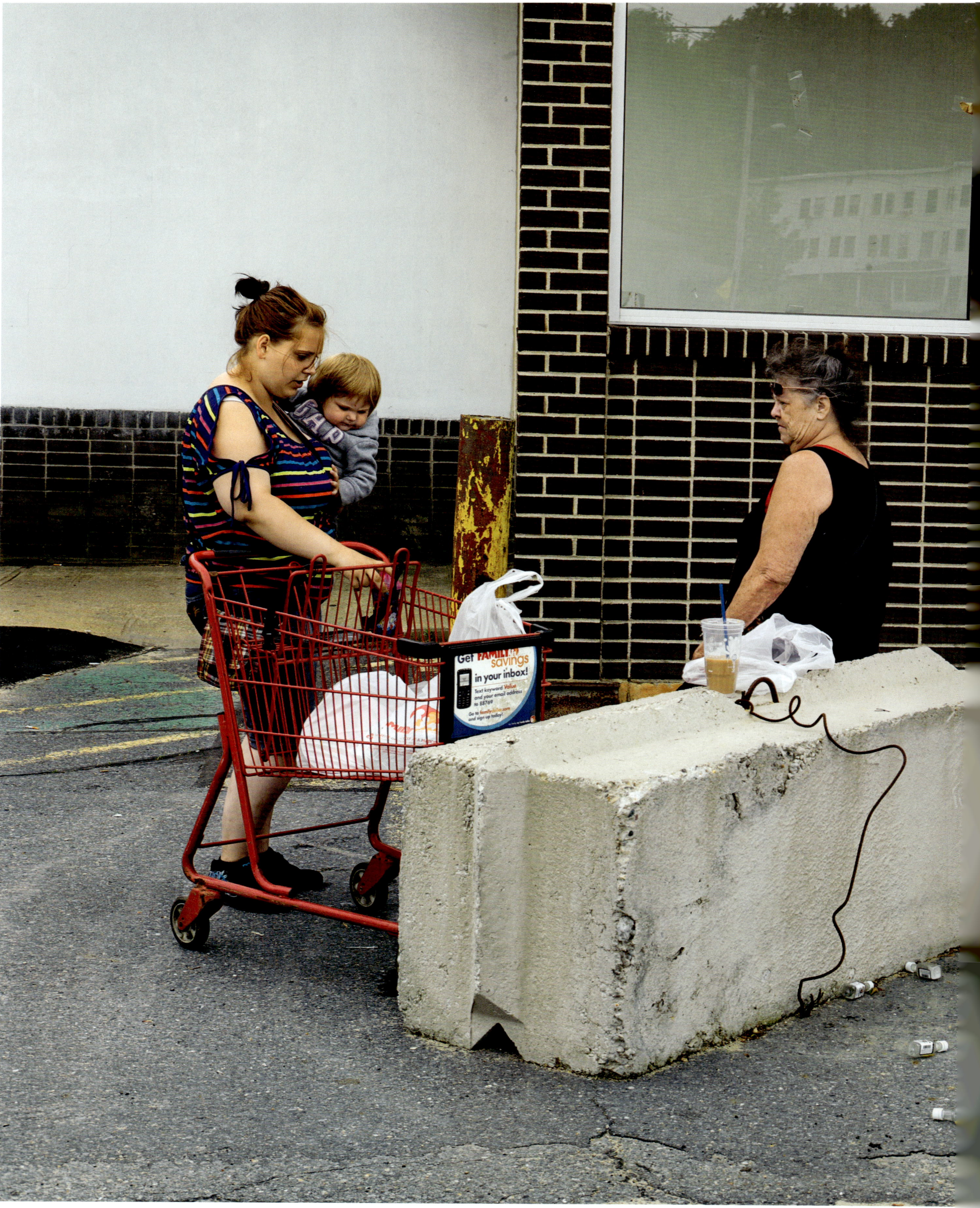
Get FAMILY savings
in your inbox!
Text keyword Value
and your email address
to 88769
Go to familydollar.com
and sign up today!

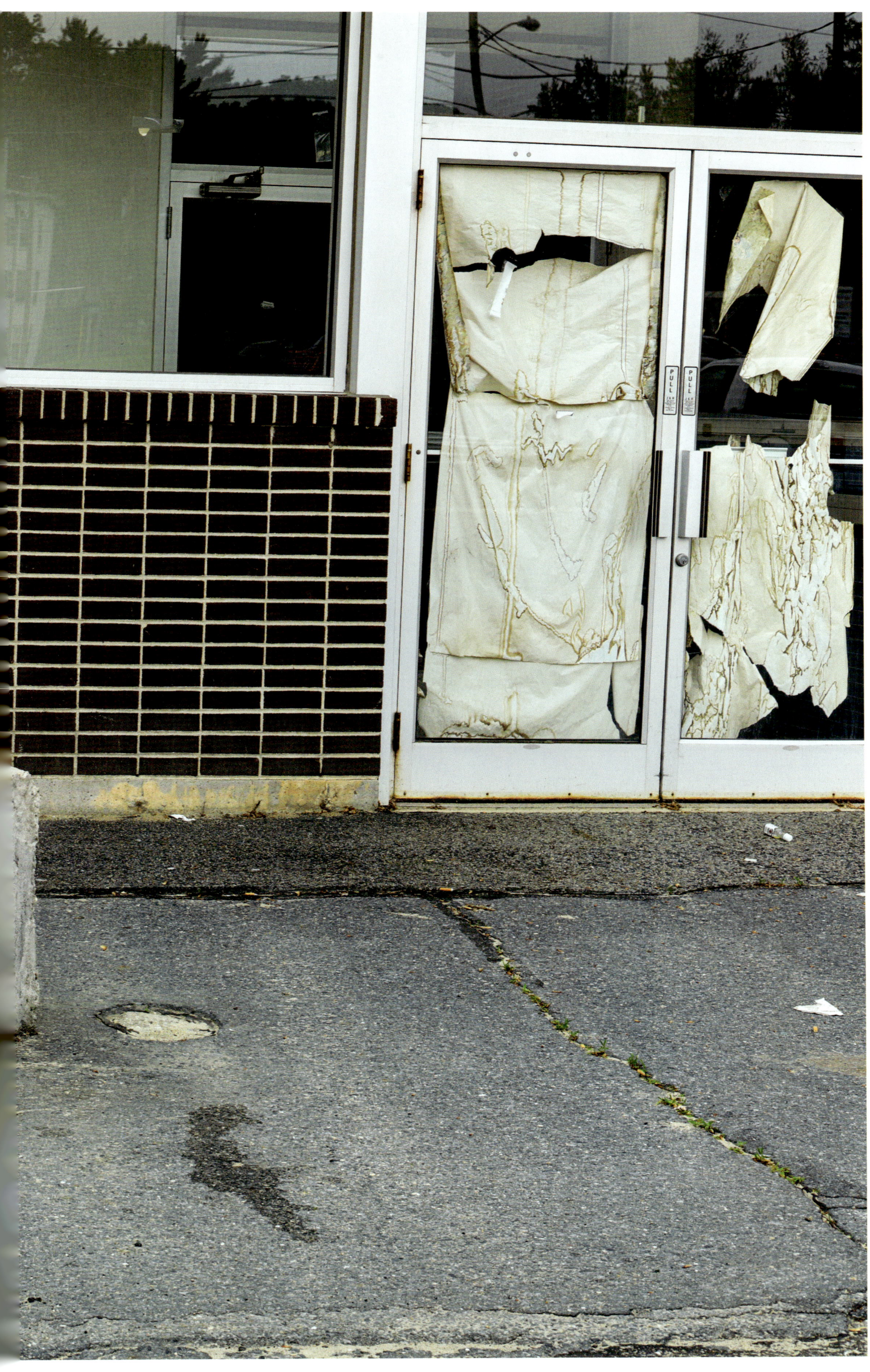

PLATE 46

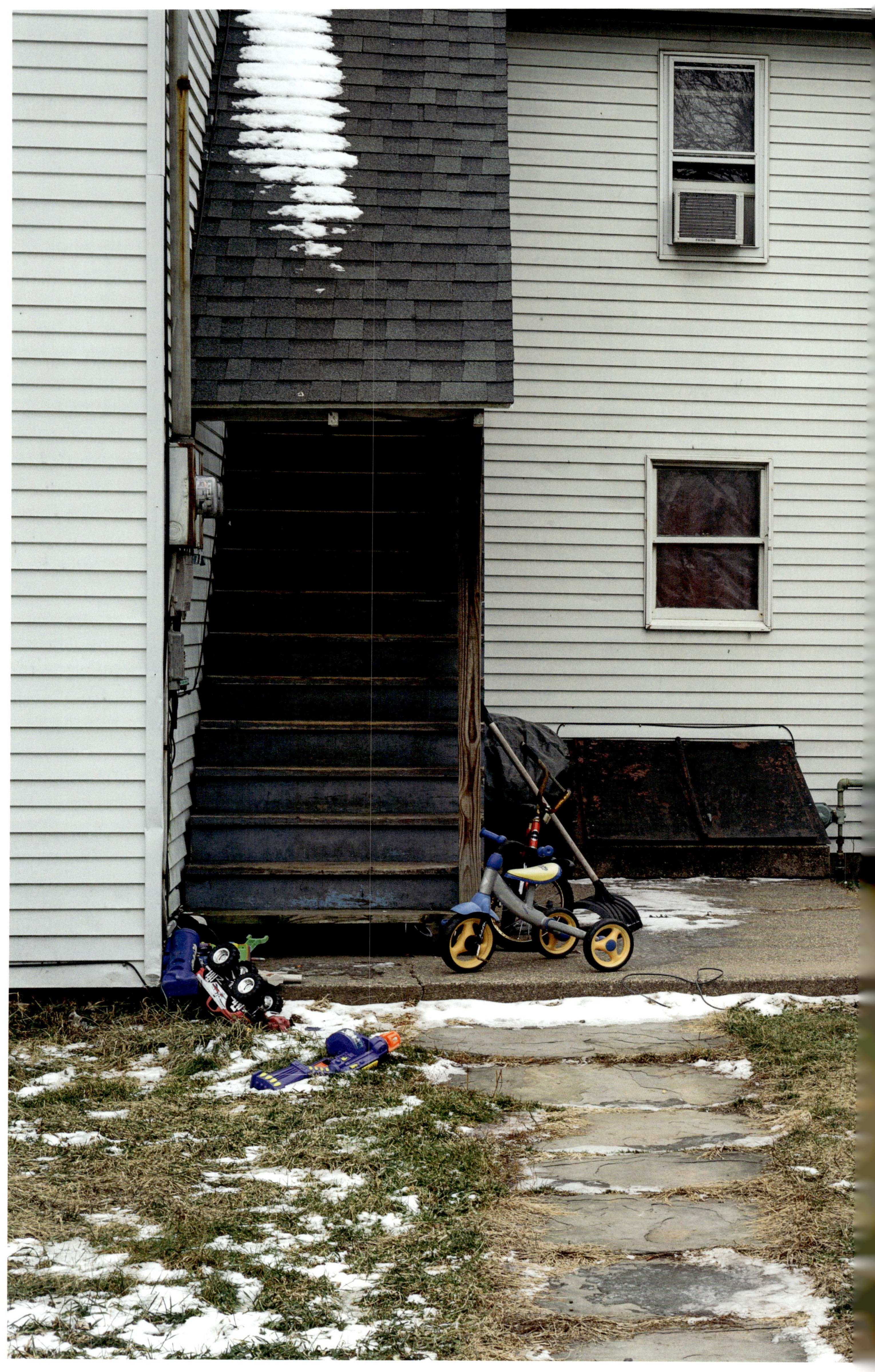

PLATE 47

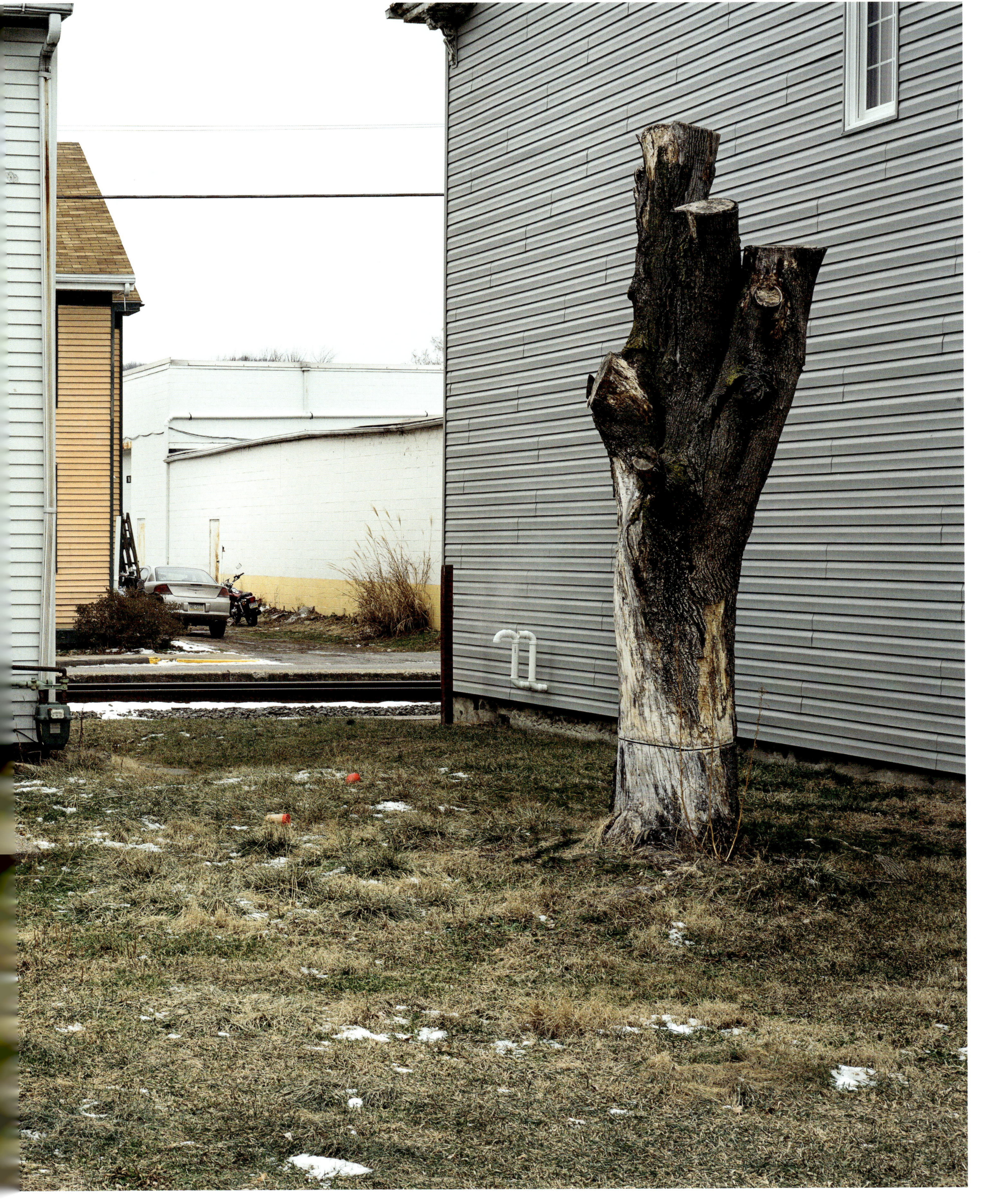

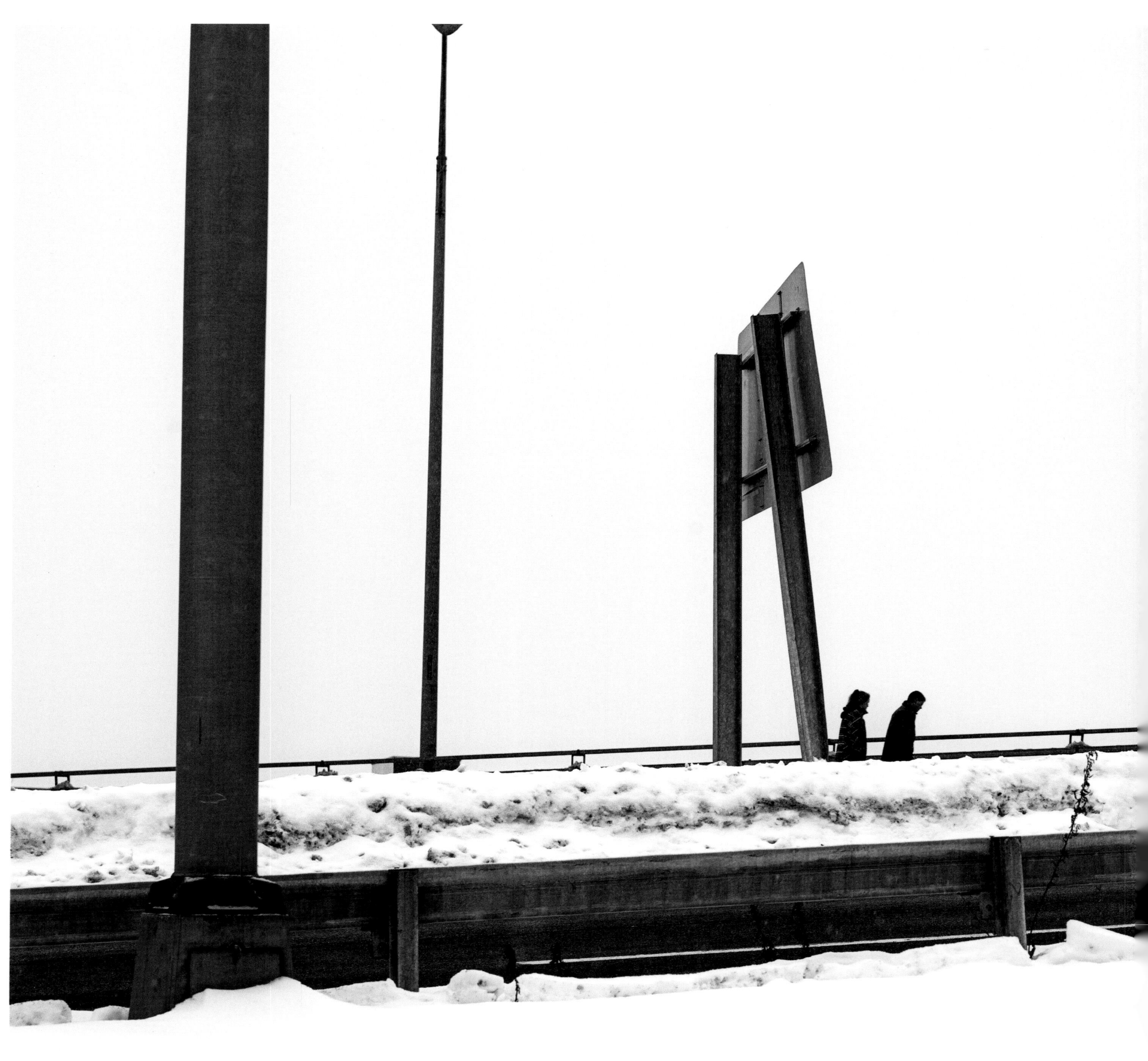

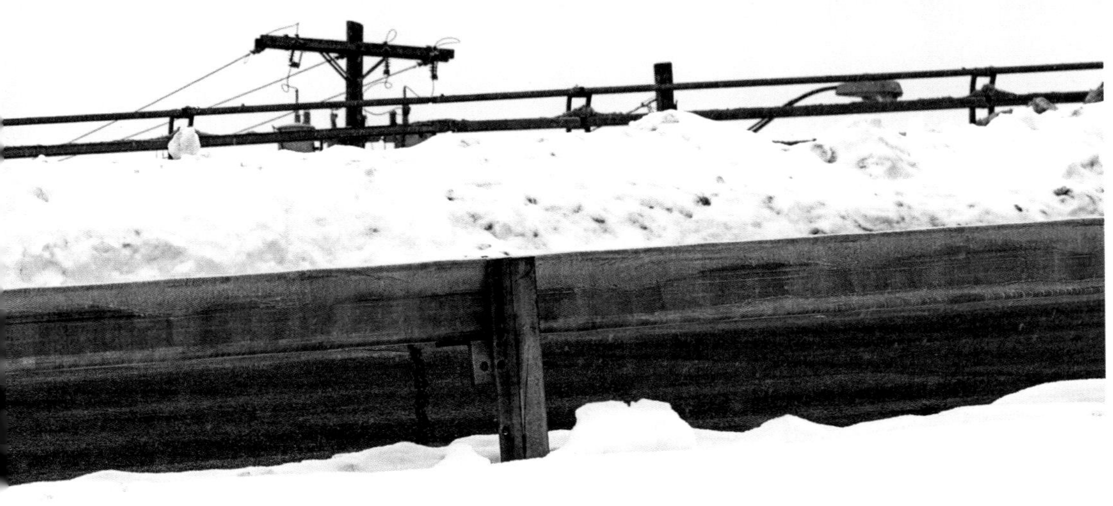

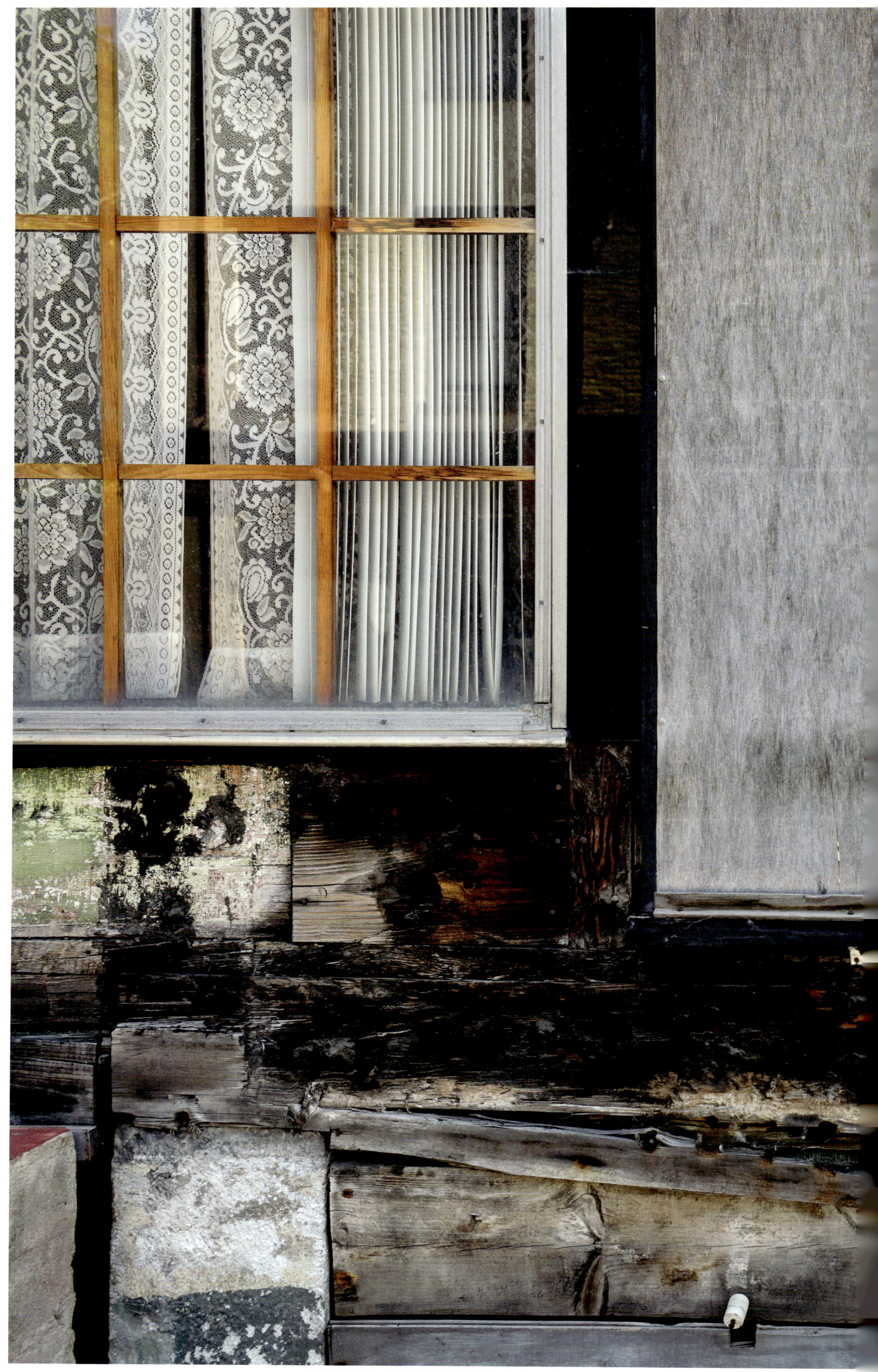

PLATE 49

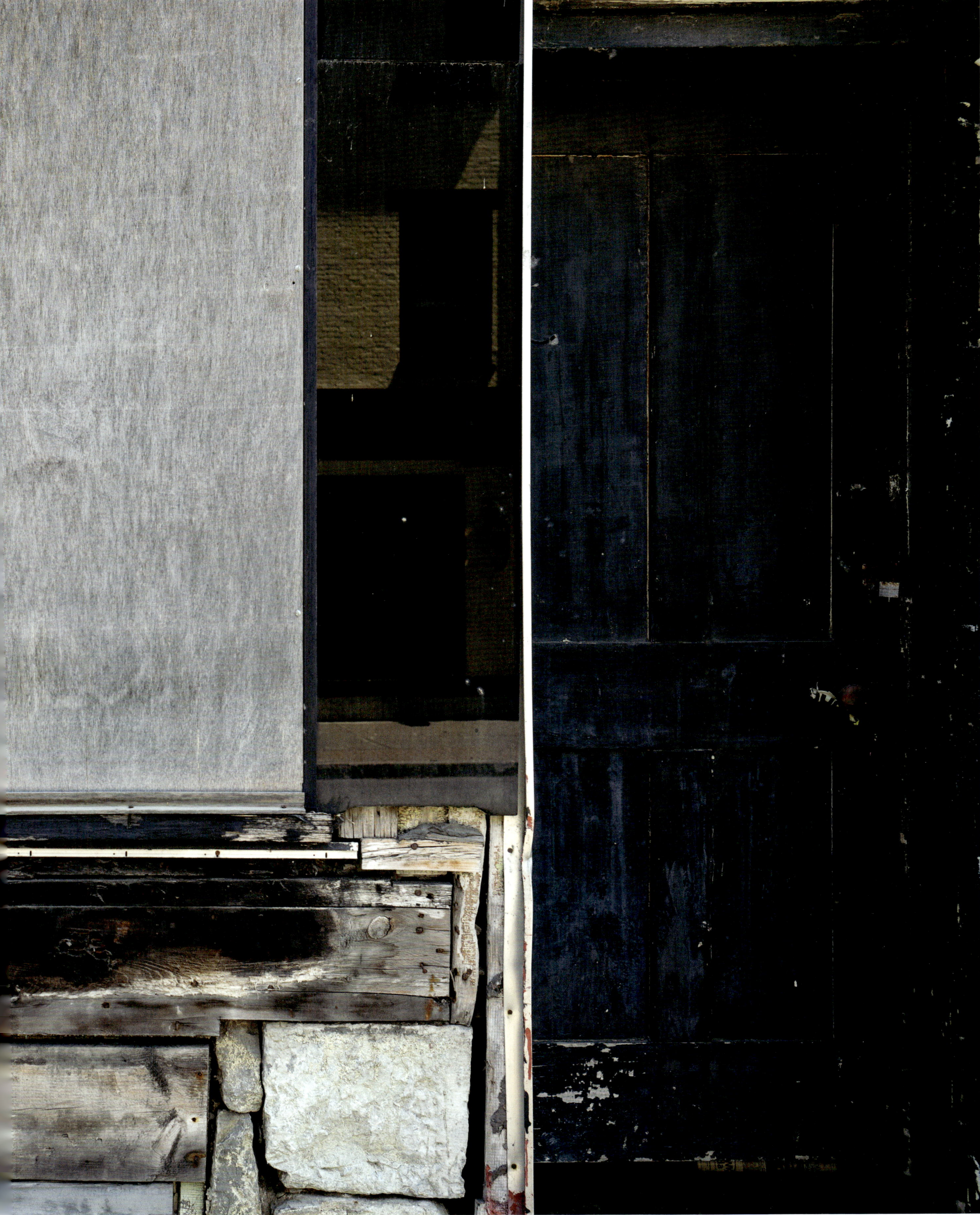

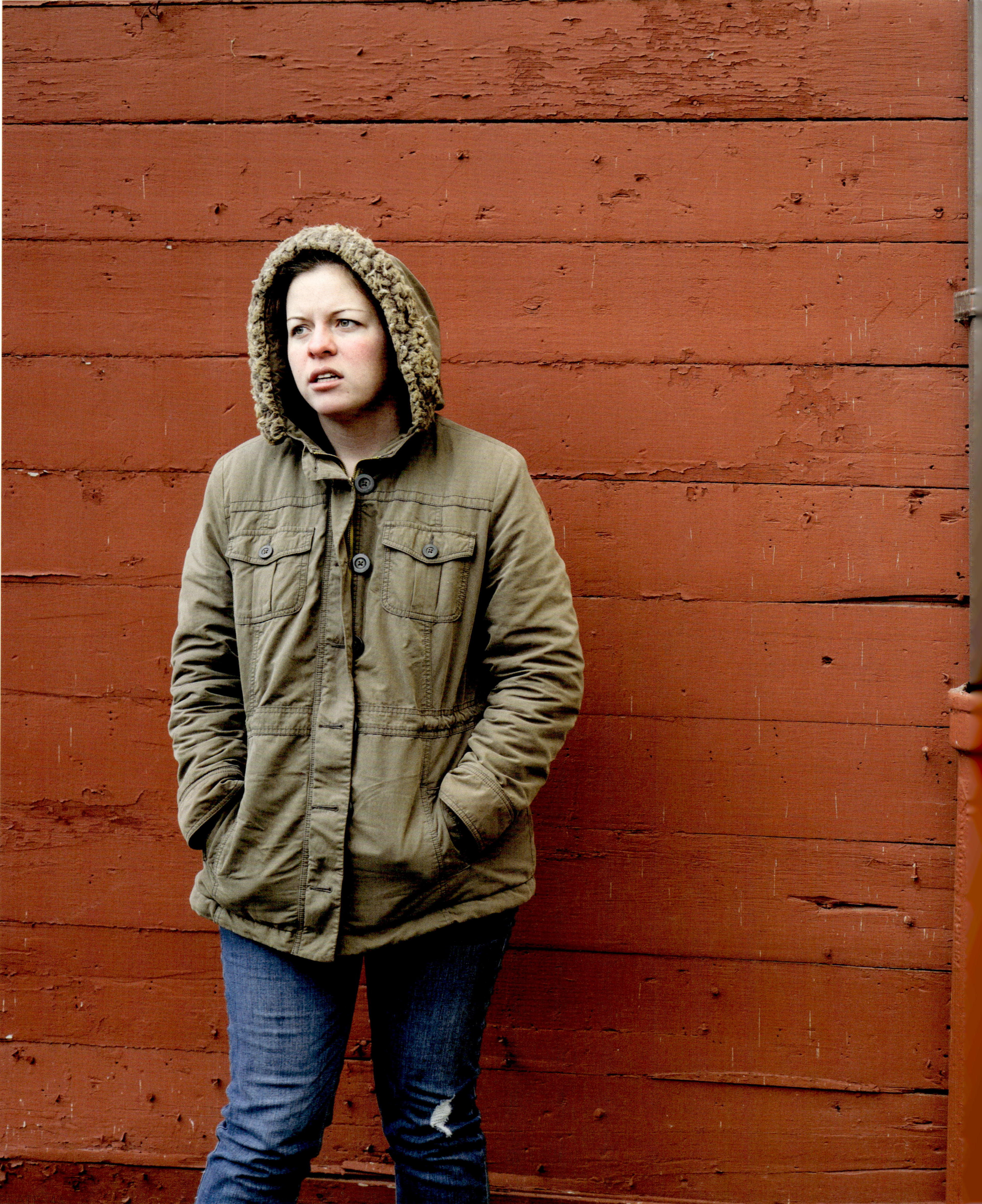

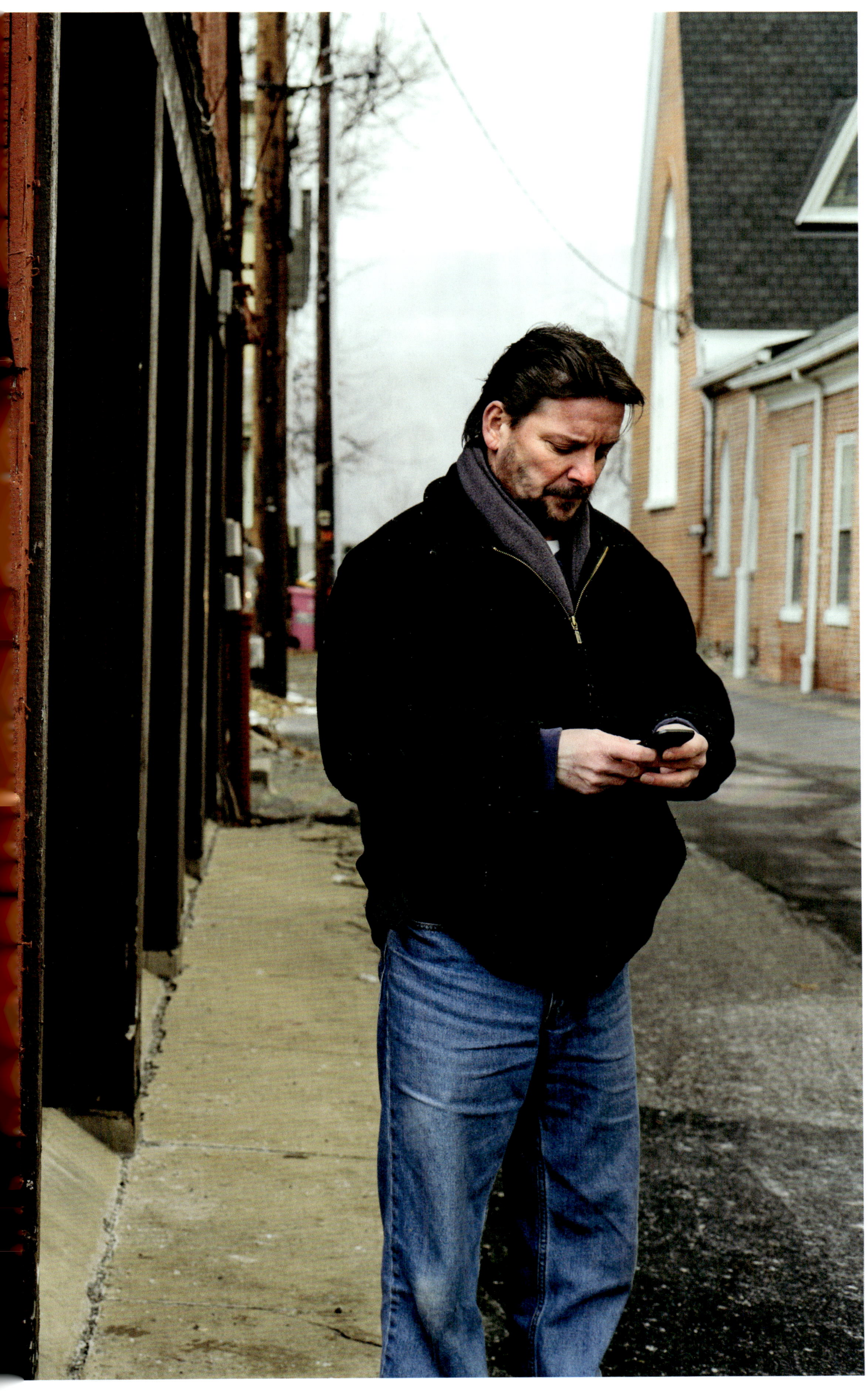

PLATE 50

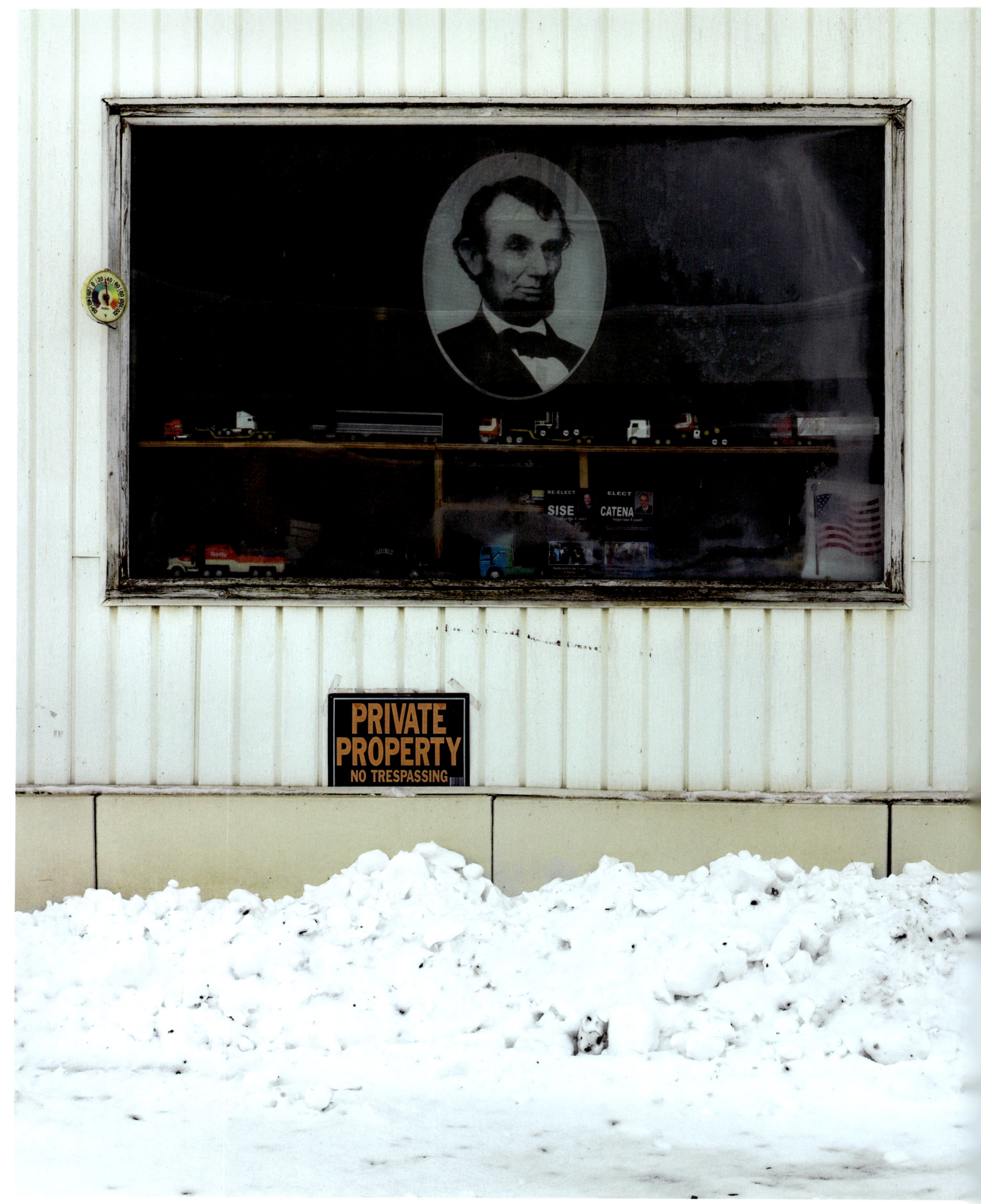
RE-ELECT
SISE
ELECT
CATENA
PRIVATE
PROPERTY
NO TRESPASSING

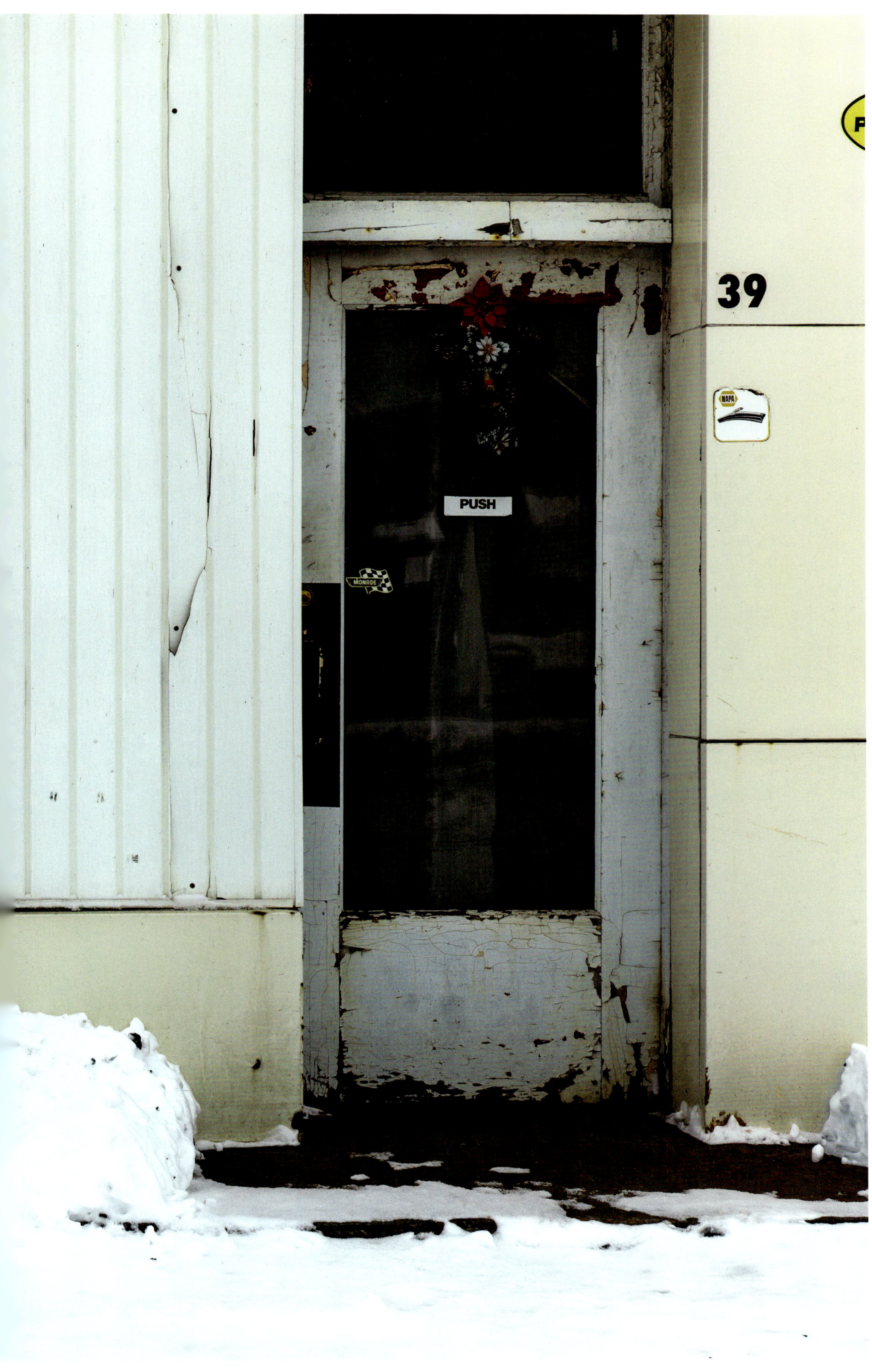
39
NAPA
PUSH
MONROE

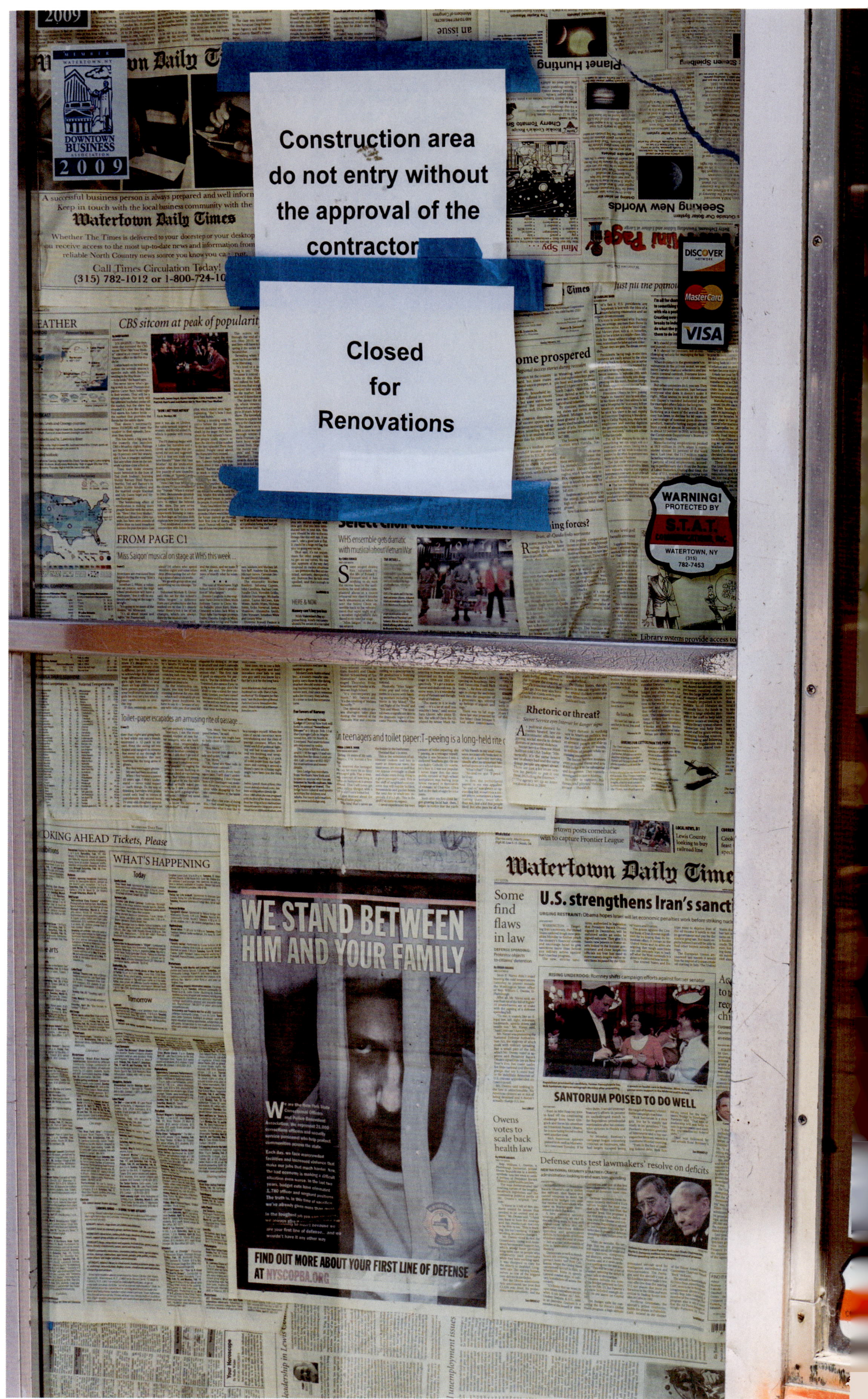
Construction area
do not entry without
the approval of the
contractor
Closed
for
Renovations
DOWNTOWN BUSINESS
2009
A successful business person is always prepared and well inforn
Keep in touch with the local business community with the
Watertown Daily Times
Call Times Circulation Today!
(315) 782-1012 or 1-800-724-10
Planet Hunting
Seeking New Worlds
DISCOVER
MasterCard
VISA
WARNING!
PROTECTED BY
S.T.A.T.
WATERTOWN, NY
(315)
782-7453
CBS sitcom at peak of popularit
FROM PAGE C1
Rhetoric or threat?
Toilet-paper escapades an amusing rite of passage
WHAT'S HAPPENING
Watertown Daily Time
U.S. strengthens Iran's sanct
Some find flaws in law
SANTORUM POISED TO DO WELL
Owens votes to scale back health law
Defense cuts test lawmakers' resolve on deficits
WE STAND BETWEEN HIM AND YOUR FAMILY
FIND OUT MORE ABOUT YOUR FIRST LINE OF DEFENSE AT NYSCOPBA.ORG

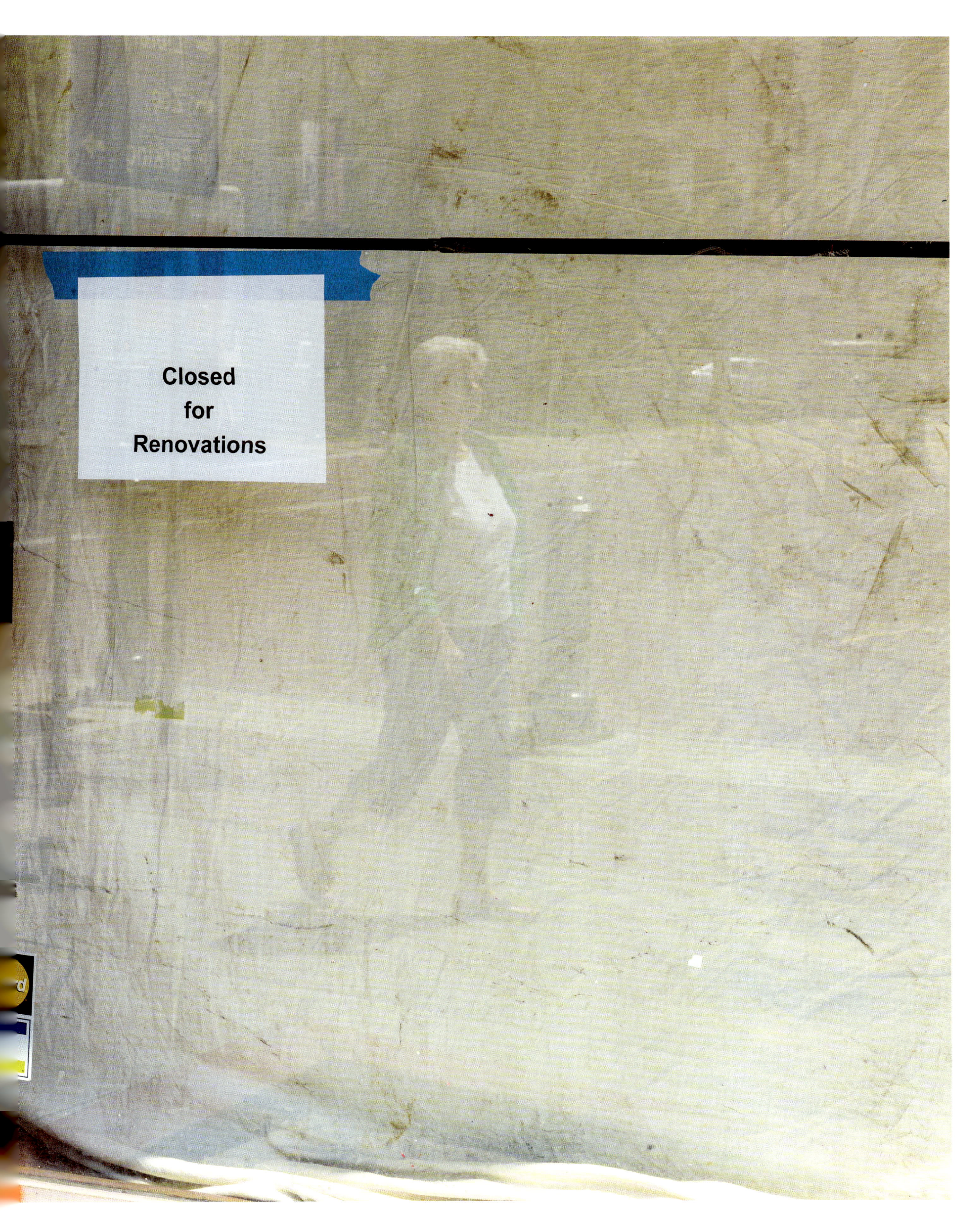
Closed
for
Renovations

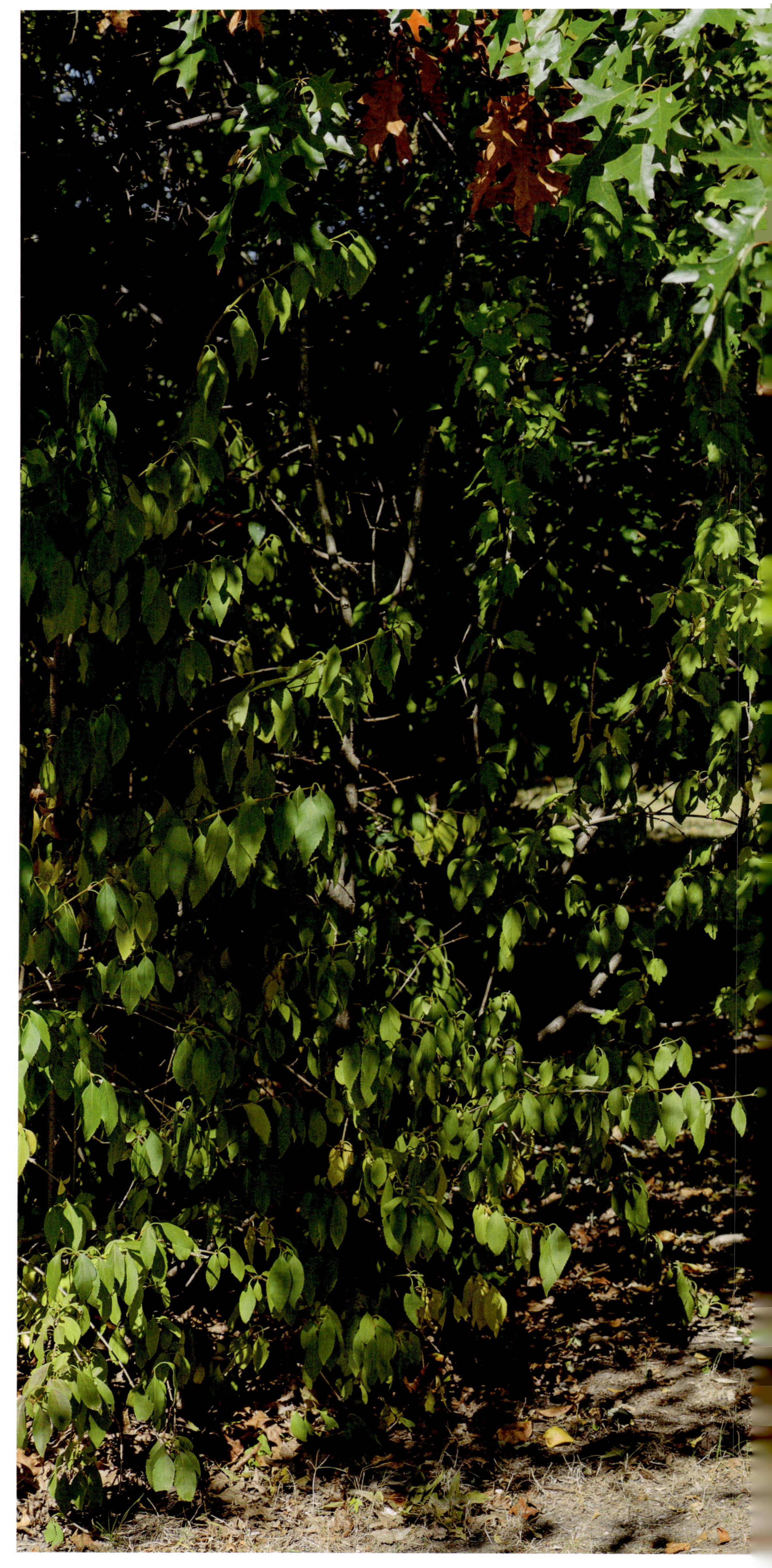

PLATE 53

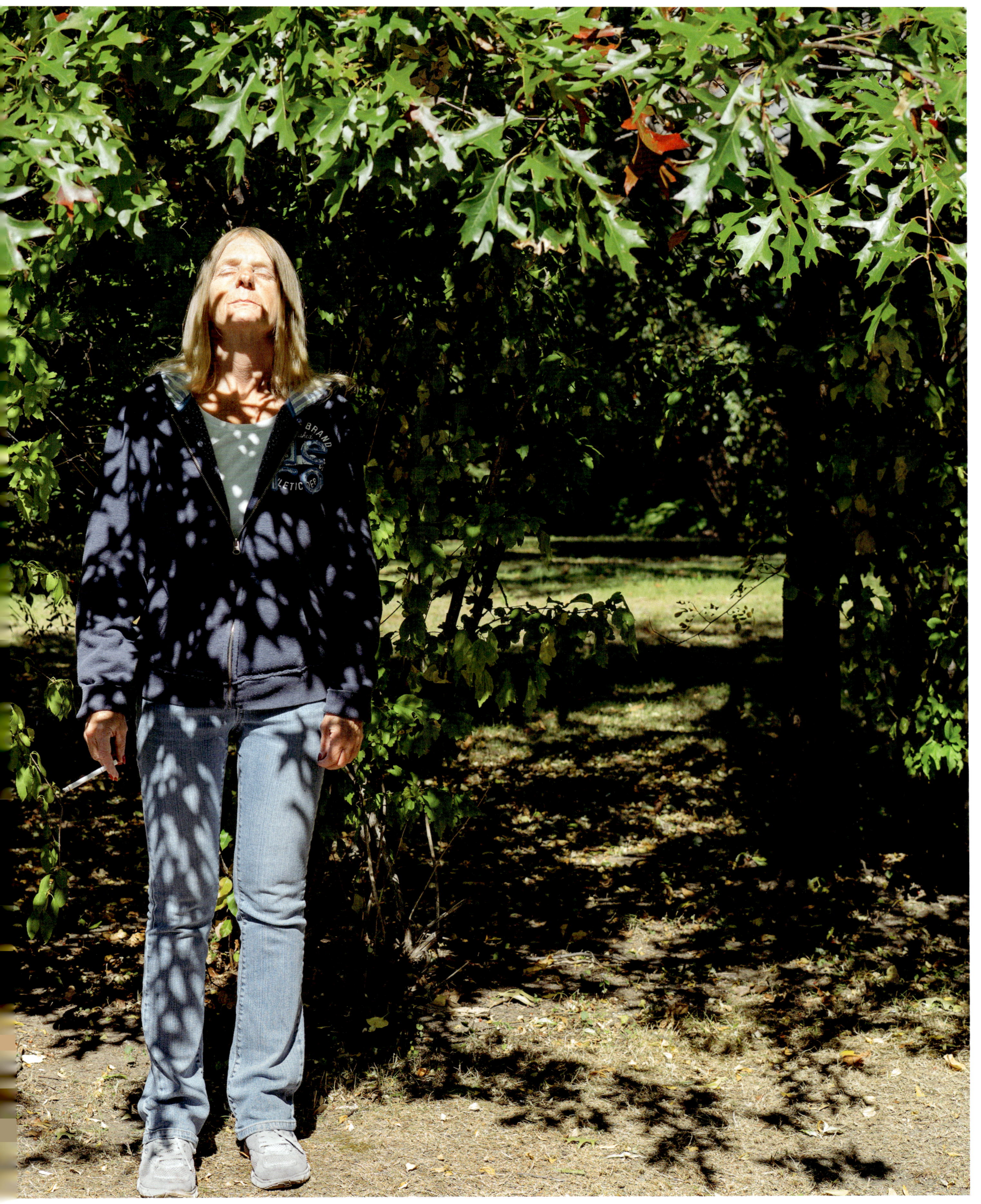

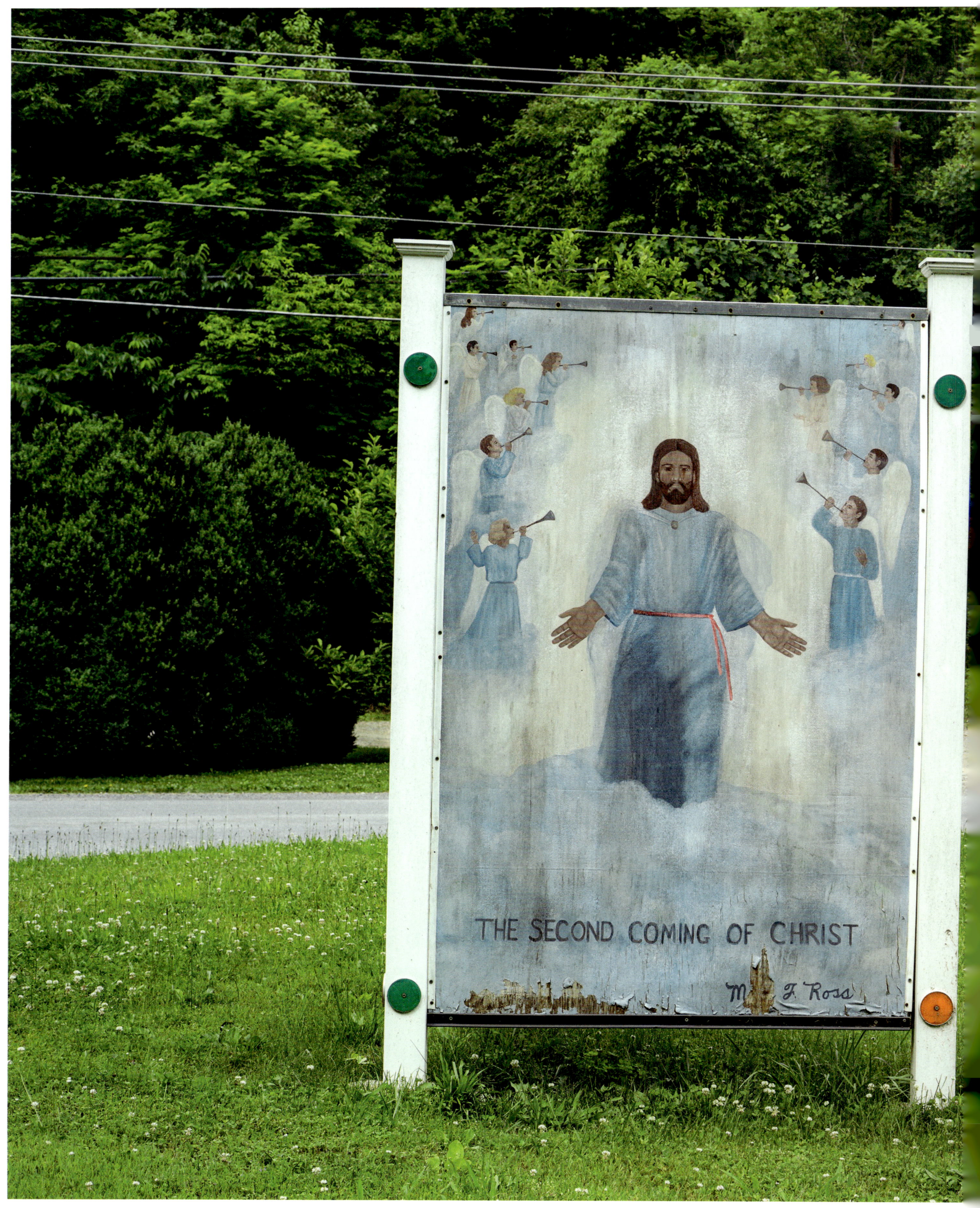
THE SECOND COMING OF CHRIST

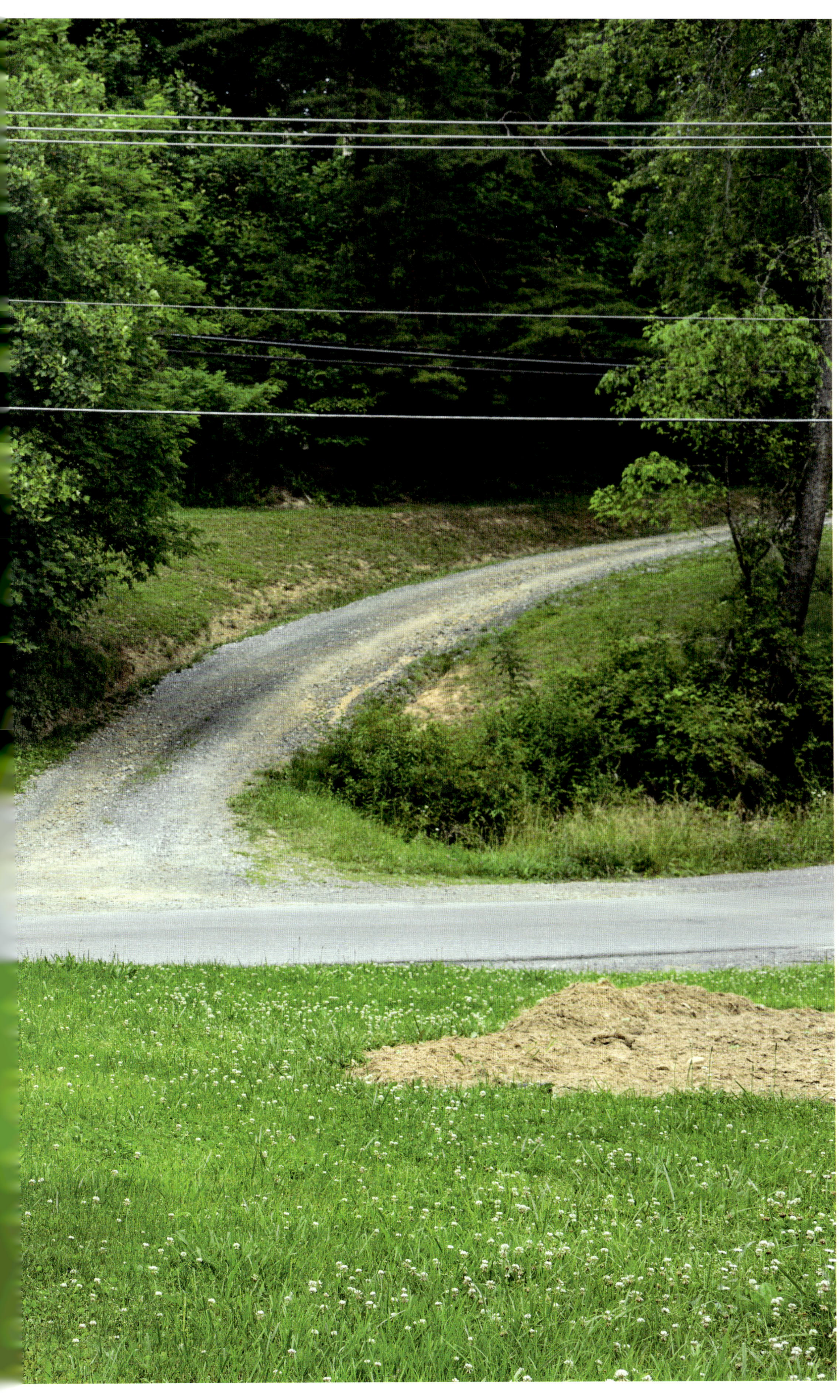

PLATE 54

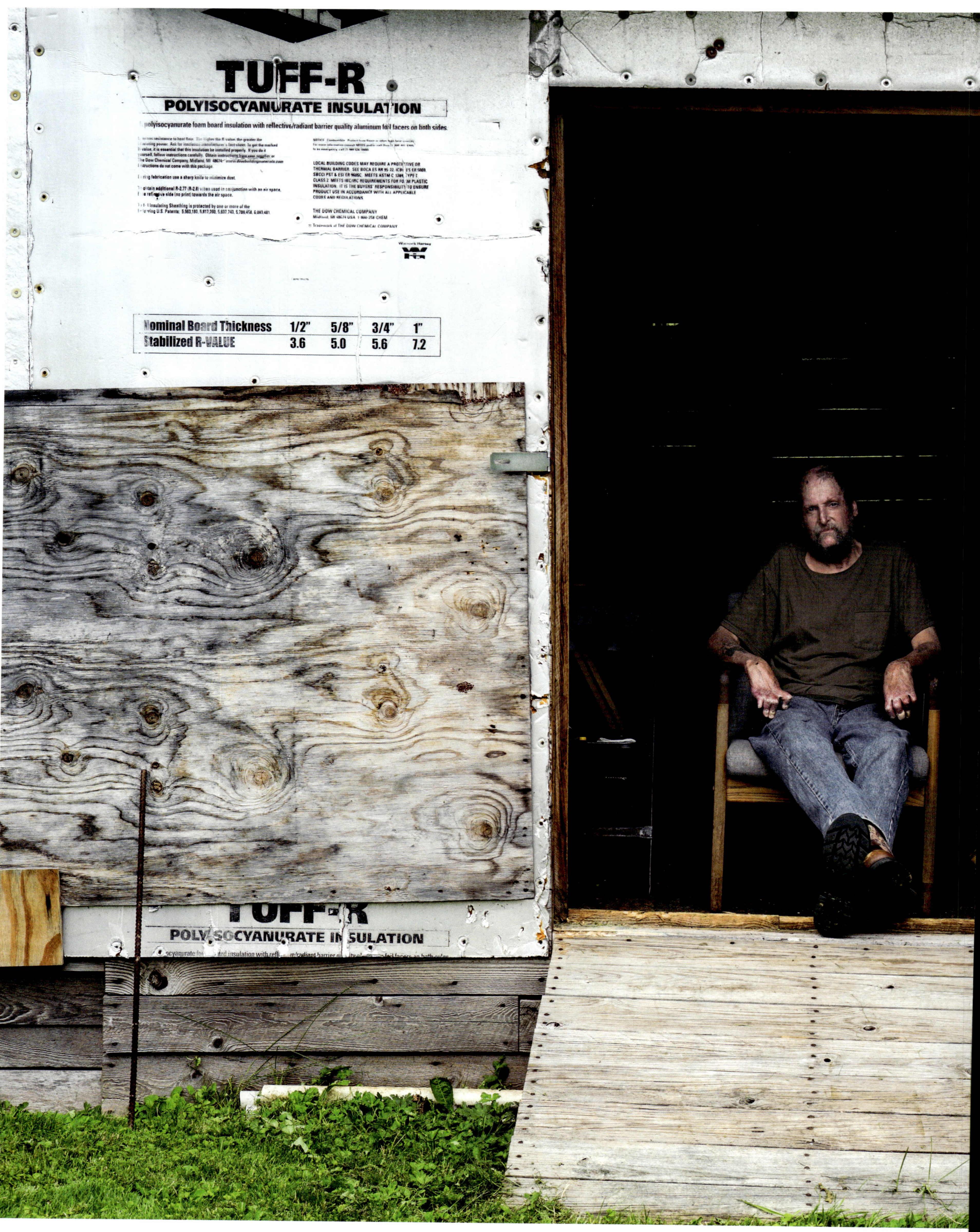
TUFF-R
POLYISOCYANURATE INSULATION
Nominal Board Thickness 1/2" 5/8" 3/4" 1"
Stabilized R-VALUE 3.6 5.0 5.6 7.2

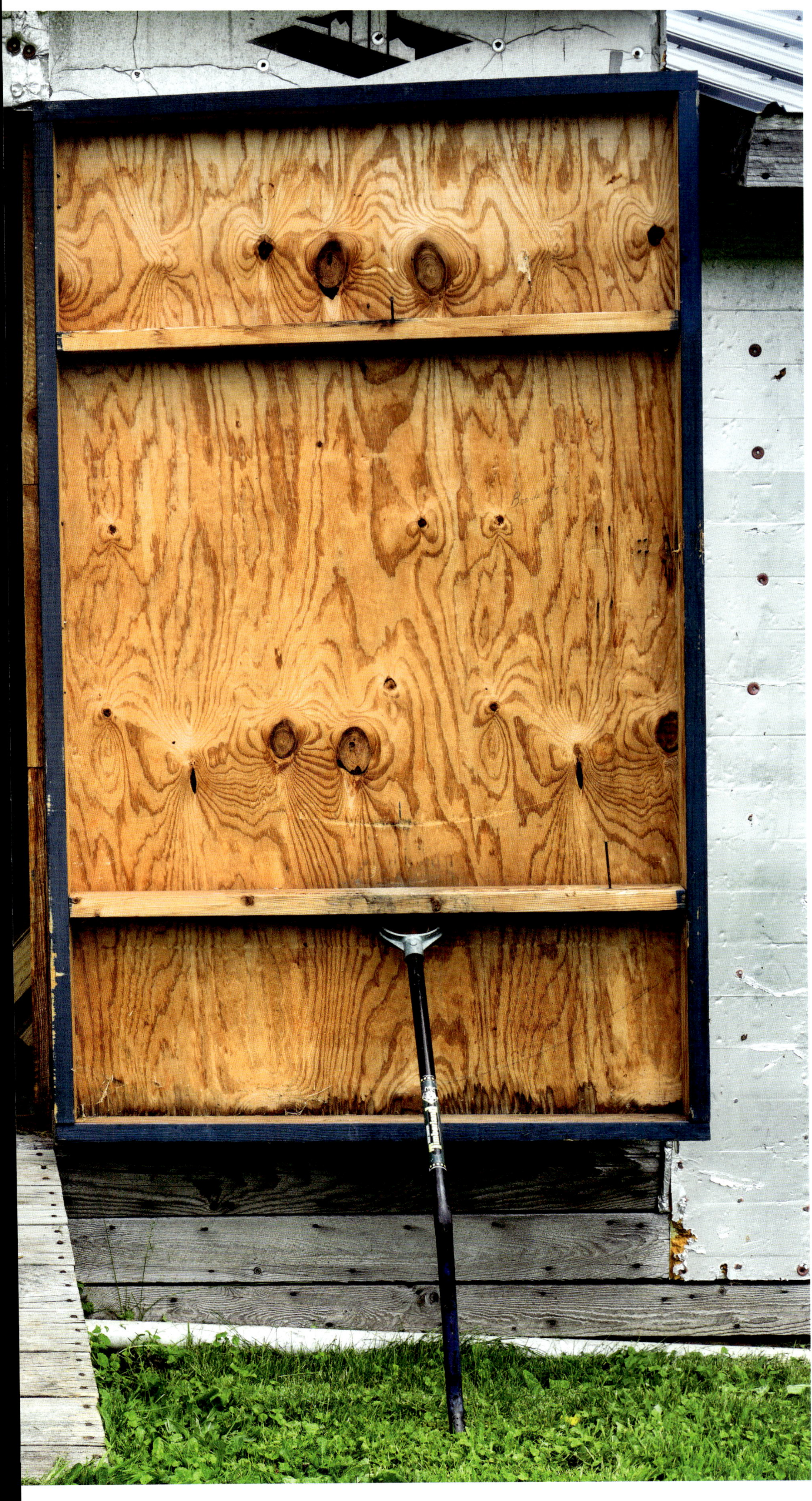

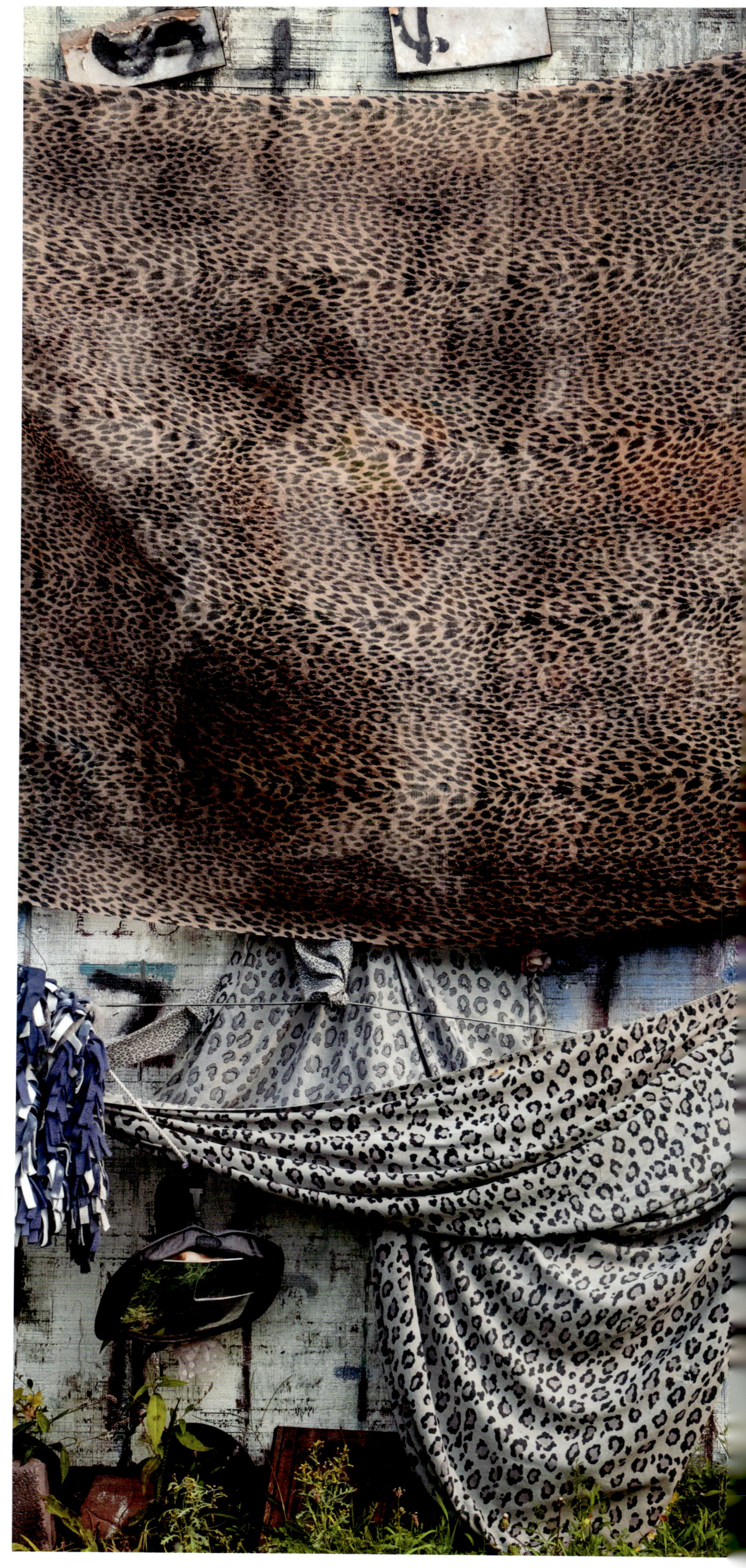

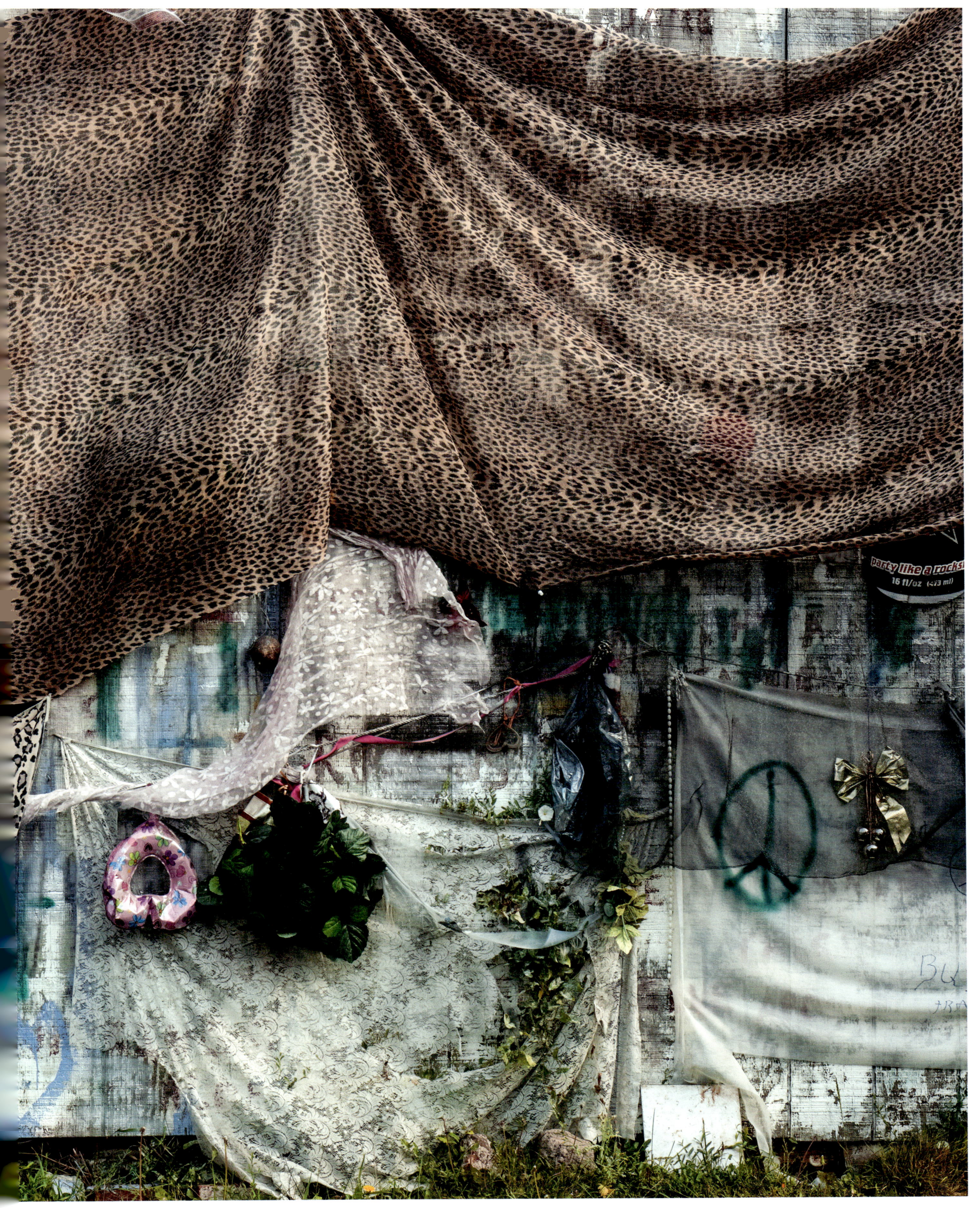
party like a rocks
16 fl/oz

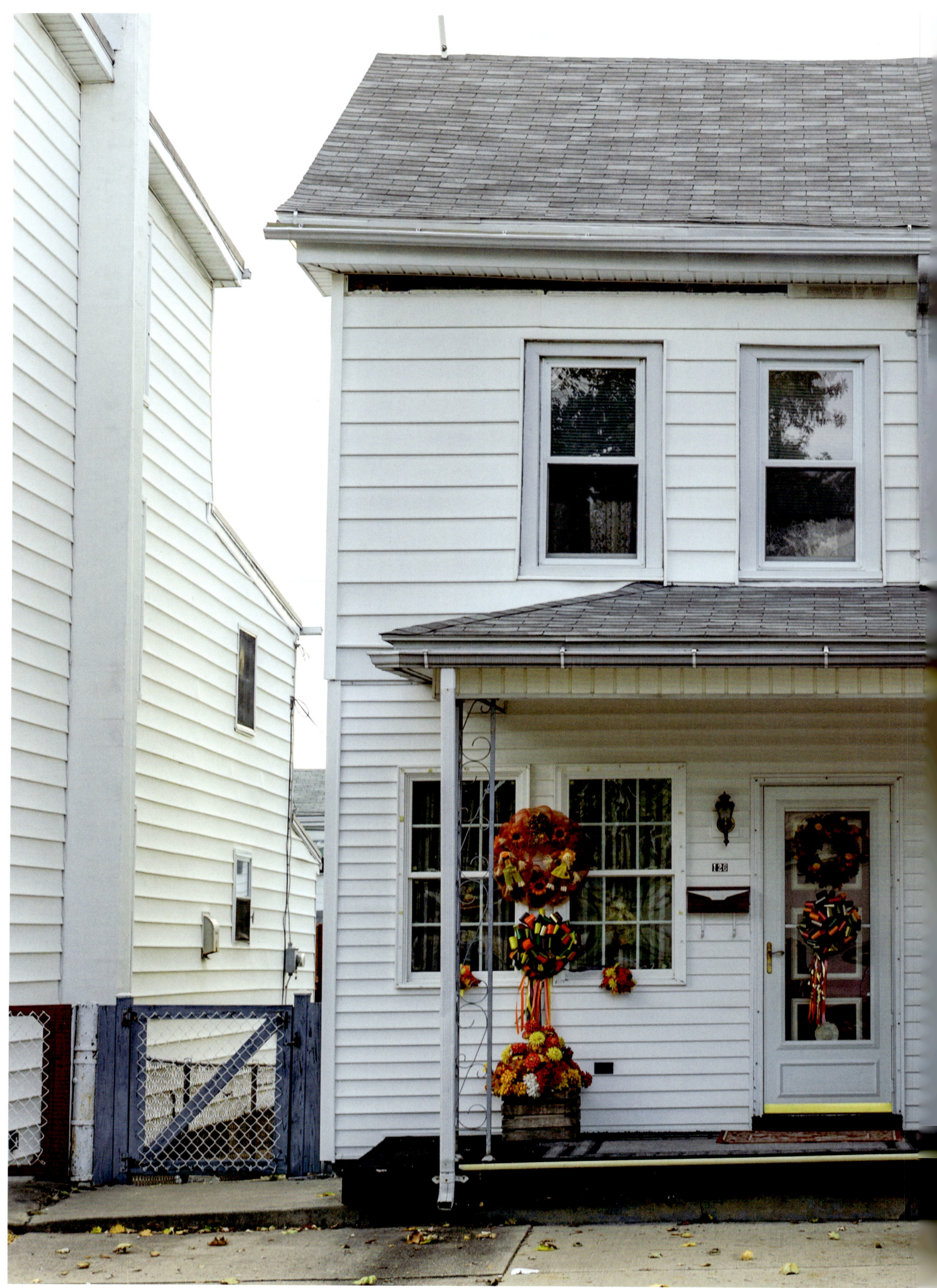
126

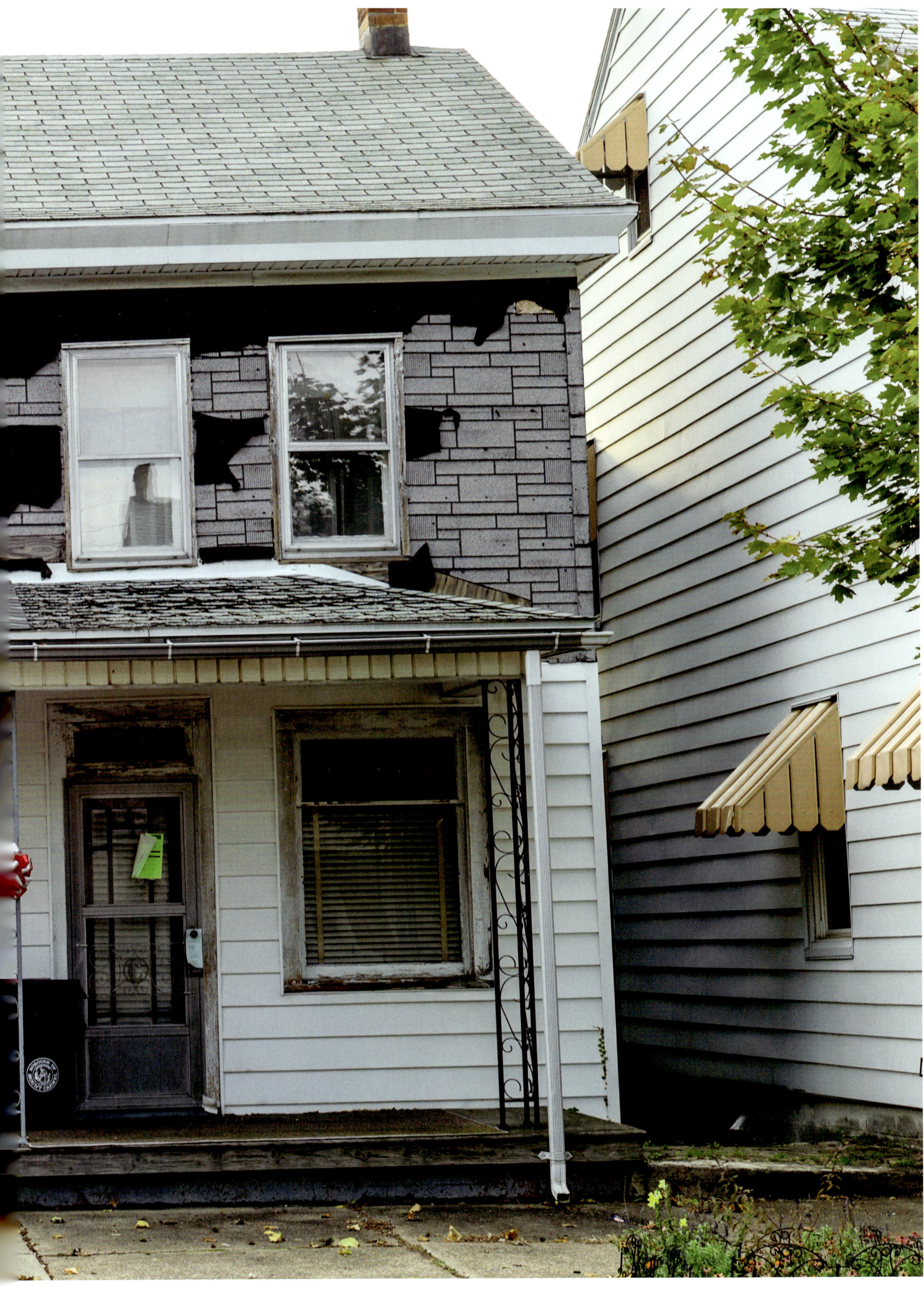

PLATE 57

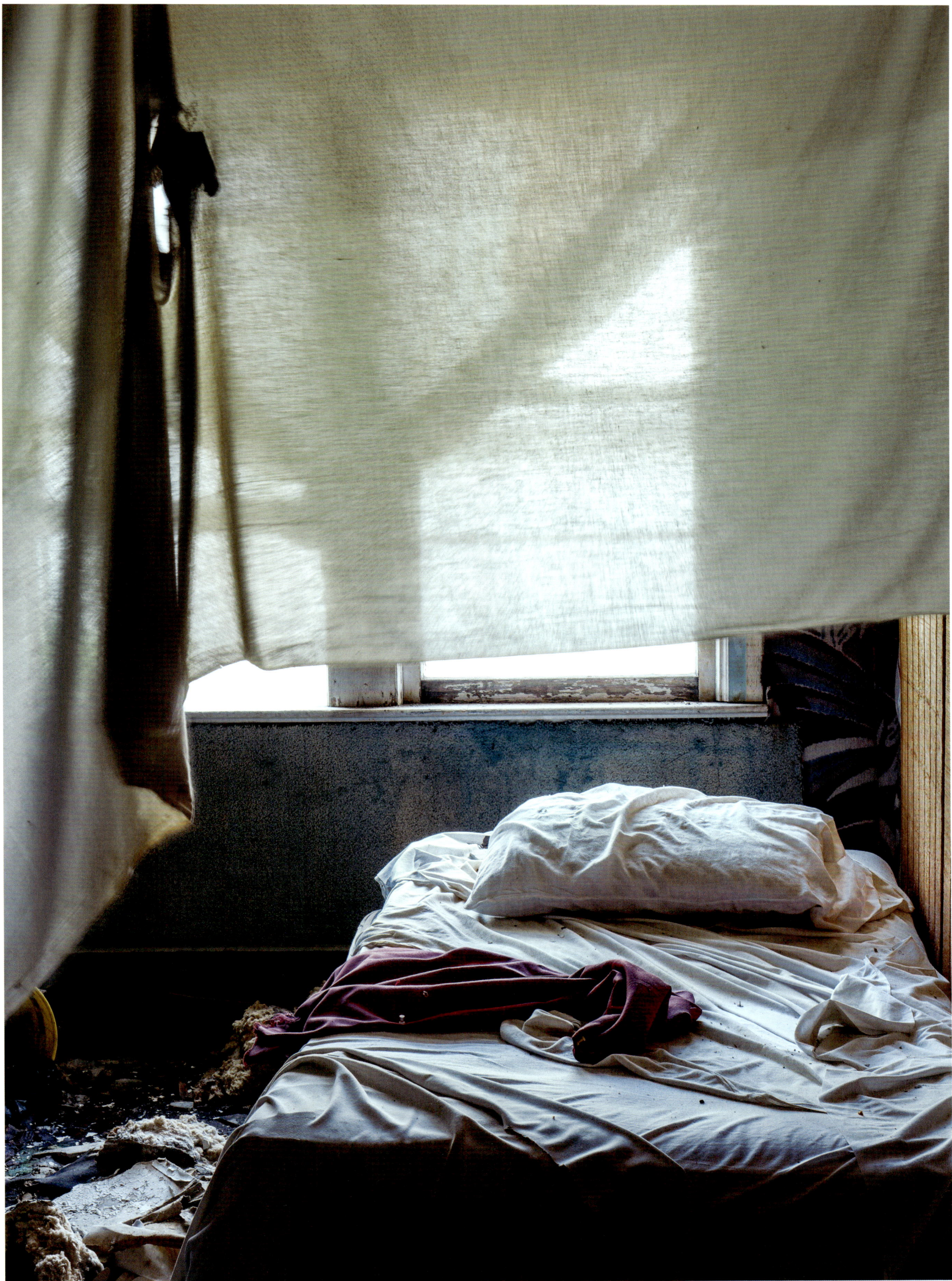

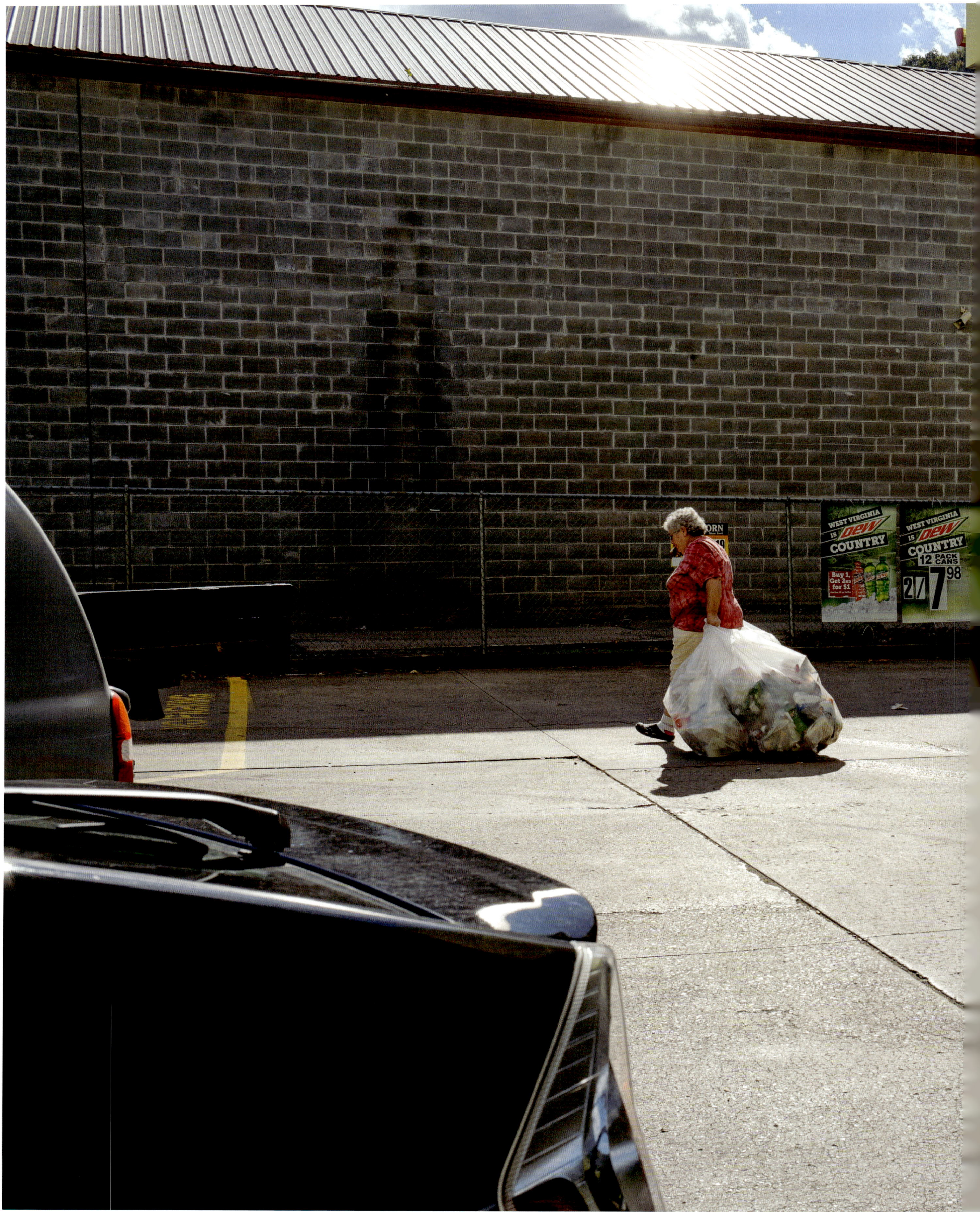
ORN
WEST VIRGINIA IS DEW COUNTRY
Buy 1, Get 2ND for $1
WEST VIRGINIA IS DEW COUNTRY
12 PACK CANS
2/7.98

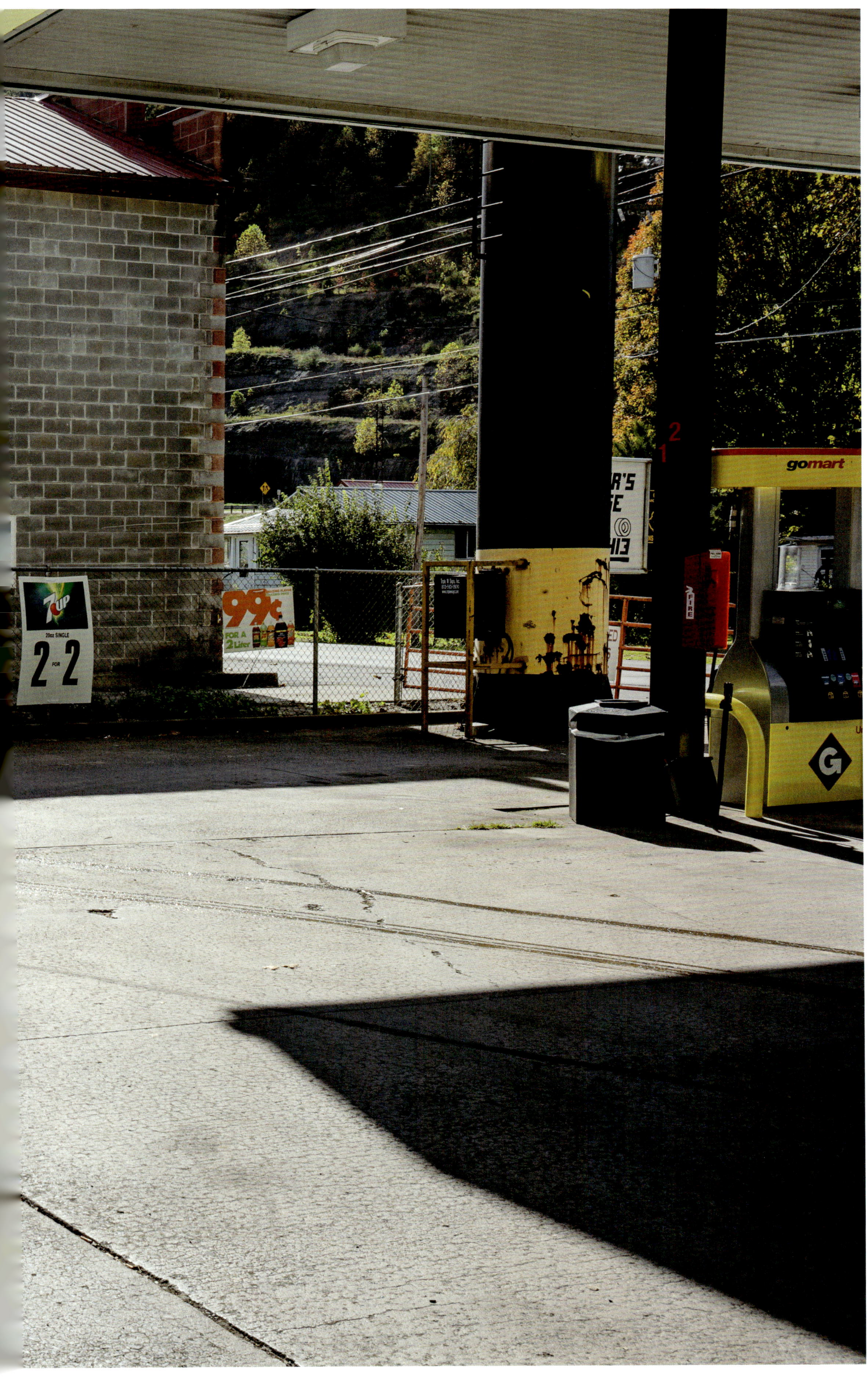

PLATE 59

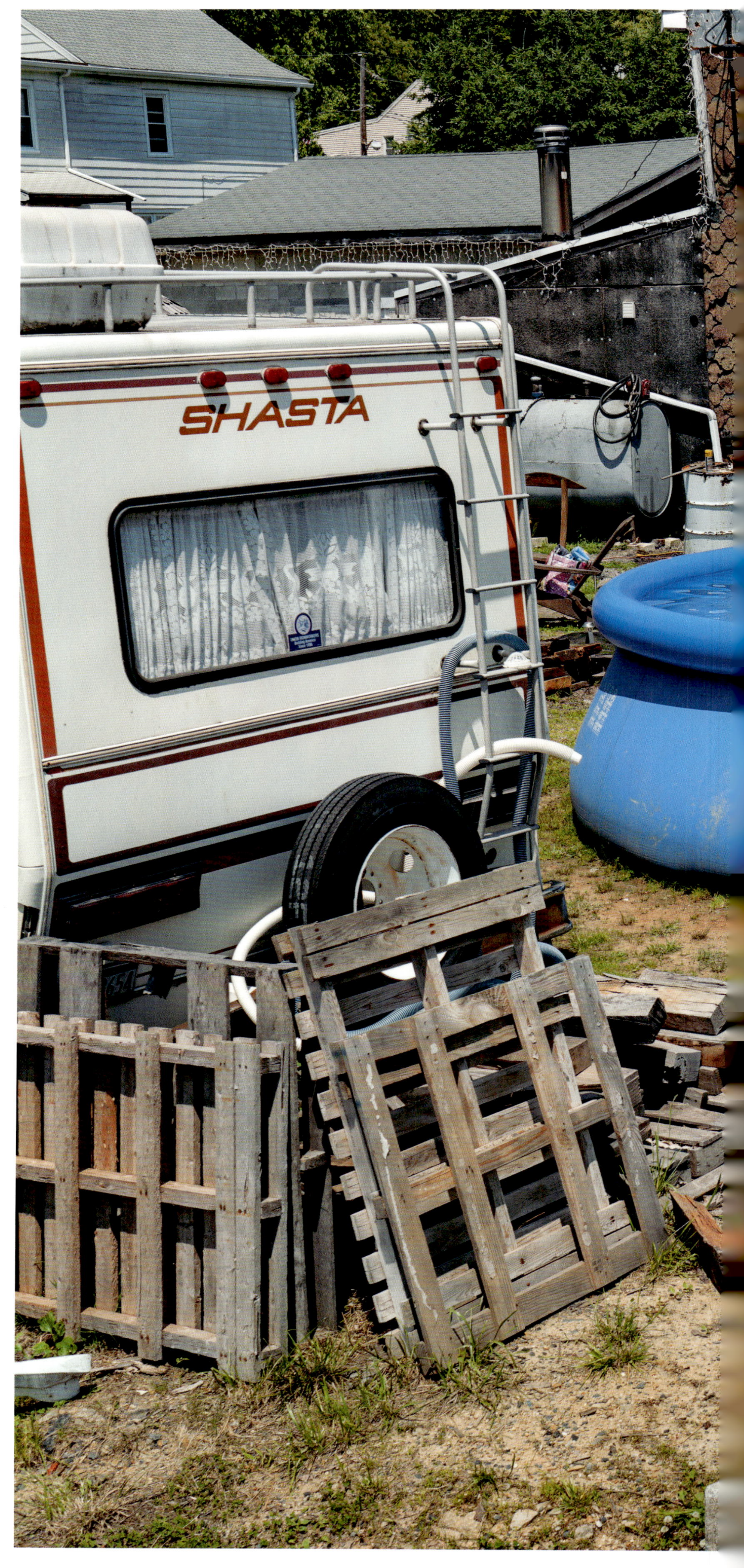

PLATE 60

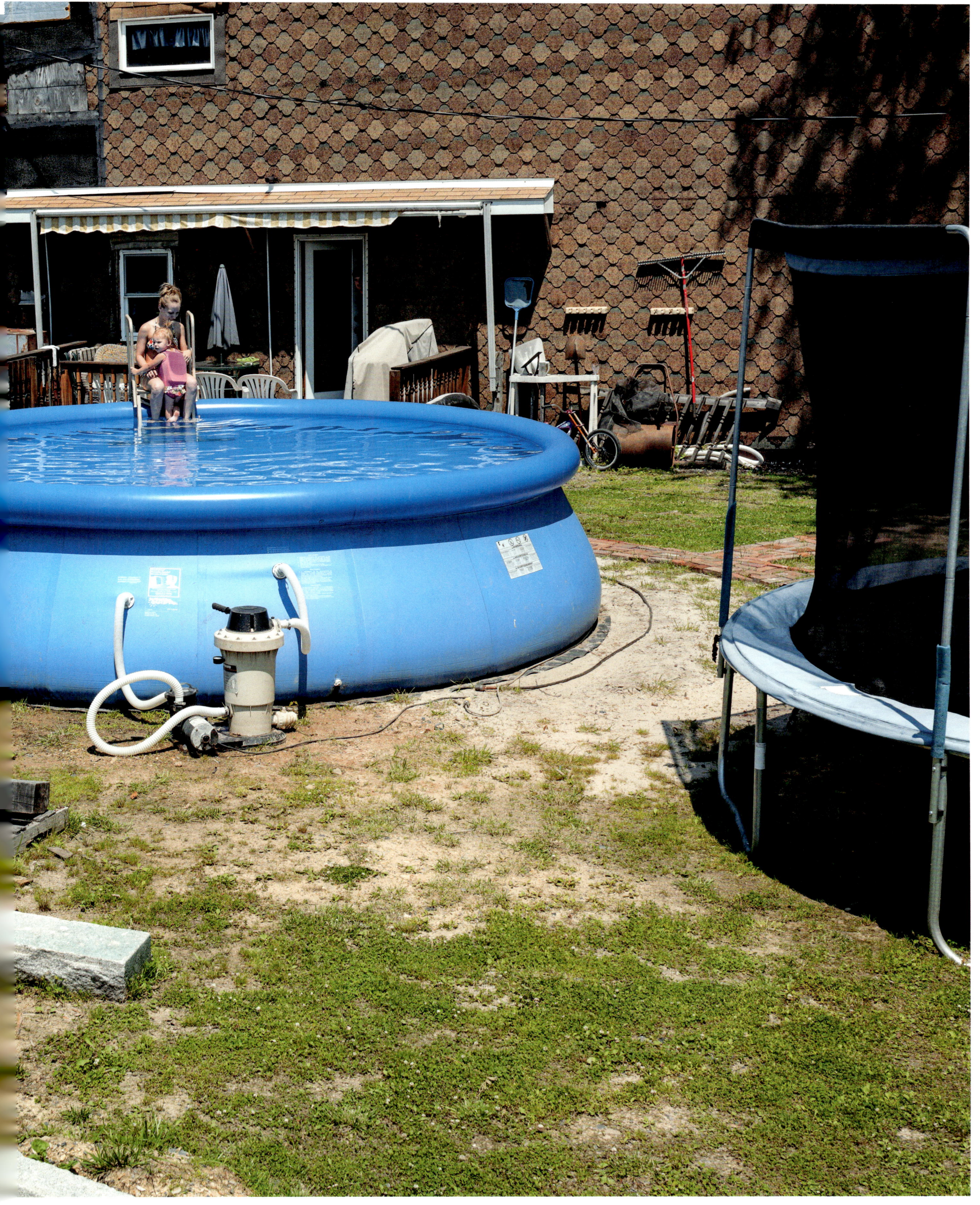

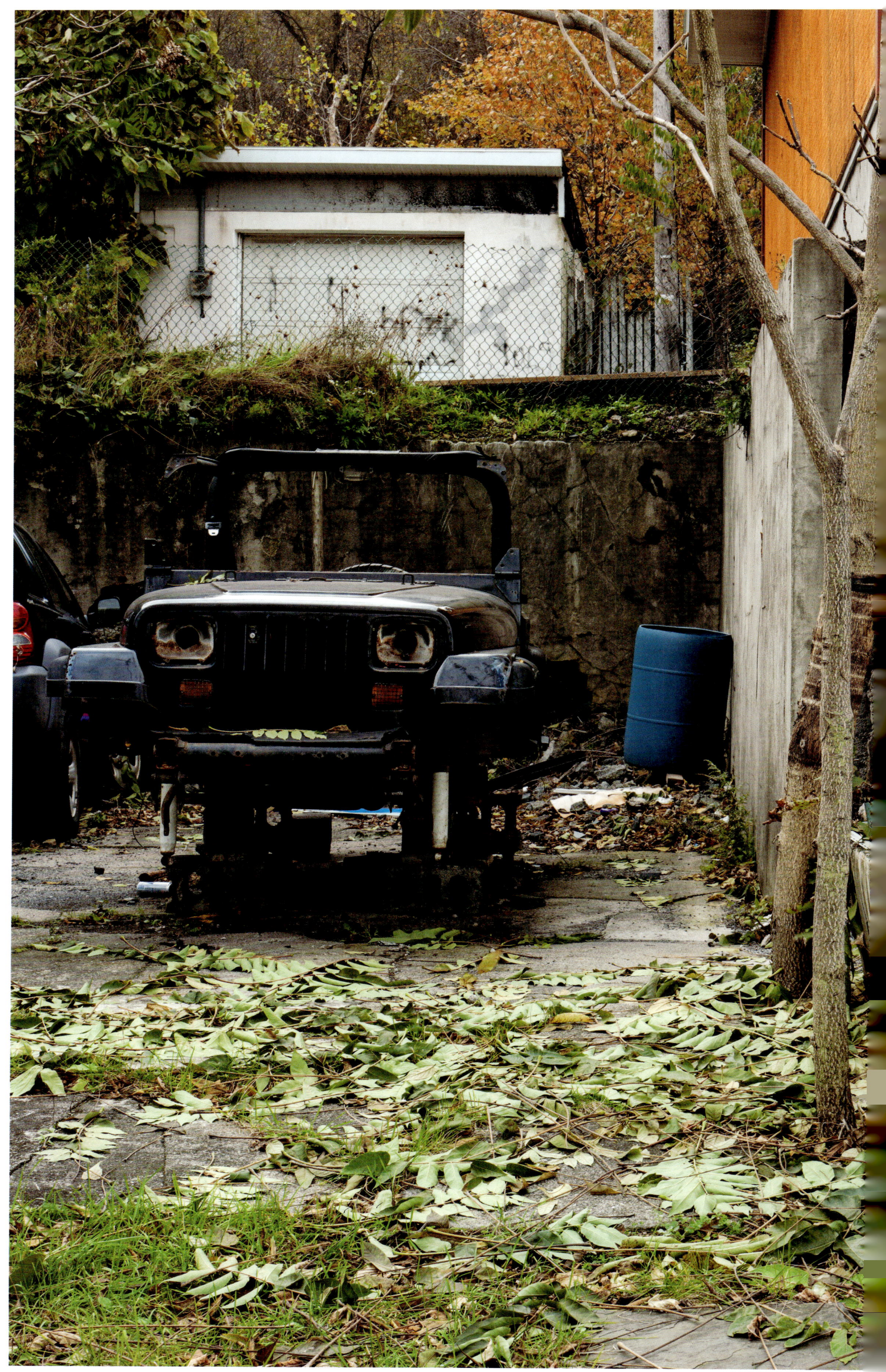

PLATE 61

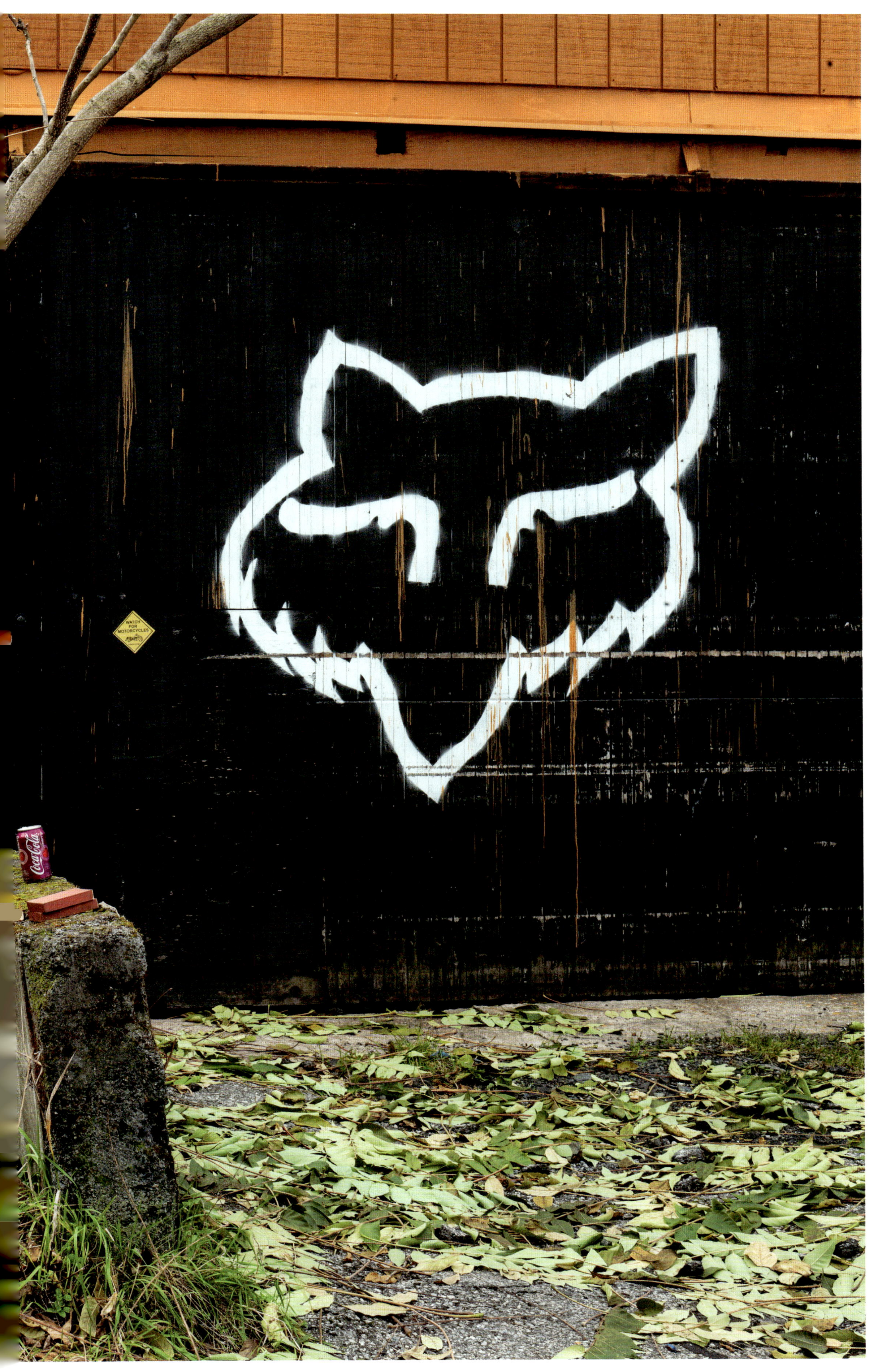
WATCH FOR MOTORCYCLES
Coca-Cola

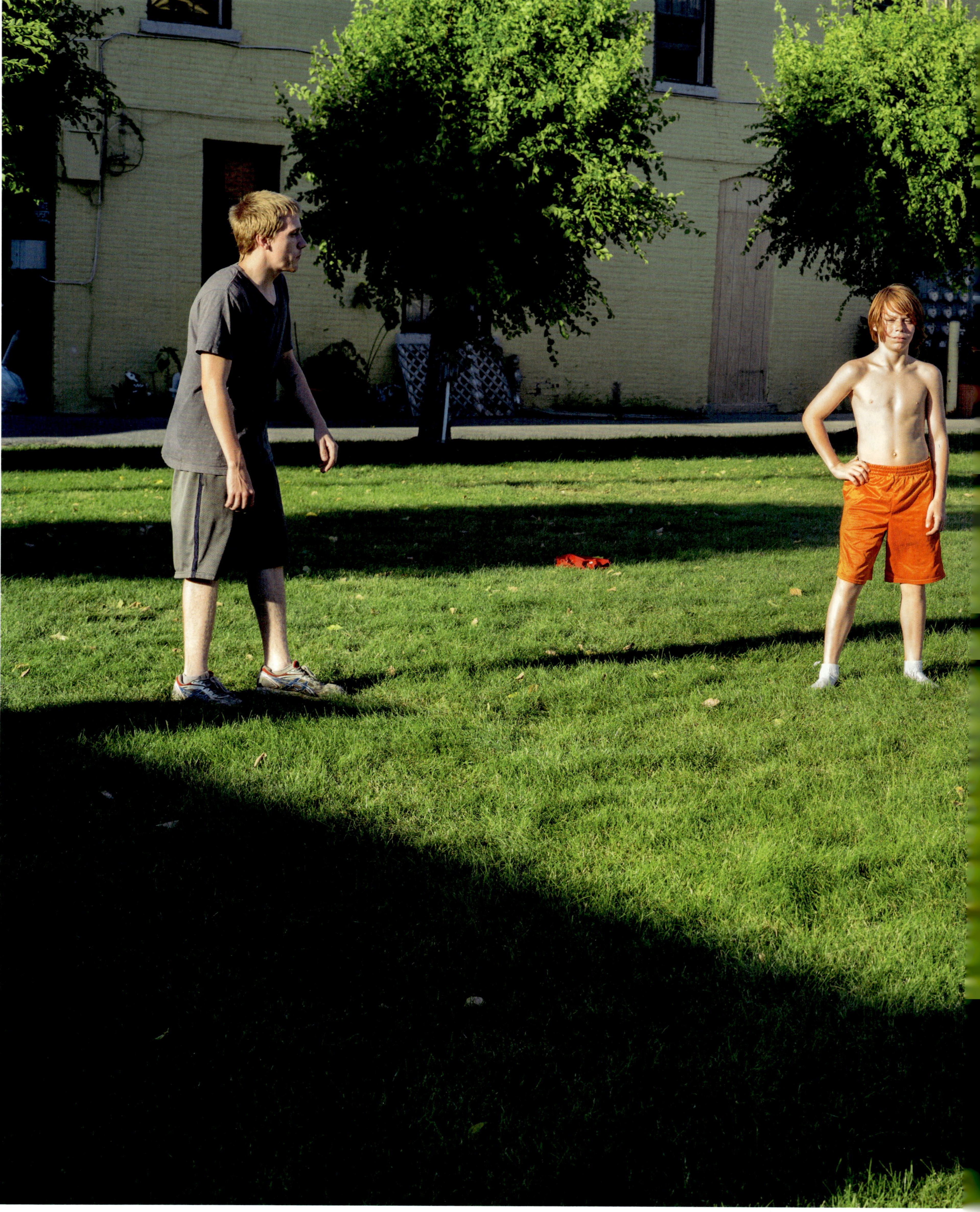

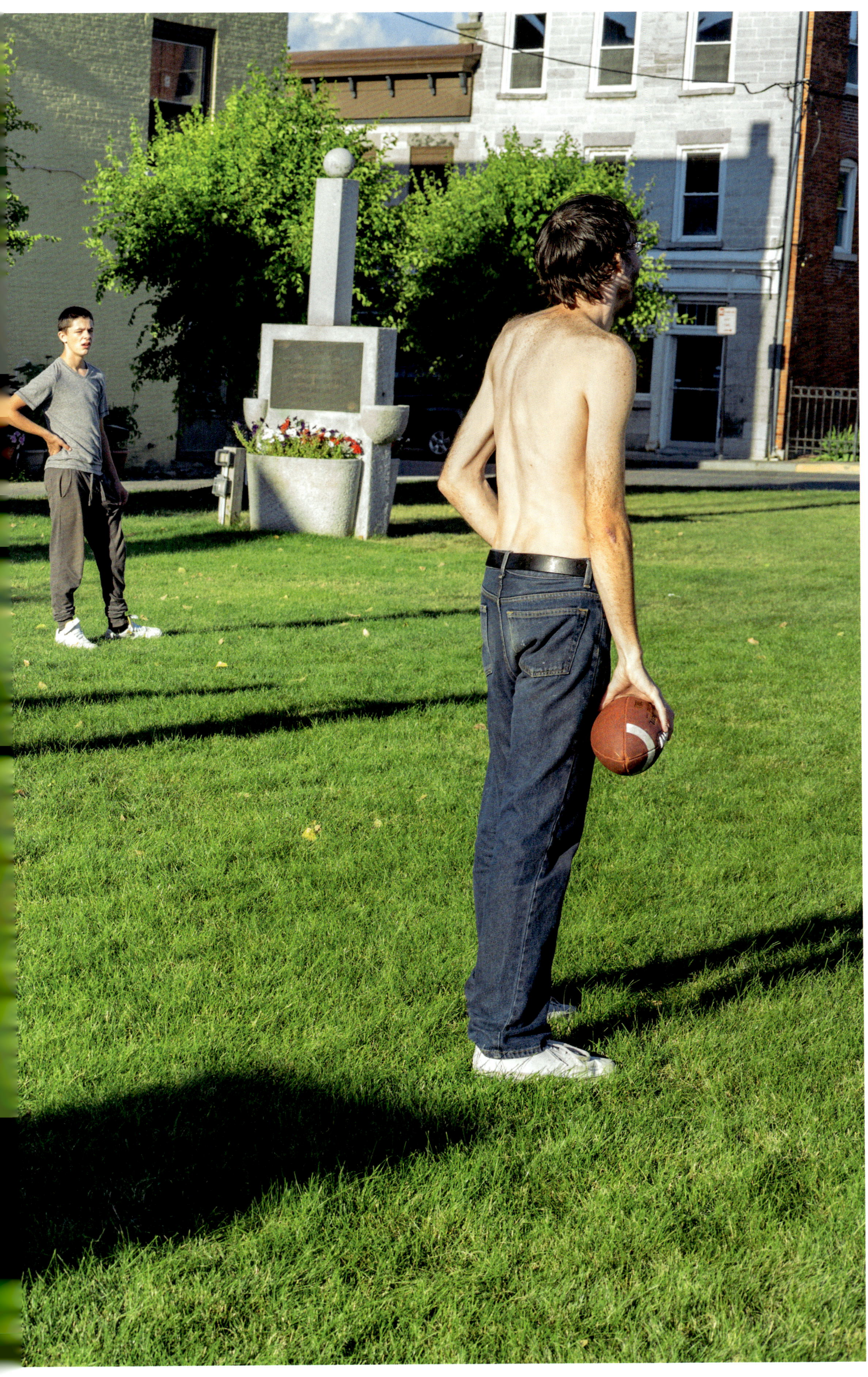

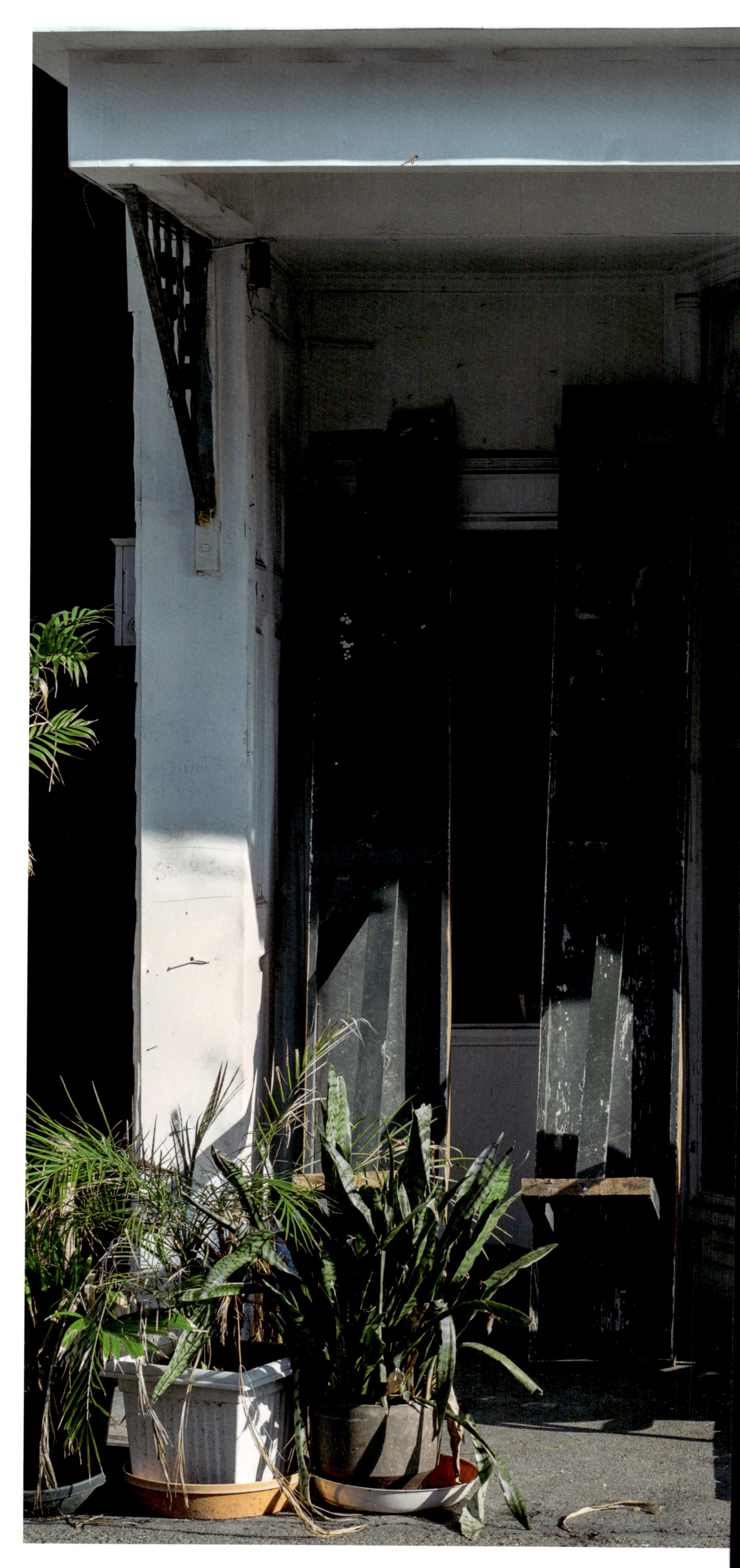

PLATE 63

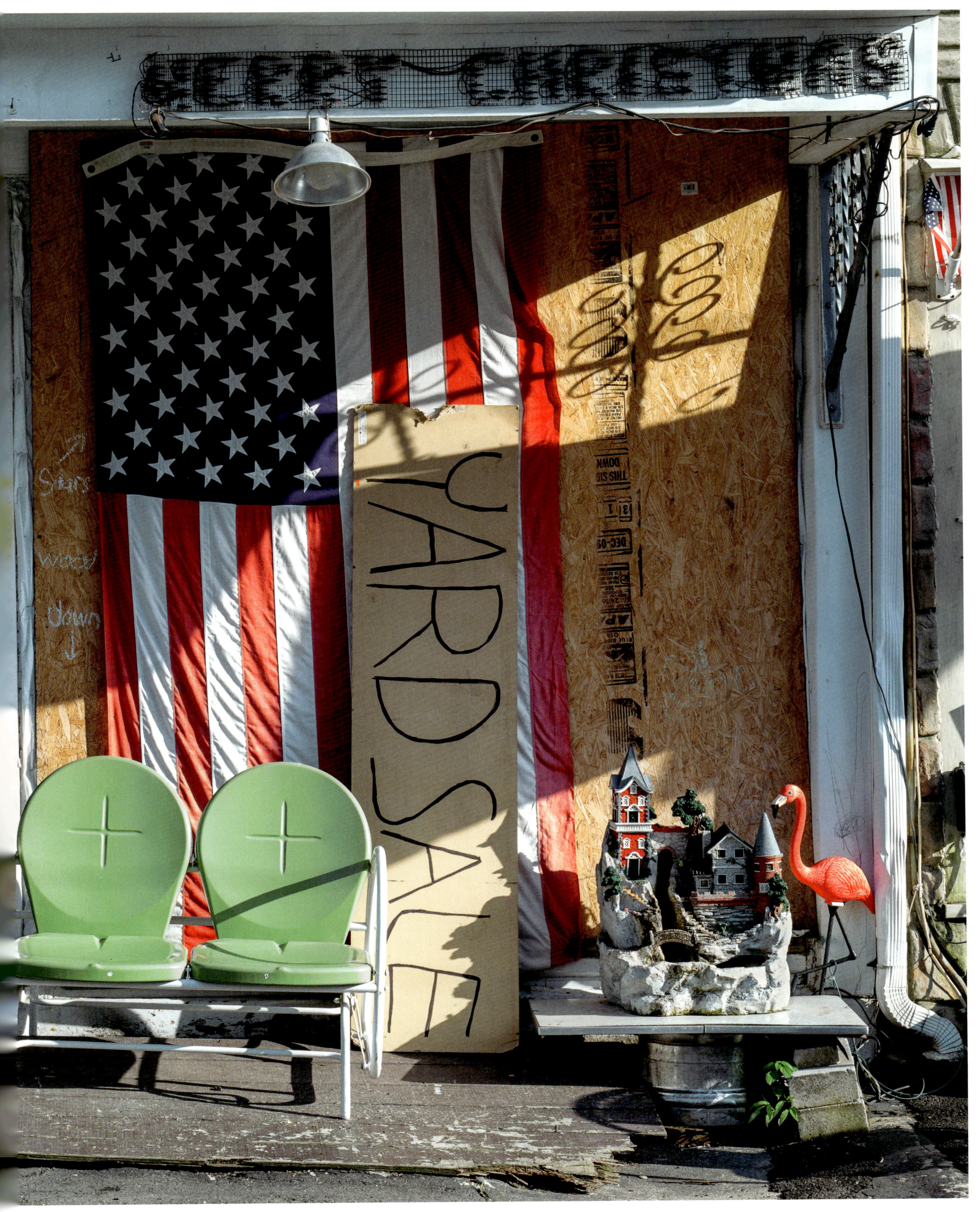
YARD SALE

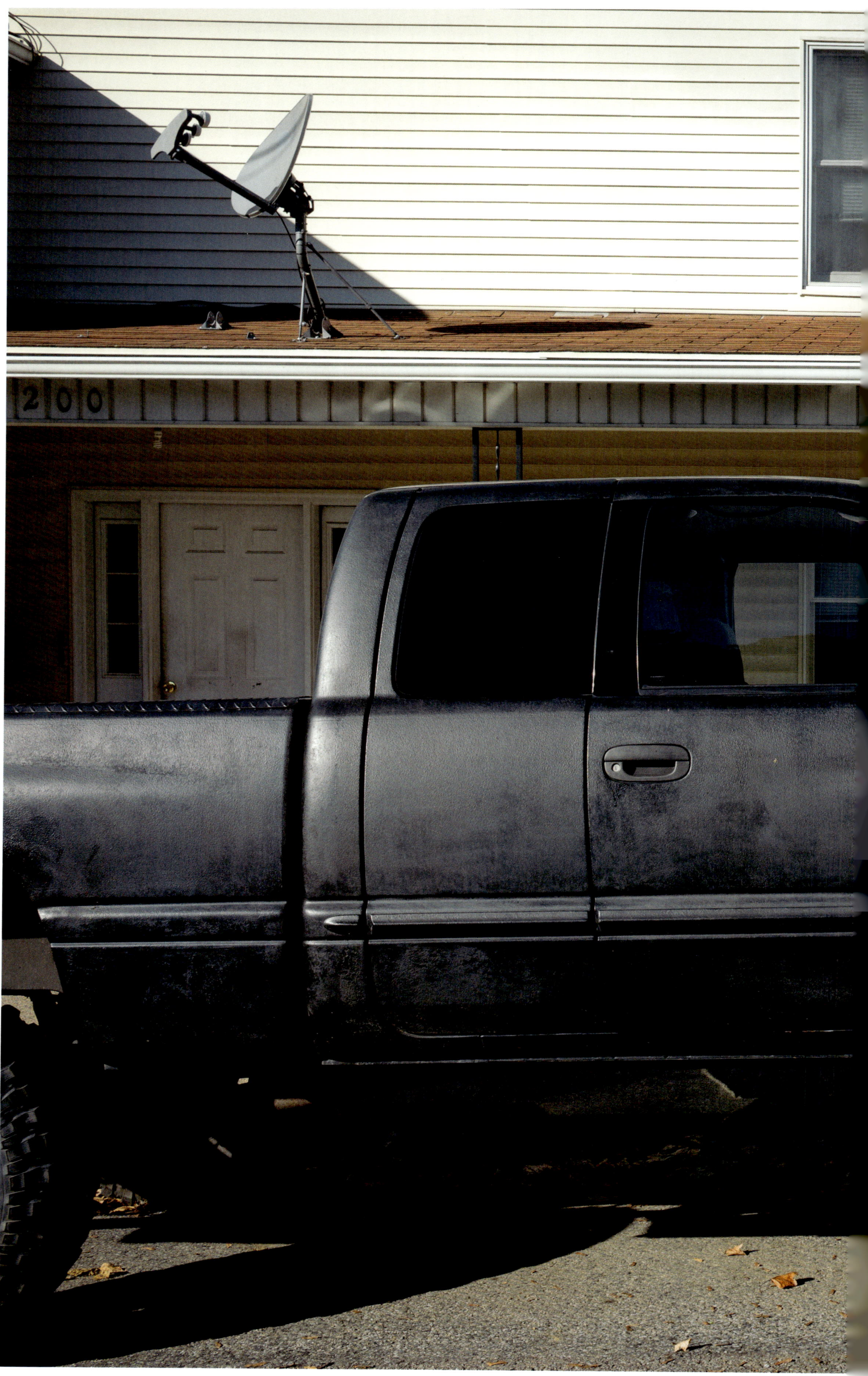

PLATE 64

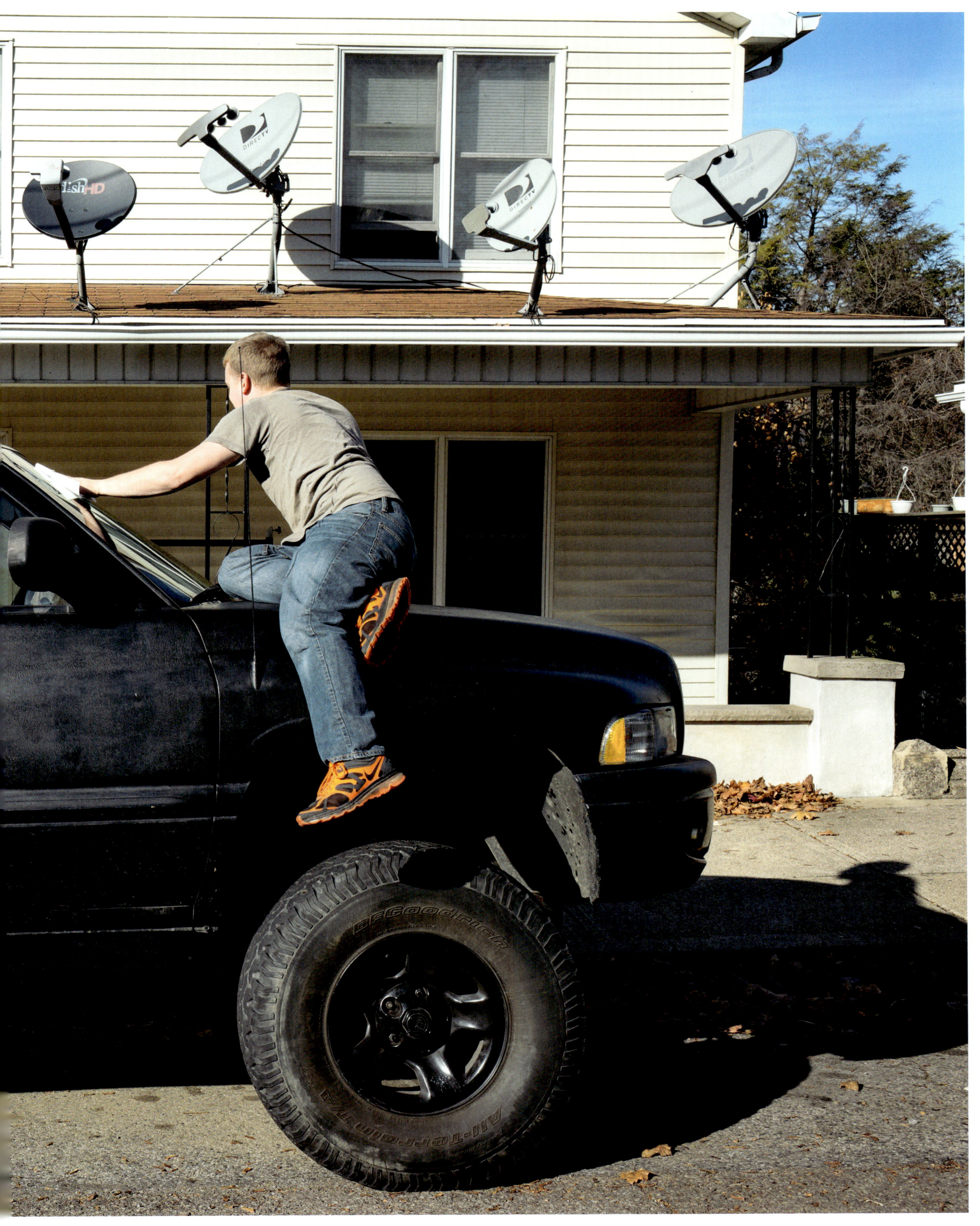
DIRECTV
DIRECTV
BFGoodrich
All-Terrain T/A

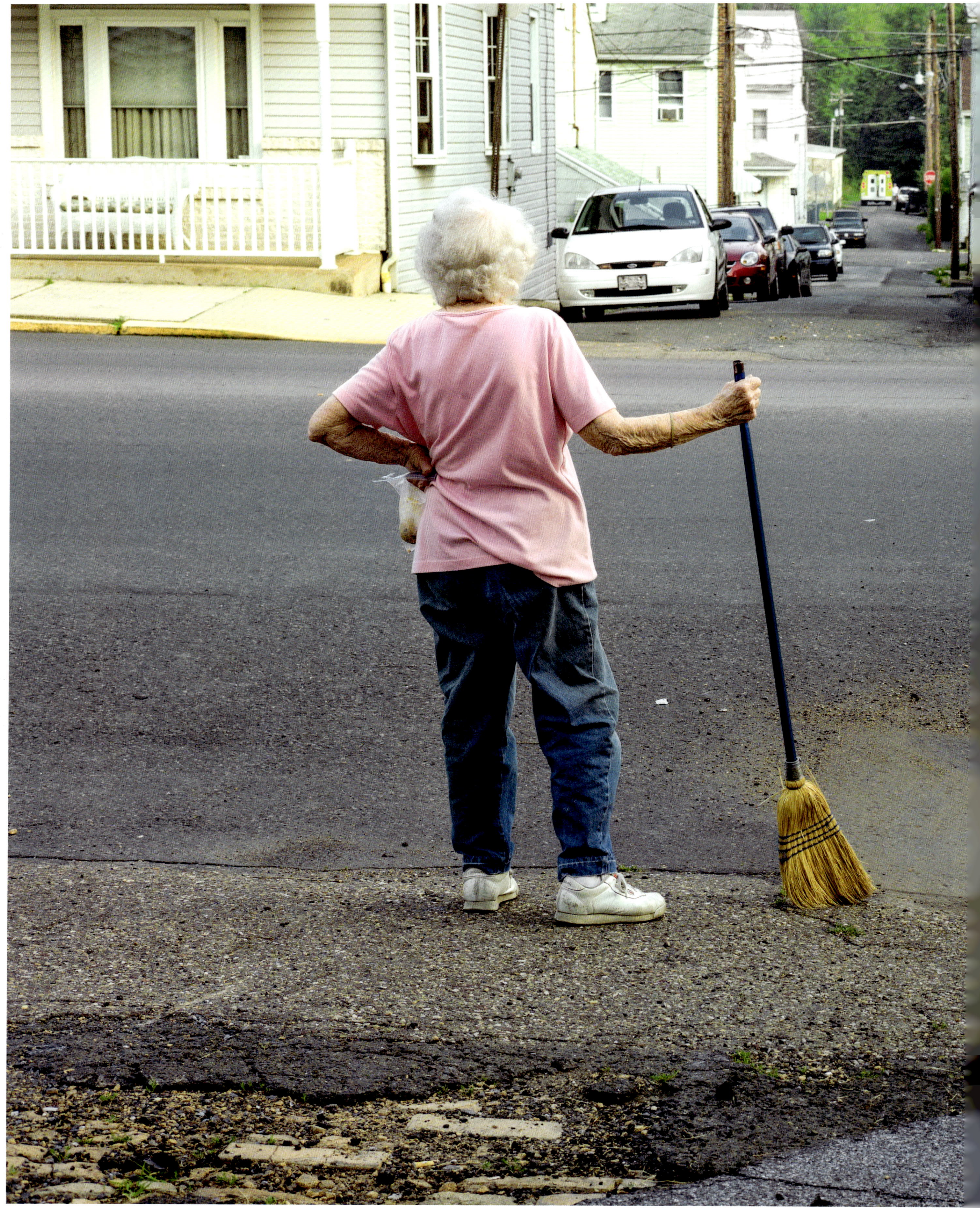

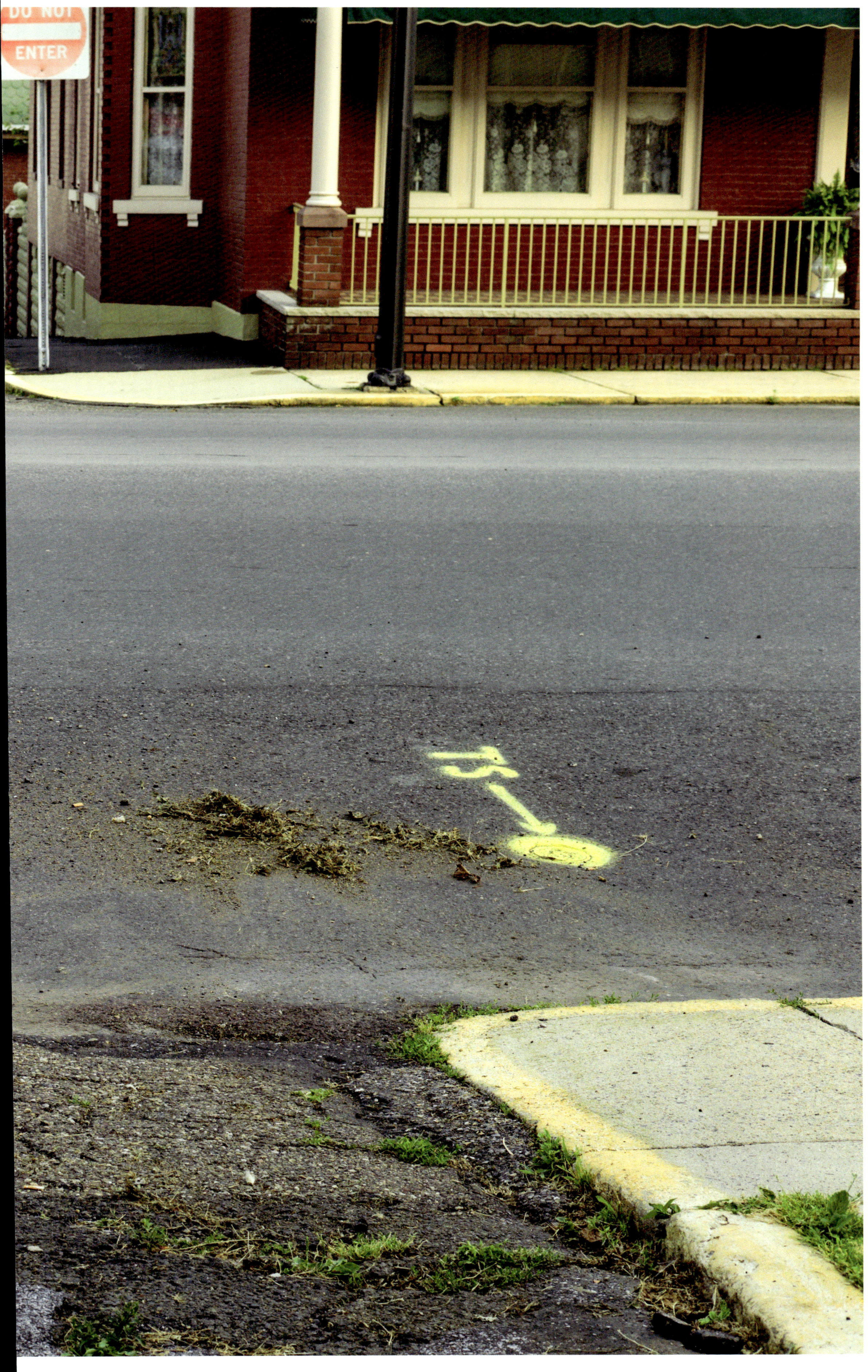

PLATE 65

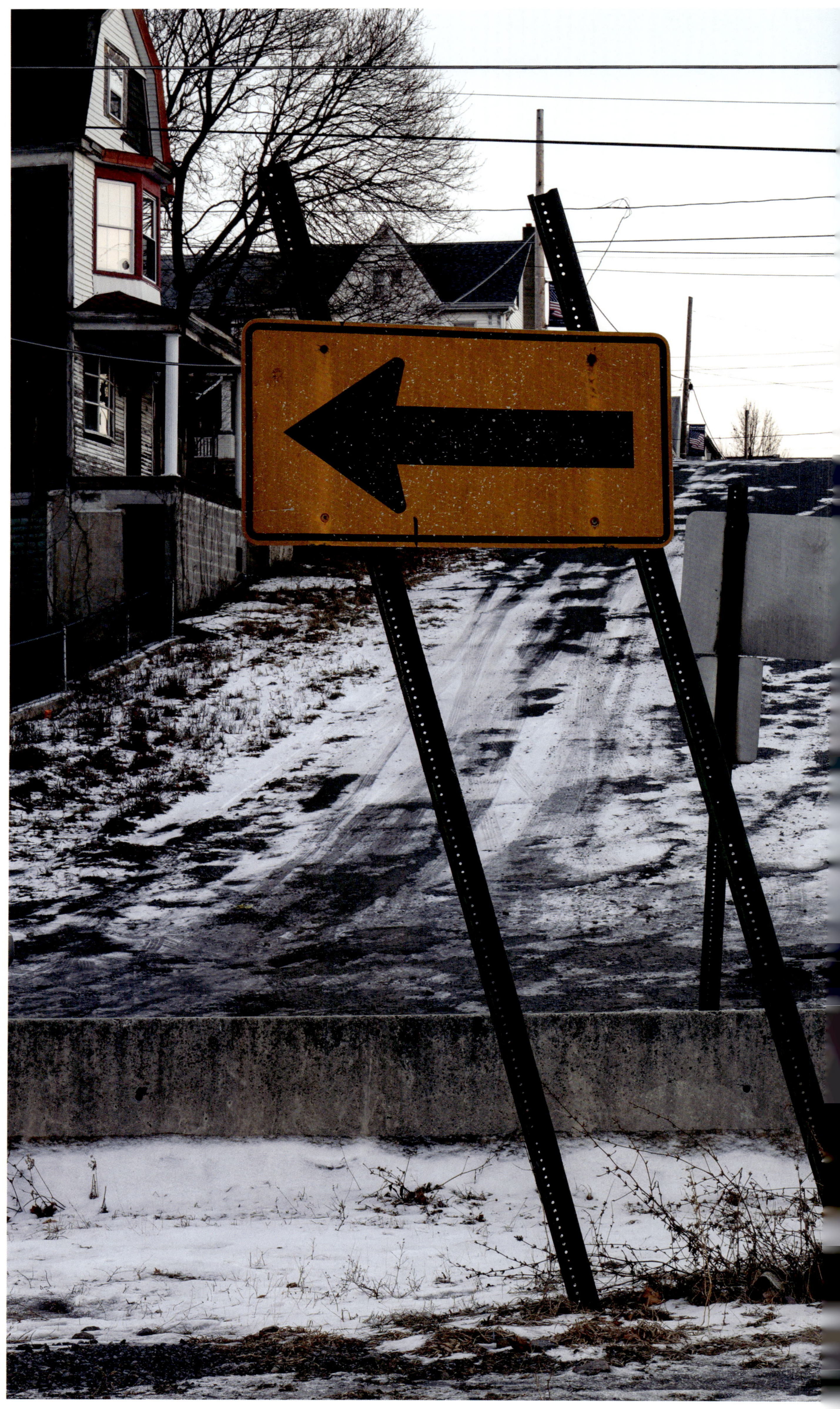

PLATE 66

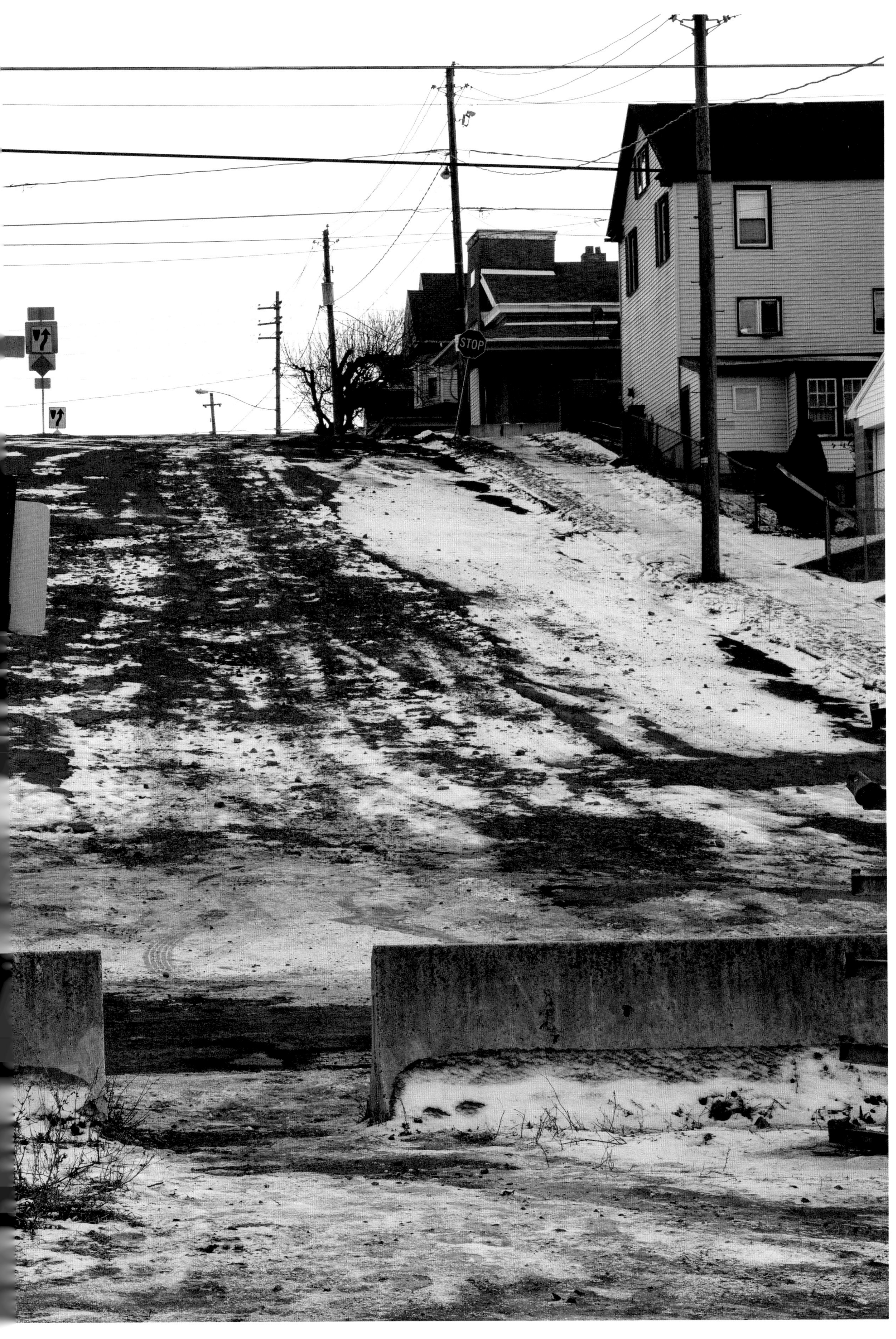
STOP

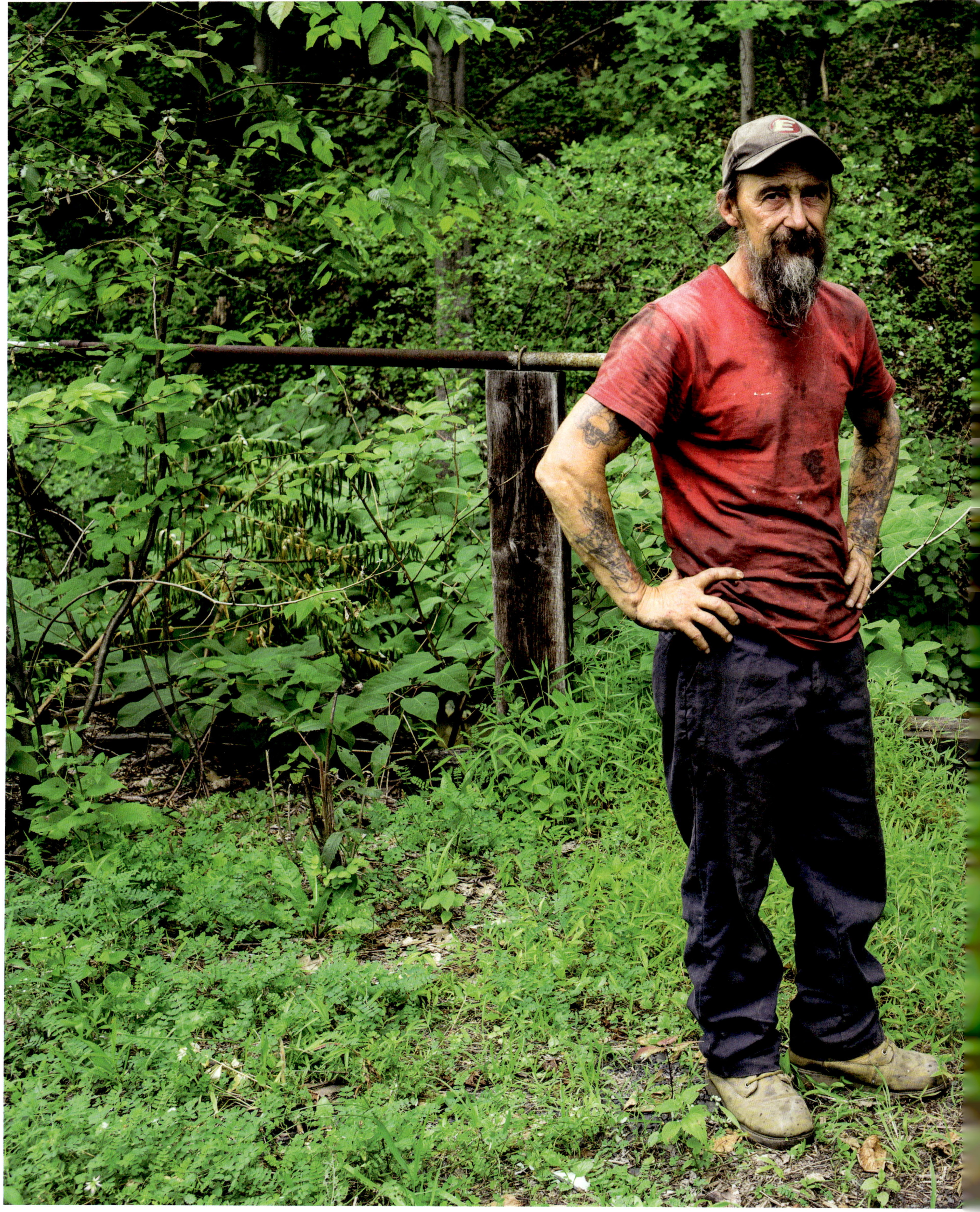

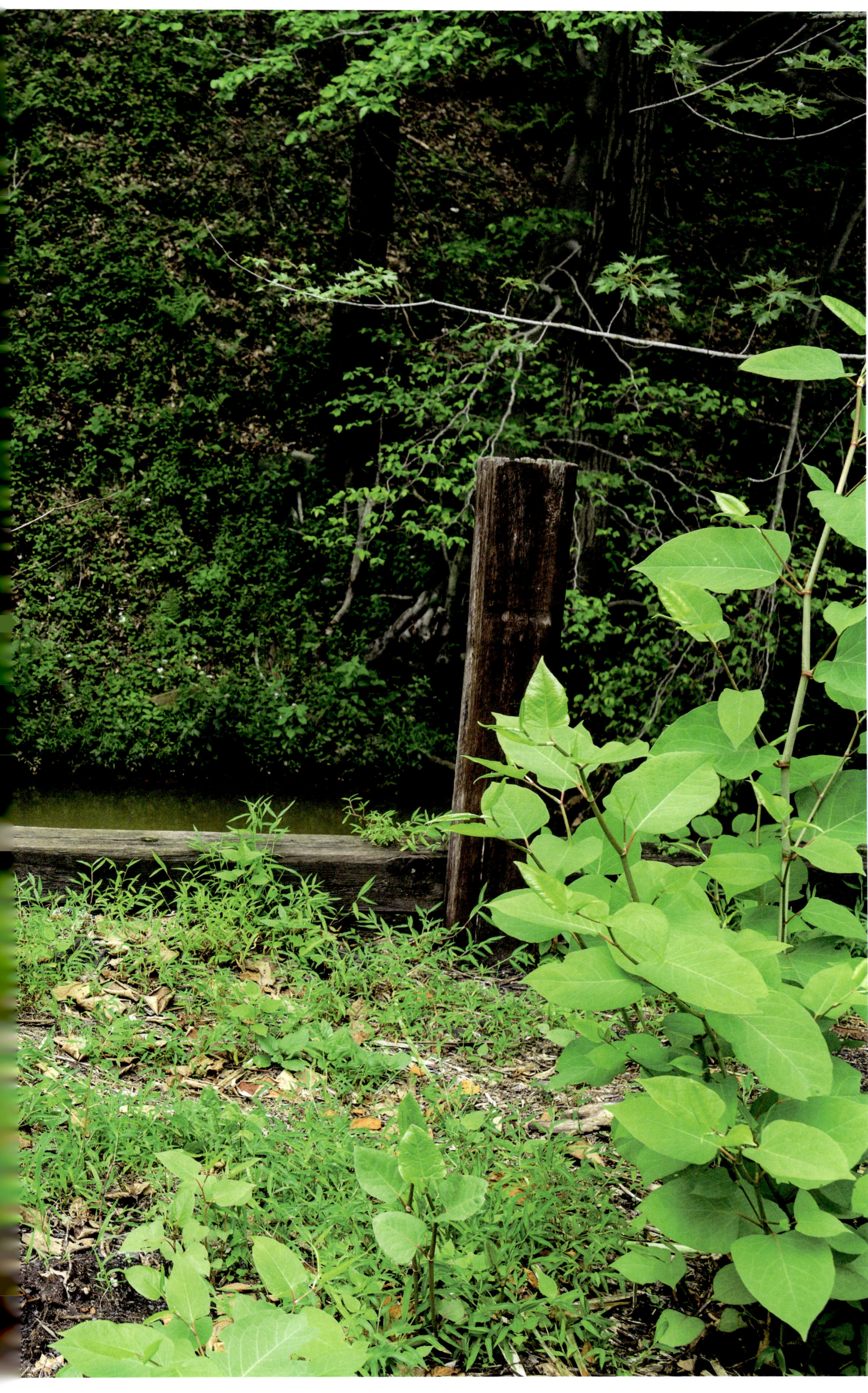

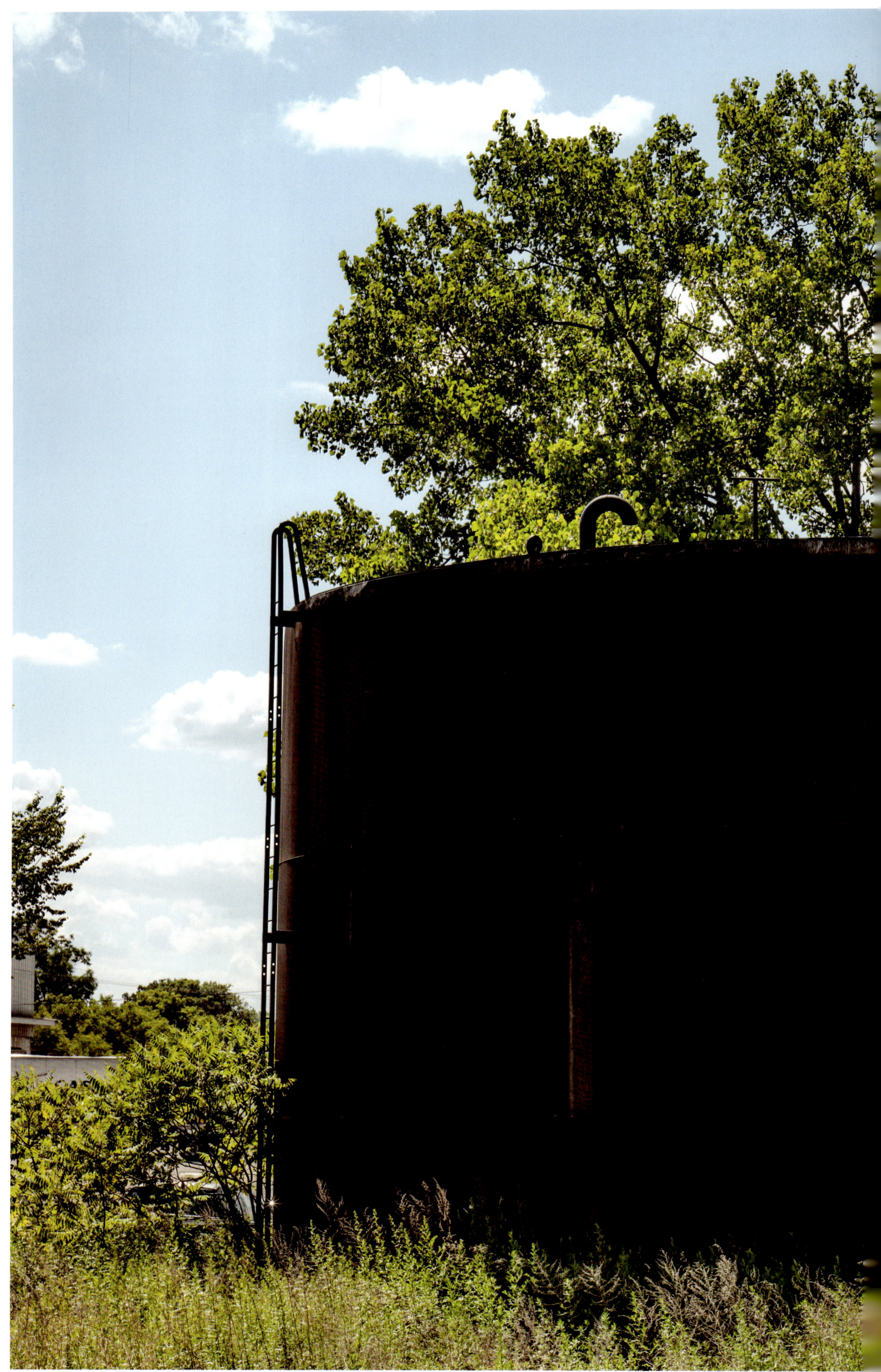

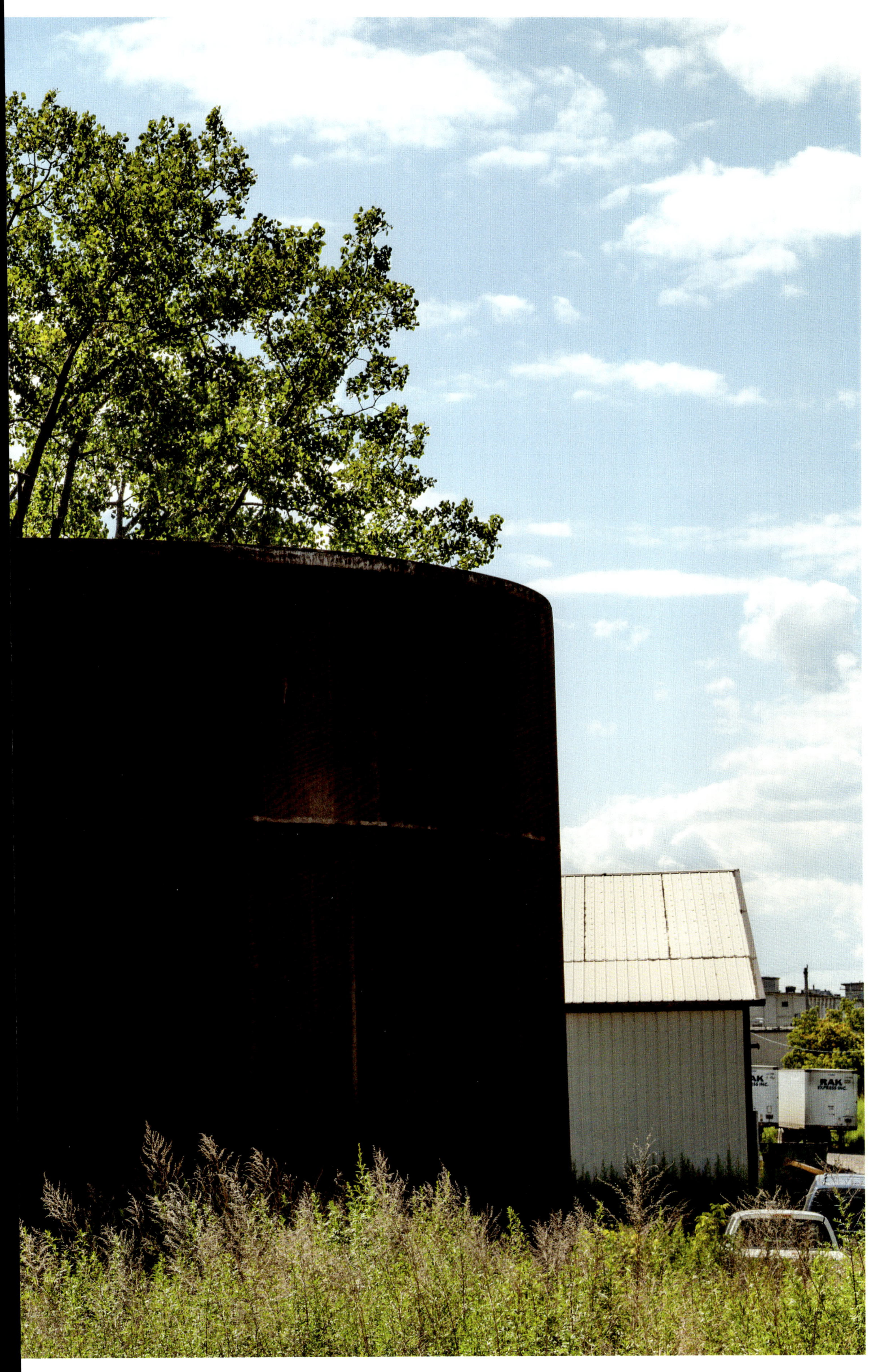

PLATE 68

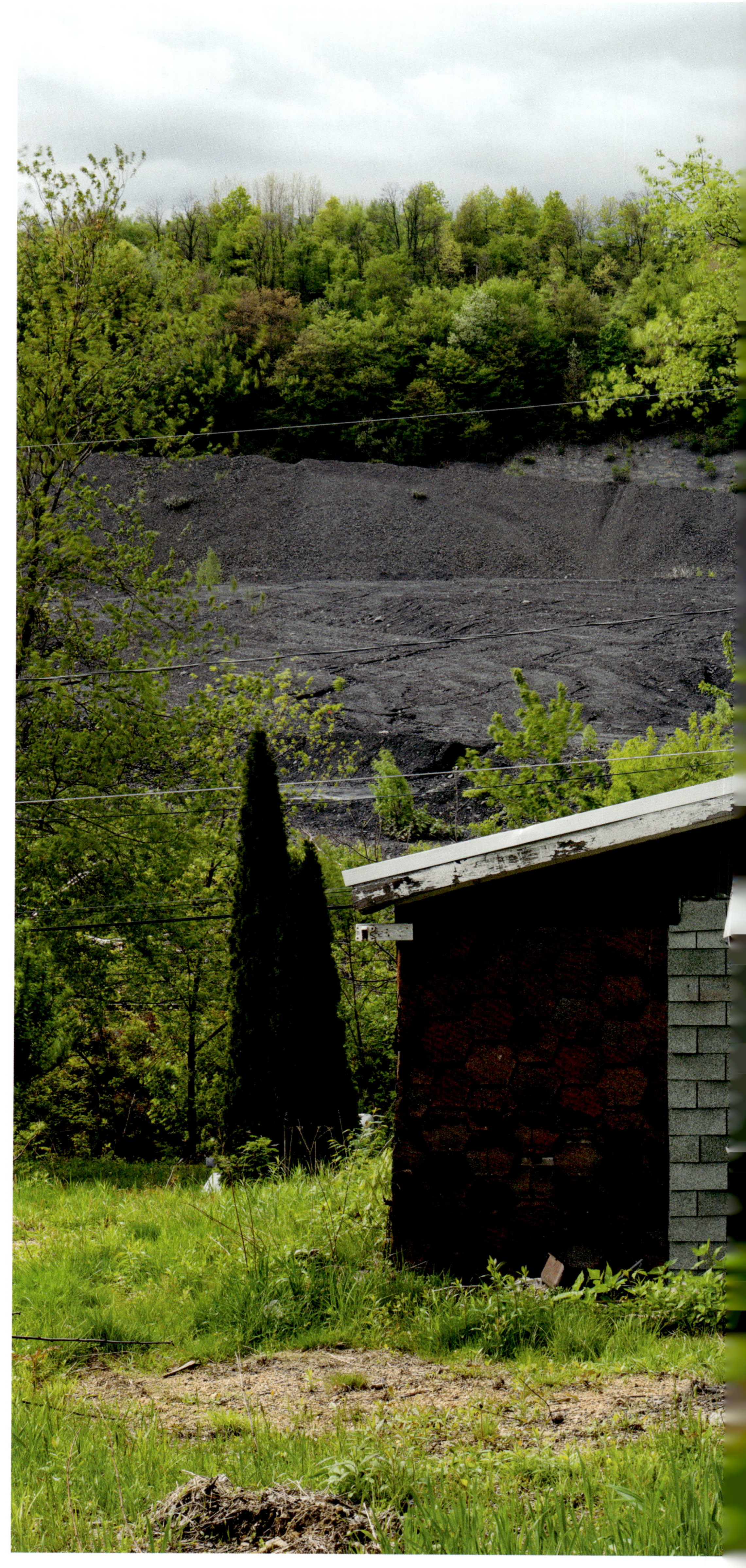

PLATE 69

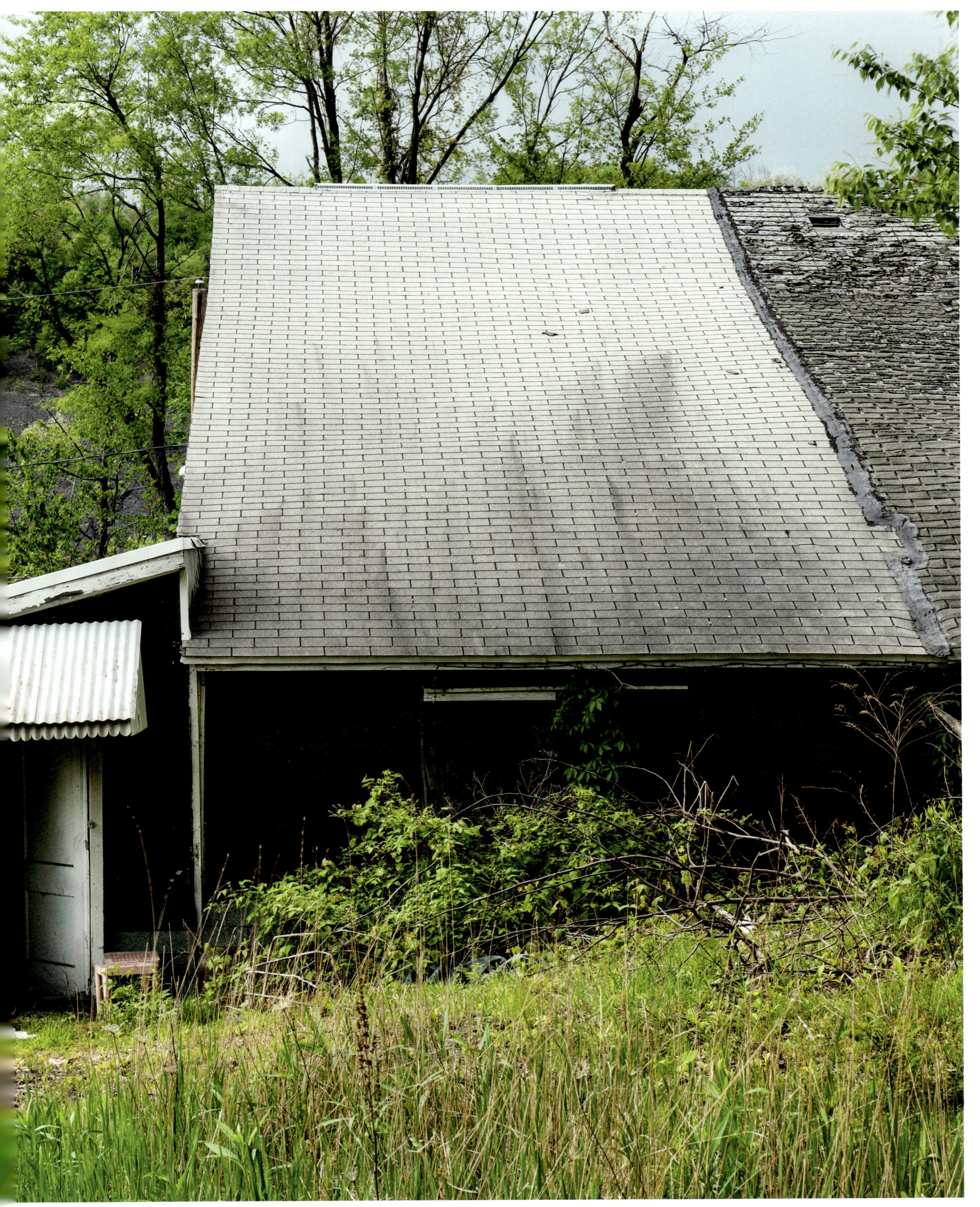

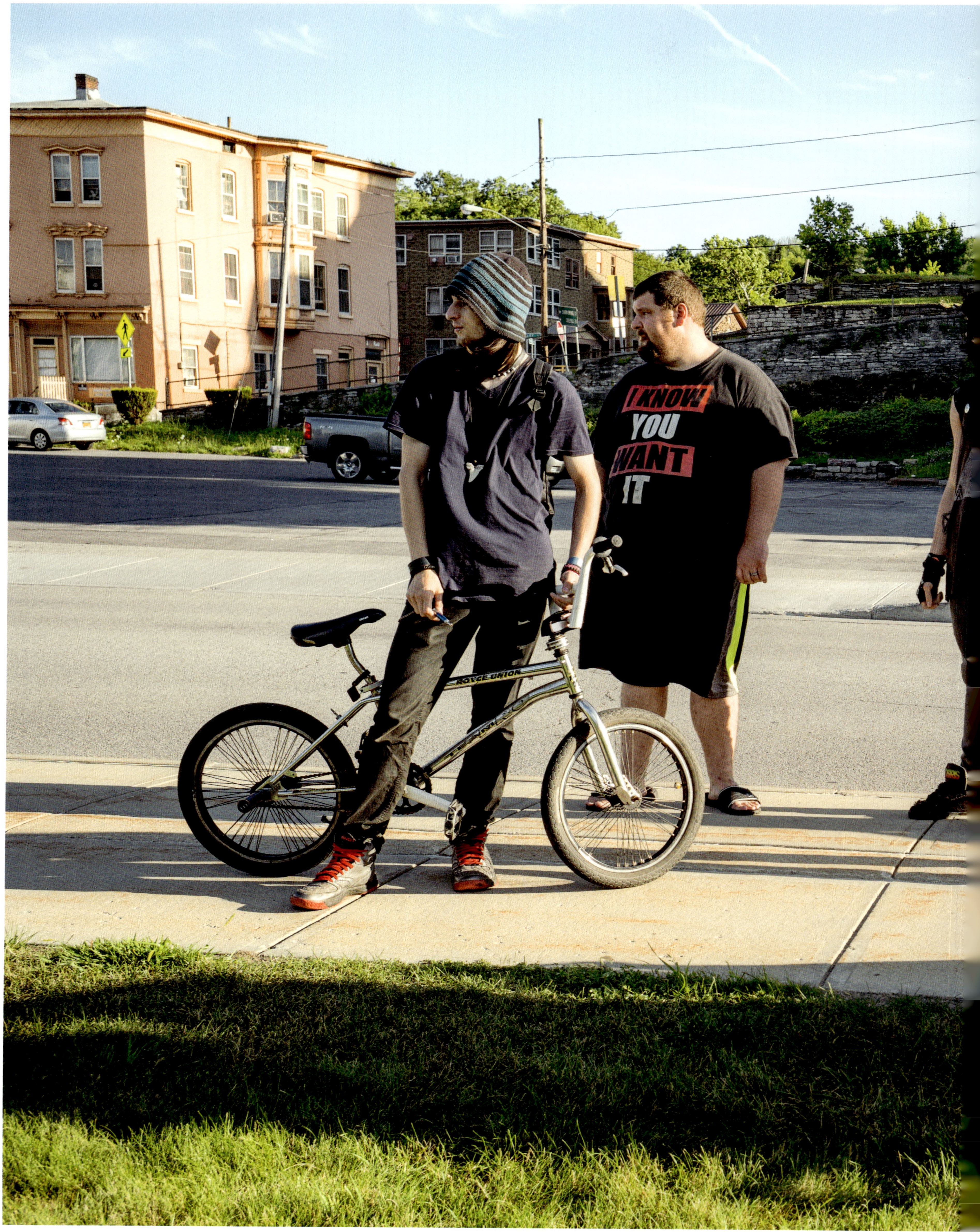
I KNOW
YOU
WANT
IT

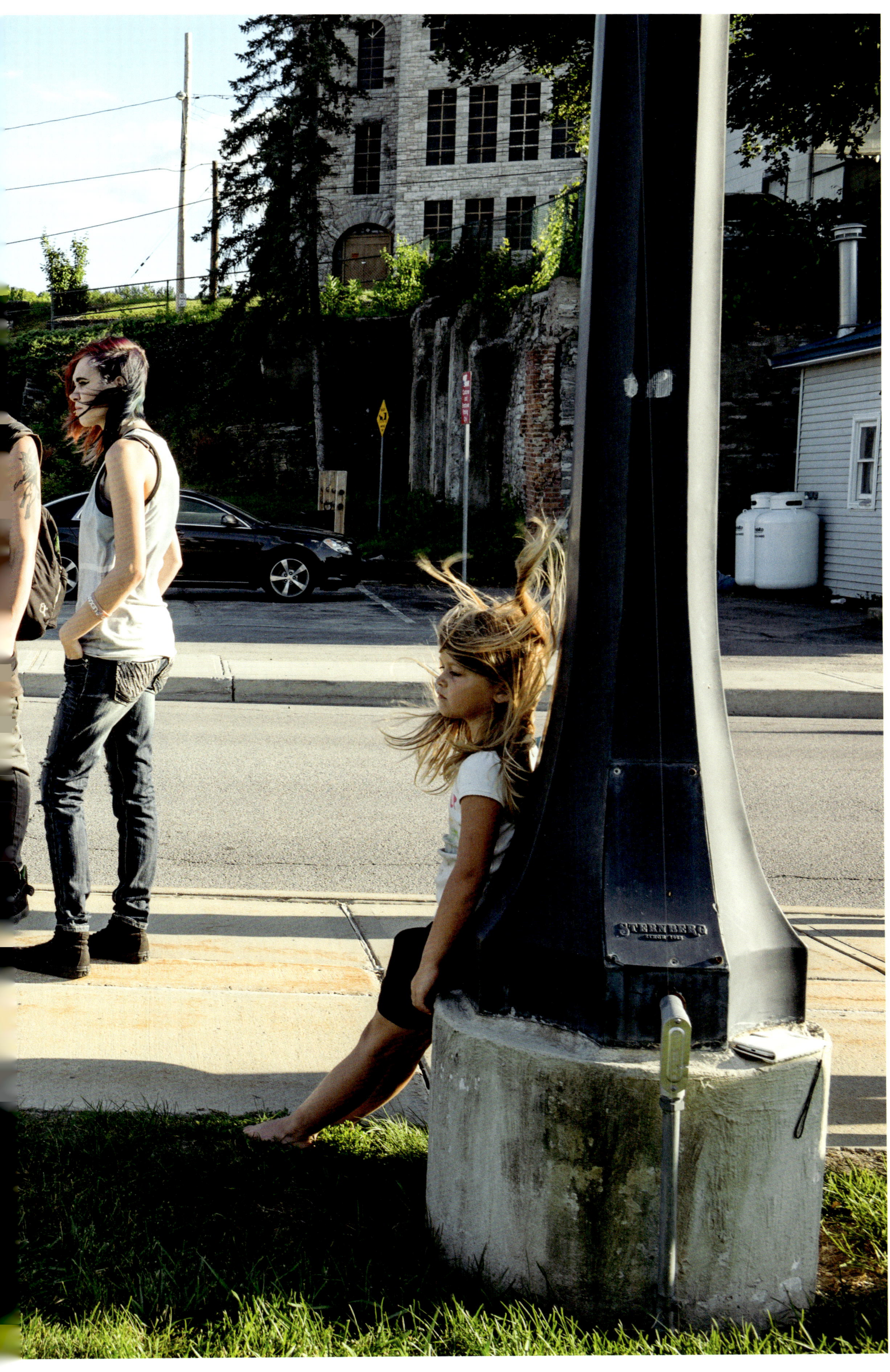

PLATE 70

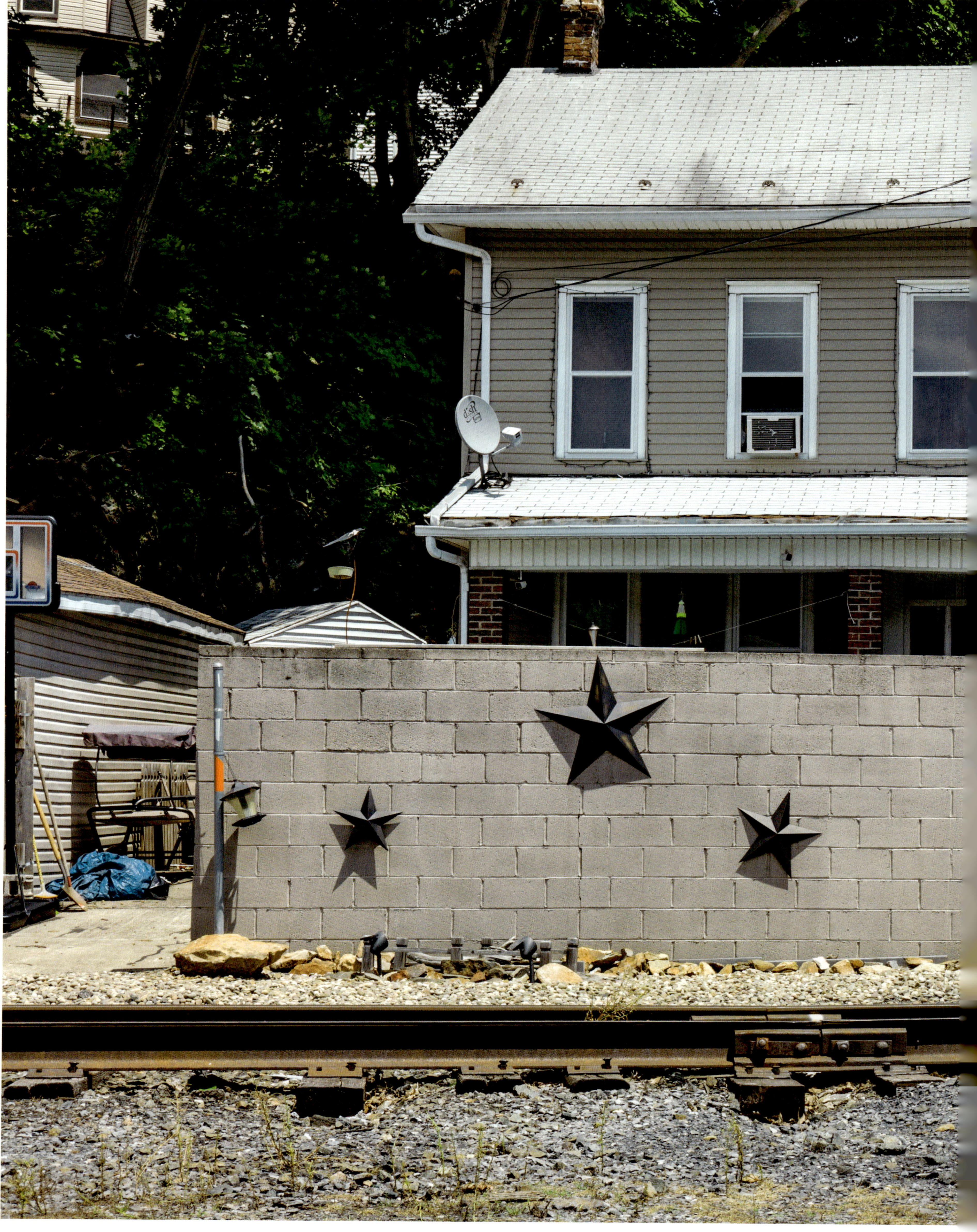

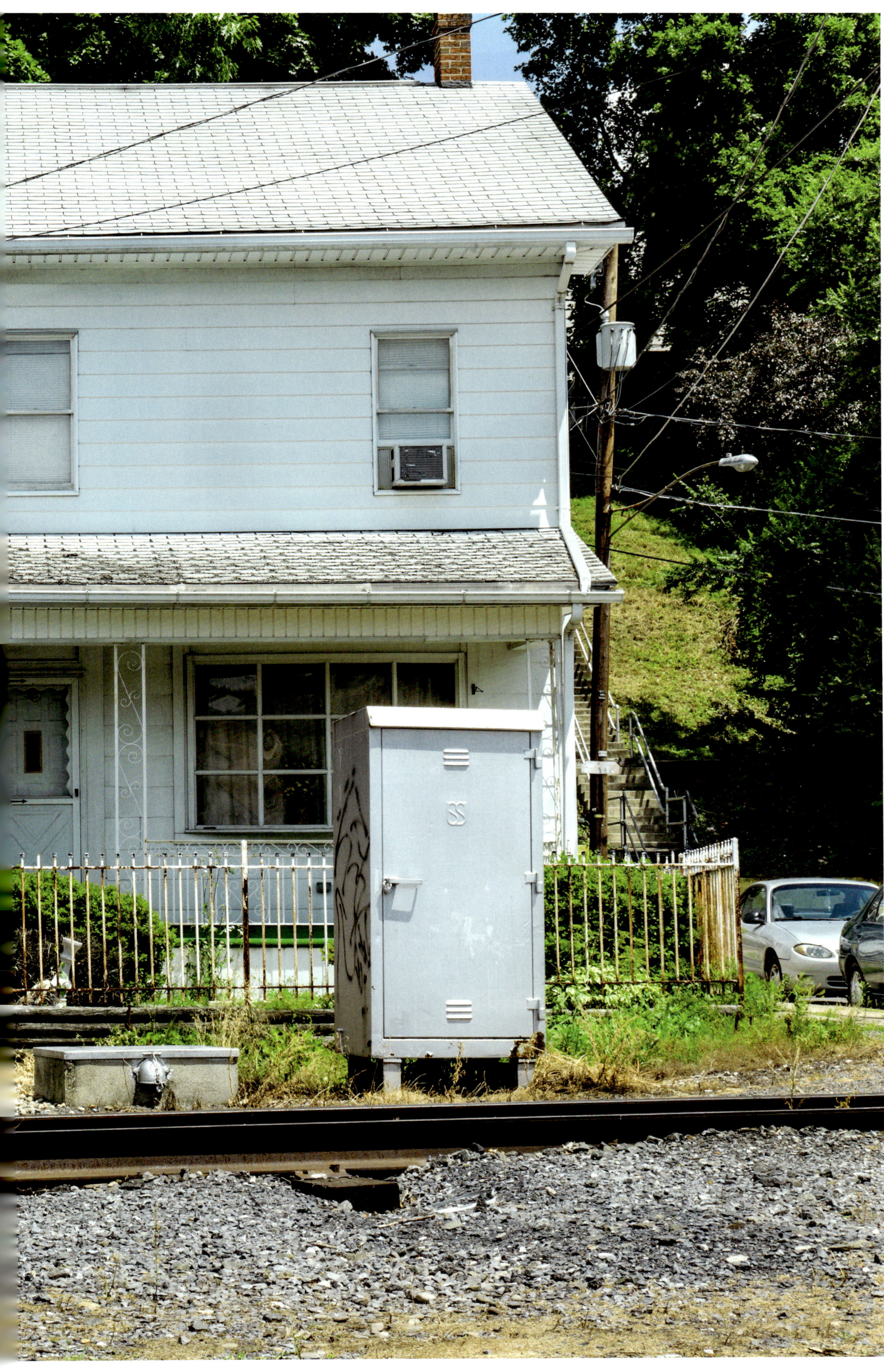

PLATE 71

Lowville
REDEMPTION
CENTER
wvville
ption Center
Thurs Hours
am - 6:00pm
y Hours
am - 6:00pm
day Hours
am - 3:00pm
Thank You
NO
Skylers Pole Stick

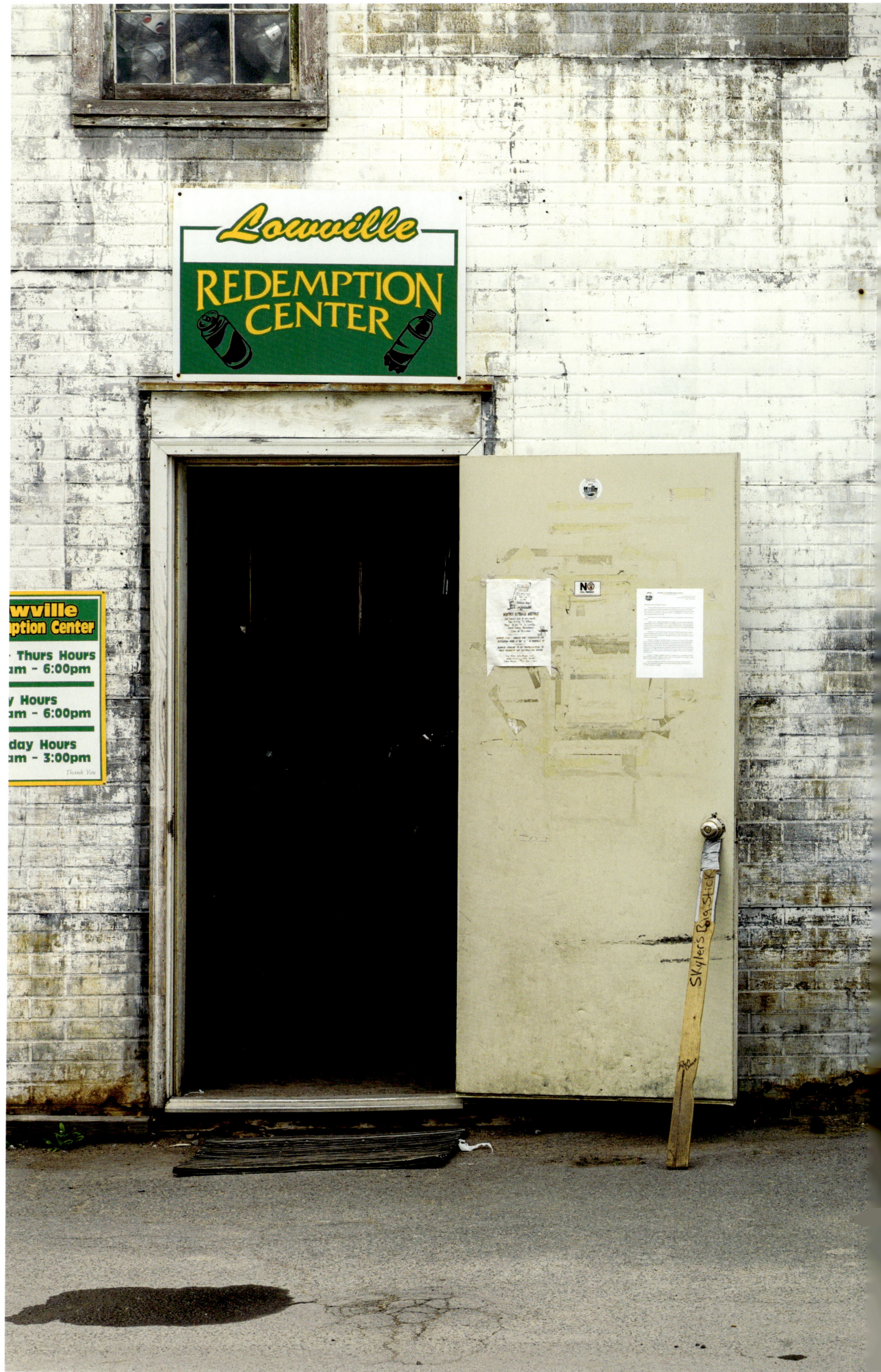

PLATE 72

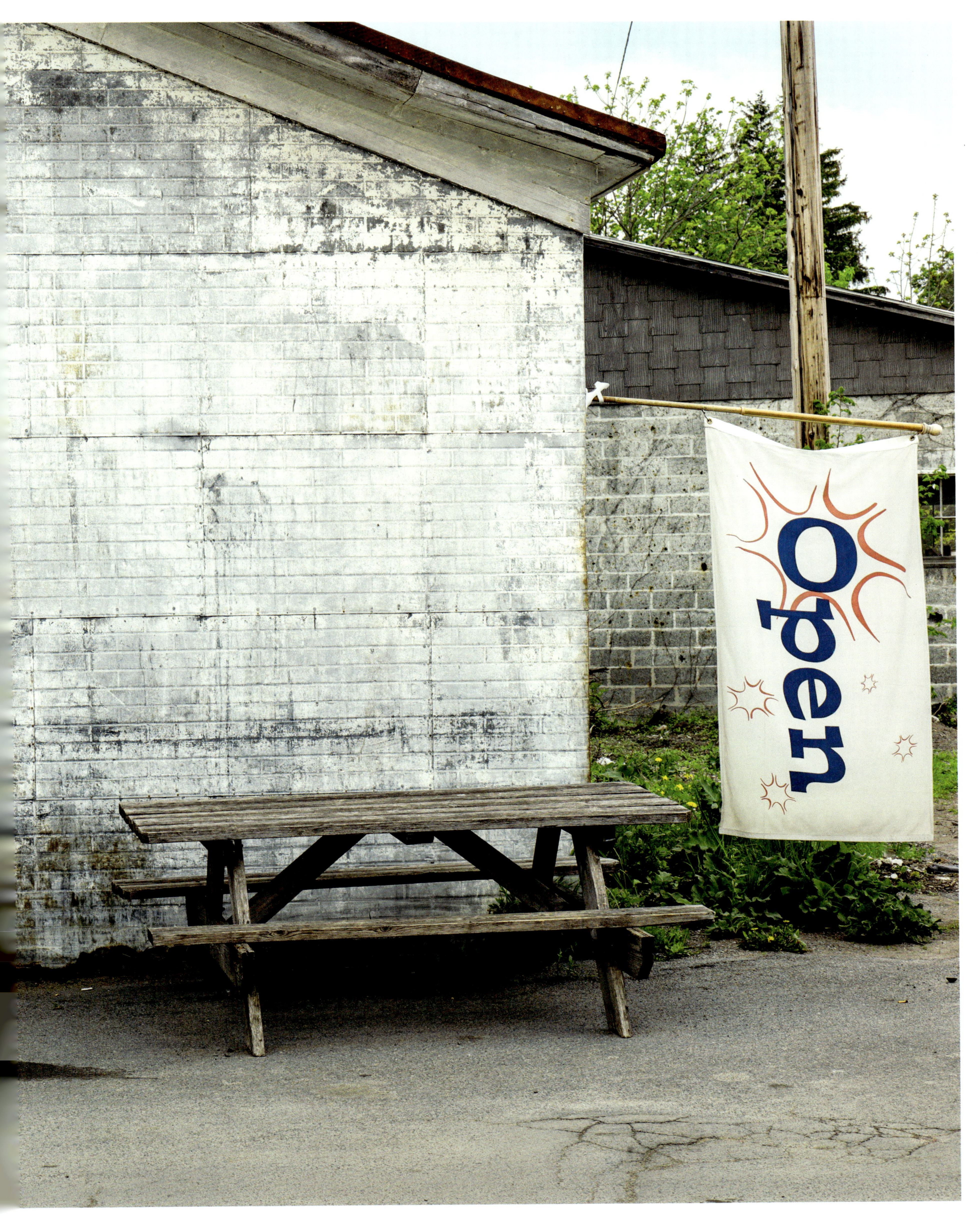
Open

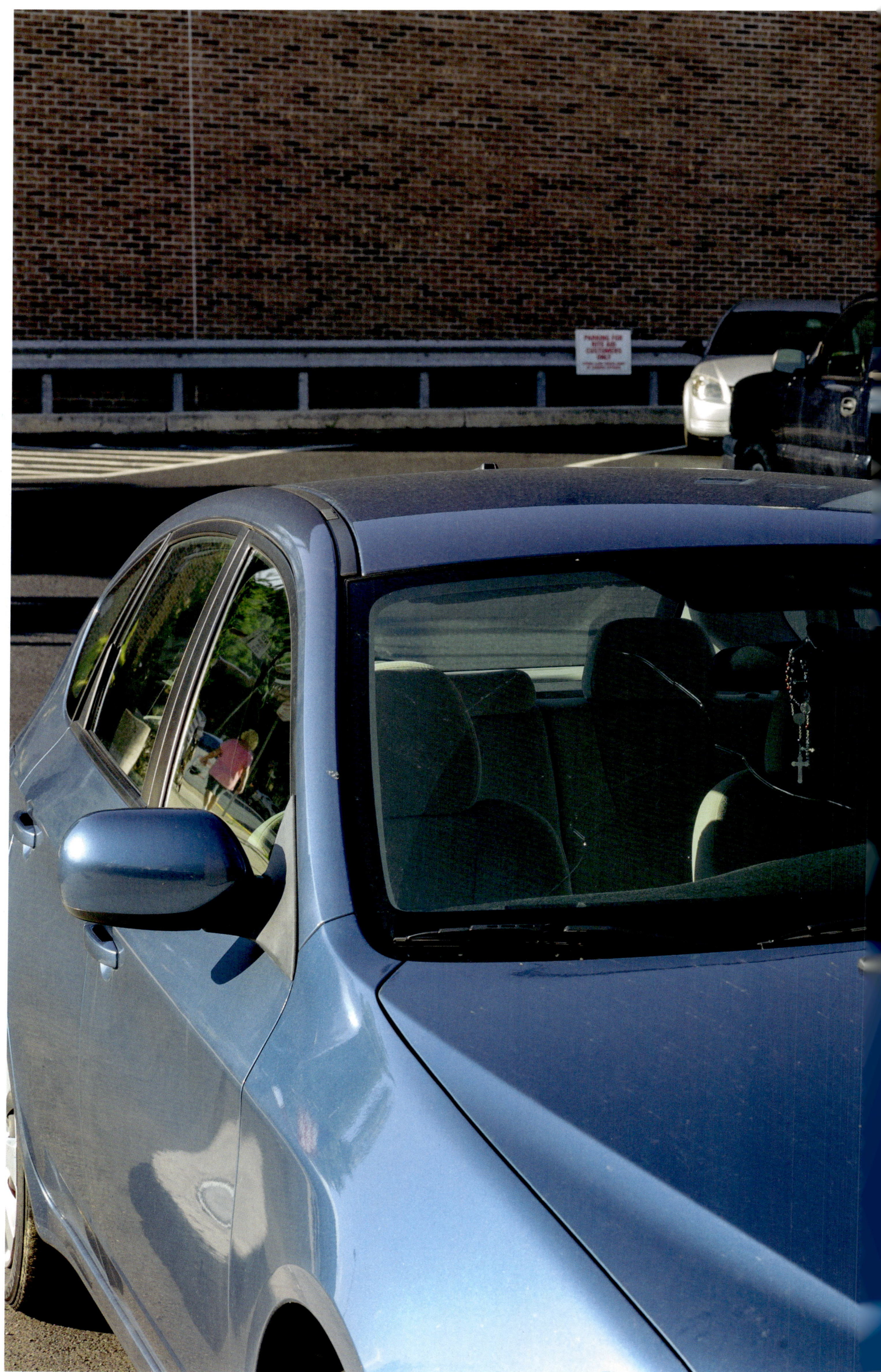

PLATE 73

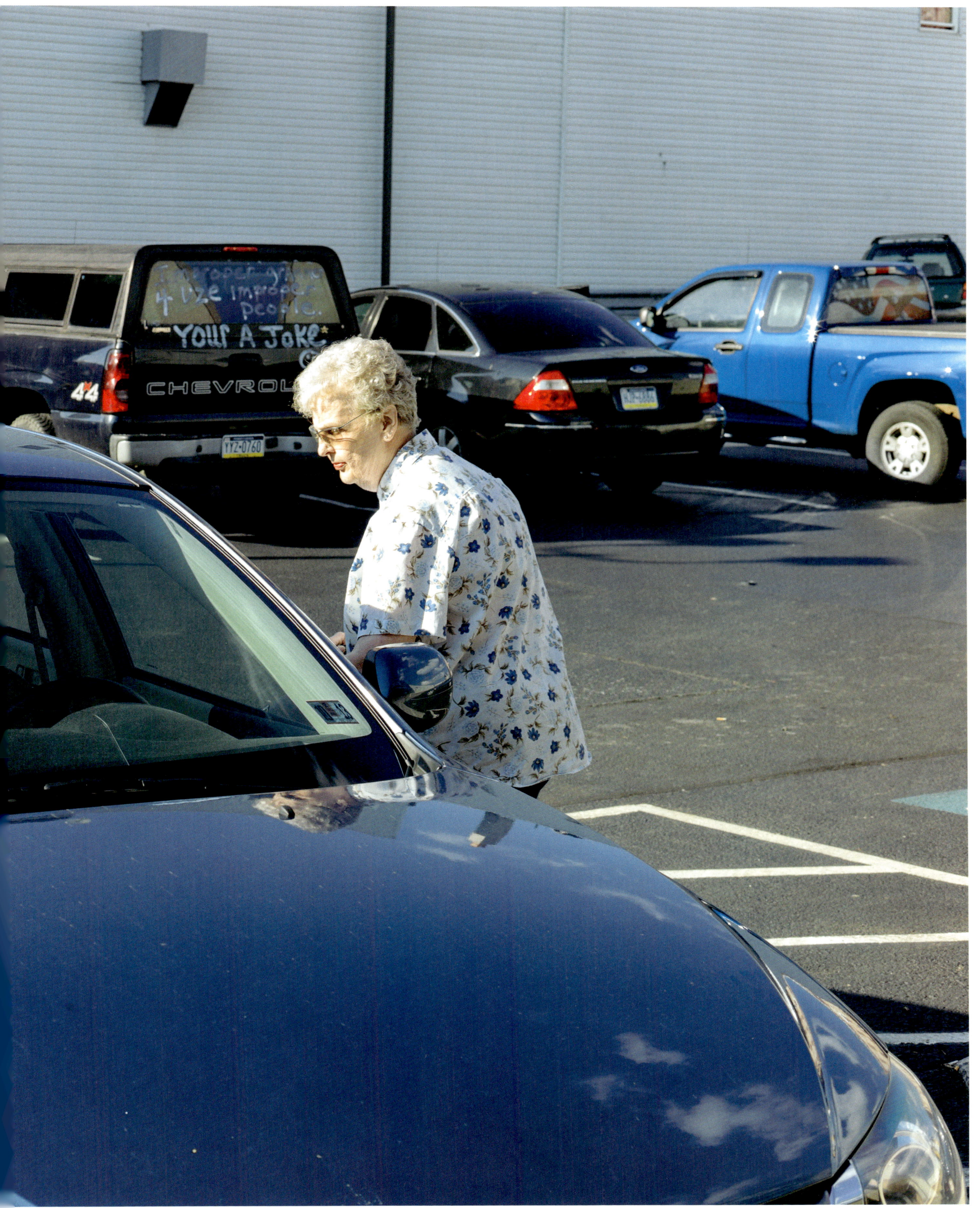
4 Uze improper
people.
YOUR A JOKE
CHEVROL
YYZ-0760

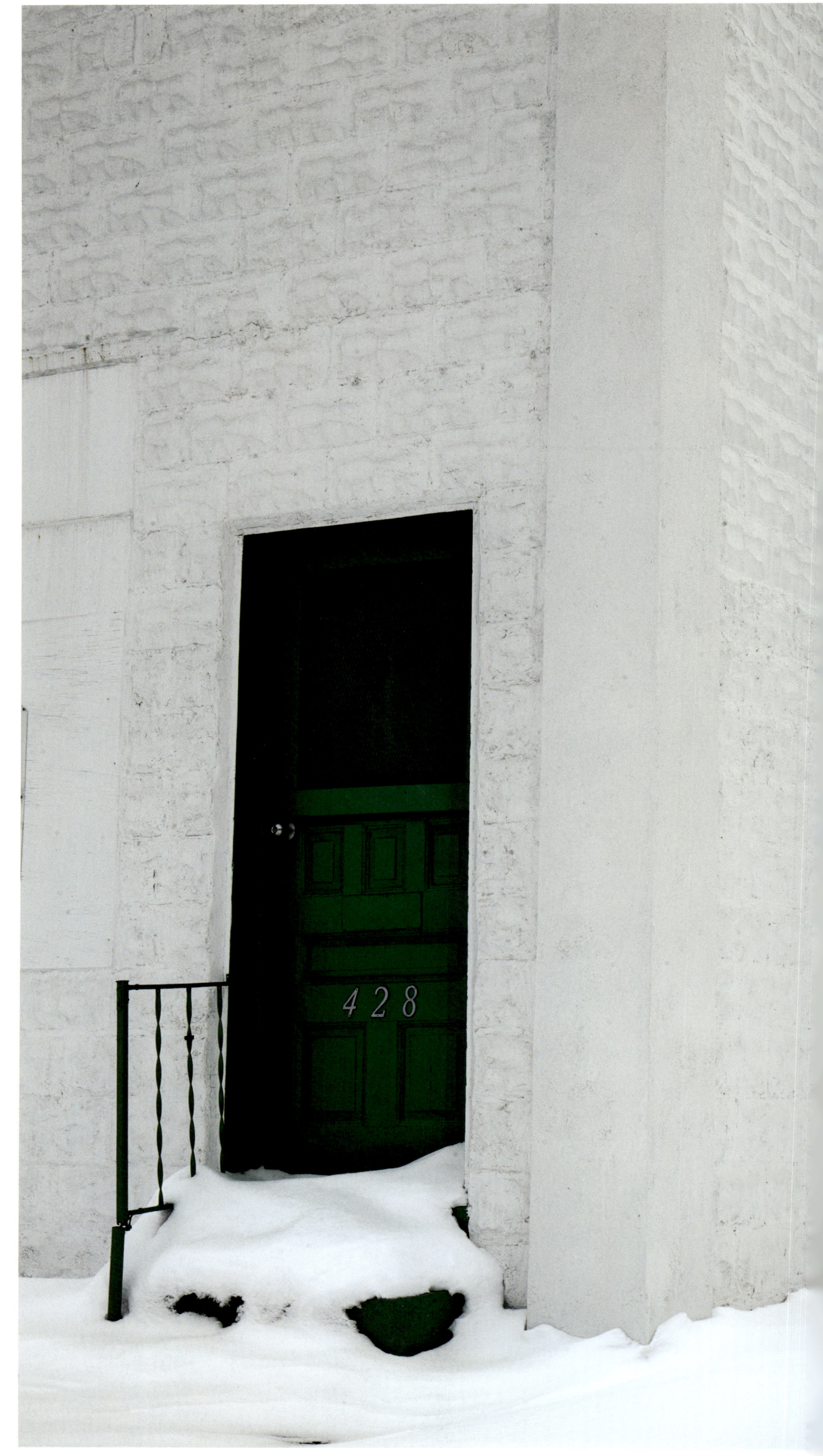

PLATE 74

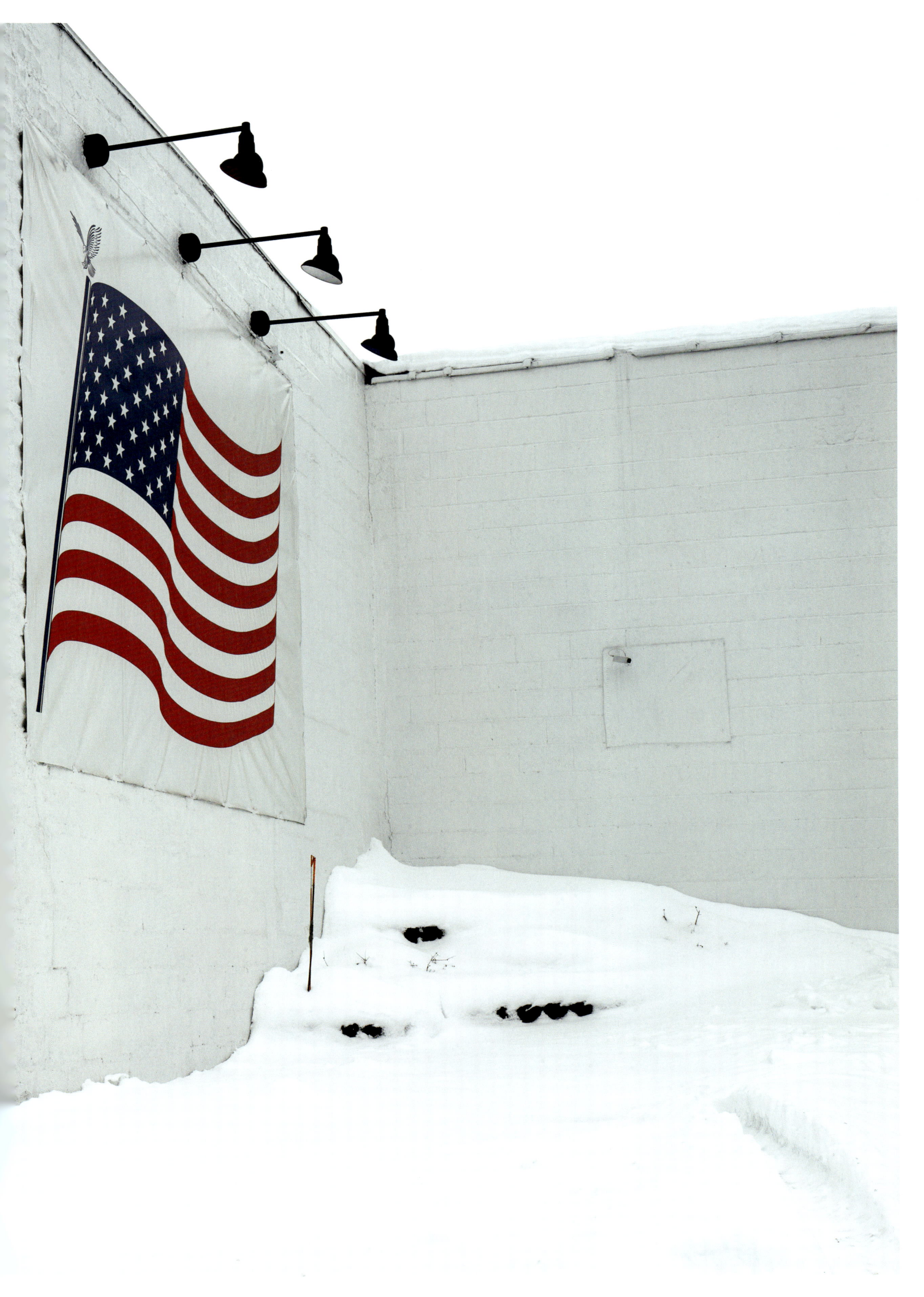

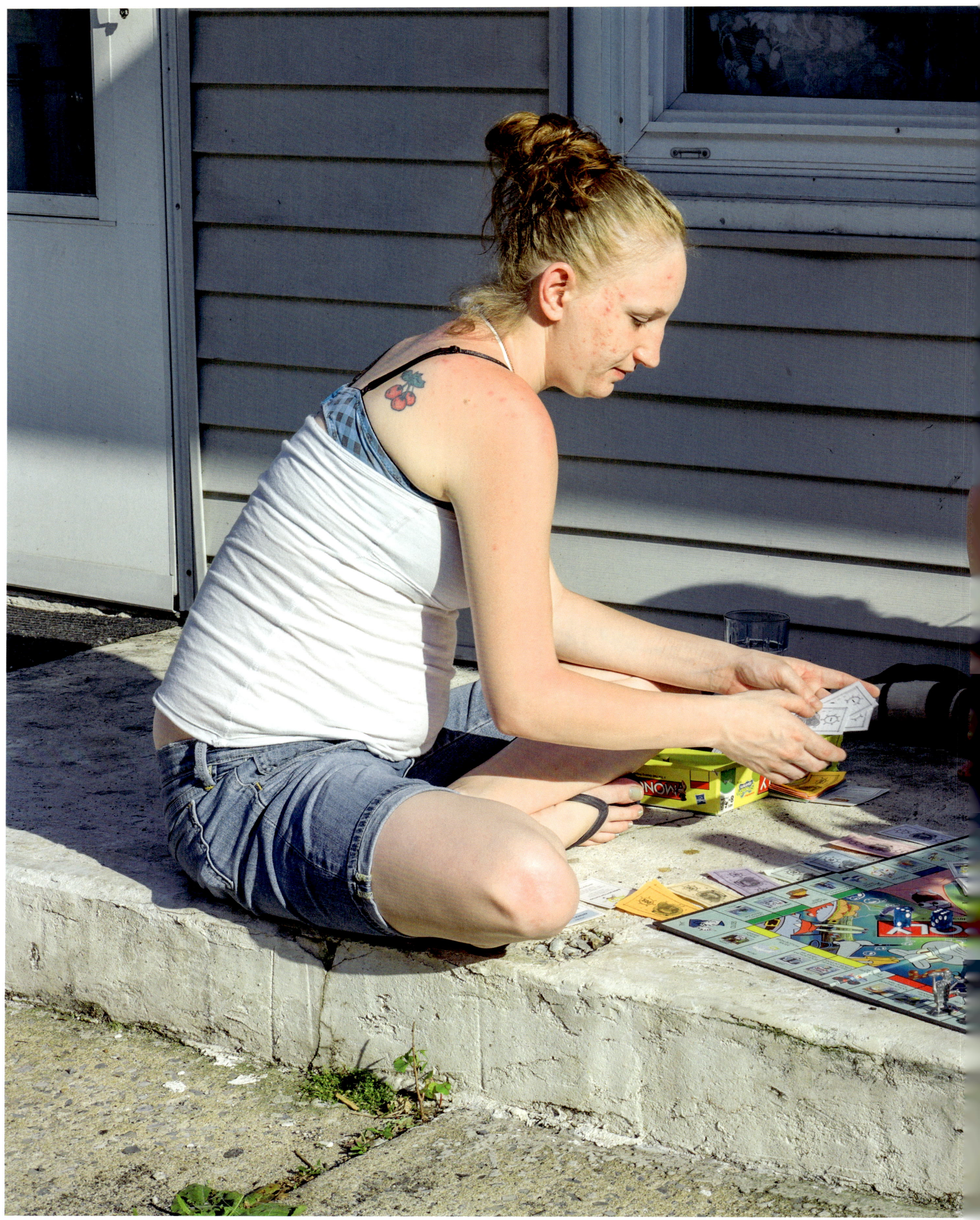

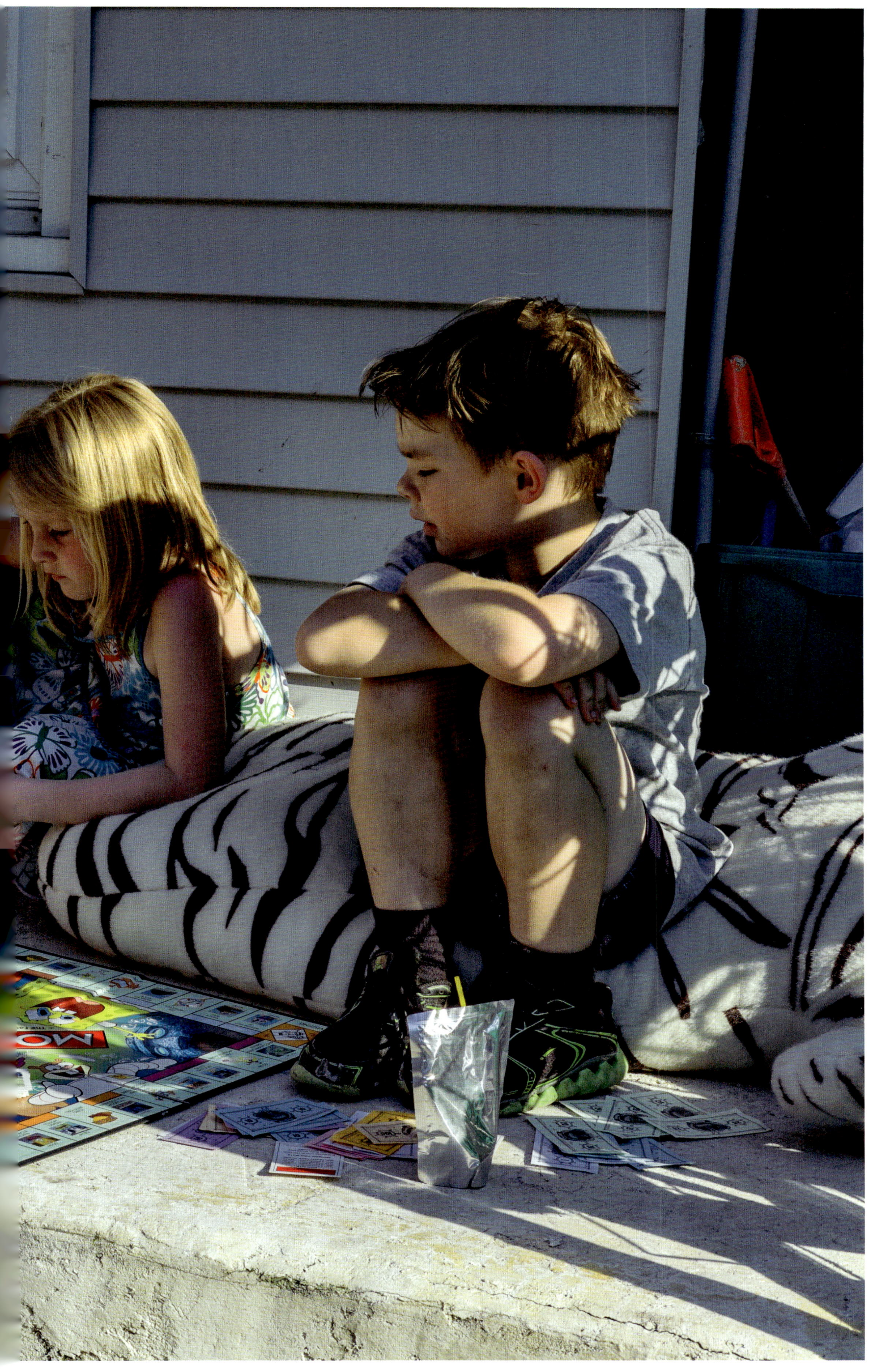

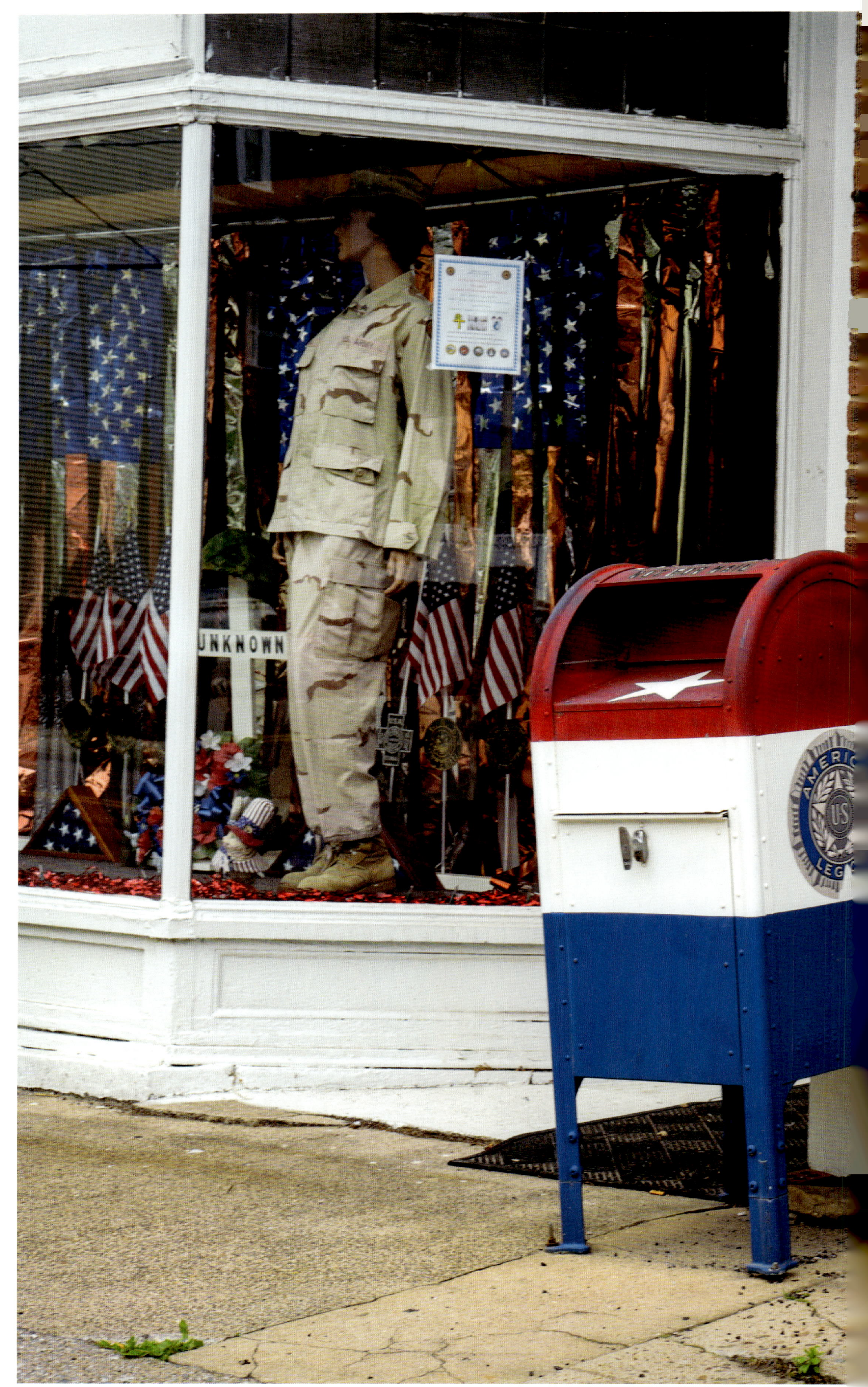

PLATE 76

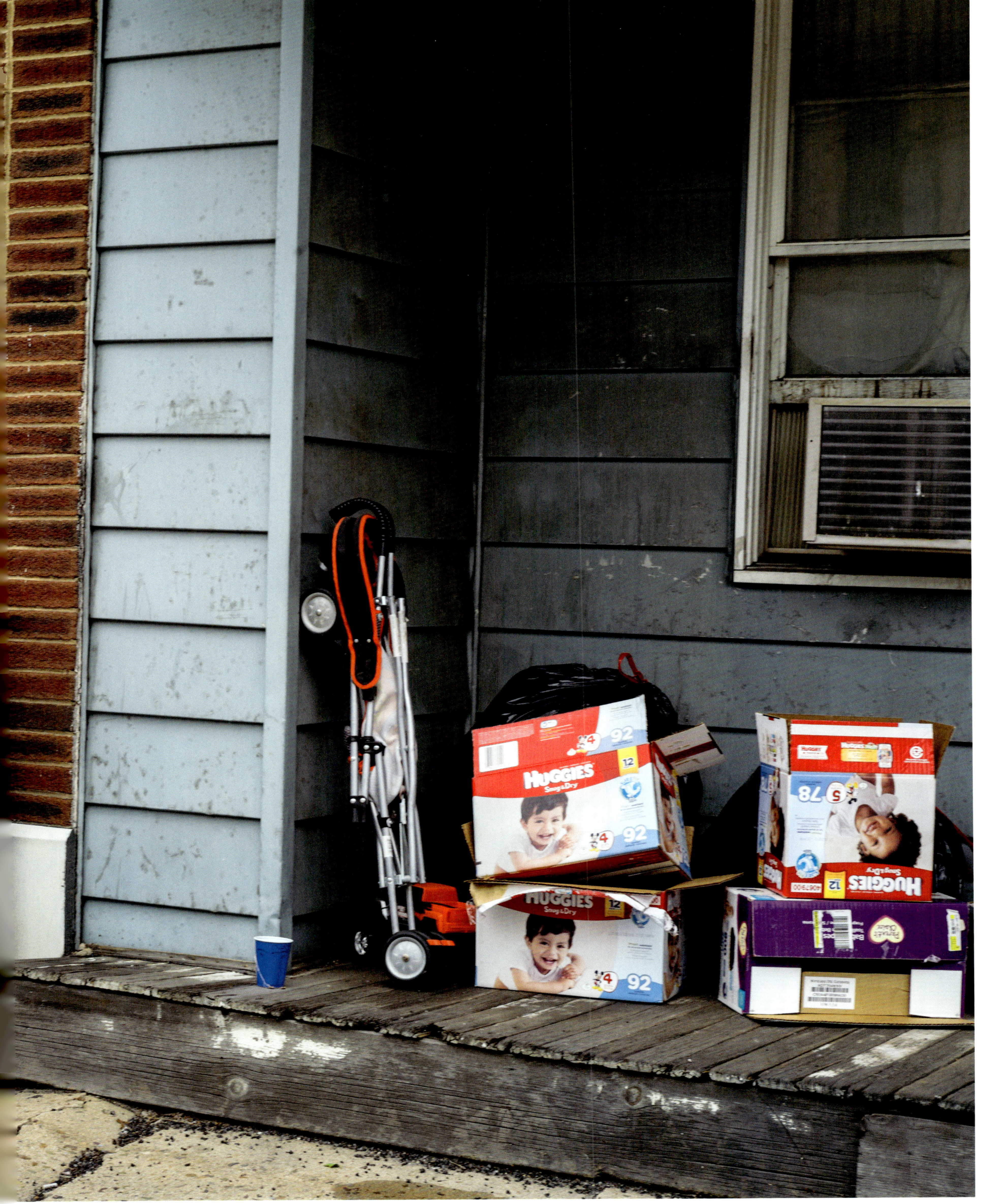
HUGGIES
Snug&Dry
12
4
92

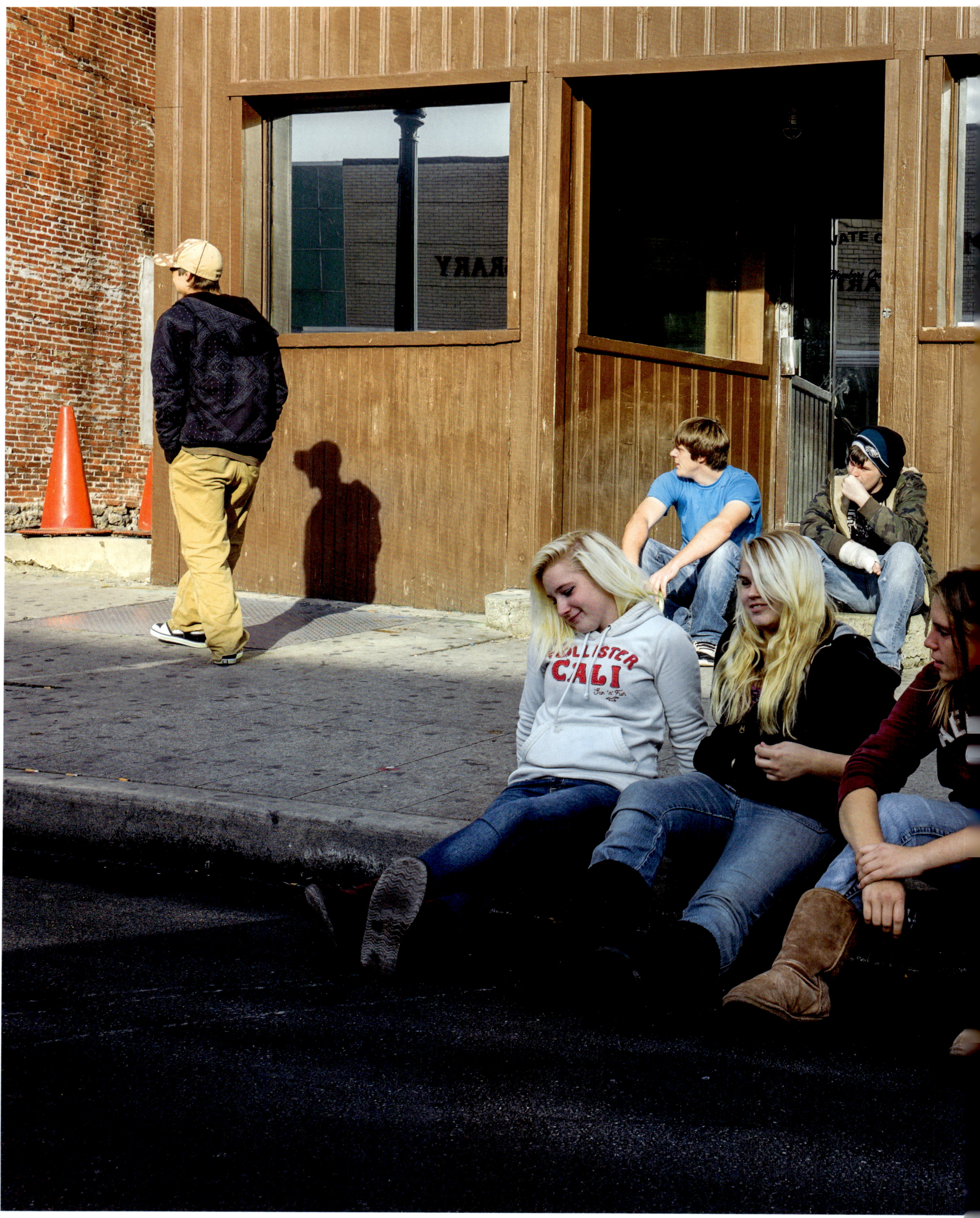
CALI

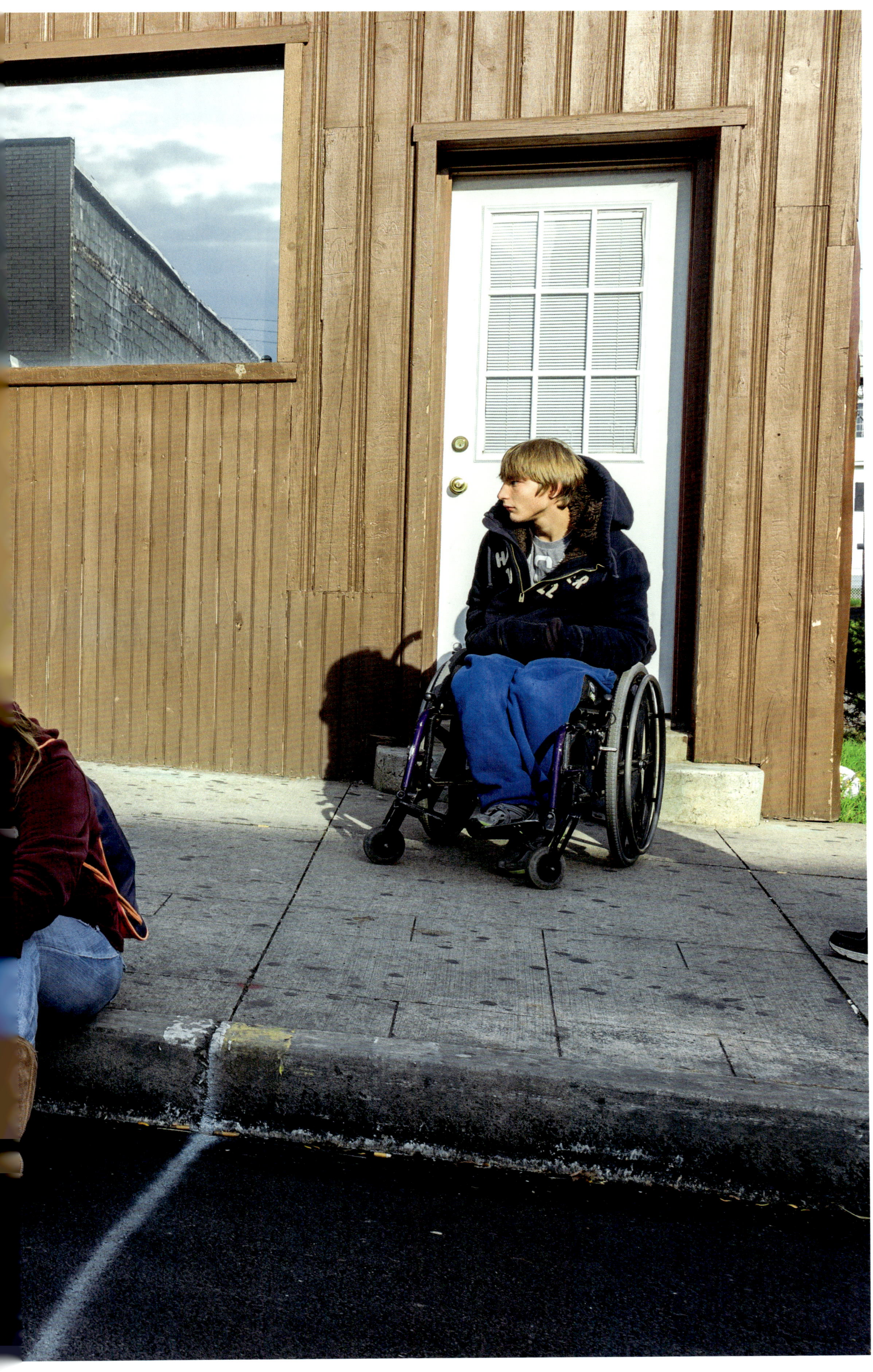

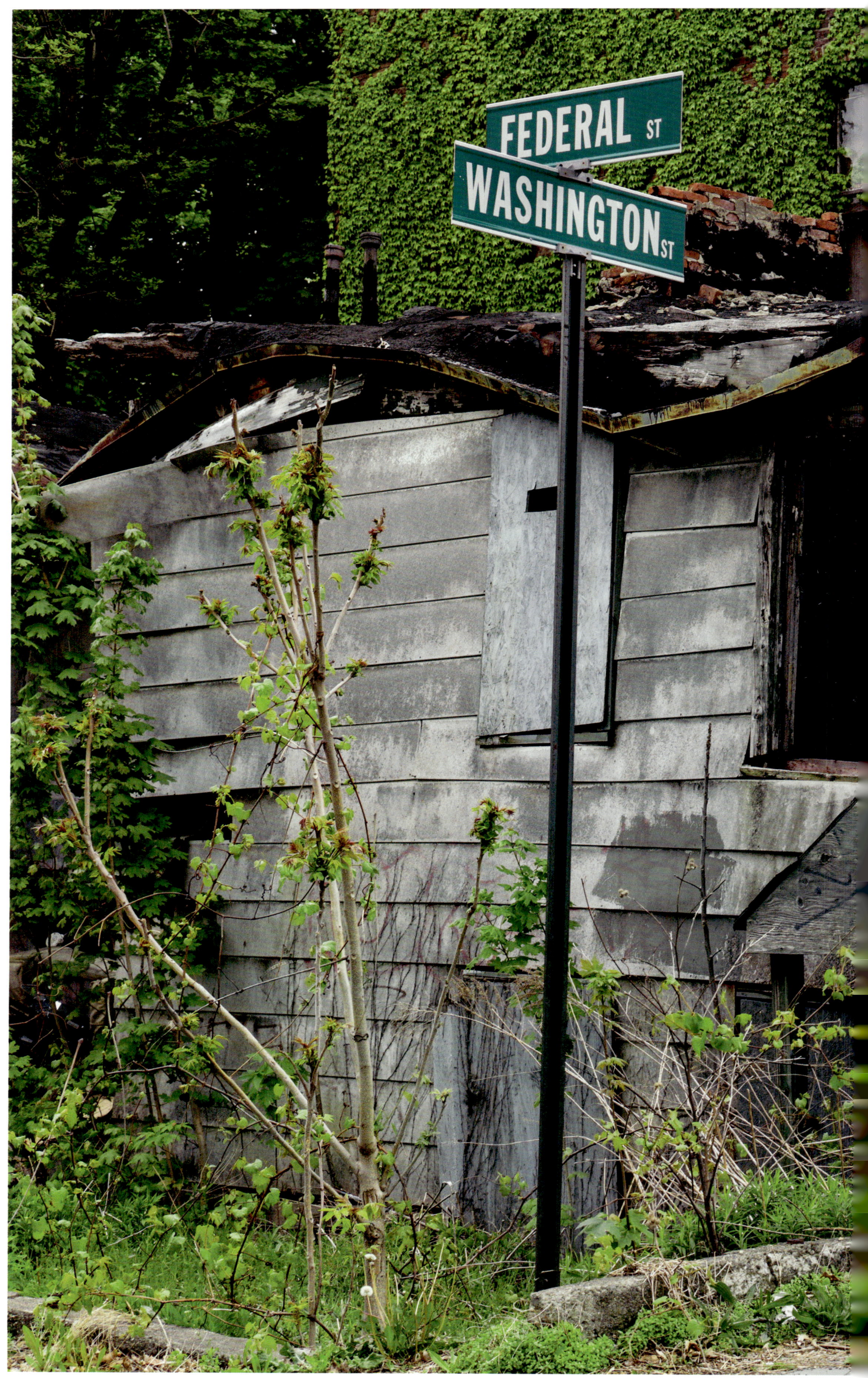

PLATE 78

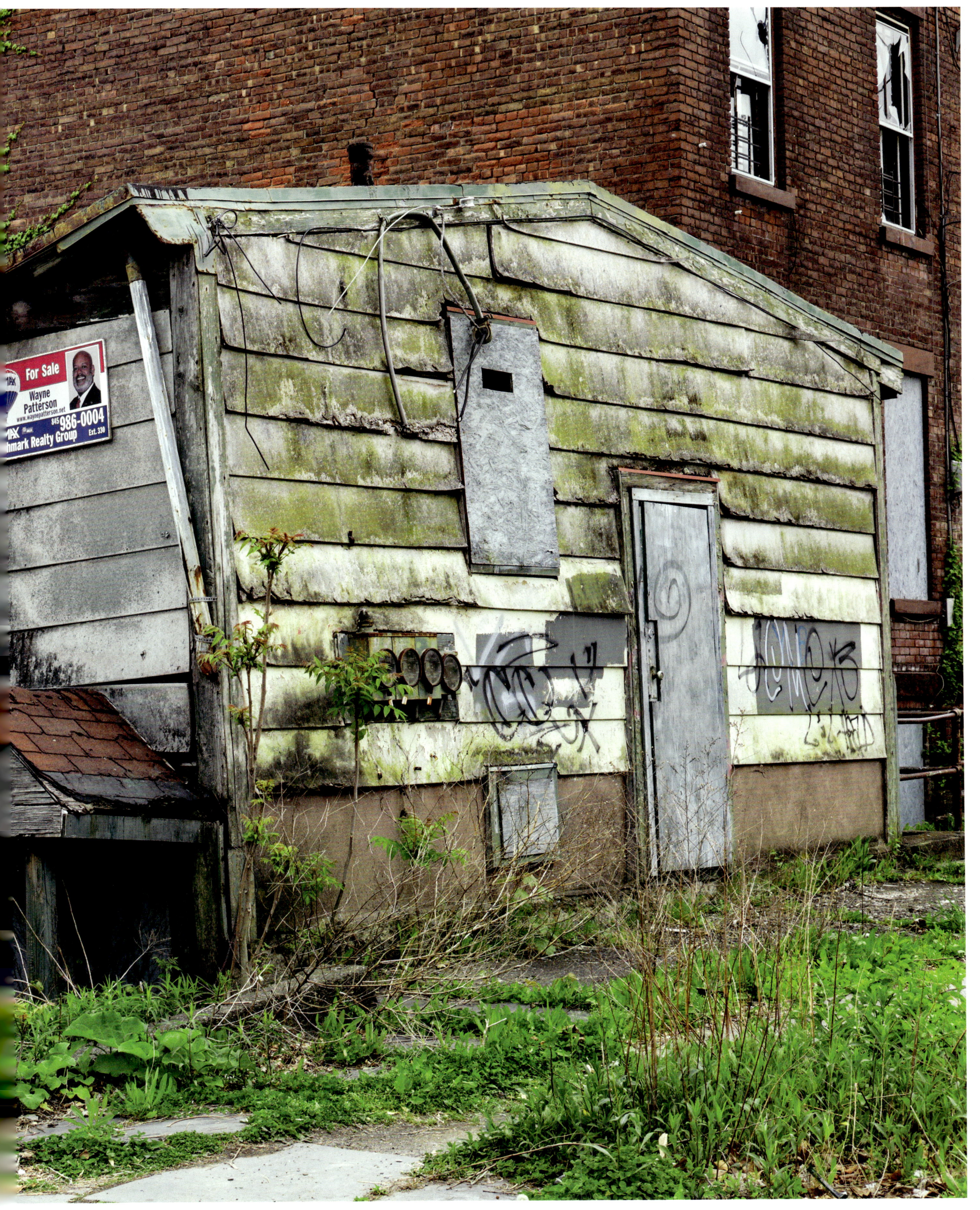
For Sale
Wayne
Patterson
www.waynepatterson.net
845 986-0004
Ext. 330

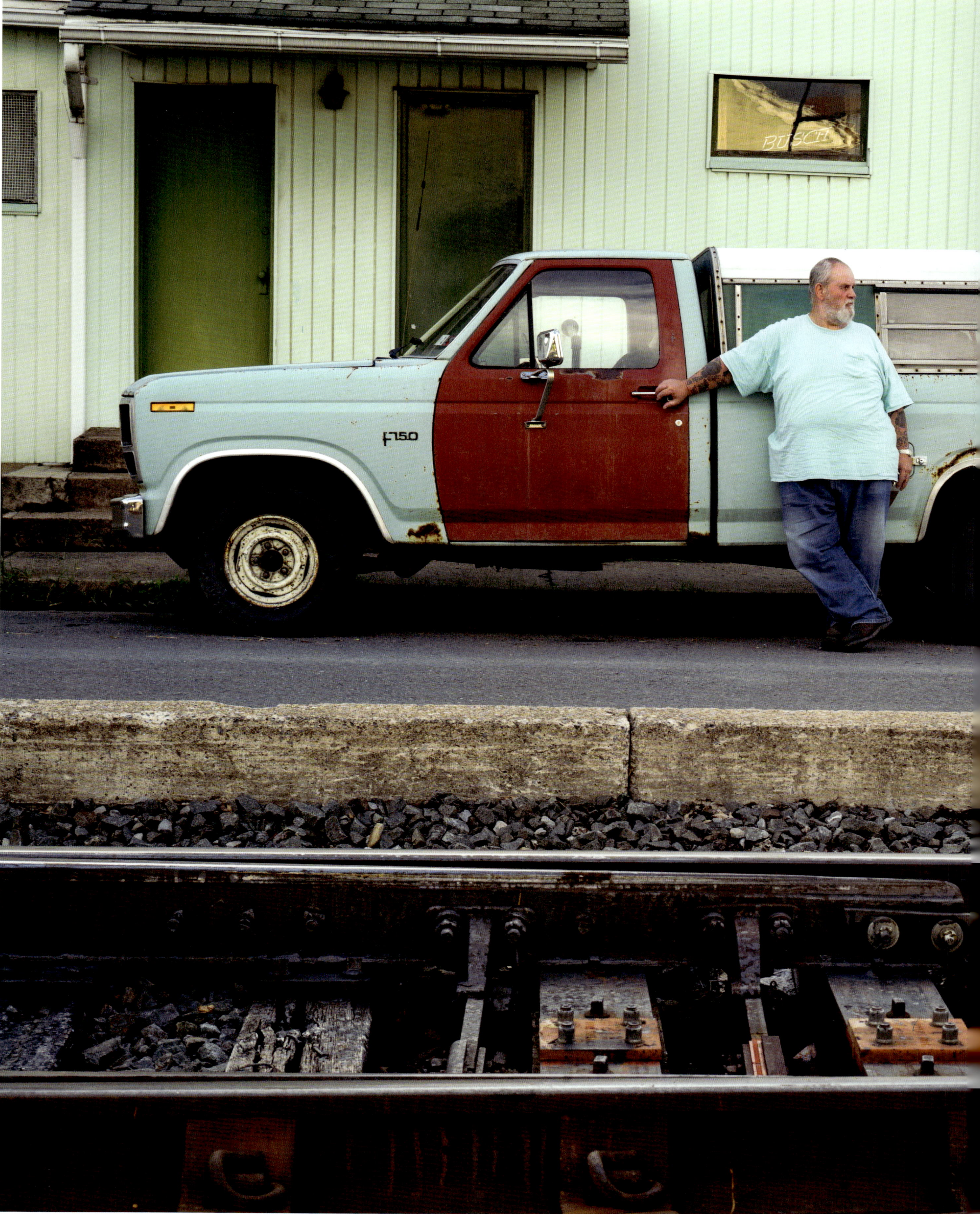
BUSCH

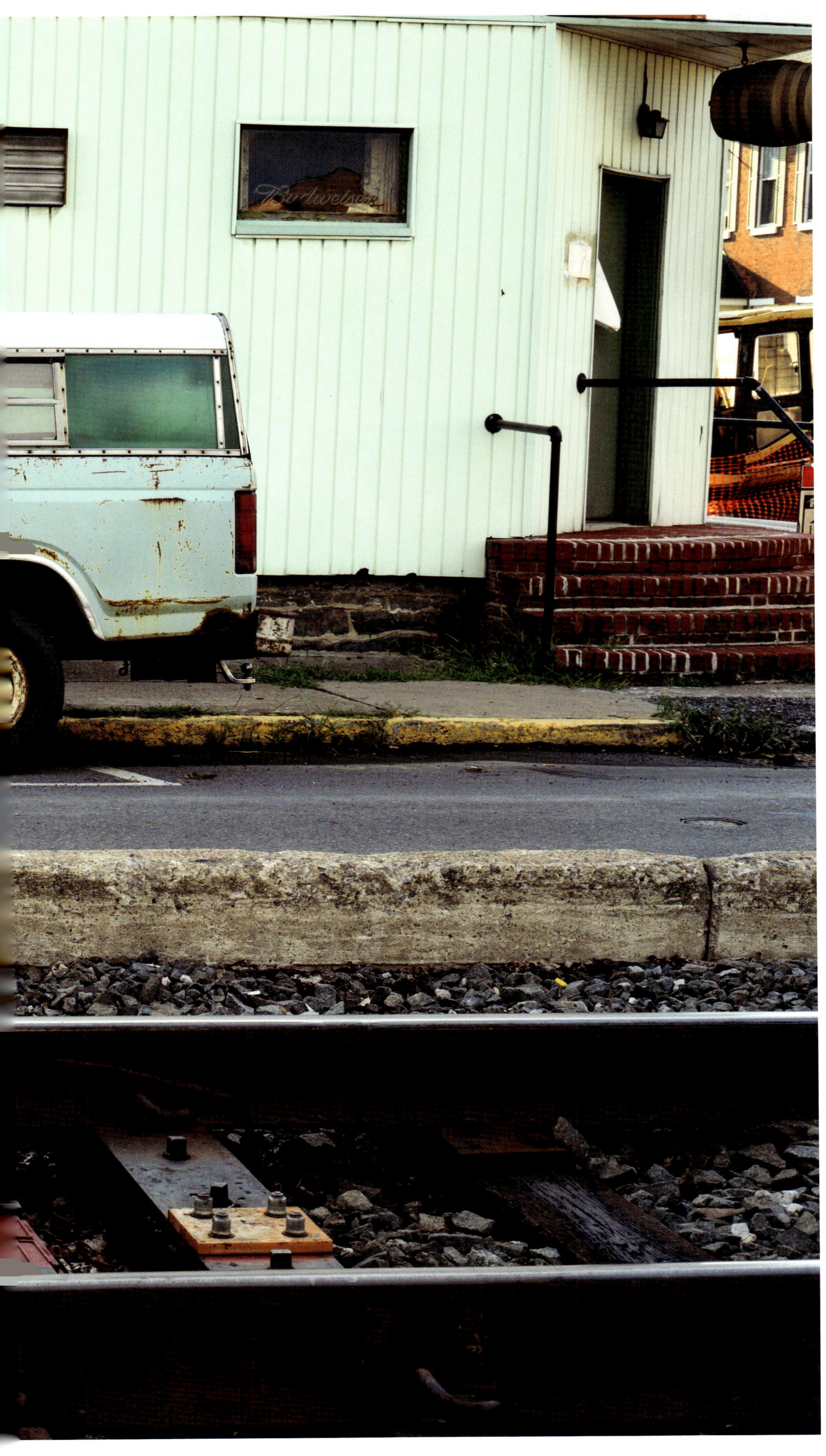
Budweiser

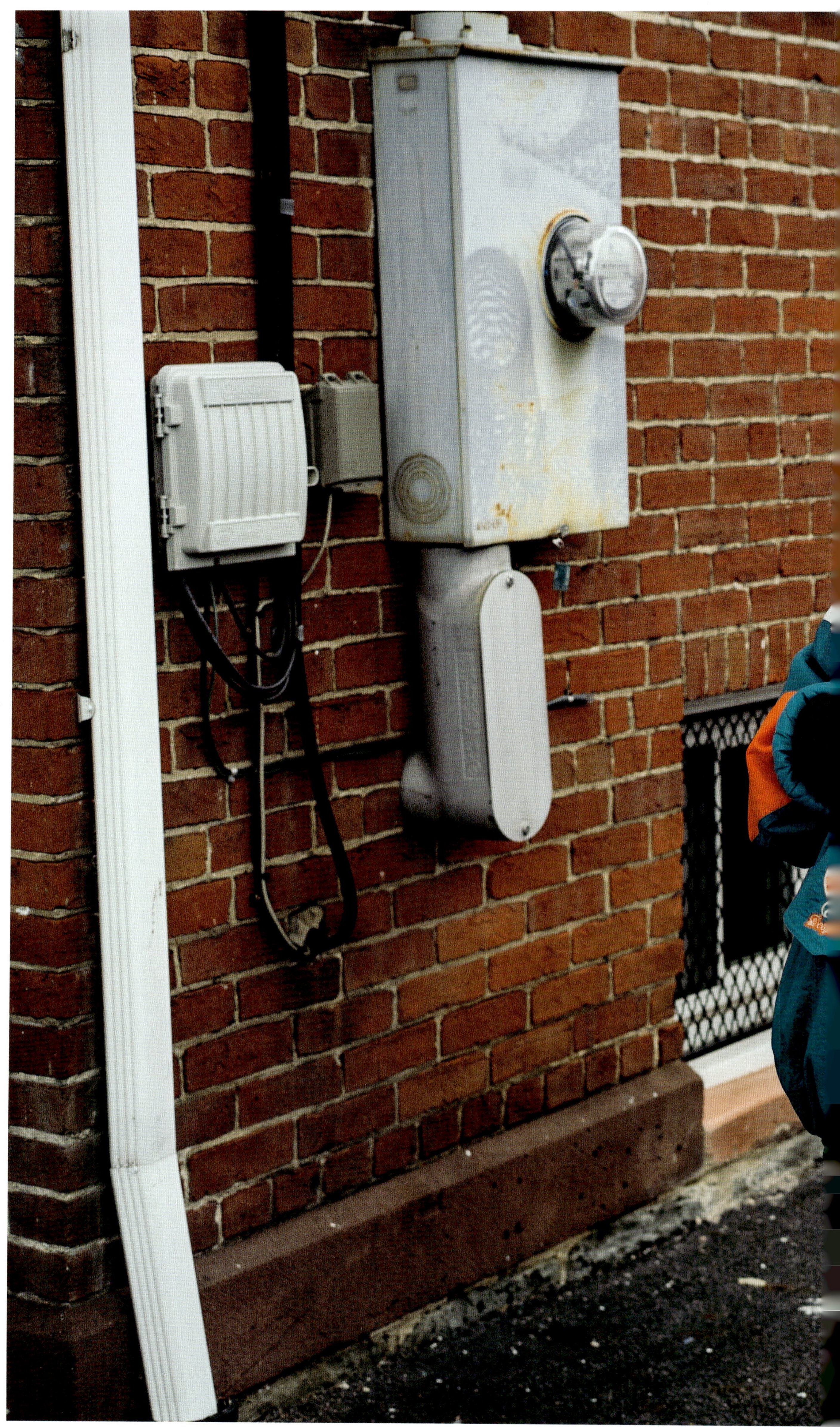

PLATE 80

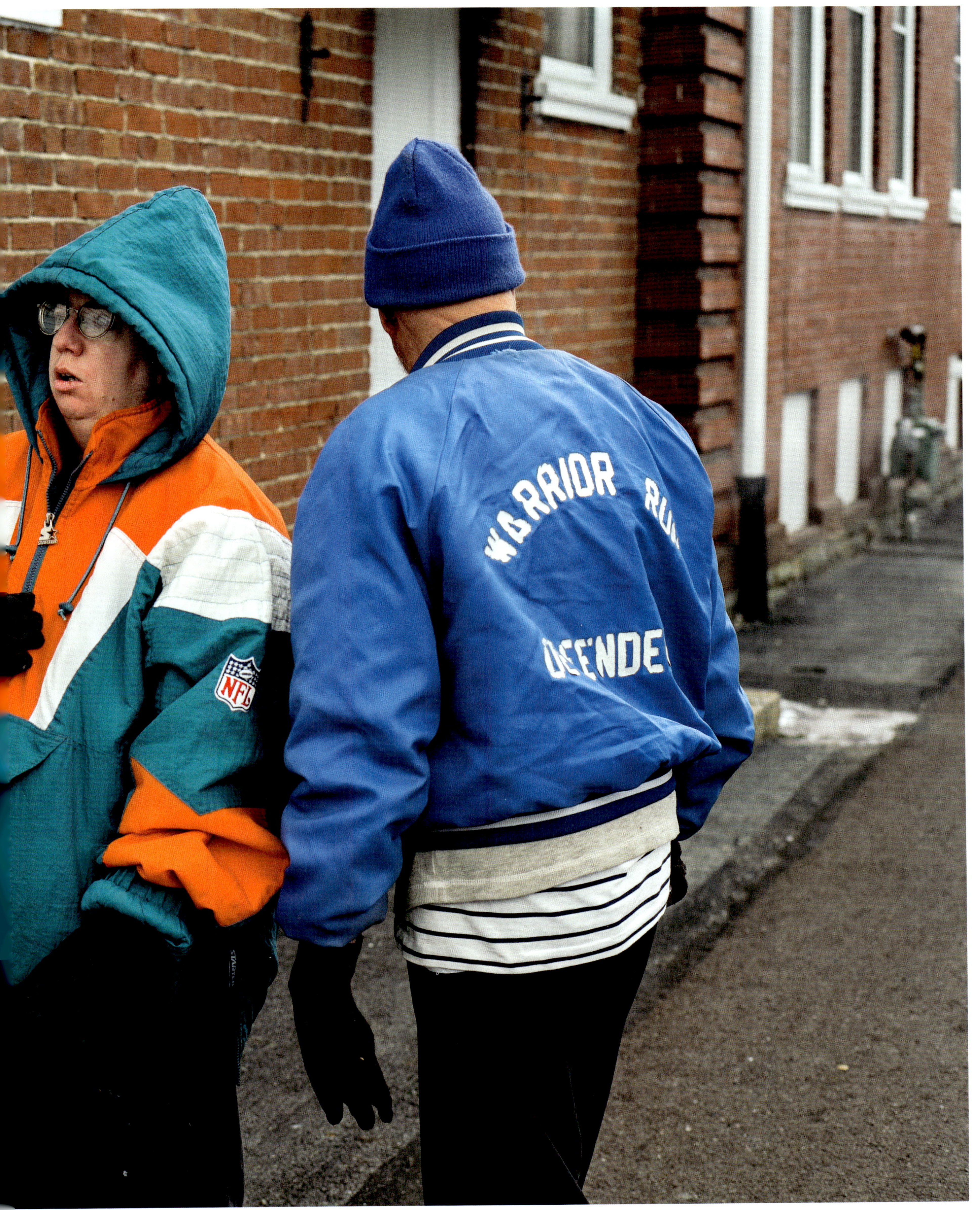
WARRIOR
NFL

PLATE 81

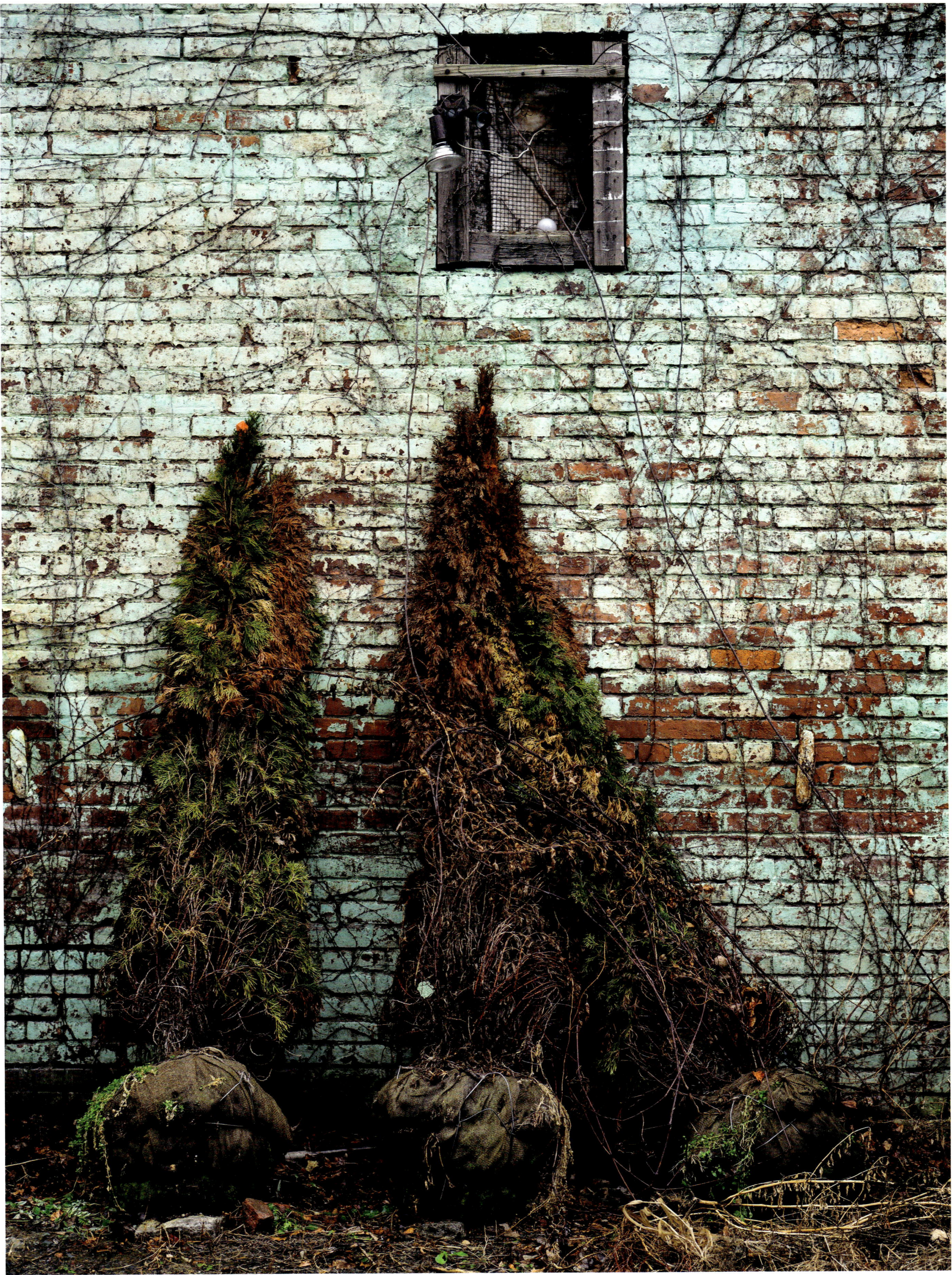

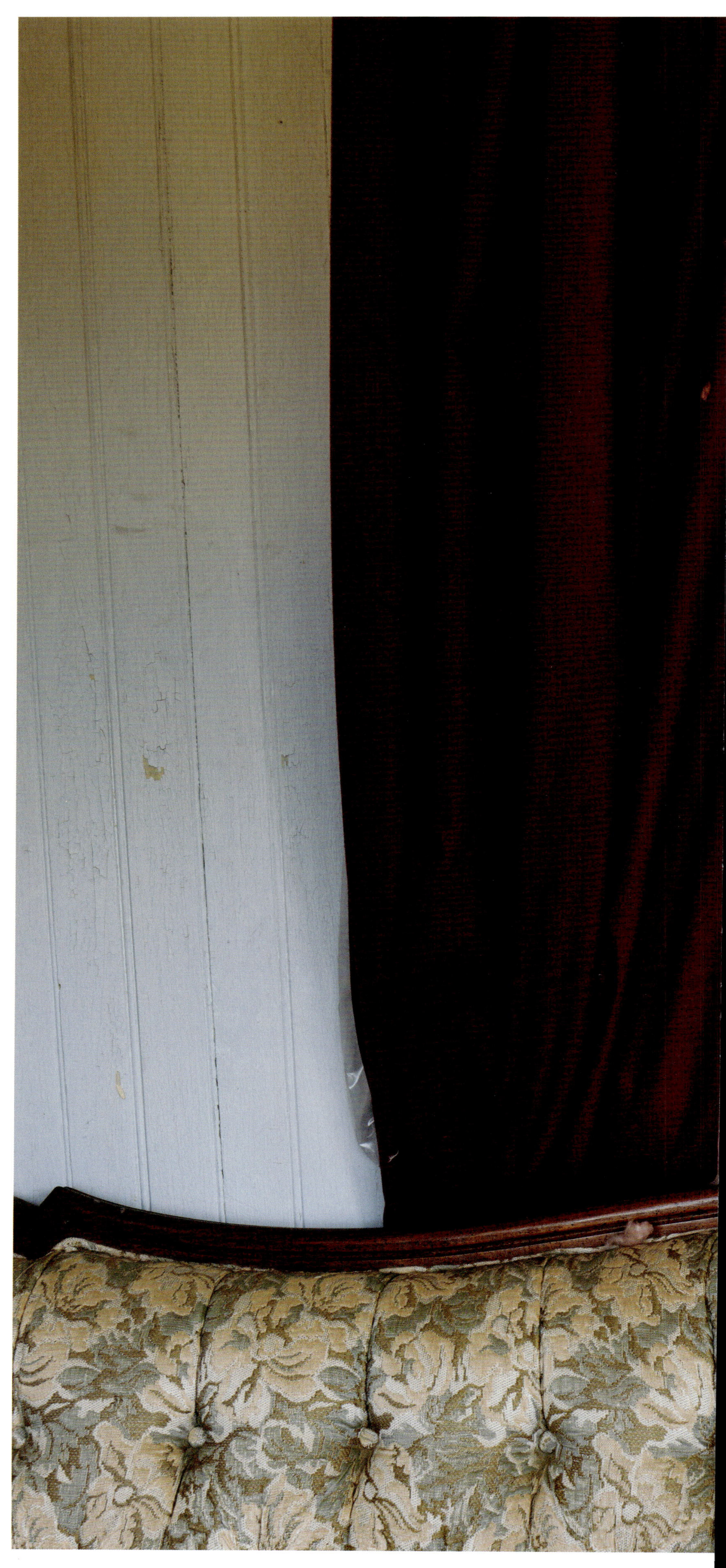

PLATE 82

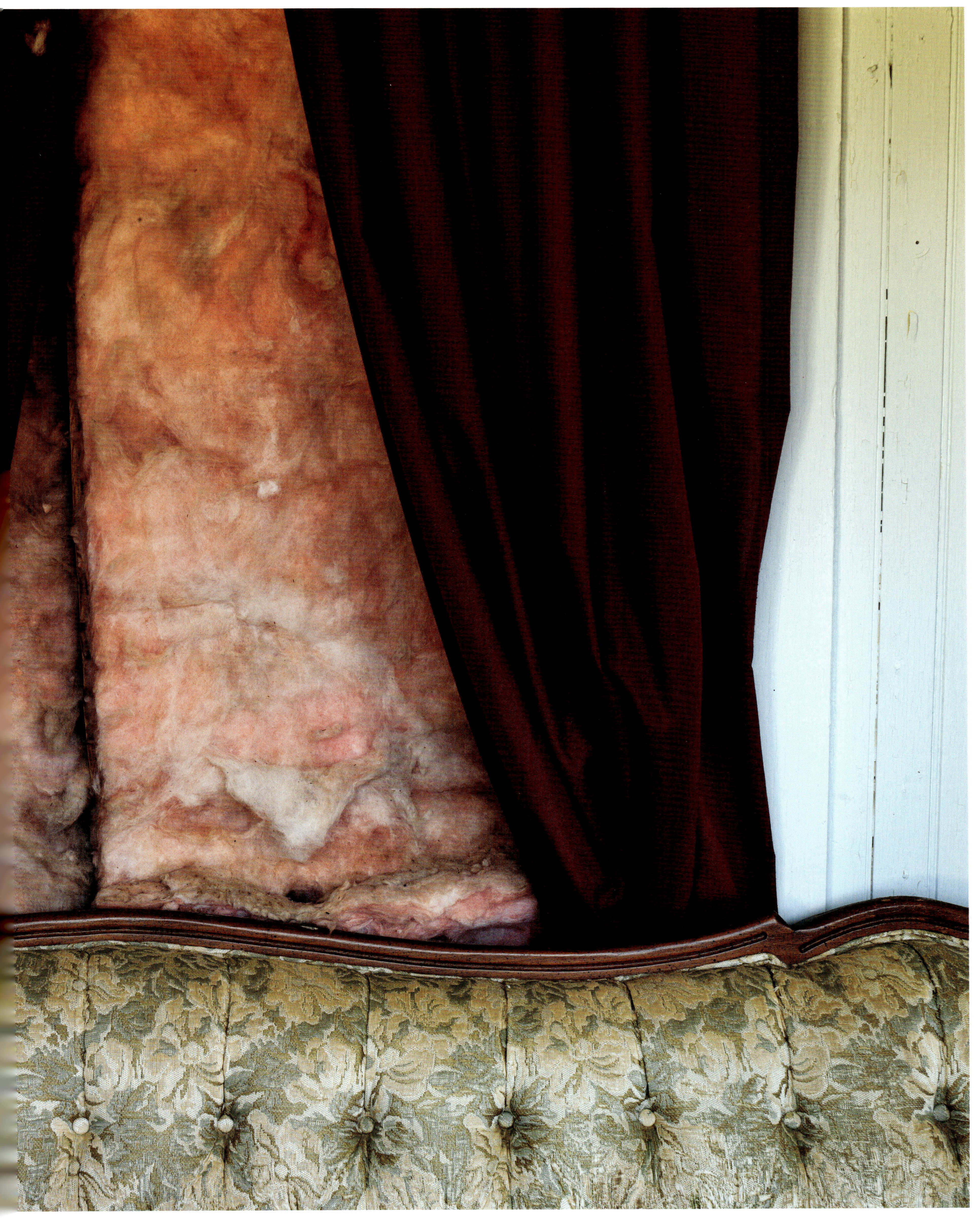

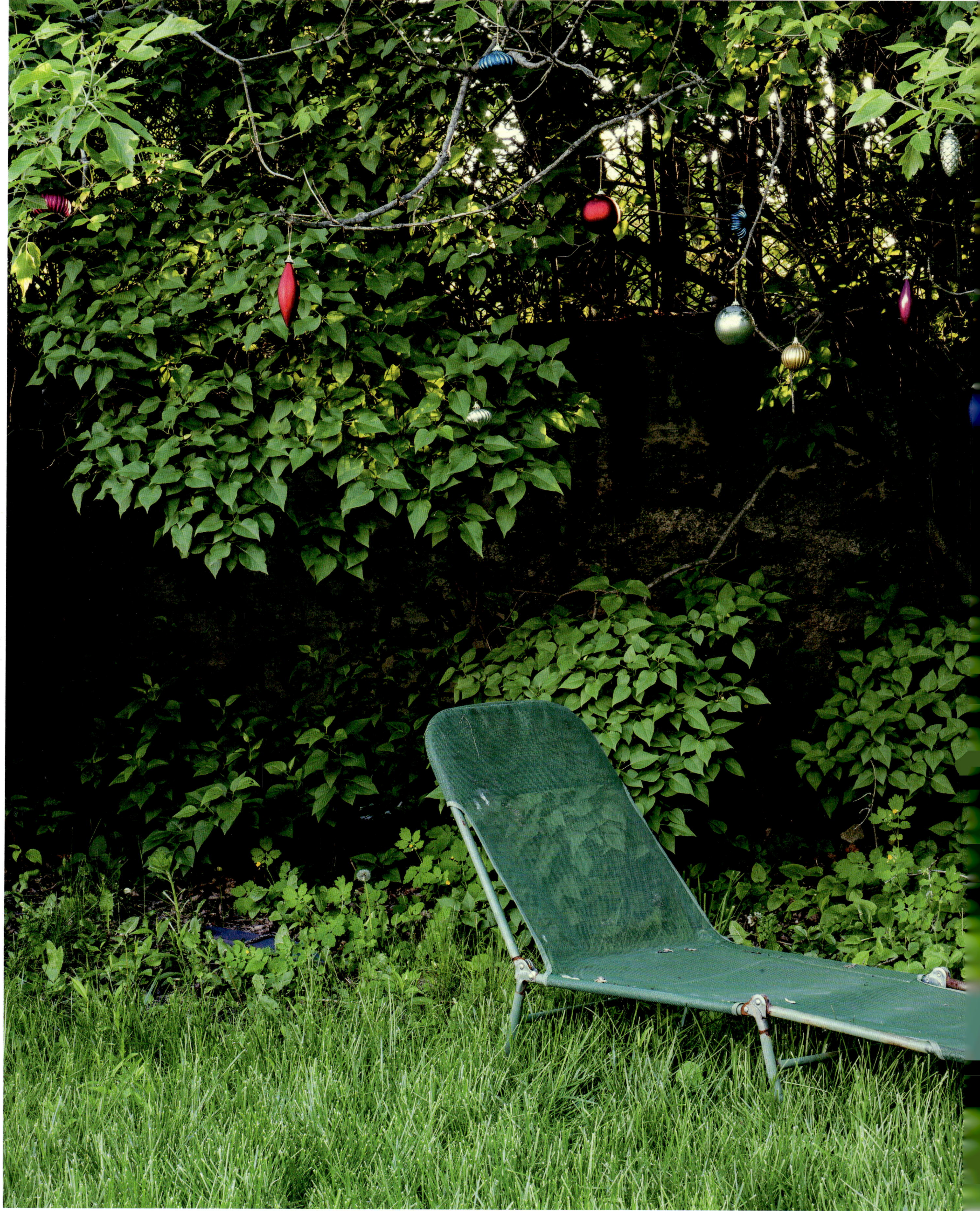

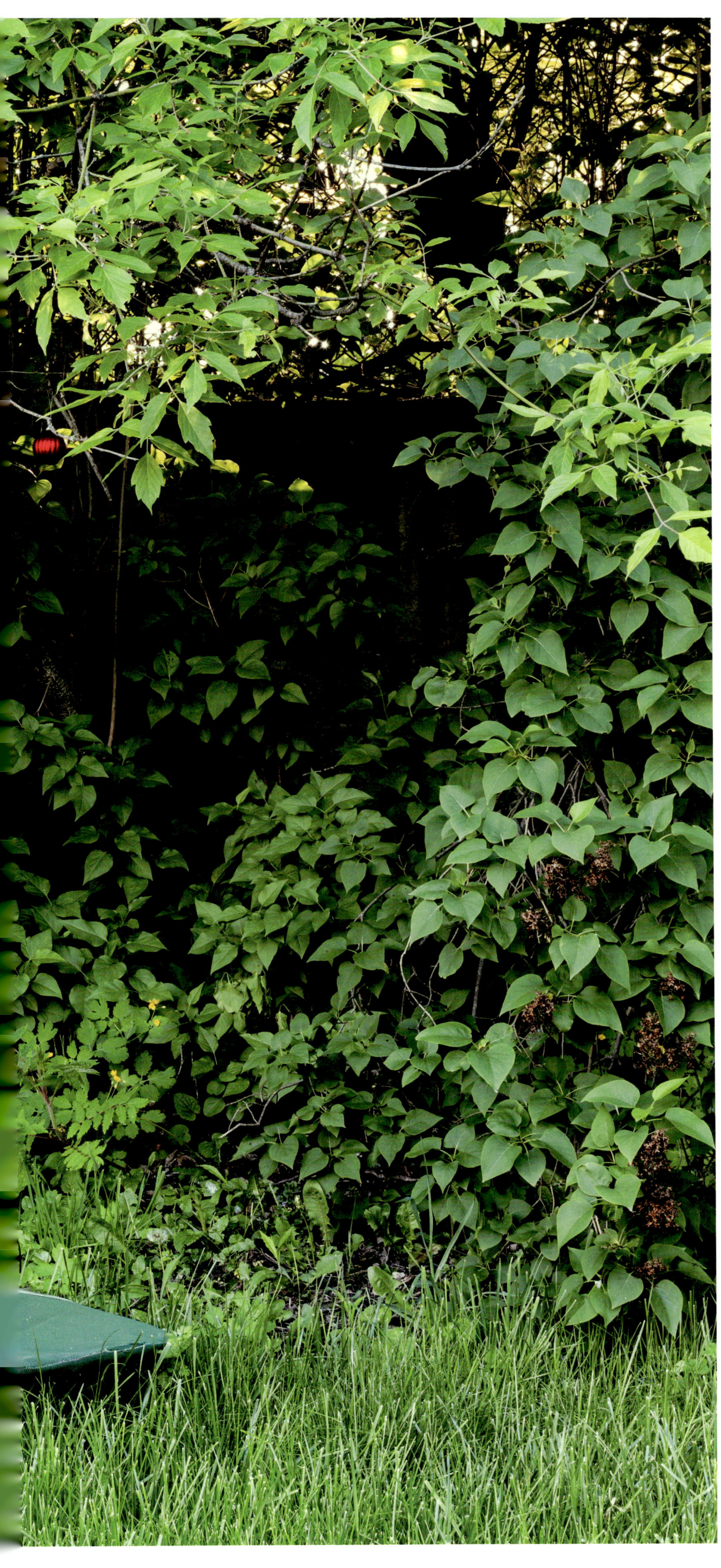

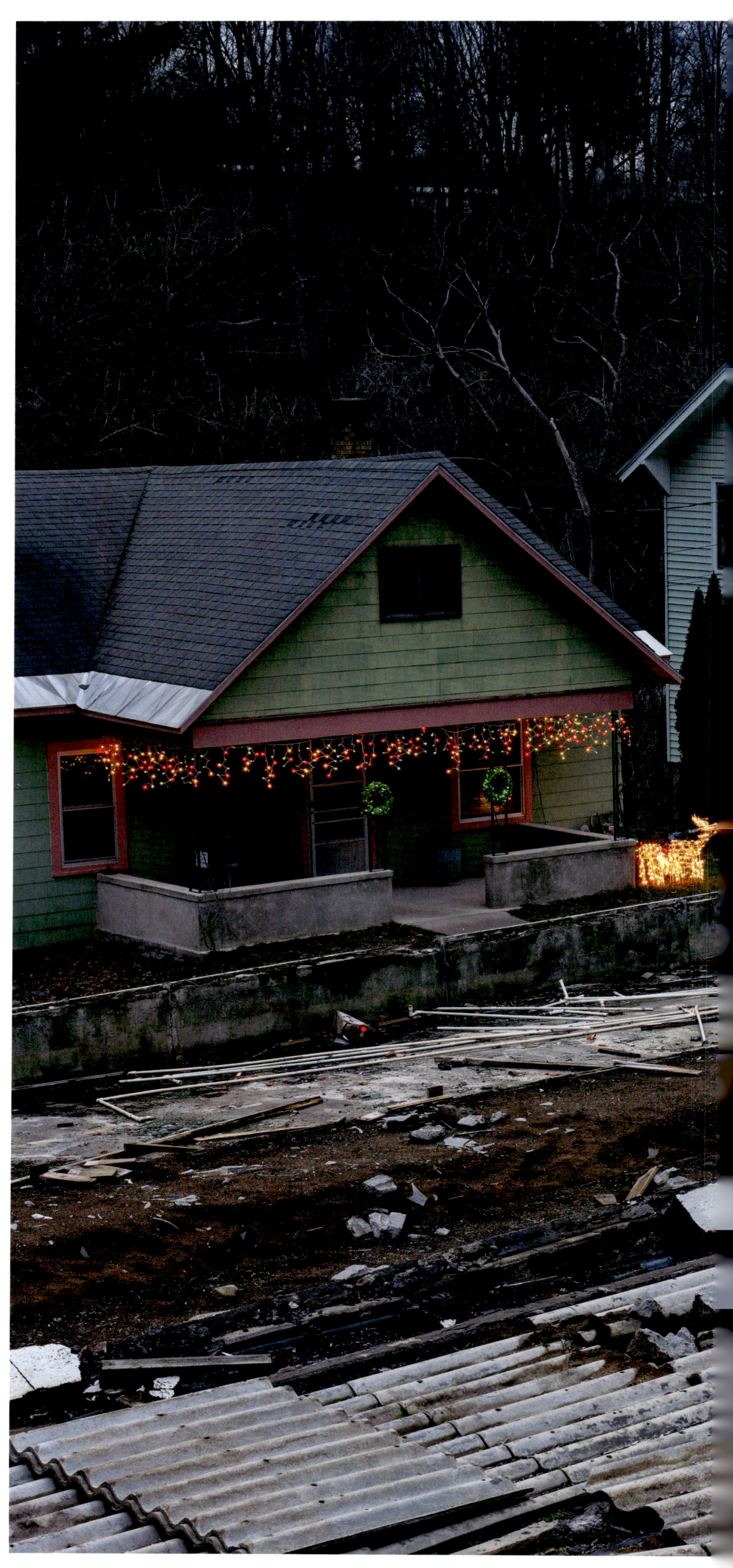

PLATE 84

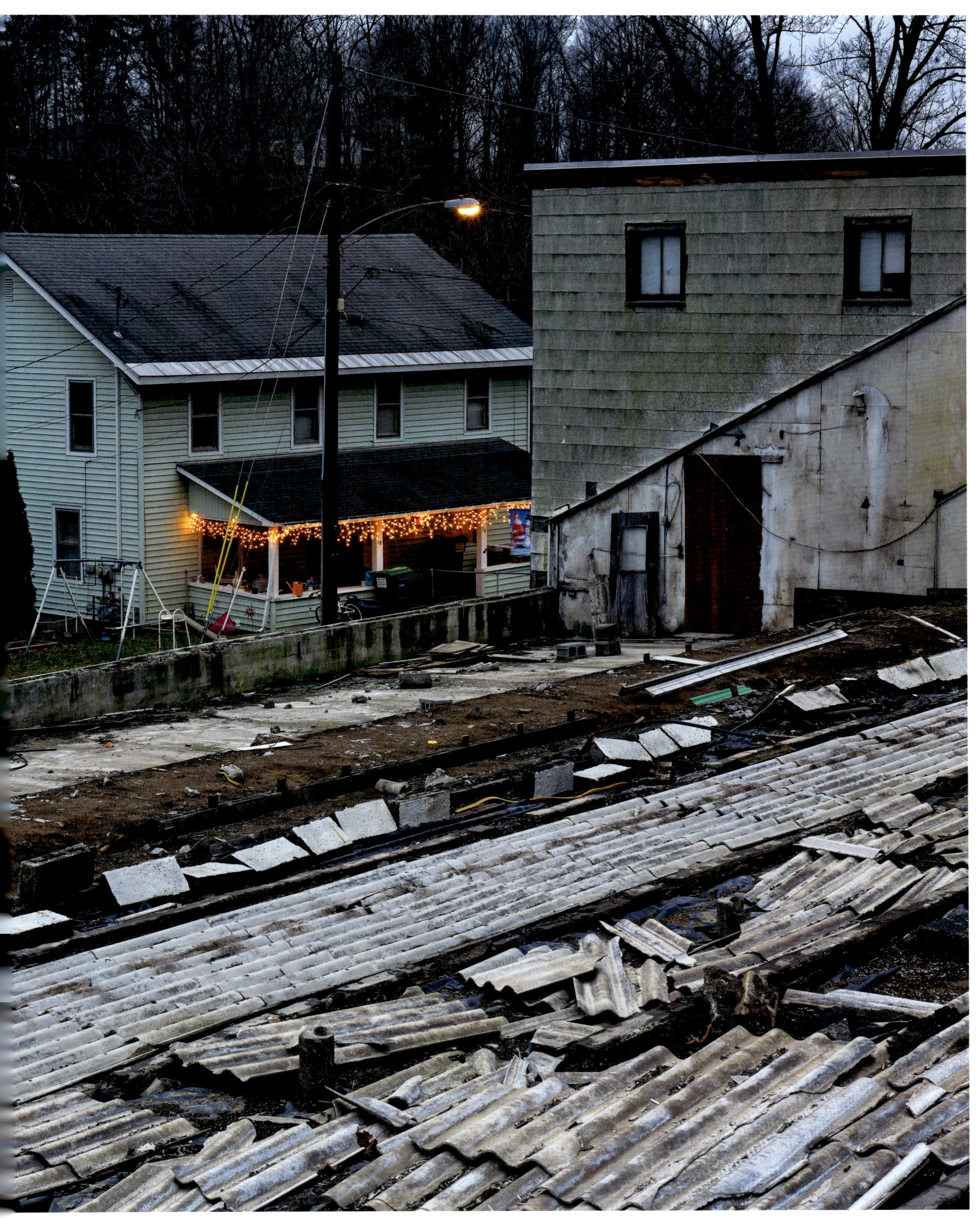

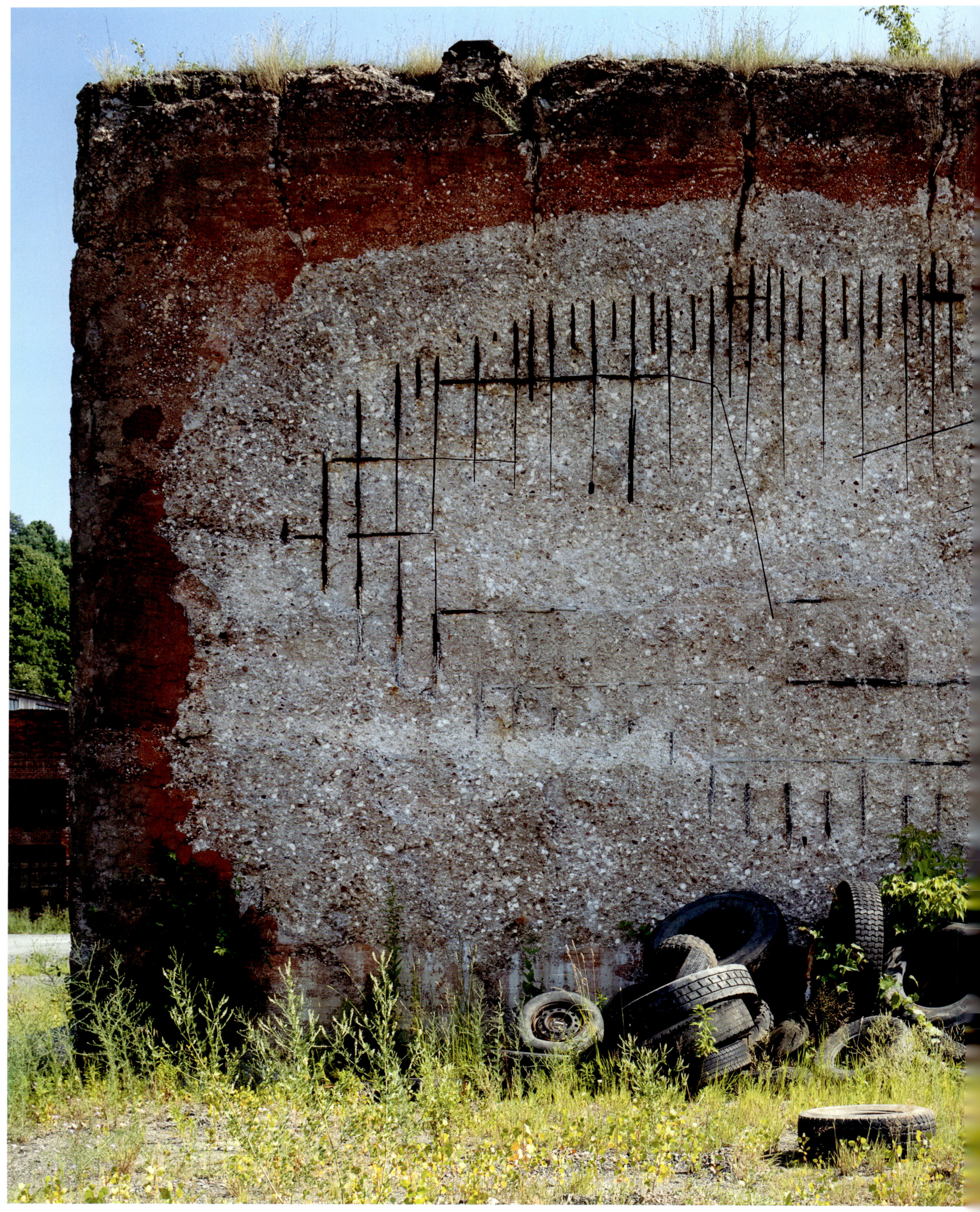

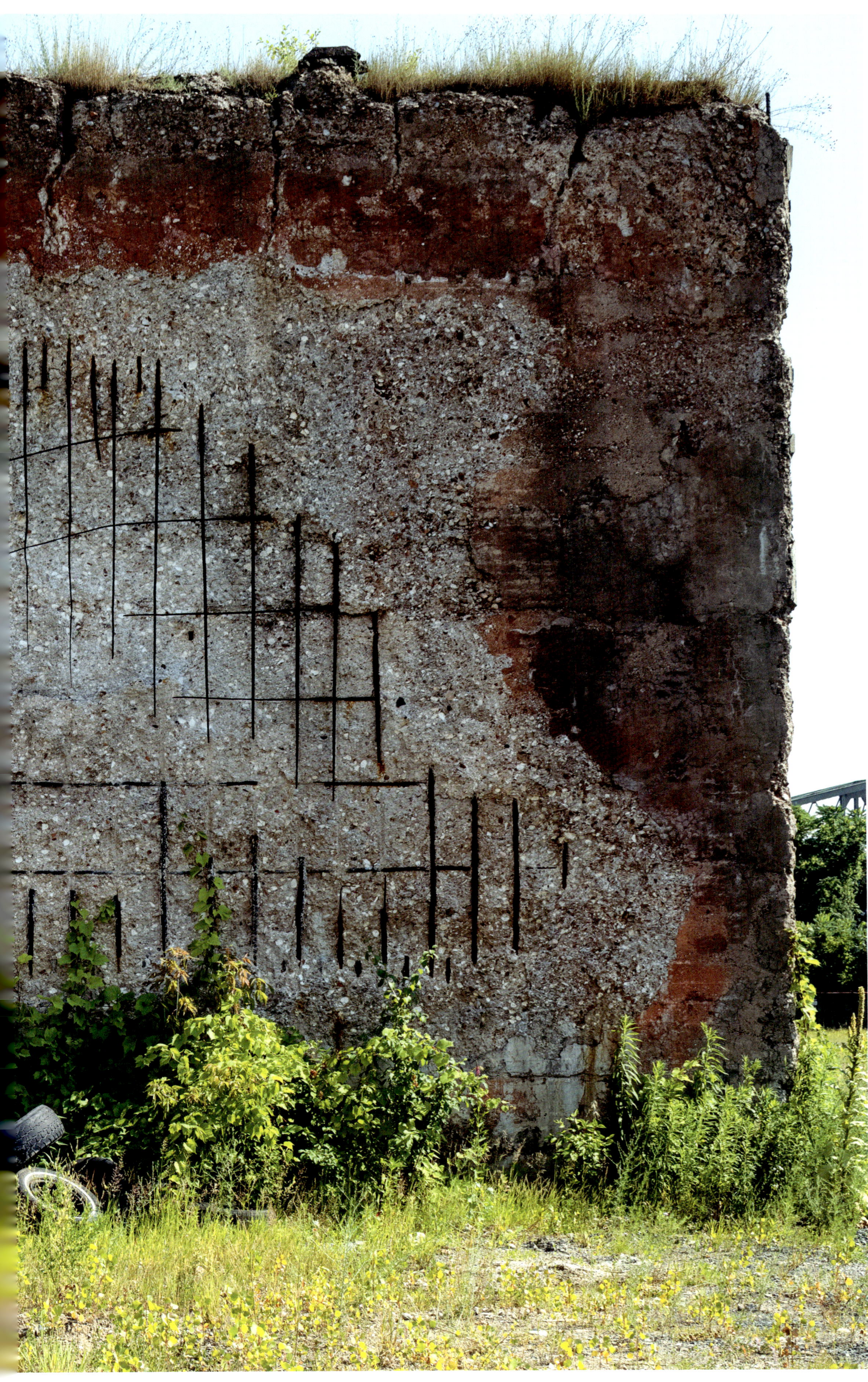

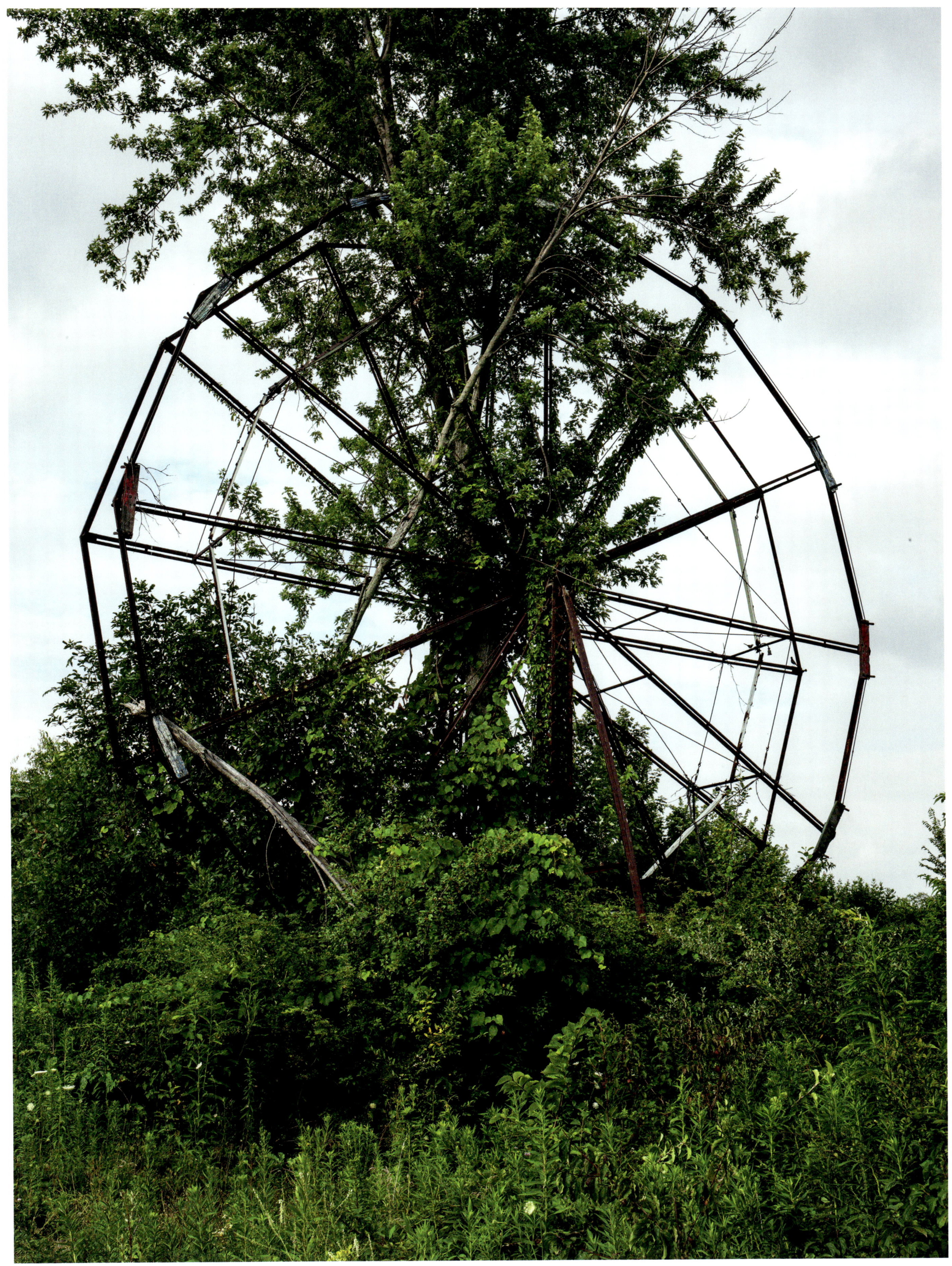

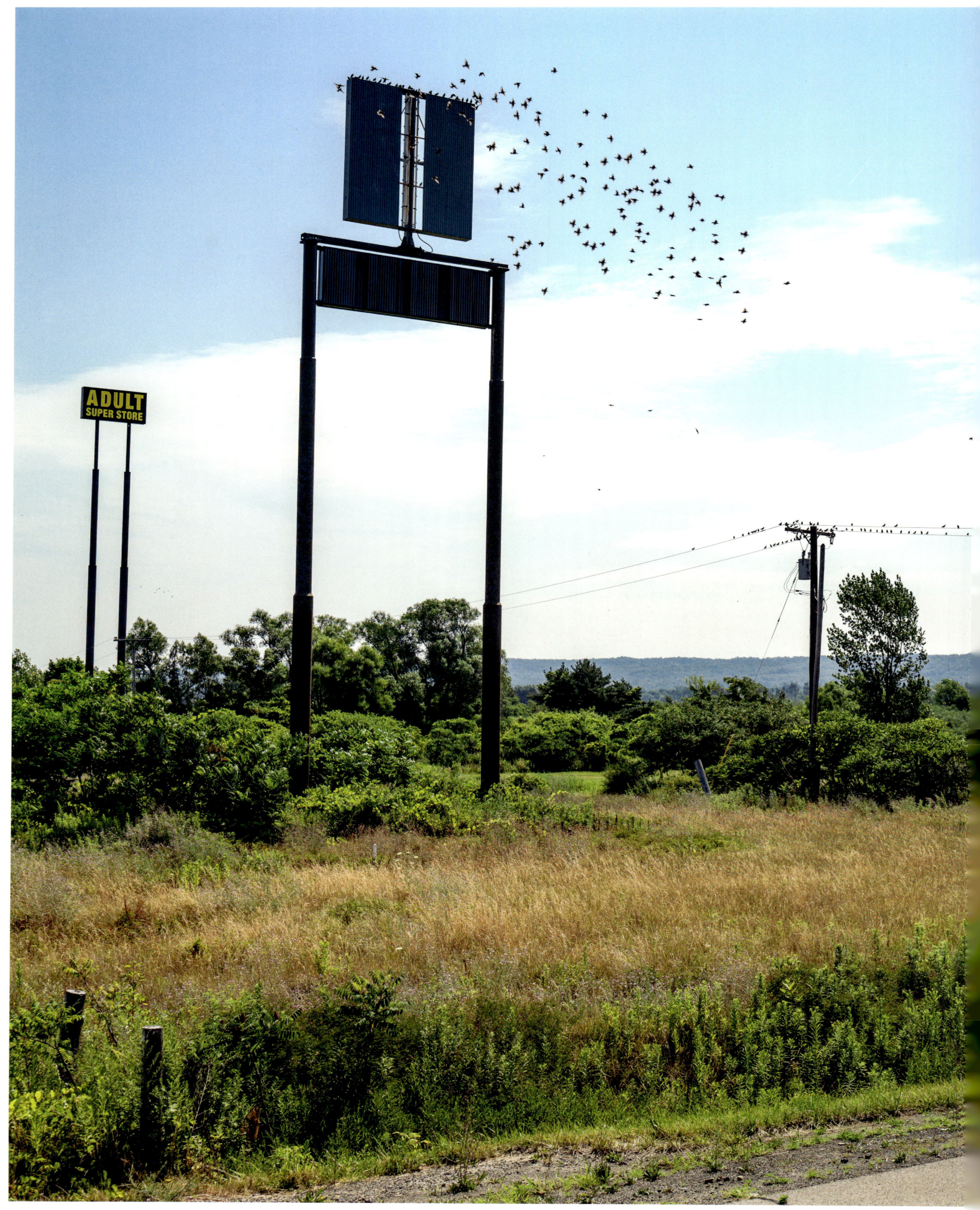
ADULT
SUPER STORE

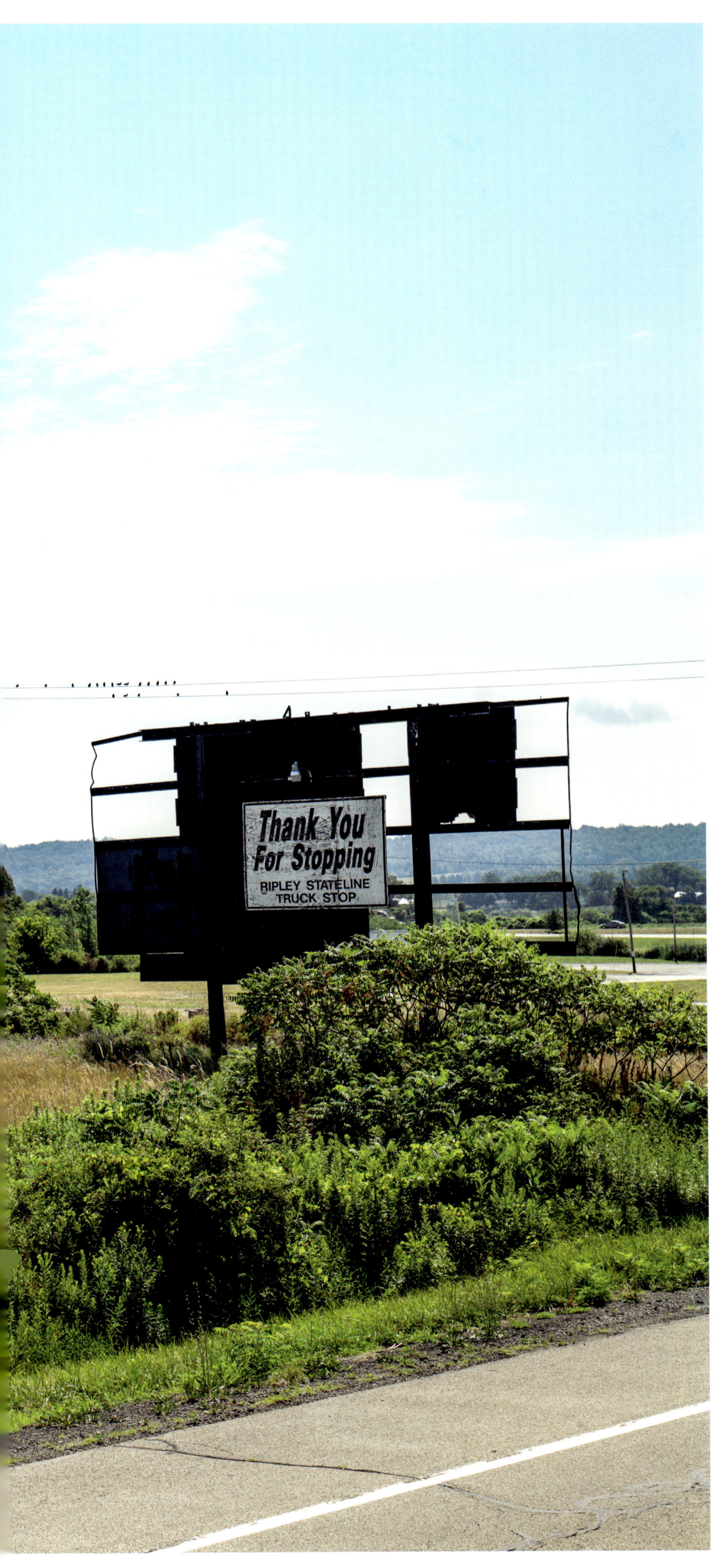
Thank You
For Stopping
RIPLEY STATELINE
TRUCK STOP

PLATE LISTING

ACKNOWLEDGMENTS

Some village-Hampden, that with dauntless breast
The little tyrant of his fields withstood;
Some mute inglorious Milton here may rest,
Some Cromwell guiltless of his country's blood.

The applause of listening senates to command,
The threats of pain and ruin to despise,
To scatter plenty o'er a smiling land,
And read their history in a nation's eyes.

— Thomas Gray, from *Elegy Written in a Country Churchyard*

For Maura

First, thank you to the kind people who allowed me to wander their towns and streets and into their backyards to make these pictures. I was met with curiosity and generosity, occasionally suspicion, a few times with hard words, and once with a big stick. I am better for each.

Thank you: Maura Glennon, Zeke Kimball, Ellie Kimball, Tom Young, Steve Smith, Brian Ulrich, Stanley Wolukau-Manambwa, Richard Benson, Joseph Carroll, Richard Woodward, Heather Bowden, Barbara Resnik, Justin H. Kimball, Heather Zullinger, Alex Kimball, and Douglas Kimball.

A special thank-you to David Chickey and the Radius crew for their unwavering support and guidance.

This book was made possible in part by the generous support of Richard S. and Jeanne Press, Ralph Segall, Harry Brandler, an Amherst College Faculty Research Award, and the Project Development Grant from CENTER Santa Fe.

RADIUS BOOKS
227 E. Palace Ave., Suite W
Santa Fe, NM 87501
t: (505) 983–4068
www.radiusbooks.org

Available through
D.A.P. / DISTRIBUTED ART PUBLISHERS
155 Sixth Ave., 2nd Floor
New York, NY 10013
t: (212) 627–1999
www.artbook.com

ISBN 978-1-942185-06-2

Library of Congress Cataloging-in-Publication Data available from the publisher upon request.

DESIGN: David Chickey, Montana Currie
PRE-PRESS: John Vokoun
PROOFING: Peg Goldstein

Printed by Editoriale Bortolazzi-Stei, Verona, Italy